SUICIDE RESEARCH: SELECTED READINGS

Volume 5

November 2010–April 2011

J. Sveticic, A. Milner, D. De Leo

Australian Institute for Suicide Research and Prevention

Griffith
UNIVERSITY

WHO Collaborating Centre for Research and Training in Suicide Prevention

National Centre of Excellence in Suicide Prevention

First published in 2011
Australian Academic Press
32 Jeays Street
Bowen Hills Qld 4006
Australia
www.australianacademicpress.com.au

ISBN: 9781921513855

Contents

Foreword

This volume contains quotations from internationally peer-reviewed suicide research published during the semester November 2010 – April 2011; it is the fifth of a series produced biannually by our Institute with the aim of assisting the Commonwealth Department of Health and Ageing in being constantly updated on new evidences from the scientific community. Compared to previous volumes, an increased number of examined materials have to be referred. In fact, during the current semester, the number of articles scrutinised has been the highest yet, with a progression that testifies a remarkably growing interest from scholars for the field of suicide research (718 articles for the first, 757 for the second, 892 for the third, and 1,121 for the forth, and 1,276 for the present volume).

As usual, the initial section of the volume collects a number of publications that could have particular relevance for the Australian people in terms of potential applicability. These researches are accompanied by a short comment from us, and an explanation of the motives that justify why we have considered of interest the implementation of studies' findings in the Australian context. An introductory part provides the rationale and the methodology followed in the identification of papers.

The central part of the volume represents a selection of research articles of particular significance; their abstracts are reported in extenso, underlining our invitation at reading those papers in full text: they represent a remarkable advancement of suicide research knowledge.

The last section reports all items retrievable from major electronic databases. We have catalogued them on the basis of their prevailing reference to fatal and non-fatal suicidal behaviours, with various sub-headings (e.g., epidemiology, risk factors, etc). The deriving list guarantees a level of completeness superior to any individual system; it can constitute a useful tool for all those interested in a quick update of what most recently published on the topic.

Our intent was to make suicide research more approachable to non-specialists, and in the meantime provide an opportunity for a vademecum of quotations credible also at the professional level. A compilation such as the one that we provide here is not easily obtainable from usual sources and can save a considerable amount of time to readers. We believe that our effort in this direction may be an appropriate interpretation of one of the technical support roles to the government that the new status of National Centre of Excellence in Suicide Prevention — which has deeply honoured our commitment — entails for us.

The significant growth of our centre, the Australian Institute for Suicide Research and Prevention, and its influential function, both nationally and internationally, in the fight against suicide, could not happen without the constant support of Queensland Health and Griffith University. We hope that our passionate dedication to the cause of suicide prevention may compensate their continuing trust in our work.

Diego De Leo, DSc

Director, Australian Institute for Suicide Research and Prevention

Acknowledgments

This report has been produced by the Australian Institute for Suicide Research and Prevention, WHO Collaborating Centre for Research and Training in Suicide Prevention and National Centre of Excellence in Suicide Prevention. The assistance of the Commonwealth Department of Health and Ageing in the funding of this report is gratefully acknowledged.

Introduction

Context

Suicide places a substantial burden on individuals, communities and society in terms of emotional, economic and health care costs. In Australia, about 2000 people die from suicide every year, a death rate well in excess of transport-related mortality. At the time of preparing this volume, the latest available statistics released by the Australian Bureau of Statistics[1] indicated that, in 2008, 2,190 deaths by suicide were registered in Australia, representing an age-standardized rate of 9.4 per 100,000.

Further, a study on mortality in Australia for the years 1997–2001 found that suicide was the leading cause of avoidable mortality in the 25–44 year age group, for both males (29.5%) and females (16.7%), while in the age group 15–24 suicide accounted for almost a third of deaths due to avoidable mortality.[2] In 2003, self-inflicted injuries were responsible for 27% of the total injury burden in Australia, leading to an estimated 49,379 years of life lost (YLL) due to premature mortality, with the greatest burdens observed in men aged 25–64.[3]

Despite the estimated mortality, the prevalence of suicide and self-harming behaviour in particular remains difficult to gauge, due to the often secretive nature of these activities. Indeed, the ABS acknowledges the difficulties in obtaining reliable data for suicides in the past few years.[4,5] Without a clear understanding of the scope of suicidal behaviours and the range of interventions available, the opportunity to implement effective initiatives is reduced. Further, it is important that suicide prevention policies are developed on the foundation of evidence-based empirical research, especially as the quality and validly of the available information may be misleading or inaccurate. Additionally, the social and economic impact of suicide underlines the importance of appropriate research-based prevention strategies, addressing not only significant direct costs on health system and lost productivity, but also the emotional suffering for families and communities.

The Australian Institute for Suicide Research and Prevention (AISRAP) has, through the years, gained an international reputation as one of the leading research institutions in the field of suicide prevention. The most important recognition came via the designation as a World Health Organization (WHO) Collaborating Centre in mid-2005. More recently (Spring 2008), the Commonwealth Department of Health and Ageing (DoHA) appointed AISRAP as the National Centre of Excellence in Suicide Prevention. This latter recognition awards not only many years of high-quality research, but also of fruitful cooperation between the institute and several different governmental agencies. The new role given to AISRAP will translate into an even deeper commitment to the cause of suicide prevention among community members of Australia.

As part of this initiative, AISRAP is committed to the creation of a databank of the recent scientific literature documenting the nature and extent of suicidal and self-harming behaviour and recommended practices in preventing and responding to these behaviours. The key output for the project is a critical biannual review of the national and international literature outlining recent advances and promising developments in research in suicide prevention, particularly where this can help to inform national activities. This task is not aimed at providing a critique of new researches, but rather at drawing attention to investigations that may have particular relevance to the Australian context. In doing so, we are committed to a user-friendly language, in order to render research outcomes and their interpretation accessable also to a non-expert audience.

In summary, this particular review serves three primary purposes:

1. to inform future State and Commonwealth suicide prevention policies

2. to assist in the improvement of existing initiatives, and the development of new and innovative Australian projects for the prevention of suicidal and self-harming behaviors within the context of the Living is for Everyone (LIFE) Framework (2008)

3. to provide directions for Australian research priorities in suicidology.

The review is presented in three sections. The first contains a selection of the best articles published in the last six months internationally. For each article identified by us (the method of chosing articles is described below), the original abstract is accompanied by a brief comment explaining why we thought the study was providing an important contribution to research and why we considered its possible applicability to Australia. The second section presents the abstracts of the most relevant literature — following our criteria — collected between November 2010 and April 2011; while the final section presents a list of citations of all literature published over this time period.

Methodology

The literature search was conducted in four phases.

Phase 1

Phase 1 consisted of weekly searches of the academic literature performed from November 2010 to April 2011. To ensure thorough coverage of the available published research, the literature was sourced using several scientific electronic databases including: Pubmed, Proquest, Scopus, Safetylit and Web of Science, using the following key words: *suicide, suicidal, self-harm, self-injury and parasuicide.*

Results from the weekly searches were downloaded and combined into one database (deleting duplicates).

Specific inclusion criteria for Phase 1 included:

- Timeliness: the article was published (either electronically or in hard-copy) between November 2010 and April 2011.

- Relevance: the article explicitly referred to fatal and/or non-fatal suicidal behaviour and related issues and/or interventions directly targeted at preventing/treating these behaviours.
- The article was written in English.

Articles about euthanasia, assisted suicide, suicide terrorist attacks, and/or book reviews, abstracts and conference presentations were excluded.

Also, articles that have been published in electronic versions (ahead of print) and therefore included in the previous volume (Volumes 1 to 4 of *Suicide Research: Selected Readings*) were excluded to avoid duplication.

Phase 2

Following an initial reading of the abstracts (retrieved in Phase 1), the list of articles was refined down to the most relevant literature. In Phase 2 articles were only included if they were published in an international, peer-reviewed journal.

In Phase 2, articles were excluded when they:

- were not particularly instructive or original
- were of a descriptive nature (e.g. a case-report)
- consisted of historical/philosophical content
- were a description of surgical reconstruction/treatment of self-inflicted injuries
- concerned biological and/or genetic interpretations of suicidal behaviour, the results of which could not be easily adoptable in the context of the LIFE Framework.

In order to minimise the potential for biased evaluations, two researchers working independently read through the full text of all articles selected to create a list of most relevant papers. This process was then duplicated by a third researcher for any articles on which consensus could not be reached.

The strength and quality of the research evidence was evaluated, based on the *Critical Appraisal Skills Programme (CASP) Appraisal Tools* published by the Public Health Resource Unit, England (2006). These tools, publically available online, consist of checklists for critically appraising systematic reviews, randomized controlled trials (RCT), qualitative research, economic evaluation studies, cohort studies, diagnostic test studies and case control studies.

Phase 3

One of the aims of this review was to identify research that is both evidence-based and of potential relevance to the Australian context. Thus, the final stage of applied methodology focused on research conducted in countries with populations or health systems sufficiently comparable to Australia. Only articles in which the full-text was available were considered. It is important to note that failure of an article to be selected for inclusion in Phase 3 does not entail any negative judgment on its 'objective' quality.

Specific inclusion criteria for Phase 3 included:

- applicability to Australia
- the paper met all criteria for scientificity (i.e., the methodology was considered sound)

- the paper represented a particularly compelling addition to the literature, which would be likely to stimulate suicide prevention initiatives and research
- inevitably, an important aspect was the importance of the journal in which the paper was published (because of the high standards that have to be met in order to obtain publication in that specific journal); priority was given to papers published in high impact factor journals
- particular attention has been paid to widen the literature horizon to include sociological and anthropological research that may have particular relevance to the Australian context.

After a thorough reading of these articles ('Key articles' for the considered timeframe), a written comment was produced for each article detailing:

- methodological strengths and weaknesses (e.g., sample size, validity of measurement instruments, appropriateness of analysis performed)
- practical implications of the research results to the Australian context
- suggestions for integrating research findings within the domains of the LIFE framework suicide prevention activities.

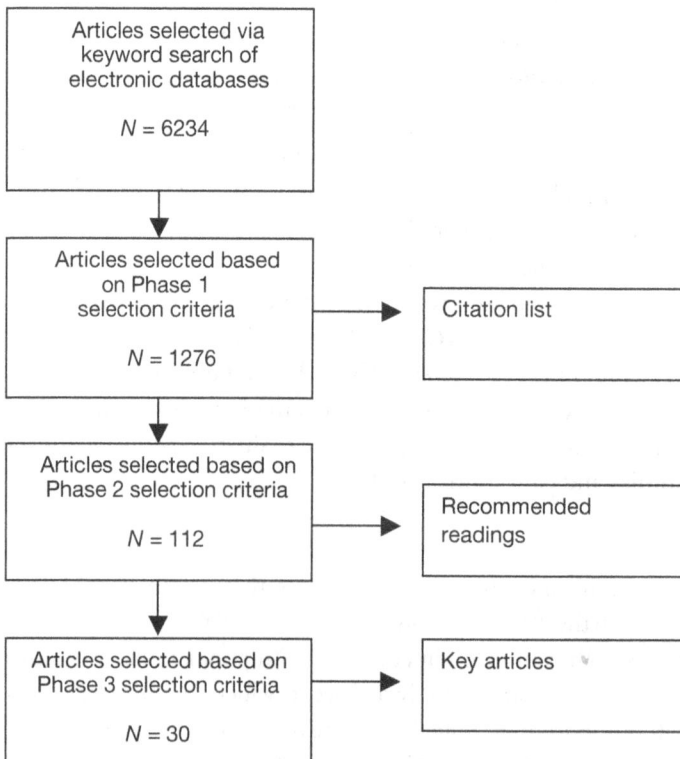

Figure 1 Flowchart of process.

Phase 4

In the final phase of the search procedure all articles were divided into the following classifications:

- *Fatal suicidal behaviour* (epidemiology, risk and protective factors, prevention, postvention and bereavement)
- *Non-fatal suicidal/self-harming behaviours* (epidemiology, risk and protective factors, prevention, care and support)
- *Case reports* include reports of fatal and non-fatal suicidal behaviours
- *Miscelleneous* includes all research articles that could not be classified into any other category.

Allocation to these categories was not always straightforward, and where papers spanned more than one area, consensus of the research team determined which domain the article would be placed in. Within each section of the report (i.e., Key articles, Recommended readings, Citation list) articles are presented in alphabetical order by author.

Endnotes

1. Australian Bureau of Statistics (2010). *Causes of death, Australia, 2008* (Cat. No. 3303.0). Canberra, Australia.
2. Page A, Tobias M, Glover J, Wright C, Hetzel D, Fisher E (2006). *Australian and New Zealand atlas of avoidable mortality.* Public Health Information Development Unit, University of Adelaide, Adelaide.
3. Begg S, Vos T, Barker B, Stevenson C, Stanley L, Lopez A (2007). *The burden of disease and injury in Australia 2003.* Australian Institute for Health and Welfare, Canberra.
4. Australian Bureau of Statistics (2009). *Causes of death, Australia, 2007, Technical note 1* (Cat. No. 3303.0). Canberra, Australia.
5. Australian Bureau of Statistics (2009). *Causes of death, Australia, 2007, Explanatory notes* (Cat. No. 3303.0). Canberra, Australia.

Key Articles

Factors influencing the decision to use hanging as a method of suicide: Qualitative study

Biddle L, Donovan J, Owen-Smith A, Potokar J, Longson D, Hawton K, Kapur N, Gunnell D (UK)

British Journal of Psychiatry 197, 320–325, 2010

Background: Hanging is the most frequently used method of suicide in the UK and has high case fatality (> 70%).

Aims: To explore factors influencing the decision to use hanging.

Method: Semi-structured qualitative interviews with 12 men and 10 women who had survived a near-fatal suicide attempt. Eight respondents had attempted hanging. Data were analysed thematically and with constant comparison.

Results: Hanging was adopted or contemplated for two main reasons: the anticipated nature of a death from hanging; and accessibility. Those favouring hanging anticipated a certain, rapid and painless death with little awareness of dying and believed it was a 'clean' method that would not damage the body or leave harrowing images for others. Materials for hanging were easily accessed and respondents considered it 'simple' to perform without the need for planning or technical knowledge. Hanging was thus seen as the 'quickest' and 'easiest' method with few barriers to completion and sometimes adopted despite not being a first choice. Respondents who rejected hanging recognised it could be slow, painful and 'messy', and thought technical knowledge was needed for implementation.

Conclusions: Prevention strategies should focus on countering perceptions of hanging as a clean, painless and rapid method that is easily implemented. However, care is needed in the delivery of such messages as some individuals could gain information that might facilitate fatal implementation. Detailed research needs to focus on developing and evaluating interventions that can manage this tension.

Comment

Main findings: This study from UK sought to explore the factors influencing the decision to use, or contemplate using, hanging as a method of suicide in a sample of 22 participants after a 'near fatal' suicide attempt (8 of which used hanging either in their index episode or past attempts). This is the first such study published internationally. In-depth interviews were performed, focusing on the perceptions of the method used, sources of information about it and the preparations involved in their attempt. In addition, a standardised instrument was used to assess the degree of suicidal intent associated with the act.

A qualitative analysis of participants' narratives confirmed two central themes related to adopting or contemplating their use of hanging: the anticipated nature of death and accessibility. Most participants using this method perceived it to be a certain method of suicide, one that could be acted upon quickly and would lead to a rapid and relatively pain-free death. In addition, all respondents agreed that the materials for hanging are highly accessible and most were aware of variety of objects that could be used for ligatures. In a few cases, the presence of usable materials actually prompted the consideration of hanging as a suicide method. On the contrary, participants that chose other methods of suicide felt hanging required specific technical knowledge and extensive preparations to ensure it was performed successfully; otherwise it could lead to a slow and traumatic dying process.

Implications: Most national suicide prevention strategies place emphasis on restricting access to commonly used methods of suicide as a means of reducing suicide rates; however, it is commonly agreed that this approach is generally not possible for hanging suicides, as the ligature points and ligatures commonly used are universally available[1]. In Australia, hanging has been gaining popularity as a suicide method over the last few decades, and currently accounts for nearly half of all self-inflicted deaths, particularly among young males[2]. An in-depth analysis of trends of suicides by hanging suggested that the observed shift could at least party been attributed to a change in social and cultural attitudes, influenced by the ending — in most countries — of capital punishment by hanging and thus removing the stigma of hanging as associated to criminal behavior[2]. Biddle and colleagues reiterated the importance of common perceptions about methods of suicide in determining whether or not they are adopted. Since hanging is currently viewed as a rapid and easily accessible method with the high likelihood of ensuing death, authors suggest that prevention strategies could focus on providing more accurate information about the processes and consequences of hanging to counter the misperception of its hygienic rapidity, and to introduce awareness of the possibility of neurological impairment in case of survival. Such messages might also include the body's appearance and the affect on family members after finding their hanging body. These subtle changes in lay knowledge could be introduced through realistic portrayals of hanging in the popular media (clearly, without undue and potentially harmful sensationalism). In addition, clinicians should be encouraged to explore reasons behind choosing a particular method of suicide in patients who have made plans for taking their lives.

Endnotes

1. Gunnell D, Bennewith O, Hawton K, Simkin S, Kapur N (2005). The epidemiology and prevention of suicide by hanging: a systematic review. *International Journal of Epidemiology* 34, 433–442.
2. De Leo D, Dwyer J, Firman D, Neulinger K (2003). Trends in hanging and firearm suicide rates in Australia: substitution of method? *Suicide and Life-Threatening Behavior* 33, 151–164.

Twelve-month prevalence of and risk factors for suicide attempts in the World Health Organization World Mental Health Surveys

Borges G, Nock MK, Abad JMH, Hwang I, Sampson NA, Alonso J, Andrade LH, Angermeyer MC, Beautrais A, Bromet E, Bruffaerts R, De Girolamo G, Florescu S, Gureje O, Hu C, Karam EG, Kovess-Masfety V, Lee S, Levinson D, Medina-Mora M (USA)

Journal of Clinical Psychiatry 71, 1617–1628, 2010

Objective: Although suicide is a leading cause of death worldwide, clinicians and researchers lack a data-driven method to assess the risk of suicide attempts. This study reports the results of an analysis of a large cross-national epidemiologic survey database that estimates the 12-month prevalence of suicidal behaviors, identifies risk factors for suicide attempts, and combines these factors to create a risk index for 12-month suicide attempts separately for developed and developing countries.

Method: Data come from the World Health Organization (WHO) World Mental Health (WMH) Surveys (conducted 2001–2007), in which 108,705 adults from 21 countries were interviewed using the WHO Composite International Diagnostic Interview. The survey assessed suicidal behaviors and potential risk factors across multiple domains, including sociodemographic characteristics, parent psychopathology, childhood adversities, DSM-IV disorders, and history of suicidal behavior.

Results: Twelve-month prevalence estimates of suicide ideation, plans, and attempts are 2.0%, 0.6%, and 0.3%, respectively, for developed countries and 2.1%, 0.7%, and 0.4%, respectively, for developing countries. Risk factors for suicidal behaviors in both developed and developing countries include female sex, younger age, lower education and income, unmarried status, unemployment, parent psychopathology, childhood adversities, and presence of diverse 12-month DSM-IV mental disorders. Combining risk factors from multiple domains produced risk indices that accurately predicted 12-month suicide attempts in both developed and developing countries (area under the receiver operating characteristic curve = 0.74–0.80).

Conclusions: Suicidal behaviors occur at similar rates in both developed and developing countries. Risk indices assessing multiple domains can predict suicide attempts with fairly good accuracy and may be useful in aiding clinicians in the prediction of these behaviors.

Comment

Main findings: This international study conducted under the auspices of the World Health Organization assessed the prevalence of non-fatal suicidal phenomena (suicide ideation, plans and attempts) across 10 developed and 11 developing countries. Participants were selected using stratified multistage probability sampling, yielding a large and representative sample from the general population exceeding 100 thousand respondents, older than 18 years (average response rate was 73% across all countries). The main aim of the study was to develop a risk index that could be used by clinicians to quickly and easily assess the risk of a patient engaging in a suicide attempt in the coming 12 months.

Results showed that, overall, the 12 month prevalence of all measured suicidal phenomena was comparable among developed and developing countries. Across all countries, approximately 15 suicide attempts occurred for every one suicide death. Further, the risk for progression from ideation, to developing a plan, and then attempting suicide was higher in the developing countries (34% of ideators developed a plan and 20% of them attempted to take their lives, as opposed to 29% and 15%, respectively, among respondents from developed countries).

This study confirms risk factors for suicidal behaviour found in many previous studies (such as female sex, lower education and income, psychiatric illnesses, etc.). At the same time, it highlights several new fascinating findings regarding the progression from suicide ideation to behaviours. Firstly, it was found that only selected mental disorders predicted attempts among those with ideation: among these, conduct disorders emerged as the most consistent and strongest predictor, followed by anxiety and substance use disorders. Secondly, a history of unplanned attempts was found to predict subsequent unplanned attempts, but not also planned ones. Thirdly, persons who have had suicidal thoughts in the past, but never carried out an attempt, were found to have lower odds of acting on these thoughts also in the future. Further exploration of this group of people and the specific characteristics that help prevent their escalation of suicidality is needed. Finally, risk factor indices for 12 month-suicide attempts (planned or unplanned) were developed with separate versions for developed and developing countries. On average, this index showed good discrimination properties, and successfully identified 74–80% of attempters from non-attempters.

Implications: The findings of this study carry significant implications for clinicians faced with suicidal patients. Despite a fast and growing body of scientific literature on the topic, one of the greatest challenges of suicide prevention efforts remains the translation of findings about suicide risk factors into clinical settings[1]. Currently, there is no empirically driven screening instrument that can accurately predict future suicidality. Suicide risk indices, derived from results of this large cross-country study, offer such an opportunity, even though their usefulness in clinical settings needs to be evaluated. However, the authors caution that these indices are not intended to be used as a suicide risk assessment tool but instead may be utilised to identify those at high risk for suicide attempt so that they can receive a more focused, in-depth assessment and adequate treatment.

Endnotes

1. De Leo D (2002). Why are we not getting any closer to preventing suicide? (Editorial). *British Journal of Psychiatry* 181, 372–374.

Repetition of suicide attempts across episodes of severe depression: Behavioural sensitisation found in suicide group but not in controls

Bradvik L, Berglund M (Sweden)

BMC Psychiatry 11, 5–12, 2011

Background: Those who die by suicide and suffer from depression are known to have made more suicide attempts during their life-span as compared to other people with depression. A behavioural sensitisation or kindling model has been proposed for suicidal behaviour, in accordance with a sensitisation model of depressive episodes. The aim of the present study was to test such a model by investigating the distribution of initial and repeated suicide attempts across the depressive episodes in suicides and controls with a unipolar severe depression.

Method: A blind record evaluation was performed of 80 suicide victims and controls admitted to the Department of Psychiatry between 1956 and 1969 and monitored to 2010. The occurrence of initial and repeated suicide attempts by order of the depressive episodes was compared for suicides and controls.

Results: The risk of a first suicide attempt decreased throughout the later episodes of depression in both the suicide group ($p < .000$) and control group ($p < .000$). The frequencies of repetition early in the course were actually higher in the control group ($p < .007$). After that, the risk decreased in the control group, while the frequencies remained proportional in the suicide group. At the same time, there was a significantly greater decreased risk of repeated attempts during later episodes in the control group as compared to the suicide group ($p < .000$). The differences were found despite a similar number of episodes in suicides and controls.

Conclusion: Repeated suicide attempts in the later episodes of depression appear to be a risk factor for suicide in severe depression. This finding is compatible with a behavioural sensitisation of attempts across the depressive episodes, which seemed to be independent of a corresponding kindling of depression.

Comment

Main findings: This Swedish study investigated the relationship between death by suicide and history of suicidal behaviours in a clinical sample of persons with long-term depressive episodes. The study design adapted two models in an attempt to explain the relationship between depression, non-fatal suicidal behaviour and eventual death by suicide: Behavioural Sensitization and the "kindling" hypothesis. The Behavioural Sensitization model suggests that every new episode of depression gives rise to negative thinking patterns and thereby increases the risk of further depression, while the "kindling" hypothesis indicates that depression becomes increasingly 'automatic' over time. In the context of suicide, these models suggest that each attempt may lead to harmful behaviours becoming an automatic response to stressors over time. Both the study and control groups in this research were obtained from inpatients at the Department of Psychiatry during the 1950s and 1960s. The study group consisted of patients who eventually died by suicide, while excluding secondary depression and other disorders. The sample of study cases ($n = 80$) were compared with living controls ($n = 80$) from the total inpatient sample of patients, matched for criteria for diagnosis (unipolar depression), gender and year of birth. The results suggest that the controls had a higher numbers of attempts in the early course of the depression; however, these reduced over the course of the illness. The authors suggest that repeated suicide attempts in controls were related to external stressors. In comparison, a greater number of persons in the study group had an ongoing history of suicide attempts throughout the course of depression. The ongoing pattern of suicide attempts in the study group may provide evidence of behavioural sensitization and "kindling".

The main strength of this study is its longitudinal design, which extended for over fifty years. However, it is necessary to consider the possible under-reporting of suicidal behaviours, as a number of persons included in either the study or control group may have attempted suicide but never presented to a health care facility.

Implications: The main clinical implication of this study comes from the finding that persons who repeat suicide later in the course of their depressive illness are particularly at risk of suicide. As suggested by the authors, the longer and more persistent the course of suicidal behavior is over an individual's life, the greater are the odds that suicidal behaviours will become "autonomised" and less related to life stressors. Therefore, if the automatic suicidal impulse can be alleviated, the likelihood of eventual death by suicide may be reduced. There is already some evidence that treatments such as Dialectic Behavioural Therapy can be effective in reducing non-fatal suicidal behaviours[1]. However, there is less evidence of the effect of such treatment on preventing death by suicide[2]. Given the findings of this study, there is a need for clinicians to pay particular attention to patients who repeat in the later course of depression. In addition, more long-term studies are required into the possible adverse effects of treatment of depressive disorders on suicidal behaviours.

Endnotes

1. Linehan MM, Comtois KA, Murray AM, Brown MZ, Gallop RJ, Heard HL, Korslund KE, Tutek DA, Reynolds SK. Lindenboim N (2006). Two-year randomized controlled trial and follow-up of dialectical behavior therapy vs. therapy by experts for suicidal behaviours and borderline personality disorder. *Archives of General Psychiatry* 63, 757–766.
2. Hepp U, Wittman L, Schnyder U, Michel K (2004). Psychological and psychosocial interventions after attempted suicide. *Crisis* 25, 108–117.

Treatment of suicidal people around the world

Bruffaerts R, Demyttenaere K, Hwang I, Chiu WT, Sampson N, Kessler RC, Alonso J, Borges G, de Girolamo G, de Graaf R, Florescu S, Gureje O, Hu C, Karam EG, Kawakami N, Kostyuchenko S, Kovess-Masfety V, Lee S, Levinson D, Matschinger H, Posada-Villa J, Sagar R, Scott KM, Stein DJ, Tomov T, Viana MC, Nock MK (Belgium)

British Journal of Psychiatry. Published online: 24 January 2011. doi:10.1192/bjp.bp.110.084129, 2011

Background: Suicide is a leading cause of death worldwide; however, little information is available about the treatment of suicidal people, or about barriers to treatment.

Aims: To examine the receipt of mental health treatment and barriers to care among suicidal people around the world.

Method: Twenty-one nationally representative samples worldwide (n = 55 302; age 18 years and over) from the World Health Organization's World Mental Health Surveys were interviewed regarding past-year suicidal behaviour and past-year healthcare use. Suicidal respondents who had not used services in the past year were asked why they had not sought care.

Results: Two-fifths of the suicidal respondents had received treatment (from 17% in low-income countries to 56% in high-income countries), mostly from a general practitioner (22%), psychiatrist (15%) or non-psychiatrist (15%). Those who had actually attempted suicide were more likely to receive care. Low perceived need was the most important reason for not seeking help (58%), followed by attitudinal barriers such as the wish to handle the problem alone (40%) and structural barriers such as financial concerns (15%). Only 7% of respondents endorsed stigma as a reason for not seeking treatment.

Conclusions: Most people with suicide ideation, plans and attempts receive no treatment. This is a consistent and pervasive finding, especially in low-income countries. Improving the receipt of treatment worldwide will have to take into account culture-specific factors that may influence the process of help-seeking.

Comment

Main findings: The article discusses the results of the World Mental Health Survey, which included 21 low, middle and high-income countries from Africa, Asia, Australasia, Europe, and North and South America. The main focus of the study was to examine the proportion of suicidal persons who received treatment for suicidal behaviours versus those who did not seek treatment, and to examine the barriers that hindered help-seeking. The results of 55,302 interviews (conducted using The World Mental Health Composite International Diagnostic Interview interviews – CIDI) showed that 39% of suicidal persons accessed treatment for emotional difficulties in the year before the survey was conducted. Those who made a suicide attempt (accounting for 49 to 55% of respondents across all participating countries) accessed care more often than those with lower levels of suicidality (i.e. ideation or plan only – 34–42% across all countries). A greater number of persons sought treatment in high-income countries than in low and middle income countries. Further, a number of differences in treatment preferences of suicidal persons were identified. Mental health care professionals were the most commonly sought treatment (23%), closely followed by general medical care (22%) and a non-health care services (11%). Non-health care services included religious counsellors, traditional healers, and complementary or alternative practitioners. Those with higher income and education and those who had never married most often attended mental health care professionals, while those who were older, had lower education and were married most often attended general medical services. Several structural barriers to help-seeking were identified, such as limited finances (12%), lack of available treatment (11%), problems with transport (4%), and inconveniences of attending treatment (4%). The perception that help was not needed for suicidality was the most common barrier in low (67%) and middle (62%) income countries, while attitudinal barriers (54%) were the primary reason for not seeking treatment in high-income countries.

While this study has a number of strengths, such as a large sample size, the validity and generalisability of its findings may be limited by problems in the reliability of self-report data and variation in the cultural understandings of suicidal behaviours.

Implications: The proportion of suicide attempters who did not seek help in high-income countries (44%) in this study was higher than has previously found in Australia (35.6%)[1]. This may because the World Mental Health Survey only assessed access to health care for the past twelve months, while the article by Milner and De Leo[1] covers the lifetime treatment seeking. Other factors contributing to this difference may be due to variations between country contexts (e.g., culture, health systems, and attitudes towards suicide). A unique finding of this study is its in-depth investigation into the reasons why some people choose not to seek help following suicide behaviour. This is certainly important, considering the past findings that those who avoid treatment are more likely to use more lethal suicide methods (Milner and De Leo, 2010). It appears that the most common barriers to persons seeking treatment for suicidal behaviours are connected to negative attitudes, rather than structural factors. This suggests the need for greater emphasis on campaigns to reduce community stigma against suicidal behaviours and to encourage the help-seeking.

Endnotes

1. Milner A, De Leo D (2010). Who seeks treatment where? Suicidal behaviours and health care: Evidence from a community survey. *Journal of Nervous and Mental Disease* 198, 412–419.

Attempted suicide among immigrants in European countries: An international perspective

Bursztein Lipsicas C, Makinen IH, Apter A, De Leo D, Kerkhof A, Lonnqvist J, Michel K, Salander Renberg E, Sayil I, Schmidtke A, van Heeringen C, Varnik A, Wasserman D (Sweden)

Social Psychiatry and Psychiatric Epidemiology. Published online: 1 January 2011. doi:10.1007/s00127-010-0336-6, 2011

Purpose: This study compares the frequencies of attempted suicide among immigrants and their hosts, between different immigrant groups, and between immigrants and their countries of origin.

Methods: The material, 27,048 persons, including 4,160 immigrants, was obtained from the WHO/EURO Multicentre Study on Suicidal Behaviour, the largest available European database, and was collected in a standardised manner from 11 European centres in 1989–2003. Person-based suicide-attempt rates (SARs) were calculated for each group. The larger immigrant groups were studied at each centre and compared across centres. Completed-suicide rates of their countries of origin were compared to the SARs of the immigrant groups using rank correlations.

Results: 27 of 56 immigrant groups studied showed significantly higher, and only four groups significantly lower SARs than their hosts. Immigrant groups tended to have similar rates across different centres. Moreover, positive correlation between the immigrant SAR and the country-of-origin suicide rate was found. However, Chileans, Iranians, Moroccans, and Turks displayed high SARs as immigrants despite low suicide rates in the home countries.

Conclusions: The similarity of most immigrant groups' SARs across centres, and the correlation with suicidality in the countries of origin suggest a strong continuity that can be interpreted in either cultural or genetic terms. However, the generally higher rates among immigrants compared to host populations and the similarity of the rates of foreign-born and those immigrants who retained the citizenship of their country of origin point to difficulties in the acculturation and integration process. The positive correlation found between attempted and completed suicide rates suggests that the two are related, a fact with strong implications for suicide prevention.

Comment

Main findings: This is one of the rare studies conducted to date that explored frequency of non-fatal suicidal behaviours among immigrant populations. It follows previous observations that immigrants tend to maintain suicide rates of their country of origin also in their new country[1], as well as reports that immigrants generally show higher suicide rates than residents of their host country due to common social and economic disadvantages brought about by migration[2]. Data for this study were drawn from the largest European database on suicidal behaviour, collected as part of a joint study performed in 20 countries (the WHO/EURO Multicentre Study); in total, more than 58 thousand cases of suicide attempts that were in contact with any health care institution in the catchment area between 1989 and 2003 were analysed.

Results showed that out of 56 studied immigrant groups, 27 had a significantly higher rate of suicide attempts (SAR) than the hosts, 25 had a similar one and four groups had a significantly lower SAR. Overall, a positive correlation was found between the SAR of immigrants (by country of birth) to the completed-suicide rates in their native countries. Of particular interest were findings pertaining to four groups that displayed high SARs as immigrants despite low suicide rates in their countries of origin: Chileans, Iranians, Moroccans and Turks.

Two theoretical frameworks have been suggested in an attempt to describe observed patterns of suicidality in immigrant populations: genetic make-up (i.e. genetic risk factors for suicidal behaviour) and cultural continuity (i.e. enduring influences of cultural origin). While the design of the study did not permit to distinguish between the these two possible causes, the authors of the study prefer to interpret the latter explanation, arguing that that varying cultural background of immigrant populations carry with them differences in collective, implicit beliefs about permissibility and adequacy of suicidal behaviour, which continue to influence their suicidal behaviours even after relocation to a different country or cultural milieu.

Implications: Relevance of this study is highlighted by the observations of increased mobility within Europe in the last decades and the subsequent focus on issues concerning immigrant's mental health. Similarly, Australia has been experiencing an unprecedented growth of immigrant populations in recent years: according to 2006 Census, 25% of Australians were first-generation immigrants, compared 20% in 1996[3]. Available research using Australian data demonstrated concurring results to those by Burzstein Lipicas and colleagues, reporting significant correlations between immigrants' suicide rates in their host countries and those of their country of birth[1.] However, in Australia another significant feature of immigration needs to be considered when conducting research on mental health and related phenomena, that is the changing composition of immigrant populations with recent influxes of immigrants from Asia, Africa and the Middle East. Undoubtedly, these represent groups with distinct cultural backgrounds and attitudes towards suicide that require future attention in studies on suicidality among immigrants. In addition, when studying patterns of non-fatal suicidal behaviours it needs to be acknowledged that different ethnic groups have different patterns of help-seeking behaviour and health-service utilisation, impacting their propensity to come in contact with health-care services.

Awareness of particular characteristics of suicidal behaviour among immigrants is of paramount importance for the development of targeted, culturally sensitive preventive initiatives, as well as provision of adequate treatment after attempted suicide.

Endnotes

1. Burvill PW (1998). Migrant suicide rates in Australia and in country of birth. *Psychological*

Medicine 28, 201–208.

2. Bhugra D (2005). Cultural identities and cultural congruency: a new model for evaluating mental distress in immigrants. *Acta Psychiatrica Scandinavica* 111, 84–93.

3. Australian Bureau of Statistics. *Picture of the Nation – 2070.0.* Camberra: Commonwealth of Australia 2006.

Very early predictors of adolescent depression and suicide attempts in children with attention-deficit/hyperactivity disorder

Chronis-Tuscano A, Molina BSG, Pelham WE, Applegate B, Dahlke A, Overmyer M, Lahey BB (USA)

Archives of General Psychiatry 67, 1044–1051, 2010

Context: Major depression and dysthymia in adolescence are associated with substantial disability, need for mental health services, and risk for recurrence. Concrete suicidal ideation and attempts during adolescence are particularly associated with significant distress, morbidity, and risk for completed suicide.

Objectives: To test the hypothesis that young children with attention-deficit/hyperactivity disorder (ADHD) are at increased risk for depression and suicidal ideation and attempts during adolescence and to identify early predictors of which young children with ADHD are at greatest risk.

Design: Prospective follow-up study.

Setting: Chicago, Illinois, and Pittsburgh, Pennsylvania.

Patients: A cohort of 125 children who met DSM-IV criteria for ADHD at 4 to 6 years of age and 123 demographically matched comparison children without ADHD were prospectively followed up in 7 structured diagnostic assessments of depression and suicidal behavior in assessment years 6 through 14, spanning 9 through 18 years of age.

Main outcome measures: DSM-IV criteria for depressive disorders and suicidal behavior.

Results: Children with ADHD at 4 to 6 years of age were at greatly increased risk for meeting DSM-IV criteria for major depression or dysthymia (hazard ratio, 4.32) and for attempting suicide (hazard ratio, 3.60) through the age of 18 years relative to comparison children. There were marked variations in risk for these outcomes among children with ADHD, however. Within the ADHD group, children with each subtype of ADHD were at risk but for different adverse outcomes. Girls were at greater risk for depression and suicide attempts. Maternal depression and concurrent child emotional and behavior problems at 4 to 6 years of age predicted depression and suicidal behavior.

Conclusions: All subtypes of ADHD in young children robustly predict adolescent depression and/or suicide attempts 5 to 13 years later. Furthermore, female sex, maternal depression, and concurrent symptoms at 4 to 6 years of age predict which children with ADHD are at greatest risk for these adverse outcomes. Identifying high-risk young children with ADHD sets the stage for early prevention trials to reduce risk for later depression and suicidal behavior.

Comment

Main findings: Existing studies examining risks for depression and suicidal behaviour among persons with childhood history of ADHD have yielded inconsistent findings. This prospective study, carried out in the United Stated, contributes to this issue by assessing several indicators of mental health in a group of 125 children diagnosed with this disorder between the ages of 4 and 6 over a longitudinal timeframe. Results suggest that by the time children were aged 18 years of age, the likelihood of depression or attempted suicide was about 4-times higher among youth who had ADHD in childhood, compared to those without such history. The risk for subsequent mood disorders was higher among girls than boys. One of the more striking results was that a third of participants who met criteria for depression had attempted suicide at least once during the follow-up period. The study differentiated between three sub-groups of ADHD: the hyperactive-impulsive type (HI), the inattentive type (I), and the combined type (CT), showing that CT and I types were associated with increased depression, and CT and HT with suicidal behaviour.

The use of standardised diagnostic measures for mental disorders based on DSM-IV criteria, high retention rate of participants, and inclusion of a wide range of child- and family-related factors as potential covariates represented the main methodological strengths of the study. However, a limitation that needs to be considered when interpreting results about gender differences was the small sample of females with ADHD.

Implications: This study provides a rare long-term investigation of the clinical significance of early childhood ADHD, highlighting the need for early intervention programs to reduce serious behavioural and emotional sequalea associated with this disorder. As with most developmental disorders and related psychopathology, factors stemming from family and broader social environment should also be closely monitored in this vulnerable group of children, particularly maternal depression. With recent controversy around the questions of epidemic growth of incidence of ADHD among children worldwide, and the questionable efficacy of the most commonly prescribed medications (Lakomski, 2009), it would be worth investigating whether the types of treatment received in early childhood might be associated with any persisting mental health problems in later life.

Endnote

1. Lakomski C (2009). ADHD as an epidemic. *The Medical Dialogue Review* 4, 24–29.

Lethal forethought: Delayed reward discounting differentiates high- and low-lethality suicide attempts in old age

Dombrovski AY, Szanto K, Siegle GJ, Wallace ML, Forman SD, Sahakian B, Reynolds CF 3rd, Clark L (USA)

Biological Psychiatry. Published online: 15 February 2011. doi:10.1016/j.biopsych.2010.12.025, 2011

Background: The decision to commit suicide may be impulsive, but lethal suicidal acts often involve planning and forethought. People who attempt suicide make disadvantageous decisions in other contexts, but nothing is known about the way they decide about the future. Can the willingness to postpone future gratification differentiate between individuals prone to serious, premeditated and less serious, unplanned suicidal acts?

Methods: Four groups of depressed participants aged 60 and older made choices between smaller immediate and larger delayed monetary rewards: 15 who had made high-lethality suicide attempts, 14 who had made low-lethality suicide attempts, 12 who seriously contemplated suicide, and 42 people with depression, but no history of suicidal thoughts. The reference group was 31 psychiatrically healthy elders.

Results: Individuals who had made low-lethality attempts displayed an exaggerated preference for immediate rewards compared with nonsuicidal depressed and healthy control subjects. Those who had carried out high-lethality suicide attempts were more willing to delay future rewards, compared with low-lethality attempters. Better planned suicide attempts were also associated with willingness to wait for larger rewards. These effects were unchanged after accounting for education, global cognitive function, substance use disorders, psychotropic medications, and possible brain injury from attempts. Discount rates were correlated with having debt, but were not significantly associated with income, hopelessness, depressive severity, premorbid IQ, age at first attempt, or choice of violent means.

Conclusions: Although clinicians often focus on impulsivity in patients at risk for suicide, these data suggest that identifying biological characteristics and treatments for nonimpulsive suicidal older people may be even more important.

Comment

Main findings: This American study examined the role of behavioural impulsivity (indicated by measures of delay financial gratification) on suicidal behavior in a small sample of elderly people diagnosed with depression. Specifically, the study assessed differences in cases of suicide ideation (thoughts of suicide with a specific plan), and suicidal behaviours (judged to be of low or high lethality based on method choice) compared to a control group (depressed but non-suicidal). Highly lethal suicide attempts included those that resulted in coma, and those that involved penetrating wounds to abdomen or chest. Impulsivity was measured via a delay discounting questionnaire which assessed an individual's preference for smaller immediate versus larger delayed monetary rewards. Higher discount rates indicated a preference for immediate rewards, while low discounting rates signified a greater ability to delay gratification and receive a larger monetary reward. Results indicated that those who had made a highly lethal attempt and those who had higher levels of attempt planning were more willing to delay future monetary rewards than those who made a low-lethality attempt. Those who made a low-lethality attempt showed a greater preference for immediate rewards compared to the non-suicidal control group. Dombrovski and colleagues explain results in terms of impulsivity, which has been shown to be an important risk factor in past studies in suicidology[1].

One important and potentially limiting factor of the methodological design is the question whether delay discounting represents a valid measure of impulsivity, which is commonly understood as a continuum of personality features or traits (Turecki, 2005). Aside from this, the small size of the study population limits the extent to which findings may be generaliazable to the general population.

Implications: In general, this study highlights the risks associated with depression and life-stressors of old age (e.g. loss, disability, chronic pain) leading to both high and low lethality suicide attempts. In Australia, elderly suicide is a serious problem, particularly among males. For example, In 2007, the male suicide rate (death per 100,000 persons) in the 75–79 year age group (16.5), 80–84 year age group (19.2), and 85 year and over age group (22.2) was markedly higher than the all-age male suicide rate of 13.9 per 100,000[2]. These high suicide rates highlight the need for further development of interventions specifically targeting to reduce suicide among the elderly.

Aside from this, one of the most positive aspects of this study was its discovery of two groups of the elderly population at particularly elevated risk of suicide: those who make poorly planned attempts and use less lethal methods, and those who make serious plans for suicide and use lethal methods. The authors speculate that individuals who react to stressors with poorly planned and less serious suicidal acts might be affected by a failure of cognitive control, resulting in more impulsive behaviours. Impulsivity and lack of ability to delay gratification could be improved through activities designed to increase cognitive control over behaviours, such as working memory training (described in more detail in the presented study).

Endnotes

1. Turecki G (2005). Dissecting the suicide phenotype: the role of impulsive–aggressive behaviours. *Journal of Psychiatry & Neuroscience* 30, 398–408.
2. Australian Institute of Health and Welfare (AIHW) (2010). *GRIM (General Record of Incidence of Mortality) Books.* AIHW: Canberra.

No-suicide contracts, no-suicide agreements, and no-suicide assurances

Edwards SJ, Sachmann MD (Australia)

Crisis 31, 290–302, 2010

Background: Suicide prevention contracting (SPC) procedures are often afforded clinical practice validity in the absence of evidence attesting to their efficacy and validity.

Aims: This study sought to develop a contemporary profile of SPC, identifying factors associated with utilization, perceived effectiveness, and to describe potentially detrimental factors when activating SPC.

Methods: A questionnaire was mailed to a sample of mental health practitioners comprising physicians, mental health nurse practitioners, and allied health practitioners to inquire about their practices and experiences with SPC.

Results: There were 420 valid responses, a response rate of 31%. Participants confirmed three types of SPC procedures in operation: (1) 355 (85%) having used verbal no-suicide assurances (NSAs); (2) 317 (76%) using verbal no-suicide agreements (NSAg); and, (3) 154 (37%) using written no-suicide contracts (NSC). The profiled procedures and their clinical application indicate that participants perceived differences in the diagnostic, therapeutic, and medico-legal utility of all three SPC procedures. Importantly, SPC procedures were shown to have a multifaceted potential for detrimental outcomes for patients and practitioners.

Conclusions: Until now, SPC had represented a poorly understood and remains a questionable clinical practice intervention. Education initiatives are required that alert mental health practitioners to the dangers of SPC for patients and practitioners alike, and to present alternative interventions containing less risk.

Comment

Main findings: Suicide prevention contracting (SPC) procedures are believed to be widely used in clinical practice, despite insufficient empirical evidence of their diagnostic and therapeutic value. The study by Edwards and Sachmann investigated the frequency of SPC use in public mental health services among a large sample of Australian mental health professionals ($n = 425$). These authors differentiated between three SPC procedures: verbal no-suicide assurances, verbal no-suicide agreements, and written no-suicide contracts. Results showed that the great majority of participants have used at least one form of SPC during their practice; the most common SPC was verbal non-suicidal assurances (85%), while the least common was written no-suicide contracts (37%). Verbal non-suicidal assurances were reported being used 'often to always' in more than half of respondents, who felt this technique assisted the process of assessing suicide risk and the overall therapeutic alliance. While a relatively high percentage of practitioners appeared to use these methods, only a low proportion of the sample had received formal training in the use of SPC (30%). Those who had never used any of the described procedures (8%) had on average about 20 years of service, which was longer than the average service of 16.5 years recorded in the total sample. They listed a variety of reasons for their non-use, such as ethical concerns and false sense of security in absence of any evidence of its efficacy. This suggests that as mental health practitioners gain more experience and knowledge — developing a suite of effective clinical practice interventions for presenting problems — the perceived effectiveness of SPC diminishes. Based on available evidence, the authors conclude that the potentially inherent risks of SPC outweigh its perceived benefits. In particular, they warn mental health practitioners of the lack of medico-legal protection that SPC offer.

Implications: There are a number of points that challenge the efficacy of suicide prevention contracting (SPC) procedures in clinical practice. First of all, there is limited evidence that these are actually effective for suicidal persons. In fact, past research has identified the profile of a patient that might benefit most from engagement in such verbal or written agreements as "one with a limited or no history of suicidal behaviour who present a positive attitude regarding SPC"[1]. In addition, it has been suggested that from the patients' perspective, such agreements/contracts weaken therapeutical alliance and are often seen as practitioners' attempt to protect themselves of any responsibility in case of an adverse clinical outcome. The article by Edwards and Sachmann also highlights a number of issues with the use of SPCs, including the ongoing difficulties faced by mental health practitioners (and researchers alike) due to: 1) unclear nomenclature in defining severity of suicidal risk, and; 2) the lack of equivocal guidance in constructing a SPC procedure.

One of the most relevant findings of the study is that only about 70% of mental health practitioners received general suicide prevention training, and even fewer have received a specialised training on no-suicide contracting. Therefore, it seems that at the moment, 'in-vivo' learning is the predominant mode for practitioners to gain an understanding of SPC practices and their potential contra-indications. Given that a great majority of these profiles frequently encounter clients at risk of suicide during their practice (in Edwards and Sachmann' study, more than 70% had seen at least five such patients in the year prior), more systematic education of mental health professionals on these issues is warranted. In addition, it might be worth expanding the scope of such trainings to health professional with a less specialised focus on mental health, such as general practitioners. Whilst GPs do not offer specialised treatment to persons at risk of suicide, a recent report by the mental health services in Australia has shown that annually GPs deliver over 13 million mental health-related consultations, which is more than double the attendances in the specialist mental health public sector[2]. Doubtlessly, among these presentations a significant number of patients report having suicidal thoughts or plans, and awareness of possible benefits, as well as harm, arising from attempting to deter such patients from their self-harming intentions would represent a valuable contribution to national suicide prevention efforts.

Until more solid evidence becomes available on the validity and efficiency of use of SPC techniques, it is essential that mental health professionals who include them into treatment protocols are aware of their limitations. SPCs should not replace other risk assessment tools nor does it guarantee patients refrain from attempting or completing suicides in the future.

Endnotes

1. Davis S, Williams IS, Hays LW (2002). Psychiatric inpatients' perceptions of written no-suicide agreements: An exploratory study. *Suicide and Life-Threatening Behavior* 32, 51–61.
2. Australian Institute of Health and Welfare (2010). *Mental health services in Australia 2007–08.* Mental Health Series No. 12. Canberra: AIHW.

Suicide among Arab-Americans

El-Sayed AM, Tracy M, Scarborough P, Galea S (USA)

PLoS One 6, e14704, 2011

Background: Arab-American (AA) populations in the US are exposed to discrimination and acculturative stress-two factors that have been associated with higher suicide risk. However, prior work suggests that socially oriented norms and behaviours, which characterize recent immigrant ethnic groups, may be protective against suicide risk. Here we explored suicide rates and their determinants among AAs in Michigan, the state with the largest proportion of AAs in the US.

Methodology/Principal Findings: ICD-9/10 underlying cause of death codes were used to identify suicide deaths from among all deaths in Michigan between 1990 and 2007. Data from the 2000 U. S. Census were collected for population denominators. Age-adjusted suicide rates among AAs and non-ethnic whites were calculated by gender using the direct method of standardization. We also stratified by residence inside or outside of Wayne County (WC), the county with the largest AA population in the state. Suicide rates were 25.10 per 100,000 per year among men and 6.40 per 100,000 per year among women in Michigan from 1990 to 2007. AA men had a 51% lower suicide rate and AA women had a 33% lower rate than non-ethnic white men and women, respectively. The suicide rate among AA men in WC was 29% lower than in all other counties, while the rate among AA women in WC was 20% lower than in all other counties. Among non-ethnic whites, the suicide rate in WC was higher compared to all other counties among both men (12%) and women (16%).

Conclusions/Significance: Suicide rates were higher among non-ethnic white men and women compared to AA men and women in both contexts. Arab ethnicity may protect against suicide in both sexes, but more so among men. Additionally, ethnic density may protect against suicide among Arab-Americans.

Comment

Main findings: The main aim of this study was to compare suicide mortality of Arab Americans living the state of Michigan in the north-east of USA to those of non-ethnic background. The topic of immigrants' mental health, including factors related to their suicidality, has been gaining increasing attention in scientific literature in recent decades, with results commonly showing that suicide rates of immigrants reflect those of their country of birth[1]. However, experiences of disadvantaged socioeconomic status, marginalisation and associated acculturative stress were found to represent additional risk factors for suicide[2]. The suicidality of Arab populations living outside their homelands has not been systematically investigated to date, making this study unique in its scope and one of high relevance. Results showed that in the period between 1990 and 2007, the Arab Americans (AAs) had significantly lower suicide rates than the non-ethnic white males (difference of 51%) and females (difference of 31%). Similar relative risks were found across all age groups, except among elderly women, where AA women had

32% higher risk of suicide than their white counterparts. Of interest is also observation that the suicide rates of AAs was lower in areas with greater ethnic density that in other contexts. This may be because this allowed stronger communal aspects and reinforcement of cultural identity, strong family bonds, and positive ethnic group identity[2]. The Islamic religion may be another protective factors, as this carries explicit religious restrictions against suicide, which is not only considered a forbidden act but also imposes families of suicide victims with ostracism within their communities.

Some methodological limitations should be considered when interpreting these findings, in particular those pertaining to uncertain generalisability of observed trends within US or internationally, and inability to account for dynamic changes in the population structure over the data collection period. It would also be worth separately investigating the rates pre- and post the terrorist attacks of September 11th 2001, after which the Arab populations have been subjected to increased marginalization from the general population.

Implications: The results of this study carry significant implications for the Australian context, which is certainly one of the culturally most diverse countries in the world. According to the 2006 Census, 25% of Australians were first-generation immigrants; an increase from 20% in 1996[3]. Migrants born in North Africa and Middle East (consisting of predominantly Muslim populations) accounted for 1.3% of the total Australian population, or about 6% of all overseas-born persons, while in 1976 they only accounted for 3.6% of immigrant population[4]. Consistent with studies conducted in the United States[2], male and female migrants born in the North Africa and Middle East have been showed to have the lowest suicide mortality of all ethnic groups residing in Australia (age standardised suicide rates in period 2004–2006: 3.9 per 100,000, compared to 12.2 per 100,000 for total population)[5]However, it needs to be acknowledged that the composition of Australia's population has changed considerably during the 20th century, with particularly marked increases in recent migrations from Asia, Africa and the Middle East (ABS, 2008). Findings from the presented study by El-Sayed and colleagues highlight the need for further investigations of the role of culture as a determinant of suicide in Arab populations, especially as the Arabs represent one of the faster growing ethnic minority groups. For example, in 2006, migrants born in North Africa and Middle East (consisting of predominantly Muslim populations) accounted for 1.3% of the total Australian population, or about 6% of all overseas-born persons, while in 1976 they accounted for 3.6% of immigrant population (ABS, 2008). Most recent study on this topic undertaken in Australia demonstrated that immigrants' suicide rates, particularly in males, are directly correlated to those of their home countries (Ide et al., under review). Consistent with studies conducted in the United States (Leong et al., 2008), male and female migrants born in the North Africa and Middle East showed the lowest suicide mortality of all ethnic groups residing in Australia (age standardised suicide rates in period 2004–2006: 3.9 per 100,000, compared to 12.2 per 100,000 for total population).

Arab immigrant populations seem to demonstrate distinctive characteristics in terms of mortality patterns, as influenced by the strong ethnic group identity and traditional interpretations of the Islamic laws[6]. However, as the authors of this study suggest, the communally-oriented features among Arab immigrants, which currently act as protective factors against suicide, may in the future deteriorate with their increasing assimilation into the culture of the dominant population. Policymakers seeking to prevent suicide among this group should therefore seek to promote community participation and civil societal growth among the ethnic minority communities, especially those in highly acculturative atmospheres. In addition, attention should be placed on mental health and suicidality experienced by the second-generation immigrants, particularly as some recent evidence suggests that second-generation immigrants may have higher rates of suicide than the first generation of immigrants compared to the majority population[7].

Endnotes

1. Burvill PW (1998). Migrant suicide rates in Australia and in country of birth. *Psychosocial Medicine* 28, 201–208.

2. Leong FTL, Leach MM (2008) Suicide *among racial and ethnic minority groups: theory, research, and practice.* New York: Routledge.

3. Australian Bureau of Statistics (2007). *Picture of the Nation, Cat. No. 2070.0.* Canberra: ABS.

4. Australian Bureau of Statistics (2008). *Migration, Australia, 2006–07, Cat. No. 3412.0* Canberra: ABS.

5. Ide N, Kolves K, Casanniti M, De Leo D (under review). Suicide of first-generation immigrants in Australia, 1974–2006.

6. Singh GK, Siahpush M (2001). All-cause and cause-specific mortality of immigrants and native born in the United States. *American Journal of Public Health* 91, 392–399.

7. Hjern A, Allebeck P (2002). Suicide in first-and second-generation immigrants in Sweden comparative study. *Social Psychiatry & Psychiatric Epidemiology* 37, 423–429.

School performance and risk of suicide in early adulthood: Follow-up of two national cohorts of Swedish schoolchildren

Gunnell D, Löfving S, Gustafsson JE, Allebeck P (Sweden)
Journal of Affective Disorder. Published online: 4 February 2011. doi:10.1016/j.jad.2011.01.002, 2011

Background: Poor school performance and low IQ are associated with an increased risk of suicide in males; it is uncertain whether cognitive performance is a risk factor for suicide in females and whether severe mental illness influences these associations.

Method: Record linkage study of Swedish education, population and census data with mortality and inpatient registers. Data were available for 95,497 males and 91,311 females born in 1972 and 1977 and followed up until 31 December 2005.

Results: 230 males and 90 females died from suicide over the follow-up period. There were strong inverse associations between school performance at age 16 and subsequent suicide risk in males (fully adjusted hazard ratio (HR) per SD increase in school performance score: 0.6 95% CI 0.6 to 0.7; $p < 0.001$)) but not females: adjusted HR. 1.1 (CI 0.9 to 1.4 $p = 0.50$). In males there were almost four fold differences in suicide risk between children in the top and bottom fifths of the range of school grade scores. Similar associations were seen with upper secondary school performance (age 18/19 years). There was no strong evidence that deterioration in school performance between ages 16 and 18 was associated with increased suicide risk. Amongst men who developed severe psychiatric illness school performance was not associated with suicide risk.

Limitations: We had limited information on the prevalence of minor psychiatric disorder in cohort members and no data on IQ for the cohort as a whole.

Conclusions: Good performance in secondary (age 16) and upper secondary (age 18) school is associated with a reduced risk of suicide in men but not women. This protective effect is not seen amongst those who develop severe psychiatric illness. These differences indicate that the aetiology of suicide differs in males and females and in those with and without severe mental illness.

Comment

Main findings: This study is distinctive in that it is the first to use a prospective population-based study design to specifically examine the association between school performance in adolescence and subsequent suicidal behaviours in early adulthood, while controlling for a range of possible confounding factors, such as socioeconomic conditions and mental illness. It represents a continuation of an earlier exploration of Swedish schoolchildren, in which it was determined that it was IQ-related performance, rather than IQ *per se* that influences suicide risk[1]. The main finding of this study was that school performance at ages 16 and 18 was strongly inversely associated with suicide risk in males, but not females. Among males, those with the highest school marks had more than 4-times lower suicide risk than those in the bottom fifth; the protective effect of good school performance appeared to be stronger in those that didn't develop severe psychiatric illness.

A large sample of two Swedish cohorts and a high retention rate (complete base-line and follow-up data were available for nearly 90% of the study populations) augment the reliability and generalisabilty of study findings. Yet, some limitations should be considered when interpreting its findings: first, information on mental health was obtained only through records of admission to inpatient care (neglecting persons treated in outpatient settings), and second, school performance results were (in part) based on teachers' experiences of the students.

Implications: Authors conclude that the strong, graded association of school performance with suicide in males, and the absence of such an association in females, requires further investigation to improve understanding of its preventive implications. It is possible that the differing associations reflect greater differences in life chances and satisfaction amongst males who perform well and those who perform badly at school, compared to such effects on women. In the latter, parenthood is believed to have a protective role against suicide even when affected by unfavourable employment or living circumstances. This study highlights children and adolescents performing poorly at school as a vulnerable population at risk for a range of adverse mental health outcomes, including suicidal behaviours. These persons should therefore be systematically assessed and monitored at regular intervals.

Endnotes

1. Andersson L, Allebeck P, Gustafsson JE, Gunnell D (2008). Association of IQ scores and school achievement with suicide in a 40-year follow-up of a Swedish cohort. *Acta Psychiatrica Scandinavica* 118, 99–105.

Electroconvulsive therapy and suicide among the mentally ill in England: A national clinical survey

Hunt IM, Windfuhr K, Swinson N, Shaw J, Appleby L, Kapur N (UK)

Psychiatry Research. Published online: 4 January 2011. doi:10.1016/j.psychres.2010.12.014, 2011

We aimed to determine the number and characteristics of psychiatric patients receiving electroconvulsive therapy (ECT) who had subsequently died by suicide. Data were collected on an 8-year (1999–2006) sample of suicide cases in England who had been in recent contact with mental health services. Of 9752 suicides, 71 (1%) were being treated with ECT at the time of death. Although the number of patients who received ECT had fallen substantially over time, the rate of suicide in these individuals showed no clear decrease and averaged 9 deaths per year, or a rate of 10.8 per 10,000 patients treated. These suicide cases were typically older, with high rates of affective disorder and previous self-harm. They were more likely to be an in-patient at the time of death than other suicide cases. Nearly half of the community cases who had received ECT had died within 3months of discharge. Our results demonstrated that the fall in the use of ECT has not affected suicide rates in patients receiving this treatment. Services appear to acknowledge the high risk of suicide in those receiving ECT. Improvements in care of these severely ill patients may include careful discharge planning and improved observation of in-patients in receipt of ECT.

Comment

Main findings: There is some existing evidence in international literature that ECT can be an effective treatment for alleviating depression and suicidal behaviours[1]. However, available studies are less clear about the effect of ECT on mortality due to suicide and, specifically, about the number of persons who have died due to suicide after receiving ECT. This may be due to the small sample size of studies, which have generally been on clinical samples. The major advantage of this study by Hunt and colleagues was its use of a large comprehensive national sample of deaths in England and Wales. This enabled the authors to conduct a relatively detailed and nationally-representative investigation of all recorded suicide death occurring under mental health care who were receiving ECT treatment at the time of death. Results showed that suicide among persons who have had ECT is rare (representing less than 1% of all in-patient suicides). The study also compared the social, behavioural and clinical features of suicide cases who had received ECT to those that had not received ECT, and found that, compared to suicide cases that had not received the treatment, suicide cases receiving ECT were significantly older than other cases and more likely to be married. Aside from this, these cases had more often engaged in previous self-harm, were in-patients at the time of death, and had a diagnosis of an affective disorder. These persons were more often receiving enhanced levels of aftercare and were receiving concomitant drug treatment.

Implications: According to Chanpatta (2002), between 2002 and 2004, the rate of ECT use in Australia was 37.8 persons per 100,000 population per annum (as assessed by the crude treated-person rate). Approximately 82% of treated cases in 136 hospitals were clinically depressed and most patient were 65 years or over (38.4%). Chanpatta (2002) found no cases of ECT-related death during a survey period. However, this could have been a reflection of the cross-sectional design of the study. Assessing the long-term outcomes of persons receiving ECT in Australia is a necessary area of future research, especially considering that these persons are often already at-risk of suicide.

Endnotes

1. Brådvik L, Berglund M (2006). Long-term treatment and suicidal behavior in severe depression: ECT and antidepressant pharmacotherapy may have different effects on the occurrence and seriousness of suicide attempts. *Depression and Anxiety* 23, 34–41.
2. Chanpatta W (2002). A questionnaire survey of ECT practice in Australia. *Journal of ECT* 23, 89–92.

Suicidality following a natural disaster

Kar N (UK)

American Journal of Disaster Medicine 5, 361–368, 2010

Objectives: It was intended to study the suicidal cognitions and behaviours following a super-cyclone.

Design: Cross-sectional evaluation study.

Setting: Community.

Participants: Using simple random procedure, 12 months after a super-cyclone, 540 victims were selected.

Main Outcome Measures: Suicidal cognitions and behaviours through the Suicidality Screening Questionnaire. This included items on whether life was worth living, death wishes, suicidal idea, plan, and attempt, and history of a suicide attempt. Self-Reporting Questionnaire was used to screen for possible psychiatric morbidity. The influence of various sociodemographic factors, degree of exposure, and clinical variables on suicidal cognitions and attempt was studied.

Results: A considerable number of victims had suicidal cognitions: death wishes (66.4 percent), suicidal ideas (38.0 percent), and suicidal plans (18.3 percent). Sixty-eight persons (12.6 percent) of the sample had made suicide attempts after the cyclone. The risk of a suicide attempt was high in persons with current psychiatric morbidity, past history of psychiatric illness, post cyclone thoughts of life not worth living, suicidal ideation and plans, and living with inadequate support.

Conclusions: There was a reported increase of suicidal cognitions and attempts within 12 months following a natural disaster. Awareness of increased suicidality, attention to associated risk factors, and support regarding these may help in the prevention of suicide following disasters.

Comment

Main findings: Most past studies on the relationship between natural disasters and suicide have been ecological and focused on suicide mortality. Unlike these, this study by Kar sought to examine the relationship between a particular type of a natural disaster — cyclone, and subsequent suicide ideation and attempts. A self-report survey was distributed in six districts in rural India, including those in 'high' exposure areas (villages that were in the centre of the eye of the cyclone) and those in 'low' exposure areas (areas not directly in the area of damage). The findings of the study suggest that those who made a suicide attempt post-cyclone more often had a psychiatric history and had received treatment for a psychiatric ailment. Factors significantly related to suicide attempts post cyclone included having thoughts that life was not worth living, and having a plan for suicide. However, results also indicated that there was actually a higher incidence of suicide attempts in low-exposure areas (not the most damaged in the disaster) rather than in high-exposure areas. The authors acknowledge a number of possible explanations for this, such as the possibility that suicidal behaviours were already more prominent in low-exposure areas before the cyclone. Further, low-exposure areas were less often the recipients of aid efforts and post-disaster intervention.

In interpreting the study findings it is necessary to consider possible contextual effects, as the rural areas under study were already experiencing substantial economic and social problems prior to the cyclone. These adverse living circumstances were worsened by the cyclone, which occurred just before the harvesting of agricultural crops, thereby severely damaging agricultural produce. Not only did the cyclone damage the main source of income in the area, it also led to an increase in unemployment, as farms no longer had the ability to hire farm labourers. Consequently, the negative impact of the cyclone may have been connected to wider social and economic losses, as well as emotional distress resulting from loss of loved ones and physical damage to homes and communities. Aside from these considerations to the methodology, the authors of the study did not explicitly ask survey participants about the perceived impact of the cyclone on their wellbeing, which limited the possibility of investigating any direct links between the studied phenomena.

Implications: While this descriptive study suffers from a few methodological problems, it adds further support to the idea that extreme weather events and disasters have an adverse effect on mental health and suicide[1]. For example, research on communities affected by Hurricane Katrina revealed high rates of suicide death and attempts following the disaster (14.7- and 78.6-times higher than in the area's baseline rate, respectively)[2]. As noted by the study authors, suicide was not only related to exposure to the event, but subsequent problems in finding stable housing, as well as a lack of access to support services and employment[2]. In the Australian context, there is increasing concern about the negative impacts of climate-related events on the affected population's wellbeing, especially the possible influence of acute weather events[3]. This emphasises the need for long term research on effects of these climatic events on suicide, as well as the ongoing support of those Australians affecting by natural disasters.

Endnotes

1. Rezaeian M (2008). Epidemiology of suicide after natural disasters: a review on the literature and a methodological framework for future studies. *American Journal of Disaster Medicine* 3, 52–6.
2. Acierno R, Ruggiero KJ, Galea S, Resnick HS, Koenen K, Roitzsch J, de Arellano M, Boyle J, Kilpatrick DG (2007). Psychological sequelae resulting from the 2004 Florida hurricanes: implications for post-disaster intervention. *American Journal of Public Health* 97, 103–108.
3. Fritze JG, Blashki GA, Burke S, Wiseman J (2008). Hope, despair and transformation: Climate change and the promotion of mental health and wellbeing. *International Journal of Mental Health Systems* 2, 13.

Increasing railway suicide acts after media coverage of a fatal railway accident? An ecological study of 747 suicidal acts

Kunrath S, Baumert J, Ladwig KH (Germany)

Journal of Epidemiology and Community Health. Published online: 19 October 2010.
doi:10.1136/jech.2009.098293, 2010

Background: While coverage of a celebrity suicide in the mass media may trigger copycat suicides, evidence for the effect of media reports of non-prominent suicides is moderate. Diversification of current media may raise further doubts as to whether their influence on suicidal acts is still present. We examined whether widespread media coverage of a railway accident, in which several people were killed while investigating a presumed railway suicide, subsequently increased the number of railway suicides.

Methods: The daily incidence of railway suicides was derived from the national accident registry on the German railway net. We estimated incidence ratios by Poisson regression, adjusting for relevant confounders (e.g., outdoor temperature, unemployment rate), for the 2 months following the accident (predefined index period) and predefined control periods (preceding 2 years of the same period and 1 month before/after the index period).

Results: The mean number of railway suicides per day in the index period increased significantly to 2.66 (95% CI 2.19 to 3.13) compared to 1.94 (95% CI 1.78 to 2.10) during both control periods. Fully adjusted Poisson regression showed a 44% daily increase in railway suicides in the index period compared to the control periods (incidence ratio 1.44, 95% CI 1.02 to 2.03). A maximum of eight suicides per day was reached about 1 week after the accident.

Conclusions: Non-fictional media coverage of a fatal accident appears to affect subsequent railway suicide numbers. Supposedly, media reports drew attention to railways as a means of suicide.

Comment

Main findings: This article examined the relationship between railway suicides and the media coverage of a rail accident that occurred in Germany in 2006, in which three police officers died while attempting to recover a body from the train tracks. The study authors examined media reports from three major nationwide televisions channels, three national subscription newspapers, and the national boulevard paper. Data on suicide occurring on railways (coded as X81 in the ICD – "intentional self harm by jumping or lying in front of a moving object") was ascertained from the Event Database Safety, which is the national central registry of accidents occurring on German railway track (excluding municipal subways). The statistical design included a study of rail suicide attempts and deaths (n = 747) during the two months after the accident (i.e. the "index" period) with a number of "control" periods occurring both before and after the incident. Results indicated that there was a marked increased in the number of fatal cases of rail suicide during the index period (at least 5 more suicides a week) than the control periods. The daily maximum was eight suicide cases, which occurred one week after the accident. There was an increase of 37% of suicide attempts in the index period compared to the control periods. After adjusting for the weekday, month and periods, the daily number of suicidal acts was between 43% and 53% higher during the two month study period after the accident. After controlling for unemployment and temperature, media coverage of the accident was related to a 44% increase in suicidal acts. The authors suggest that the media created the perception that death by suicide on the railway tracks was a "certain and painless death", therefore making it is more attractive option for vulnerable persons contemplating suicide.

However, several methodological problems in this study lessen the strength of its findings. For example, the study does not provide information on whether individuals who died by rail suicide were exposed to the media information on the accident. Further, the authors did not provide any data on other suicide in other locations (e.g. bridges) and therefore it is impossible to ascertain whether they had been any instances of "means substitution" of suicide.

Implications: The findings of this study expand the scope of current understanding regarding media reporting and suicide. It appears that it is not only reporting of suicidal behaviours cases that may be related to other instances of suicide, but also media reports about accidents in general. The authors suggest that the relationships between accidents and suicide reflect a "choice-structuring" preference for suicide methods likely to result in death and that are relatively painless. This means that media reporting on rail-accidents provided vulnerable individuals with ideas about possible locations and methods for death or harm. Before the findings of this study can be applied to the Australian context, we suggest replication studies to be conducted, using instances of rail-accidents and suicides in Australia.

The scope of nonsuicidal self-injury on YouTube

Lewis SP, Heath NL, St Denis JM, Noble R (Canada)
Pediatrics. Published online: 21 February 2011. doi:10.1542/peds.2010-2317, 2011

Objective: Nonsuicidal self-injury, the deliberate destruction of one's body tissue (eg, self-cutting, burning) without suicidal intent, has consistent rates ranging from 14% to 24% among youth and young adults. With more youth using video-sharing Web sites (eg, YouTube), this study examined the accessibility and scope of nonsuicidal self-injury videos online.

Methods: Using YouTube's search engine (and the following key words: "self-injury" and "self-harm"), the 50 most viewed character (ie, with a live individual) and noncharacter videos (100 total) were selected and examined across key quantitative and qualitative variables.

Results: The top 100 videos analyzed were viewed over 2 million times, and most (80%) were accessible to a general audience. Viewers rated the videos positively (M = 4.61; SD: 0.61 out of 5.0) and selected videos as a favorite over 12 000 times. The videos' tones were largely factual or educational (53%) or melancholic (51%). Explicit imagery of self-injury was common. Specifically, 90% of noncharacter videos had nonsuicidal self-injury photographs, whereas 28% of character videos had in-action nonsuicidal self-injury. For both, cutting was the most common method. Many videos (58%) do not warn about this content.

Conclusions: The nature of nonsuicidal self-injury videos on YouTube may foster normalization of nonsuicidal self-injury and may reinforce the behavior through regular viewing of nonsuicidal self-injury–themed videos. Graphic videos showing nonsuicidal self-injury are frequently accessed and received positively by viewers. These videos largely provide nonsuicidal self-injury information and/or express a hopeless or melancholic message. Professionals working with youth and young adults who enact nonsuicidal self-injury need to be aware of the scope and nature of nonsuicidal self-injury on YouTube.

Comment

Main findings: Online social interactions, including online video sharing, have become an integral part of most youths' and young adults' lives. In recent years, there has been increased attention to the possible negative impacts of online sharing of content about non-suicidal self-injury (NNSI). Some researchers have gone as far to suggest that online communications about NSSI may lead to nor-malisation of self-harming behaviours and exacerbate the risk for repetition via contagion effects[1]. To date, studies in this area have been limited to text-based sites, with absence of analysis of such contents on videos posted on the Internet.

Lewis and colleagues conducted a pioneering study that examined the 100 most-viewed videos on self-harm on YouTube, the largest and fastest growing video-sharing Web site. Descriptive results indicated that videos were most often posted by young adult female users (though the accuracy of their demographic information, in particular age, cannot be verified on YouTube and it is suspected many user lie about their age to gain access to contents restricted to minors). While many of these videos tended to portray neutral educational or factual information, over half did not include a warning that the contents may be upsetting to the viewers. This is particularly problematic given that 80% of the videos were accessible to general audiences. Non-character videos (including text, photography and music) received a larger number of comments and votes than character videos (including a living individual). As suggested by the study authors, non-character videos were richer in artistic expression, and may normalise or "glamorise" NSSI, and therefore may be associated with a higher risk of NSSI than character videos.

Implications: Non-suicidal self-injury (NSSI) is a growing clinical problem, especially among adolescents and young adults. The current estimates of the lifetime prevalence of such acts in high school students average at about 20%, although they vary significantly across samples[2] (the alarming proportions of the prevalence of self-injury in Australia is discussed in more detail in another key article in this volume by Martin and colleagues[3]). Research suggests that there is often no suicidal intent behind such acts, rather these are used to lessen a distressing affect, inflict self-punishment or signal personal grief; nevertheless, NNSI has been suggested to increase risk of attempted or completed suicide through habituation to self-inflicted harm[4].

While the need for development of prevention and early intervention programs for adolescent NNSI is clear, at the moment, no such program exists in Australia. Lewis and colleagues provided evidence of the growing number of self-harming images currently shared among youth through the Web, and the potentially detrimental effects of normalising and even sensationalising self-harm. At the same time, the Authors of this study identified the Internet as the platform which should be utilised more heavily in any future strategies targeting self-harm. From a policy perspective, electronic searches for NSSI videos should provide the person with helpful resources, similar to how Google now provides suicide crisis numbers for specific searchers relating to suicide (e.g. "suicidal thoughts"). In addition, health professionals working with youth engaging in self-injuries behaviours, as well as their parents and teachers, are encouraged to enquire about their Internet use and facilitate more open and informed discussions about its potential harms. However, more empirical research is needed on the impacts of exposure to self-harming visual imagery on youth, and the identification of factors (e.g. music or images) and mechanisms (e.g. behaviour or peer modelling) involved in the process of increasing the risk for repetitive actions.

Endnotes

1. Whitlock JL, Powers JP, Eckenrode JE (2006). The virtual cutting edge: adolescent self-injury and the Internet. *Developmental Psychology* 42, 404–417.

2. Muehlenkamp J, Kerr PL (2010). Untangling a complex web: how non-suicidal self-injury and suicide attampts differ. *The Prevention Researcher* 17, 8–10.

3. Martin G, Swannell SV, Hazell PL, Harrison JE, Taylor AW (2010). Self-injury in Australia: a community survey. *Medical Journal of Australia* 193, 506–510.

4. Joiner TE (2006). *Why people die by suicide.* Cambridge: Harvard University Press.

Self-injury in Australia: A community survey

Martin G, Swannell SV, Hazell PL, Harrison JE, Taylor AW (Australia)

Medical Journal Australia 193, 506–510, 2010

Objective: To understand self-injury and its correlates in the Australian population.

Design, Participants and Setting: Cross-sectional survey, using computer-assisted telephone interview, of a representative sample of 12 006 Australians from randomly selected households.

Main Outcome Measures: Data on demographics, self-injury, psychiatric morbidity, substance use, suicidality, disclosure and help-seeking.

Results: In the 4 weeks before the survey, 1.1% of the sample self-injured. For females, self-injury peaked in 15–24-year-olds; for males, it peaked in 10–19-year-olds. The youngest self-injurers were nine boys and three girls in the 10–14-year age group, and the oldest were one female and one male in the 75–84-year age group. Mean age of onset was 17 years, but the oldest age of onset was 44 years for males and 60 years for females. No statistically significant differences existed between those who did and did not self-injure on sex, socioeconomic status or Indigenous status. Most common self-injury method was cutting; most common motivation was to manage emotions. Frequency of self-injury during the 4-week period ranged from 1 to 50 instances (mean, 7). Self-injurers were significantly more psychologically distressed, and also more likely to use substances. Adults who self-injured were more likely to have received a psychiatric diagnosis. Self-injurers were more likely to have experienced recent suicidal ideation (OR, 11.56; 95% CI, 8.14–16.41), and have ever attempted suicide (OR, 8.51; 95% CI, 5.70–12.69). Most respondents told someone about their self-injury but fewer than half sought help.

Conclusion: The prevalence of self-injury in Australia in the 4 weeks before the survey was substantial and self-injury may begin at older ages than previously reported. Self-injurers are more likely to have mental health problems and are at higher risk of suicidal thoughts and behaviour than non-self-injurers, and many self-injurers do not seek help.

Comment

Main findings: This research contributes to health research and prevention in Australia by identifying the number of persons who engaged in self-injurious behaviours (defined as deliberately hurting themselves without intent to die) in the general population (12,010 interviews). Results indicated that the lifetime prevalence (inclusive of the 4 weeks prior to the survey) of self-injury was 8.1%; the lifetime prevalence of self-injury was observed to be higher in females (8.7%) than males (7.5%). Females who reported a history of self-injury were a found be to slightly older (in the 15 to 19 year age range, and in the 20 to 25 years age range) than males, who were more often in the 10 to 14 years and 15 to 19 year age range. Cutting (40.6%) was the most commonly used method of self-harm, followed by scratching (39.8%), hitting (36.8%), and punching, hitting and slapping (33.8%). The most frequent motives associated with self-injury were management of emotions, followed by the need to punish oneself. There was a strong link between suicidality and self-injury, with over 48% of the sample of those who had engaged in self-harm in the four weeks prior to the survey also experiencing suicide ideation. Further, over one-quarter of those who self-injured in the four weeks leading to the survey also reported of a lifetime suicide attempt. Persons who self-injured were more likely to have received a psychiatric diagnosis, experience psychological distress, and more often reported drug and alcohol use than those that did not report self-injury. Few of those who engaged in self-harm in the four weeks prior to the survey had received medical treatment (14.3%); however, most (71.4 %) had communicated their self-injury to family and friends.

One limitation of this study is that it did not consider the possible problems in asking participants to retrospectively report the intent behind engaging in self-injurious behaviours injuries, such as the possibility of ambiguous intent where the person may not be clear on the underlying motivations for their behavior[1].

Implications: The main finding of this study is that self-injury is highly prevalent in the Australian community. This is concerning given that self-injury may result in medically serious injuries. Further, while there is likely to be significant distress associated with self-injurious behaviours, it appears that few sufferers seek medical interventions for their problems. There may be a number of structural and individual level factors that prevent those who engage in self-injury from seeking help, such as cost and transportation issues. As identified by another key article on this topic[2], these persons may avoid treatment due to the perception that it is not necessary, or because of stigma associated with such acts. It is necessary to understand more about reasons why people avoid treatment after engaging in self-injurious behaviours, as this would be paramount in the design of appropriately targeted prevention practices.

Endnotes

1. De Leo D, Burgis S, Bertolote JM, Kerkhof AJ, Bille-Brahe U (2006). Definitions of suicidal behavior: Lessons learned from the WHO/EURO multicentre Study. *Crisis* 27, 4–15.
2. Bruffaerts R, Demyttenaere K, Hwang I, Chiu WT, Sampson N, Kessler RC, Alonso J, Borges G, de Girolamo G, de Graaf R, Florescu S, Gureje O, Hu C, Karam EG, Nawakami N, Kostyuchenko S, Kovess-Masfety V, Lee S, Levinson D, Matschinger H, Posada-Villa J, Sagar R, Scott KM, Stein DJ, Tomov T, Viana MC, Nock MK (2011). Treatment of suicidal people around the world. *British Journal of Psychiatry.* Published online: 24 January 2011. doi:10.1192/bjp.bp.110.084129, 2011.

Socio-economic determinants of suicide: an ecological analysis of 35 countries

Milner A, McClure R, De Leo D (Australia)

Social Psychiatry & Psychiatric Epidemiology. Published online: 17 November 2010. doi:10.1007/s00127-010-0316-x, 2010

Purpose: A long tradition of research has shown a relationship between suicide rates and socio-economic factors. However, most investigations have neglected to account for country-specific influences. The purpose of this study was to clarify the association between socio-economic variables and gender-specific suicide rates in 35 countries, using analytic techniques able to control for effects embedded within different country contexts.

Method: Data relating to male and female age-standardised suicide rates (obtained from the WHO Statistical Information System) were analysed using fixed-effect regression. The possible associations between suicide rates and social variables were tested using data for 35 countries over the period 1980–2006.

Results: Findings indicated that higher male and female suicide rates were associated with increased female labour force participation, unemployment, and the proportion of persons over 65 years. Reductions in male and female suicide rates were associated with increased health spending per capita. The study also revealed that higher fertility was associated with a reduction in male suicide. Female labour force participation had a stronger effect on male suicide rates.

Conclusions: The results of this study suggest that variables related to the labour market and the economy were better explanatory factors of suicide rates than population-level indicators of interpersonal relationships. Although results were generally similar for males and females, males appeared to be more sensitive to changes in the social environment than women.

Comment

Main findings: This ecological cross-country study examined the effect of social and economic determinants on suicide and included a sample of 35 countries (including Australia). One of the main results of the study was that that unemployment had important influences on suicidal behaviours at the population level, thus confirming similar past suggestions[1]. Aside from loss of income, the relationship between unemployment and suicide may be connected to the damaging effects of job loss on self-esteem and self-value[2]. The proportion of elderly persons in the population was also found to be a significant correlate of suicide mortality, which may reflect the fact that elderly persons have higher suicide rates in many of the countries included in this sample. There were some gender specific differences, as males in particular appear to be strongly affected by the rate of participation of females in the workplace, as well as by the presence of families within the population (measured indirectly through the proxy variable of fertility)[3]. There was no relationship between female suicide with either of these variables.

Therefore, it appears that some social conditions have a greater effect on male suicide, rather than female suicide.

Implications: The findings of this study confirm the importance of several population-level factors on suicidality. These include employment (with unemployed persons being recognised to be at higher risk of suicide), and the presence of family (found to be a protective factor). The study also confirms the recent data that there are higher suicide rates in the elderly. Therefore, at the population level, there is a need to address the potential for suicidality in vulnerable persons who have become unemployment, as well as increasing the interventions available in the elderly. However, as noted by Eliason and Storrie[2], further research needs to be conducted to increase the understanding of the pathways through which factors such as employment are related to suicidality.

Endnotes

1. Corcoran P, Arensman E (2011). Suicide and employment status during Ireland's Celtic Tiger economy. *European Journal of Public Health* 21, 209–214.
2. Eliason M, Storrie D (2009) Job loss is bad for your health — Swedish evidence on cause-specific hospitalization following involuntary job loss. 1396–1406.
3. Stack S (2001). Suicide: A 15-year review of the sociological literature. Part II: Modernization and social integration perspectives. *Suicide & Life-Threatening Behavior* 30, 163–176.

Exposure to parental mortality and markers of morbidity, and the risks of attempted and completed suicide in offspring: An analysis of sensitive life periods

Niederkrotenthaler T, Floderus B, Alexanderson K, Rasmussen F, Mittendorfer-Rutz E (Sweden)

Journal of Epidemiology & Community Health. Published online: 5 October 2010.
doi:10.1136/jech.2010.109595, 2010

Background: There is evidence of parental risk factors for suicidal behaviour in offspring, but research on variations in their effects with offspring's age at first exposure is sparse. Aims To explore the effects of age at exposure to parental mortality and markers of morbidity on the risks of suicide and attempted suicide in offspring.

Methods: This was a case-control study effected through record linkage between Swedish registers. Individuals born 1973–83 who committed suicide ($n = 1407$) or were hospitalised due to an attempted suicide ($n = 17159$) were matched to ≤ 10 controls by sex, month and county of birth. ORs were measured in time windows representing age at first exposure.

Results: A general pattern of increasing risks of suicide and attempted suicide in offspring with decreasing age at exposure to parental risk factors emerged. Adjusted suicide risk (OR (95% CI)) was most pronounced in the youngest exposure window for parental psychiatric disability pension (3.1 (1.6 to 5.8)), somatic disability pension (1.9 (1.0 to 3.4)), psychiatric inpatient care (2.5 (2.0 to 3.1)), parental attempted suicide (2.9 (2.0 to 4.1)) and suicide (2.9 (1.7 to 5.2)). For parental non-suicidal deaths, the general pattern was the opposite. Patterns in offspring attempted suicide were similar to completed suicide for parental disability pension, psychiatric inpatient care and non-suicidal death. Attempted suicide risk after parental suicide showed an increasing trend with increasing age at exposure.

Conclusion: Parental morbidity and parental suicidal behaviour show the most detrimental effects on completed suicide among offspring when they appear early in life. Early interventions in families at risk are necessary to prevent suicide in offspring.

Comment

Main findings: This article focuses on the relationship between suicidal behaviours and disability in parents and the subsequent risk of suicide in their offspring. The sample used in this study came from a nationally representative database called the Multi-Generation Register, while information on parental/child morbidity and mortality came from the Cause of Death Register and the National Patient Register. Results indicate that exposure to parental attempted suicide was associated with a 2.6 increased risk of fatal or non-fatal suicidal behaviours in offspring, while exposure to parental death by suicide increased the risk by 2.5 and 1.8-times, respectively. The risk of death by suicide in offspring was most pronounced in those exposed to parental suicide when younger than three years, while the risk of non-fatal suicidal behaviours increased with the age of offspring. However, there were notable differences based on method used in suicidal acts, with persons who engaged in violent suicide methods more often being aged under 10 years when exposed to parental attempted suicide. Parental disability pension, past inpatient care, and death due to other causes were also associated with an elevated risk of fatal and non-fatal suicidal behaviours.

The findings need to be interpreted in the light of several methodological limitations. Firstly, study design only included persons who sought medical intervention following non-fatal suicidal behaviours. Secondly, the authors could not control for multiple exposures, for example where suicidality and psychiatric disorders occurs in several family members, even though this is suspected to have a significant impact on relationship with later suicidality. Lastly, statistical analysis and the data available did not allow for the investigation of the casual pathways linking parental exposures to suicide in children.

Implications: One of the most prominent findings of this study was the increased risk of fatal and non-fatal suicidal behaviours in offspring exposed to parental morbidity. These relationships were retained after controlling for the possible influence of socioeconomic conditions and marital status. The authors of this study suggest that there may be a genetic component linking the risk behaviours in parent the subsequent fatal or nonfatal suicidal behaviour in children. However, the differences in risk based on age of the child when exposed suggests a possible "sensitization period"[1]. These results suggest the importance of providing early intervention for vulnerable families, such as those with a history of suicidal behaviours or psychiatric/somatic disability.

Endnote

1. Lynch J, Davey Smith G (2005). A life course approach to chronic disease epidemiology. *The Annual Review of Public Health* 26, 1–35.

Excess mortality rate during adulthood among Danish adoptees

Petersen L, Sorensen TIA, Mortensen EL, Andersen PK (Denmark)

PLoS One 5, 12, 2010

Background and objective: Adoption studies have been used to disentangle the influence of genes from shared familial environment on various traits and disease risks. However, both the factors leading to adoption and living as an adoptee may bias the studies with regard to the relative influence of genes and environment compared to the general population. The aim was to investigate whether the cohort of domestic adoptees used for these studies in Denmark is similar to the general population with respect to all-cause mortality and cause-specific mortality rates.

Methods: 13,111 adoptees born in Denmark in 1917, or later, and adopted in 1924 to 1947 were compared to all Danes from the same birth cohorts using standardized mortality ratios (SMR). The 12,729 adoptees alive in 1970 were similarly compared to all Danes using SMR as well as cause-specific SMR.

Results: The excess in all-cause mortality before age 65 years in adoptees was estimated to be 1.30 (95% CI 1.26–1.35). Significant excess mortality before age 65 years was also observed for infections, vascular deaths, cancer, alcohol-related deaths and suicide. Analyses including deaths after age 65 generally showed slightly less excess in mortality, but the excess was significant for all-cause mortality, cancer, alcohol-related deaths and suicides.

Conclusion: Adoptees have an increased all-cause mortality compared to the general population. All major specific causes of death contributed, and the highest excess is seen for alcohol-related deaths.

Comment

Main findings: This study examined the relationship between adoption and suicide deaths through the use of the Danish Adoption Register and the Cause of Death Register. The control group consisted of Danish residents of the same birth cohorts who were not adopted. Cases were compared to controls regarding all cause mortality as well as cause specific conditions, such as: infections, vascular causes, cancer, alcohol-related deaths and suicide. Adoptees were found to have a higher mortality rate due to suicide than non-adoptees, as well as being at increased risk of other causes of deaths such as cancer and alcohol related deaths. The authors suggest a number of possible explanations for the higher rates of mortality in adopted persons. Some of these may include genetic predispositions within the biological family, or adverse experiences occurring within the gestational conditions that adversely affect the risk of suicide. The adoption process itself may also be a factor that increases the risk of suicide, particularly if the disclosure of the adoption by the host family is not handled appropriately.

A notable limitation of this study was the fact that it could not control for possible confounding influences such as mental illness, adverse social circumstances or alcohol or drug use.

Implications: This study confirmed the results found in a past Swedish study con-ducted on adoptees[1]. The reasons for the higher risk of suicide in adoptees remain unclear, however are believed to be tied to a range of prenatal (e.g. genetic and biological factors, problems experienced during gestation), pre-adoption factors (e.g. physical care, experiences after birth) and post-adoption factors (e.g. family environment, etc.). To date, the only Australian study on the relationship between adoption and suicide in Australia was a small qualitative study by Gair[2], which found that rejection, feelings of being disposable, grief, loss, and prolonged low self-worth were key themes linking suicidality to adoption. When these potential relationships between suicidality and adoption are considered in combination with the findings of the study by Petersen and colleagues, the need to progress research on suicidality in adoptees in the Australian context is all the more neces-sary.

Endnotes

1. von Borczyskowski A, Hjern A, Lindblad F, Vinnerljung B (2006). Suicidal behaviour in national and international adult adoptees: a Swedish cohort study. *Social Psychiatry and Psy-chiatric Epidemiology* 41, 95–102.
2. Gair S (2008). The psychic disequilibrium of adoption: Stories exploring links between adop-tion and suicidal thoughts and actions. *Australian e-Journal for the Advancement of Mental Health* 7, 207–216.

Increasing deaths involving oxycodone, Victoria, Australia, 2000–09

Rintoul AC, Dobbin MD, Drummer OH, Ozanne-Smith J (Australia)

Injury Prevention. Published online: 7 January 2011. doi:10.1136/ip.2010.029611, 2011

Objective: In light of an emerging epidemic identified in the United States and Canada, to identify trends in fatal drug toxicity involving oxycodone and the demographic characteristics and indicators of socioeconomic disadvantage of the deceased.

Study design: Population-based observational study in Victoria, Australia. Population Decedents whose death was reported to the Victorian Coroner between 2000 and 2009 and where oxycodone was detected. Main outcome measures Association between supply of oxycodone and deaths. Demographic characteristics of decedents. Rate ratios of the rural or metropolitan location and socioeconomic indicators of disadvantage of the deceased.

Results: Supply to Victoria has increased nine-fold from 7.5–14mg per capita in 2000 to 67.5–14mg per capita in 2009. Detection of oxycodone in deaths reported to the Victorian Coroner has increased from 4 (0.08/100,000 population) in 2000 to 97 (1.78/100,000 population) in 2009-a 21-fold increase in deaths. Of the 320 cases described, 53.8% (172) were the result of drug toxicity. Of these, 52.3% were unintentional and 19.8% intentional self-harm; the remaining 27.9% are either still under investigation by the coroner or intent is unknown. Drug toxicity deaths were overrepresented in both rural areas and areas indexed with high levels of disadvantage.

Conclusions: The substantial increase in the number of deaths involving oxycodone is strongly and significantly associated with the increase in supply. Most drug toxicity deaths involving oxycodone were unintentional. This newly identified trend in fatalities in Victoria supports concerns that a pattern of increasing deaths involving oxycodone is emerging globally.

Comment

Main findings: Australia has experienced an increase in the number of prescriptions of strong pain-medication such as oxycodone over the past two decades. The study by Rintoul et al. (2011) sought to examine the increased supply of this opiod analgesic in relation to trends of deaths involving oxycodone over the period 2003 to 2009. The study design relied on the data available through the National Coroners Information System (NCIS), Victorian Drugs Module and The Office of Chemical Safety and Environmental Health. The information obtained from the NCIS database found 327 cases where oxycodone was detected in toxicology; death in 172 of these cases was attributed to the drug toxicity alone. Over 19% of these 127 cases were judged to be due to intentional self-harm (suicide). Results indicated a 21% increase in the rate of oxycodone-related deaths from 0.19 per 100,000 in 2003 to 1.78 per 100,000 in 2009. The rise in oxycodone deaths was found to be significantly related to the supply of the drug, which increased nine-fold over the studied period. Results showed that deaths due to drug toxicity occurred more often in the most disadvantaged, rural areas of Victoria, even though these areas had the lowest rate of oxycodone prescriptions. This suggests that these medications may have been obtained illegally.

The observational design of the study made it impossible to determine whether there was a causal relationship between the increased supply of oxycodone and deaths due to this medication. A further problem was that data records were obtained from corpses and, because of this, readings and interpretations of the drug presence may have been affected by individual variability in the tolerance to the drug, influences of the location of sampling, and elapsed time between death and data collection. It is also necessary to indicate that the study findings represent a specific sample of "reportable" cases (i.e. those cases reported to a coroner), and are therefore not representative of the wider population of deaths where oxycodone may have been involved.

Implications for Australia: While it is difficult to design prevention and intervention strategies for persons obtaining oxycodone illegally, there are a number of possible pathways to reach those who overdose on prescribed medication. Rigorous risk assessment of patients is one possible strategy to alleviate the potential for suicide in those prescribed with oxycodone. Another strategy, as suggested by the study authors, is to initiate a drug monitoring programs that can provide medical practitioners and pharmacists with 'real time' information on a patient's medication supply history. This would require data linkages between bodies such as Medicare Australia and health care facilities. A similar type of drug monitoring program already exists in the USA[1]. This additional information on prescribing behaviours would help to identify persons at-risk due to drug misuse.

Endnote

1. Prescription Monitoring Programs, Pain and Policy Studies Group Website, University of Winconsin, Madison, Winconsion, USA, 2010. http://painpolicy.wisc.edu/domestic/ pmp.htm

Suicide and unintentional poisoning mortality trends in the United States, 1987–2006: Two unrelated phenomena?

Rockett IR, Hobbs GR, De Leo D, Stack S, Frost JL, Ducatman AM, Kapusta ND, Walker RL (USA)

BMC Public Health 10, 705, 2010

Background: Two counter trends in injury mortality have been separately reported in the US in recent times — a declining suicide rate and a rapidly rising unintentional poisoning mortality rate. Poisoning suicides are especially difficult to detect, and injury of undetermined intent is the underlying cause-of-death category most likely to reflect this difficulty. We compare suicide and poisoning mortality trends over two decades in a preliminary assessment of their independence and implications for suicide misclassification.

Methods: Description of overall and gender- and age-specific trends using national mortality data from WISQARS, the Web-based Injury Statistics Query and Reporting System, maintained by the Centers for Disease Control and Prevention (CDC). Subjects were the 936,633 residents dying in the 50 states and the District of Columbia between 1987 and 2006 whose underlying cause of death was classified as suicide, unintentional poisoning, or injury mortality of undetermined intent.

Results: The official US suicide rate declined 18% between 1987 and 2000, from 12.71 to 10.43 deaths per 100,000 population. It then increased to 11.15 deaths per 100,000 by 2006, a 7% rise. By contrast to these much smaller rate changes for suicide, the unintentional poisoning mortality rate rose more than fourfold between 1987 and 2006, from 2.19 to 9.22 deaths per 100,000. Only the population aged 65 years and older showed a sustained decline in the suicide rate over the entire observation period. Consistently highest in gender-age comparisons, the elderly male rate declined by 35%. The elderly female rate declined by 43%. Unlike rate trends for the non-elderly, both declines appeared independent of corresponding mortality trends for unintentional poisoning and poisoning of undetermined intent. The elderly also deviated from younger counterparts by having a smaller proportion of their injury deaths of undetermined intent classified as poisoning. Poisoning manifested as a less common method of suicide for this group than other decedents, except for those aged 15–24 years. Although remaining low, the undetermined poisoning mortality rate increased over the observation period.

Conclusions: The official decline in the suicide rate between 1987 and 2000 may have been a partial artifact of misclassification of non-elderly suicides within unintentional poisoning mortality. We recommend in-depth national, regional, and local population-based research investigations of the poisoning-suicide nexus, and endorse calls for widening the scope of the definition of suicide and evaluation of its risk factors.

Comment

Main findings: Past research suggests that official statistics understate the true scope of suicide[1]. To answer the question whether the changing mortality rates of suicides in the United States over the last couple of decades have been influenced by the rates of deaths by unintentional poisoning or poisoning of undetermined intent, Rockett and colleagues examined corresponding trends for selected causes of death. The results of this study convincingly point out contrasting trends of overall decreasing suicide rates (a drop of 18% between 1987 and 2000) and sharply increasing rates of 'unintentional poisonings' (fourfold rise between 1987 and 2006). The effect of misclassification under 'poisoning of undetermined intent' appeared minimal, yet this may be due to its very low rate. The breakdown of these trends by age and gender showed that the underestimation of poisoning suicides primarily involved persons younger than 65 year. The authors propose several possible systemic problems that may have led to the underreporting of suicide, such as underfunding of agencies collating cause-of-death statistics, changing policies influencing medical examiners and their willingness to determine suicide, or in fact a genuine epidemic of unintentional poising deaths (though the latter seems unlikely).

A methodological strength of the study is certainly the inclusion of very large number of cases whose cause of death was coded using an internationally standardised system over a sufficient time period to allow for reliable statistical analysis of temporal trends. However, the absence of a national database with results of toxicological investigations prevented more in-depth analysis of actual toxic substances involved in these deaths.

Implications: The study makes a valuable contribution to the existing debate on the accuracy of suicide mortality statistics not only in the United States but worldwide by emphasizing the need for greater scrutiny of the suicide-poisoning nexus. As suggested by the study authors, the compilation of suicide statistics need to consider information from multiple sources, including death certificates, reports by medical examiners, coroners, emergency response services and police, augmented by psychological autopsies and community-based surveys and ethnographic studies of suicide. In addition, it is recommended that all cases of deaths by poisoning, be it of intentional or unintentional manner, are subjected to postmortem autopsy and toxicological analysis of blood and/or urine. Accessibility of these reports would enable coroners to not only more accurately assess the intentionality behind the death but also the type and dose of toxin ingested. An improved ability to delineate suicidal intent in ambiguous cases of poisoning-related deaths would generate radical improvements in suicide surveillance, identification of risk factor and vulnerable risk group, designing of prevention and intervention programs, and finally the introduction of more stringent monitoring of availabilities of drugs most commonly used in suicidal overdoses.

Several parallels could be made between the reported findings of this American study and recent debate surrounding under-counting of suicides in Australia[2]. While the under-enumeration of suicide deaths in Australian national suicide statistics has been attributed to delays in coronial processes and the coding practices of the Australian Bureau of Statistics, undoubtedly a significant percentage of deaths remains misclassified due to inadequate analysis of toxicological reports. Establishment of nationally coordinated efforts to strengthen communications between coroners, pathologists, forensic counselling services and researchers is of paramount relevance.

Endnotes

1. Andriessen K (2006). Do we need to be cautious in evaluating suicide statistics? *European Journal of Public Health* 16, 445–447.
2. De Leo D (2010). Australia revises its mortality data on suicide. *Crisis* 31, 169–173.

Is a history of school bullying victimization associated with adult suicidal ideation? A South Australian population-based observational study

Roeger L, Allison S, Korossy-Horwood R, Eckert KA, Goldney RD (Australia)
Journal of Nervous and Mental Disease 198, 728–733, 2010

The objective of this research was to determine whether a history of school bullying victimization is associated with suicidal ideation in adult life. A random and representative sample of 2907 South Australian adults was surveyed in Autumn, 2008. Respondents were asked "When you were at school, did you experience traumatic bullying by peers that was particularly severe, for example, being frequently targeted or routinely harassed in any way by 'bullies'?" Depression was determined by the mood module of the PRIME-MD which includes a suicidal ideation question; "In the last 2 weeks, have you had thoughts that you would be better off dead or hurting yourself in some way?" The overall prevalence of suicidal ideation in postschool age respondents was 3.4% (95% confidence interval: 2.8%–4.2%) in 2008. Bullying by peers was recalled by 18.7% (17.2%–20.3%). Respondents with a history of being bullied were approximately 3 times (odds ratio: 3.2) more likely to report suicidal ideation compared with those who did not. The association between being bullied and suicidal ideation remained after controlling for both depression and sociodemographic variables (odds ratio: 2.1). The results from the present research suggest that there is a strong association between a history of childhood bullying victimization and current suicidal ideation that persists across all ages. Bullying prevention programs in schools could hold the potential for longer lasting benefits in this important area of public health.

Comment

Main findings: The aim of this study was to explore the link between experiences of being a victim of bullying during schooling years and subsequent suicidal ideation in adult life. Nearly 3,000 participants older than 15 years were recruited through a well-controlled randomised sampling design, conducted as part of the annual Health Omnibus survey in South Australia. Results showed that nearly a fifth of respondents (18.7%) recalled severe and traumatic bullying by peers in school; among them, 7.5% reported having suicidal ideation in last two months, compared to 2.5% of people who were not bullied at school. After controlling for effects of depression and sociodemographic characteristics (such as age, sex, and unemployment), there was a 2.1 greater risk of suicide ideation among those with a history of being victimised at school compared to persons without such history. This effect varied little across different levels of socioeconomic statuses and three age groups: 18–34, 35–55 and 56+ years. These results suggest that the negative impacts of bullying in childhood can endure across the lifespan, and are not just a transient phenomenon that ameliorates with time.

A methodological strength of the study was its use of a large and nationally-representative sample. However, it should be acknowledged the retrospective and self-reported nature of information on bullying may have led to it's under- or over-representation. While this is the first study conducted on the long-term effects of childhood bullying victimisations on suicidality in adulthood, longitudinal studies are needed to confirm its findings and further assess impacts of specific types of bullying (e.g. verbal vs. physical, isolated events vs. continuing frequency).

Implications: It is a well-known fact that children who are victims of bullying tend to have lower self-esteem and report feeling more depressed, lonely, anxious, and insecure than other children[1]. Results of this original Australian study by Roeger and colleagues corroborate the need for the implementation of national bullying prevention programs in Australia, especially since such strategies could have longer lasting benefits than previously anticipated. In addition, it would be advantageous to incorporate more stringent screening for bullying behaviours into primary school curricula in order to identify children who may be at later risk of suicide. Children identified as victims of bullying should be enrolled into school programs aimed at increasing resilience (e.g. teaching stress coping strategies and social skills, enhancing self-esteem), while parents, caregivers, education staff should be systematically educated about what constitutes bullying and how to best respond to it.

With the unprecedented advancement of internet-based communication tools, recent years have witnessed an emergence of a new form of bullying in many developed countries worldwide: 'cyber-bullying'. One Australian study found about 14% of students reported being victims of such actions; however, it did not explore potential consequences of bullying on mental wellbeing and suicide[2]. While yet to be determined, it seems likely that similar detrimental outcomes can befall those involved in cyber bullying.

Endnotes

1. Bond L, Carlin JB, Thomas L, Rubin K, Patton G (2001). Does bullying cause emotional problems? A prospective study of young teenagers. *British Medical Journal* 323, 480–484.
2. Campbell MA (2005). Cyber bullying: An old problem in a new guise? *Australian Journal of Guidance and Counselling* 15, 68–76.
3. Hinduja S, Patchin JW (2010). Bullying, cyberbullying, and suicide. *Archives of Suicide Research* 14, 206–212.

Combination of family history of suicidal behavior and childhood trauma may represent correlate of increased suicide risk

Roy A (USA)

Journal of Affective Disorders. Published online: 12 October 2010. doi:10.1016/j.jad.2010.09.022, 2010

Background: There is a need to try to identify patients at highest risk for suicidal behavior. A family history of suicidal behavior (FHS) and childhood trauma are two important risk factors for suicidal behavior. It was therefore decided to combine them and examine if the combination would identify patients at even increased risk for suicidal behavior.

Methods: Two hundred and eighty one substance dependent patients with a FHS completed the Childhood Trauma Questionnaire (CTQ) and were interviewed about their lifetime history of suicidal behavior. Patients with the combination of a FHS and CTQ score above the mean were examined and compared with FHS patients with a CTQ score below the mean.

Results: One hundred and two of the 129 (79.1%) FHS patients with a CTQ score above the mean had attempted suicide. Thirty five of the 40 female (87.5%) FHS patients with a CTQ score above the mean had attempted suicide. Patients with a CTQ score above the mean were found significantly more among FHS patients who had attempted suicide than among FHS patients who had never attempted. FHS attempters with a CTQ score above the mean had a significantly earlier age of first attempting and had made more attempts than FHS attempters with a CTQ score below the mean.

Limitations: Childhood trauma data derived from self-report questionnaire. No consistent collateral information about FHS.

Conclusion: The combination of a FHS and childhood trauma may represent a correlate of increased risk of attempting suicide, attempting earlier, and making more attempts.

Comment

Main findings: Several studies have demonstrated that adverse events in one's early childhood, such as abuse, domestic violence, and a family history of suicidal behaviour, may have long-term consequences and increase vulnerability for suicide later in life[1]. The author of this cross-sectional study aimed to examine the combined impacts of childhood trauma and family history of attempted/completed suicide on a sample of 281 adults, recruited through substance abuse treatment programs (however, the inclusion criteria was abstinence at time of participation in the study). Results confirmed that the combination of these two risk factors increased the lifetime odds of attempting suicide. Further, compared to those without childhood trauma, the study indicates that adverse events in childhood were related to a history of making multiple attempts at a younger age.

The author offers a couple of possible explanations for the observed links, based on previous research: firstly, family history of suicide and childhood trauma may lead to greater impulsive aggression and neuroticism, both important predisposing diatheses for suicidality, and secondly, genetic predisposition towards suicide might aggravate the adverse effects exposure to childhood trauma would have on an individual.

Implications: As evident from results of this study, exposure to trauma and suicidality in one's social network, particularly when perpetrated by a family member, can have long-reaching and detrimental consequences on mental health. Indeed, past research has shown that survivors often experience a range of different emotions like guilt, blame, responsibility, rejection, depressive feelings, and anger intermingled with social responses such as social stigma and isolation[2], all known factors increasing vulnerability to suicidal outcomes. Undoubtedly, more attention should be placed on individuals faced with such a trauma in their childhood.

Another relevant implication from this study is the realisation that both clinicians and researchers should consider as many risk factors as possible when evaluating an individuals' risk for suicide, not only those concerning their present life or immediately precipitating suicidal crisis (proximal factors), but also those originating from one's early childhood (predisposing or distal factors). In addition, the role of protective factors should be considered equally important in assessing vulnerability to suicide; however, this study and in general great part of research in the field of suicidology tend to overlook their significance.

Endnotes

1. Dube SR, Anda RF, Felitti VJ, Chapman D, Williamson DF, Giles WH (2001). Childhood abuse, household dysfunction and the risk of attempted suicide throughout the life span: findings from the Adverse Childhood Experiences Study. *Journal of American Medical Association* 286, 3089–3096.

2. Sveen CA, Walby FA (2008). Suicide survivors' mental health and grief reactions: A systematic review of controlled studies. *Suicide and Life-Threatening Behavior* 38, 13–29.

Suicide prevention in primary care: General practitioners' views on service availability

Saini P, Windfuhr K, Pearson A, Da Cruz D, Miles C, Cordingley L, While D, Swinson N, Williams A, Shaw J, Appleby L, Kapur N (UK)

BMC Research Notes 3, 246, 2010

Background: Primary care may be a key setting for suicide prevention. However, comparatively little is known about the services available in primary care for suicide prevention. The aims of the current study were to describe services available in general practices for the management of suicidal patients and to examine GPs views on these services. We carried out a questionnaire and interview study in the North West of England. We collected data on GPs views of suicide prevention generally as well as local mental health service provision.

Findings: During the study period (2003–2005) we used the National Confidential Inquiry Suicide database to identify 286 general practitioners (GPs) who had registered patients who had died by suicide. Data were collected from GPs and practice managers in 167 practices. Responses suggested that there was greater availability of services and training for general mental health issues than for suicide prevention specifically. The three key themes which emerged from GP interviews were: barriers accessing primary or secondary mental health services; obstacles faced when referring a patient to mental health services; managing change within mental health care services.

Conclusions: Health professionals have an important role to play in preventing suicide. However, GPs expressed concerns about the quality of primary care mental health service provision and difficulties with access to secondary mental health services. Addressing these issues could facilitate future suicide prevention in primary care.

Comment

Main findings: The presented study was conducted with 286 GPs who have lost a patient due to suicide, of whom 56% were interviewed about their perceptions of suicide prevention and the availability of services for suicide prevention. Descriptive analysis indicated that most GPs had a psychiatric liaison process in place, but reported of a lack of training specific to suicide and self-harm awareness (67.7%), inadequate risk assessment protocols (68.3%), and a shortage of significant services specifically catered for suicidal persons. A majority of GPs reported being effected following the death of a patient due to suicide (61%), and almost half reported a lack of professional support in the aftermath of this tragedy (43%). Some of the key barriers to the care of suicidal persons included a lack of services able to adequately meet patients' needs, the inability to access mental health services, long waiting lists, and closed patient lists. There were also a number of problems identified regarding referrals, including rigid criteria for patients to be admitted to mental health services, a high number of referrals back to the primary care services, and under-resourcing and high turnovers among staff at secondary mental health services.

Implications: Understanding the experiences of GPs in relation to their treatment of suicidal persons is particularly relevant in the light of a recent the shift from deinstitutionalization towards "community based care" in the primary setting in Australia[1,2]. In the presented study, GPs identified limited access to high-quality health care facilities and a lack of support from mental health services as the largest barriers in managing care of suicidal persons. This problem could be addressed by designing more structured pathways of referral and communication between GPs and secondary care services. An additional study finding was that a large number of GPs reported a lack of professional support following the death of one of their clients to suicide. Attending to the personal experiences of GPs is important on both a personal and professional level, as adverse experiences may flow through to negatively impact the care GPs provide to future clients. Learning more about GPs experiences with suicide could be an important area of work in Australia; specifically, there needs to be greater research into how many GPs have experience with suicidal clients, their reactions to these cases, and how GPs feel the care of suicidal clients can be improved.

Endnotes

1. Andersen UA, Andersen M, Rosholm JU, Gram LF (2000). Contacts to the health care system prior to suicide: a comprehensive analysis using registers for general and psychiatric hospital admissions, contacts to general practitioners and practising specialists and drug prescriptions. *Acta Psychiatrica Scandinavica* 102, 126–134.
2. Rosen A (2006). The Australian experience of deinstitutionalization: interaction of Australian culture with the development and reform of its mental health services. *Acta Psychiatrica Scandinavica* 113, 81–89.

Are suicidal phenomena in children different to suicidal phenomena in adolescents? A six-year review

Sarkar M, Byrne P, Power L, Fitzpatrick C, Anglim M, Boylan C, Morgan S (Ireland)
Child and Adolescent Mental Health 15, 197–203, 2010

Background: There has been little published about the nature and frequency of suicidal phenomena in children compared to that of adolescents.

Method: Standardised information on all presentations with suicidal phenomena to the Children's University Hospital, Dublin from 2002 to 2008 were retrospectively analysed from a centralised database.

Results: During the time period of the study, 401 young people presented for assessment, of whom 21.9% (N = 88) were under 12 years of age. Children differed from adolescents in terms of gender distribution, method of self-harm, and risk factors present.

Conclusion: Children under 12 are capable of displaying suicidal phenomena and differ considerably to adolescents in this regard.

Comment

Main findings: This is the first study to compare the socio-demographic characteristics and risk factors for suicidality in children (< 12 years) and adolescents (13–16 years). This study sample consisted of 435 presentations to a paediatric emergency department involving suicidal phenomena, ranging from suicidal thoughts to suicide attempts. A marked increase in the number of presentations involving self-harm was noted over the 6 years period of the study, rising from 19 cases in 2002 to 86 in 2008, though it remains unclear whether this was due to a genuine increase in these acts or an improvements in the referral systems within mental health care units. Children were more likely to present with suicidal ideation (53%), while adolescents more often presented with acts of self-harm (54%). When engaging in self-harm, both age groups most frequently used overdose with medications (23% of children and a third of adolescents), with the older group also frequently using drug and/or alcohol overdoses (20%) or cutting (9%). However, compared to adolescents, children employed somewhat less complex and more easily accessible methods such as of attempted hanging or strangulation (13% vs. 10%). In terms of risk factors, children were more likely to have a history of family psychopathology (37%) and reported being bullied (16%), while adolescents more frequently had a history of previous self-harm (47%).

A limitation of this study lies in the classification of 'self-harm', which combined all non-fatal acts of harming oneself regardless of suicidal ideation. While there is little doubt that self-harming represents one of the biggest risk factors for subsequent non-fatal or non-fatal suicidal acts[1], caution should be taken interpreting findings of this study pertaining to the cohort of paediatric presentations to emergency departments following acts of self-harm. This is particularly important, considering several studies have demonstrated that children and adolescents that engage in self-injuries behaviours differ in their characteristics and psychopathology depending on the presence of the underlying wish to die[2]. Secondly, the authors acknowledge that results cannot be generalised to the community sample of youth who self-harm, since it is a well-known fact that only a small minority of them present for medical treatment (De Leo & Evans, 2003) and much remains unknown about the characteristics and associated risks of children and adolescents who never seek professional help.

Implications: Suicide is a leading cause of death in children younger than 15 years of age worldwide, with rising rates observed in several countries, including Australia. Data indicates that suicide in children is an increasing problem showing an upward trend of 92% for the 1960 to 1990 period[3]. Whilst some previous studies provided a broad overview of the phenomenon of child suicide[4], little is known about the specific pathways to suicide for children, the ways developmental process influences suicide, and which issues need to be addressed in future suicide prevention programs.

The findings of this study clearly demonstrate that suicidal ideation and self-harm can occur very early in children's life, even in those younger than 12 years old. A significant implication of these results is the recommendation that all (mental) health professionals faced with these vulnerable populations should receive psychological education about the differing risk-factors affecting children and adolescents, and about the differing presentations of suicidal phenomena in young children. In order to prevent escalation to more life-threatening forms of self-harming behaviours, it is imperative to effectively respond and treat all children presenting with suicidal phenomena, including seemingly fleeting or passive thoughts of wishing to be dead. This could be achieved by providing them with more efficient coping skills for facing stressors stemming from unfavourable living conditions or other developmental difficulties. Further qualitative study should be initiated to find out more about the perception and reasoning that occurs in children considering self-harm and suicide, as well as longitudinal studies to identify their outcomes. In the Australian context, there is a particular need for improved understanding of the specific pathways to suicide occurring in children and adolescents of Aboriginal and/or Torres Strait Island ethnicities, who display an at least 7-fold higher risk for suicide than other Australian children[5].

Endnotes

1. Chen VC, Tan HK, Chen CY, Chen TH, Liao LR, Lee CT, Dewey M, Stewart R, Prince M, Cheng AT (2011). Mortality and suicide after self-harm: Community cohort study in Taiwan. *British Journal of Psychiatry* 198, 31–36.
2. Muehlenkamp JJ, Gutierrez PM (2007). Risk for suicide attempts among adolescents who engage in non-suicidal self-injury. *Archives of Suicide Research* 11, 69–82.

3. De Leo D, Evans R (2003). *International suicide rates. Recent trends and implications for Australia.* Australian Institute for Suicide Research and Prevention, Griffith University.

4. Shaw D, Fernandes J, Rao C (2005). Suicide in children and adolescents. A 10-year retrospective review. *American Journal of Forensic Medicine and Pathology* 26, 309–315.

5. Queensland Commission for Children and Young People and Child Guardian Queensland. *Annual report: deaths of children and young people, Queensland, 2006–07.* Commission for Children and Young People and Child Guardian Queensland.

Epidemiology of suicide attempts among persons with psychotic disorder in the general population

Suokas JT, Perälä J, Suominen K, Saarni S, Lönnqvist J, Suvisaari JM (Finland)

Schizophrenia Research 124, 22–28, 2010

Objective: To establish the epidemiology of suicide attempts in persons with psychotic disorder identified from the general population and to investigate the associations of suicidal behavior with other clinical characteristics and with physical violence against other people.

Method: A random sample of 9922 Finnish persons aged 18 years or over was screened for psychotic disorder using multiple sources of information. All screen positives and random sample of screen negatives were invited to an SCID interview. Diagnostic assessment, lifetime history of suicide attempts and violence against others were based on all available systematically evaluated information from the questionnaire, interview and/or case records.

Results: Of persons with a lifetime history of any primary or substance-induced psychotic disorder ($n = 264$), 34.5% (women: 34.1%, men: 34.9%) had a history of at least one suicide attempt. There were no suicide attempts among persons with delusional disorder, while the rate of suicide attempts was higher among persons with substance-induced psychotic disorders (48.8%) than in persons with other psychotic disorders 41.8%) ($\chi(2)=4.4$, d.f.=1, P=0.036). Suicide attempts were associated with younger age, comorbid substance use disorders, depressive symptoms, and physical violence against other people.

Conclusion: Suicide attempts are common in all psychotic disorders except for delusional disorder. They are particularly common in substance-induced psychotic disorder and in persons with comorbid substance use disorders. They are associated with severe depressive symptoms but not with the severity of psychotic symptoms. Suicidal behavior correlates with physical violence against other people.

Comment

Main findings: The main aim of this Finnish study was to identify the prevalence of suicide attempts among persons with psychotic disorders. The article also sought to examine specific clinical characteristics and history of physical violence among this sub-population. This information was obtained from a general population sample of 9,922 persons, who were screened with a mental health survey. Results indicated that approximately one-third of all persons with psychotic disorder had a history of at least one suicide attempt. When considered across the broad spectrum of psychotic disorders, results indicated that the lifetime rate of suicide attempt was between 30% and 49% (with the exception of those with delusional psychotic disorders, who reported no history of suicidal behaviours). Multivariate testing showed that physical violence, substance use disorder, depressive symptoms, and a history of physical violence were each independently associated with increased risk of suicide attempt among those with a diagnosis of psychotic disorder. Many of these findings align with past research, with the exception of the noted association between physical violence and suicide, which is a new finding. The authors suggest that the substantial and additional risk associated with aggressive behavior towards others and self-inflicted harm may reflect a serotonergic hypofunction, which predisposes individuals to impulsive and violent behaviours. In addition, impulsivity, violence and substance use may interact to create a greater risk of aggression.

This study has a number of strengths, as it is based on a community-wide sample of persons reporting psychotic symptoms. The main limitation of the study is that it was based on retrospective self-reports of suicidal behaviours which might have underestimated the size of the problem.

Implications: Research to date has confirmed that persons with psychotic disorder are at heightened risk of suicide[1]. While there is some evidence that early intervention may be effective in reducing suicidality in these patients[2], there have been no interventions developed yet that particularly address the link between aggression and suicidality in this group. Developing strategies to address the high risk of suicide within the subpopulation of aggressive persons, as well as the wider population of persons with a psychosis, could be an important area of future clinical research.

Endnotes

1. McGorry PD, Yung AR (2003). Early intervention in psychosis: an overdue reform. *Australian and New Zealand Journal of Psychiatry* 37, 393–398.
2. Power PJ, Bell RJ, Mills R, Herrman-Doig T, Davern M, Henry L, Yuen HP, Khademy-Deljo A, McGorry PD (2003). Suicide prevention in first episode psychosis: the development of a randomised controlled trial of cognitive therapy for acutely suicidal patients with early psychosis. *Australian and New Zealand Journal of Psychiatry* 37, 414–420.

Childhood physical abuse, aggression, and suicide attempts among criminal offenders

Swogger MT, You S, Cashman-Brown S, Conner KR (USA)

Psychiatry Research 185, 363–367, 2011

Childhood physical abuse (CPA) has numerous short and long-term negative effects. One of the most serious consequences of CPA is an increased risk for suicide attempts. Clarifying the mechanisms by which CPA increases risk for suicidal behavior may enhance preventive interventions. One potential mechanism is a tendency toward aggression. In a sample of 266 criminal offenders, ages 18–62, we examined the relationships among CPA, lifetime aggression, and suicide attempts and tested lifetime history of aggression as a mediator of the relationship between CPA and suicide attempts. Results indicated that CPA and aggression were associated with suicide attempts. Consistent with our hypothesis, lifetime aggression mediated the CPA and suicide attempts relationship. Findings suggest that aggression may be an important mediator of the relationship between CPA and suicide attempts among criminal offenders, and are consistent with the possibility that treating aggression may reduce risk for suicide attempts.

Comment

Main findings: This study sought to explore the relationships between experiences of physical abuse in childhood (a well-know distal risk factor for a variety of negative outcomes, including mental ill-health) and suicidal behaviour in adulthood. A substantial sample of criminal offenders from the United States has been chosen as a population of interest in which to study mediators of CPA-suicidal behaviour relationship since they have previously been found to report of high rates of childhood physical abuse as well as suicide attempts. Results showed that CPA was associated with lifetime suicide attempts, after controlling for age, gender, marital status and education. However, after controlling for the effects of lifetime aggression, the link became statistically non-significant, confirming a model whereby the experience of CPA leads to a vulnerability to aggression that confers risk for suicide attempt. Authors suggest that among abused individuals, the presence or absence of certain psychosocial variables (e.g. hopelessness, family cohesion) determine whether an individual directs underlying aggressive impulses towards others or self.

Implications: The study findings highlighted the need for routine assessment of suicide risk among individuals who exhibit trait aggression. In addition, Swogger and colleagues raise the possibility that successful treatment of aggressive behaviour among offenders with history of childhood abuse (for example through use of pharmacological agents or dialectical behaviour therapy) may also have a positive impact on lowering risks for suicide attempts. However, there remains a need for further research into the specific types of aggression that mediates the relationship between childhood trauma and subsequent suicidality, which could increase the specificity of suicide risk assessments. Finally, inclusion of the nonoffender sample will help to clarify the robustness of the findings of this study and their generalisability to other high/risk populations.

National study of suicide in all people with a criminal justice history

Webb RT, Qin P, Stevens H, Mortensen PB, Appleby L, Shaw J (Denmark)

Archives of General Psychiatry. Published online: 7 February 2011. doi:10.1001/archgenpsychiatry. 2011.7, 2011

Context: Previous research has focused on suicide among male prisoners and ex-prisoners, but little is known about risk in the wider offender population.

Objective: To examine suicide risk over 3 decades among all people processed by a national criminal justice system.

Design: Nested case-control study.

Setting: The whole Danish population.

Participants: Interlinked national registers identified all adult suicides during 1981 to 2006 according to any criminal justice system contact since 1980. Exposure was defined according to history of criminal justice adjudication, up to and including each subject's last judicial verdict before suicide (or date of matching for controls). There were 27 219 suicides and 524 899 controls matched on age, sex, and time, ie, controls were alive when their matched case died.

Main Outcome Measure: Suicide.

Results: More than a third of all male cases had a criminal justice history, but relative risk against the general population was higher for women than men. Independent effects linked with criminal justice exposure persisted with confounder adjustment. Suicide risk was markedly elevated with custodial sentencing, but the strongest effects were with sentencing to psychiatric treatment and with charges conditionally withdrawn. Risk was raised even in people with a criminal justice history but without custodial sentences or guilty verdicts. It was especially high with recent or frequent contact and in people charged with violent offenses.

Conclusions: We examined a section of society in which major health and social problems frequently coexist including offending, psychopathology, and suicidal behavior. The need for developing more far-reaching national suicide prevention strategies is indicated. In particular, improved mental health service provision is needed for all people in contact with the criminal justice system, including those not found guilty and those not given custodial sentences. Our findings also suggest that public services should be better coordinated to tackle co-occurring health and social problems more effectively.

Comment

Main findings: Past studies on criminal behaviours and suicide have been confined to specific sample groups within prison populations[1]. Compared to these studies, the main advantage of this Danish study was that it was able to identify the potential risk associated with criminal offence type across a large nationally-representative sample, resulting in a sample of 27,219 cases matched for date of birth and sex to 524,899 control cases. The analytic approach of the study was also able to account for the potential effect of mental health and social adversity on the relationship between criminal justice history and suicide, providing more robust research findings. Results suggest that the presence of criminal justice history was linked with more than a 2-fold higher suicide rates in men and greater than 3-fold increase in women. A strong relationship was also seen in persons with suspended sentences, charges conditionally withdrawn, acquittals, "other verdicts", and in persons sentenced for psychiatric treatment. Further, there was an increasing and linear relationship identified between number of contacts with the justice system and an increasing risk of suicide, even after adjusting for mental health or social background. A secondary analysis investigated the influence of past psychiatric treatment on the relationship between criminal justice history and suicide and found that almost half of all males with a criminal justice history had received secondary care psychiatric treatment compared with three-quarters of women with such history. Persons who were sentenced to receive psychiatric treatment and those with charges conditionally withdrawn had a notably higher prevalence of past treatment for a mental illness. Also, those younger than 35 years had an observably higher risk than older groups.

Implications: In terms of suicide prevention, it appears that it is not only those who are actually imprisoned who are at-risk of suicide, but also those who have never received a custodial sentence or a guilty verdict. This suggests the need for better assessment and treatment for all those who have ever been in contact with the justice system, particularly those who have had multiple contacts with the justice system. One possible implication of these results is that exposure to the system itself may constitute a risk, rather than this relationship wholly depending on individual circumstances or mental health (although the latter undoubtedly mediate the relationship). Indeed, as suggested in this study, there may be a socially and economically disadvantaged group in society who are at particularly elevated risk of suicide after contact with the justice system. Addressing the adverse social and economic circumstances associated with both suicidality and criminality therefore represents a potential intervention strategy. Another important consideration is that those who may be particularly at risk of suicide are persons who have been prosecuted for property crimes and traffic offences. These findings align with Australian research[2], which has found that risk of death by suicide was highest in prison psychiatric hospitals, violent offenders and repeat offenders. The authors suggest that violent offenders may be particularly at-risk due to an underlying predisposition towards impulsive-aggressive behavior, which is also thought to be related to a greater risk of suicide[3]. Therefore, there is a particular need to address violence which, in turn, may lead to lowered impulsivity and risk of suicide.

Endnotes

1. Fazel S, Cartwright J, Norman-Nott A, Hawton K (2008). Suicide in prisoners: a systematic review of risk factors. *Journal of Clinical Psychiatry* 69, 1721–1731.

2. Kariminia A, Law MG, Butler TG, Corben SP, Levy MH, Kaldor JM, Grant L (2007). Factors associated with mortality in a cohort of Australian prisoners. *European Journal of Epidemiology* 22, 417–428.

3. Turecki G (2005). Dissecting the suicide phenotype: the role of impulsive–aggressive behaviours. *Journal of Psychiatry & Neuroscience* 30, 398–408.

Research participation experiences of informants of suicide and control cases: Taken from a case-control psychological autopsy study of people who died by suicide

Wong PWC, Chan WSC, Beh PSL, Yau FWS, Yip PSF, Hawton K (Hong Kong)

Crisis 31, 238–246, 2010

Background: Ethical issues have been raised about using the psychological autopsy approach in the study of suicide. The impact on informants of control cases who participated in case-control psychological autopsy studies has not been investigated.

Aims: (1) To investigate whether informants of suicide cases recruited by two approaches (coroners' court and public mortuaries) respond differently to the initial contact by the research team. (2) To explore the reactions, reasons for participation, and comments of both the informants of suicide and control cases to psychological autopsy interviews. (3) To investigate the impact of the interviews on informants of suicide cases about a month after the interviews.

Methods: A self-report questionnaire was used for the informants of both suicide and control cases. Telephone follow-up interviews were conducted with the informants of suicide cases.

Results: The majority of the informants of suicide cases, regardless of the initial route of contact, as well as the control cases were positive about being approached to take part in the study. A minority of informants of suicide and control cases found the experience of talking about their family member to be more upsetting than expected. The telephone follow-up interviews showed that none of the informants of suicide cases reported being distressed by the psychological autopsy interviews.

Limitations: The acceptance rate for our original psychological autopsy study was modest.

Conclusions: The findings of this study are useful for future participants and researchers in measuring the potential benefits and risks of participating in similar sensitive research. Psychological autopsy interviews may be utilized as an active engagement approach to reach out to the people bereaved by suicide, especially in places where the postvention work is underdeveloped.

Comment

Main findings: This is the first international study to examine the subjective experiences of informants participating in a case-control psychological autopsy study. It addresses a relevant ethical consideration on this particular study design, following a basic ethical principle of minimising any risk of harm or discomfort befalling study participants. Its findings reiterated that partaking in such interviews is a predominantly positive experience for both proxies and control cases. In fact, when contacted again within a month after participation in the PA interview, about half of informants of suicide (45%) and control cases (54%) said they found the experience better than they had expected. When asked about their feelings of being approached to participate in the study, more suicide informants in reported having positive feelings about it than control informants (91% vs. 84%) – this might be explained through greater sense of contributing to the suicide prevention cause in the group of people that have lost somebody through suicide. An additional reason for participation, suggested by 12% of suicide informants, was the wish to better understand the reasons behind their loved one's act.

Another striking findings of this study (although it may not have been one of its aims) was the fact that less than a third of informants of suicide cases had sought professional help after the suicide death, yet 72% said they would find support group helpful. Given the considerable scientific evidence that people bereaved by suicide suffer qualitative differences in their bereavement compared to those bereaved by loss of a loved one due to other causes[1], yet often underutilise professional help[2], it is clear that the needs of the vulnerable population of suicide survivors should be more effectively targeted by adequate support programs.

In interpreting the study's findings, one should consider factors specific to Chinese context that might have impacted on the experiences of participating information in interviews about the deceased's life and factor preceding their death. Talking about death is considered taboo in the Chinese culture, therefore it is reasonable to assume that most participants have not had many opportunities to discuss these topics and ventilate their distress with a sympathetic listener. This could have enhanced their positive feelings about having participated. A transcultural study comparing experiences of informants participating in PA studies is needed to provide more insight into these questions. A relevant factor reported that can be believed to transcend cultural differences is the participants' wish to contribute to suicide prevention research.

Implications: The results of this study carry several practical implications for future improvements of study designs employing this approach, mainly through provision of relevant information about both benefits and risks of participating in such studies to the contacted next-of-kins. Albeit rarely reported, some participants nevertheless experience overwhelmingly negative feelings when participating in such studies and this possibility should be included in the informed consent procedure. As a way of identifying and potentially alleviating any potential negative effects from participation in PA studies, brief telephone follow-up evaluations should be conducted with informants of all deceased, regardless of their manner of death. This would also provide them with a valuable opportunity to voice their concerns or recommendations for refinements of the study method and provision of adequate help services. Given that about 8% of the informants of suicides and control expressed interest in being informed about the study findings, it is recommended that study's results are offered to participants after conclusion of the study (e.g. through a system of notification about the publication of research articles). Lastly, the authors suggest it would be worth routinely offering PA interviews to all families and friends of persons who died by suicide, especially in places where postvention work is underdeveloped as this study has confirmed many participants find the experience of talking about their loved one's life and death helpful in their grieving process.

Endnotes

1. Sveen CA, Walby FA (2008). Suicide survivors' mental health and grief reactions: A systematic review of controlled studies. *Suicide and Life-Threatening Behavior* 38, 13–29.
2. Wilson A, Marshall AM (2010). The support needs and experiences of suicidally bereaved family and friends. *Death Studies* 34, 625–640.

Employment status and suicide: The complex relationships between changing unemployment rates and death rates

Yip PSF, Caine ED (Hong Kong)

Journal of Epidemiology and Community Health. Published online: 28 November 2011.
doi: 10.1136/jech.2010.110726.

Background: Existing studies have described a strong correlation between unemployment rates and suicide rates, but the exact mechanisms through which they may interact with one another remain unknown.

Method: This study examined the complex relationships between suicide rates and both regional unemployment rates and individual employment status during times of economic recession (2000–3) and recovery (2003–6) in Hong Kong.

Results: Despite the strong correlation (0.86) between the unemployment rates and suicide rates for 2000–6, the rates of suicides within the employed and unemployed groups moved in the opposite direction from the overall population trend. That is, the suicide rate among the unemployed decreased during economic recession and increased during recovery.

Conclusion: It is important to be able to distinguish precisely between population-level concepts, such as rates, and individual-level characteristics, such as employment status, when considering the development of evidence-based suicide prevention strategies.

Comment

Main findings: Several past studies conducted in Australia and abroad[1,2] have found a strong correlation between unemployment rates and suicide. However, the exact mechanisms of how employment conditions influence suicide remains insufficiently understood. The study by Yip and Caine sought to explore the transitional trends of suicide rates in Hong Kong among the employed and unemployed populations during the period 2000 to 2006, half of which was marked by times of economic recession, followed by a time of recovery. The authors applied statistical analysis that allowed for a separate monitoring of relationships between employment and suicide at both an individual and population-level. Results showed a strong correlation ($\rho = 0.82$) between the employment rate and suicide rate across the period 2000–2006; however, when the overall working population was separated to employed and unemployed group, they showed divergent trends. Specifically, the suicide rate for the employed rose during a time of economic downturn and decreased during a time of economic recovery, as contrasted by the reverse trend noted among the unemployed.

A limitation of the study design is that it did not include several community or individual level factors, related to suicidal outcomes (such as mental illness, help-seeking behaviours, availability of treatment, other stressful life events, social support, etc.). Also, it would be of great interest to compare associations between unemployment and suicidality in males and females, particularly following findings of a recent study by Milner et al.[3] (see comments to this study among Key

Articles) following which males appear to be more sensitive to changes in the social environment than women.

Implications: The widespread financial crisis in 2008 had significant impacts on rates of employment in most industrialised countries worldwide, including Australia. The effects of the recession extended well beyond the unemployment statistics, and carried detrimental consequences on population's psychological well-being due to the fear of job loss and financial worries. In the past, unemployment has been conclusively linked to an increased risk of poor mental health outcomes, such as depression, anxiety, psychosomatic symptoms, poor subjective well-being and self esteem, and higher rates of several specific causes of mortality, including suicide[4].

Australia, as a high-income country and one with a robust economy that is already showing signs of a recovery from recent recession[5], may therefore experience similar trends of suicide mortality among the employed and unemployed groups as observed in Hong Kong. To minimise the possible elevation in the national suicide rate among the unemployed, it would be reasonable to provide suicide and mental health assessment, followed by tailor-designed intervention programmes ameliorating unemployment-related distress. Generalisability of the findings from Hong Kong could be tested in Australian context by either replicating the study design, or, preferably, by expanding it to include exploration of economic instability and changing rates of unemployment in certain other groups suspected of being particularly vulnerable to its detrimental effects: members of ethnic minority groups, long-term-unemployed, and youth just entering work force.

Endnotes

1. Chen VC, Chou JY, Lai TJ, Lee CT (2010). Suicide and unemployment rate in Taiwan, a population-based study, 1978–2006. *Social Psychiatry & Psychiatric Epidemiology* 45, 447–452.

2. Morrell S, Taylor R, Quine S, Kerr C (1993). Suicide and unemployment in Australia 1907–1990. *Social Science & Medicine* 136, 749–756.

3. Milner A, McClure R, De Leo D (2010) Socio-economic determinants of suicide: an ecological analysis of 35 countries. *Social Psychiatry & Psychiatric Epidemiology.* Published online: 17 November 2010. doi:10.1007/s00127-010-0316-x.

4. Paul KI, Moser K (2009). Unemployment impairs mental health: Meta-analyses. *Journal of Vocational Behavior* 74, 264–283.

5. ABC News (2010). Australia leads global economic recovery. Retrieved on 30 March 2011 from http://www.abc.net.au/news/stories/2010/04/22/2879454.htm.

Association of Internet search trends with suicide death in Taipei City, Taiwan, 2004-2009

Yang AC, Tsai SJ, Huang NE, Peng CK (Taiwan)

Journal of Affective Disorders. Published online: 1 March 2011. Doi: 10.1016/j.jad.2011.01.019.

Background: Although Internet has become an important source for affected people seeking suicide information, the connection between Internet searches for suicide information and suicidal death remains largely unknown. This study aims to evaluate the association between suicide and Internet searches trends for 37 suicide-related terms representing major known risks of suicide.

Methods: This study analyzes suicide death data in Taipei City, Taiwan and corresponding local Internet search trend data provided by Google Insights for Search during the period from January 2004 to December 2009. The investigation uses cross correlation analysis to estimate the temporal relationship between suicide and Internet search trends and multiple linear regression analysis to identify significant factors associated with suicide from a pool of search trend data that either coincides or precedes the suicide death.

Results: Results show that a set of suicide-related search terms, the trends of which either temporally coincided or preceded trends of suicide data, were associated with suicide death. These search factors varied among different suicide samples. Searches for "major depression" and "divorce" accounted for, at most, 30.2% of the variance in suicide data. When considering only leading suicide trends, searches for "divorce" and the pro-suicide term "complete guide of suicide," accounted for 22.7% of variance in suicide data.

Conclusions: Appropriate filtering and detection of potentially harmful source in keyword-driven search results by search engine providers may be a reasonable strategy to reduce suicide deaths.

Comment

Main findings: This ecological study investigated a possible temporal relationship between suicide-related terms on a popular Internet search engine (Google) and trends of suicide mortality over a period of 5 years in Taipei. Results indicated a number of possible lagged trends between 37 key terms (covering 5 areas: psychiatric, medical, familial, socioeconomic factors, and pro-suicide terms) and suicide mortality. Search terms signifying medical, familial, and socioeconomic terms preceded suicide deaths by one to two months, while psychiatric terms tended to coincide with the monthly suicide count. The authors suggest that this finding may reflect a sequence of acts associated with suicide. For example, searches for divorce preceded suicide by two months (triggering life event), while the "complete guide to suicide" preceded increased tends of suicide by one month (ascertaining and planning suicidal act). Suicide trends related to the "complete guide to suicide" was particularly associated with violent suicides, which may be a reflection of the highly lethal and aggressive methods promoted in this online material. Searches for "major depression" and "divorce" accounted for 30.2% of the variance in male suicide and adult data, while search terms related to "anxiety" were more strongly related to female suicide. Non-violent suicides were associated with internet terms such as "insomnia".

While the findings of this study hold potential in terms of identifying the aspects of Internet searchers related to greater risk of suicide, they should be interpreted in light of several methodological limitations. For example, it was impossible to assess how many persons who died by suicide had actually access to the Internet or used the search terms investigated in this study. The study also did not control for other possible explanation of suicide trends, such as changes in economic and social situations, geography (urban versus rural residence), and access to lethal means used to suicide. Further, the authors of the article only considered a limited number of search terms for suicide.

Implications: The findings of this study provide justification for greater attention to relationship between suicide and internet use, particularly given the increasing internet use in Australia. According to the Australian Bureau of Statistics[1], internet access has quadrupled in recent years, from 16% of Australian households in 1998 to 64% in 2006–07. It is also pertinent to invest more resources in this area of work given rising concerns about issues such as "cyber suicide"[2]. From a public health perspective, the findings of this article suggest the need for greater of filtering and detection of pro-suicide information in order to protect vulnerable persons from accessing dangerous internet content about suicide methods.

Endnotes

1. Australian Bureau of Statistics (2008). *Australian Social Trends.* Catalogue number 4102.0. Canberra: Australian Bureau of Statistics.
2. Auxemery Y, Fidelle, G (2010). Internet and suicidality. A googling study about mediatic view of a suicidal pact. *Annales Medico-Psychologiques* 168, 502–507.

Recommended Readings

Emotional dysregulation and interpersonal difficulties as risk factors for nonsuicidal self-injury in adolescent girls

Adrian M, Zeman J, Erdley C, Lisa L, Sim L (USA)

Journal of Abnormal Child Psychology. Published online: 16 October 2010. doi:10.1007/s10802-010-9465-3, 2010

The purpose of this study was to examine a model of factors that place psychiatrically hospitalised girls at risk for non-suicidal self-injury (NSSI). The role of familial and peer interpersonal difficulties, as well as emotional dysregulation, were examined in relationship to NSSI behaviors. Participants were 99 adolescent girls (83.2% Caucasian; M age = 16.08) admitted to a psychiatric hospital. Structural equation modeling indicated the primacy of emotional dysregulation as an underlying process placing adolescents at risk for NSSI and mediating the influence of interpersonal problems through the family and peer domains. When family and peer relationships were characterized by conflict and lack of support for managing emotions, adolescents reported more dysregulated emotion processes. Family relational problems were directly and indirectly related to NSSI through emotional dysregulation. The indirect processes of peer relational problems, through emotional dysregulation, were significantly associated with NSSI frequency and severity. The findings suggest that the process by which interpersonal difficulties contribute to NSSI is complex, and is at least partially dependent on the nature of the interpersonal problems and emotion processes.

Testing the hypothesis of the natural suicide rates: Further evidence from OECD data

Andres AR, Halicioglu F (Denmark)

Economic Modelling 28, 22-26, 2010

This paper provides further evidence on the hypothesis of the natural rate of suicide using the time series data for 15 OECD countries over the period 1970–2004. This hypothesis suggests that the suicide rate of a society could never be zero even if both the economic and the social conditions were made ideal from the point of view of suicide (Yang and Lester, 1991). This research relates the suicide rates to harmonized unemployment and divorce rates to test the natural hypothesis statistically. We also address methodological flaws by earlier suicide studies by employing autoregressive-distributed lag (ARDL) approach to cointegration advocated by Pesaran et al. (2001). In majority of regression equations, the constant term was positive and statistically significant, indicating a non-zero natural suicide rate. In particular, we find evidence that at aggregate level, Turkey has the lowest (3.64) and Japan has the highest (13.98) natural rate of suicides. In terms of the male natural suicide rates, the United Kingdom ranks the lowest (4.73) and Belgium ranks the top (15.44). As for the female natural suicide rates, Japan takes the lead (16.76) and Italy has the lowest (5.60). The results are also compared and contrasted to each other with a view to drawing plausible policy conclusions.

Detecting suicide risk at psychiatric emergency services

Bertolote JM, de Mello-Santos C, Botega NJ (Brazil)
Revista Brasileira De Psiquiatria 32, 87-95, 2010

Objective: Guide the health professional to identify risk factors and forms of protection, together with handling such patient throughout a clinical interview within the emergency service context.

Method: Selected literature revision so as to identify relevant and illustrative key cases.

Results: The clinical interview is the best method to evaluate the suicidal risk and has two different aims: (1) emotional support and creation of a bond; (2) collecting information. There is a substantial amount of information to be collected during the clinical interview, such as: risk factors and protection, epidemiologic data, act characterisation, psychical dynamics aspects, personal and familial historic patterns, identification models, data on physical wealth and social net support. Difficulties are to emerge throughout the clinical interview, but a trained and informed professional will be able to approach and adequately add the patient. Although several scales have been proposed, none of them have been efficient to deter the suicidal risk.

Conclusion: There is no method to predict who is to commit suicide, nevertheless, it is possible to evaluate the individual risk of each patient with regards to a detailed and empathic clinical interview. Prevent the patient to commit suicide is the preliminary and fundamental rule.

Deliberate self-harm patients in the emergency department: Factors associated with repeated self-harm among 1524 patients

Bilen K, Ottosson C, Castren M, Ponzer S, Ursing C, Ranta P, Ekdahl K, Pettersson H (Sweden)
Emergency Medicine Journal. Published online: 12 November 2010. doi:10.1136/emj.2010.102616, 2010

Objectives: (1) investigate risk factors associated with repeated deliberate self-harm (DSH) among patients attending the emergency department due to DSH, (2) stratify these patients into risk categories for repeated DSH and (3) estimate the proportion of repeated DSH within 12 months.

Design: A consecutive series of individuals who attended one of Scandinavia's largest emergency departments during 2003–2005 due to DSH. Data on sociodemographic factors, diagnoses and treatment, previous DSH at any healthcare facility in Sweden (2002–2005) and circumstances of the index DSH episode were collected from hospital charts and national databases. A nationwide register based on follow-ups of any new DSH or death by suicide during 2003–2006.

Main outcome measure: Repeated DSH episode or suicide.

Results: 1524 patients were included. The cumulative incidence for patients repeating DSH within 12 months after the index episode was 26.8% (95% CI: 24.6 to 29.0). Risk factors associated with repeating DSH included previous DSH, female gender, self-injury as a method for DSH and if the self-injury required a surgical procedure, current psychiatric or antidepressant treatment and if the patient suffered from a substance use disorder or adult personality disorder or did not have children under the age of six.

Conclusion: Patients attending an emergency department due to DSH have a high risk of repeating their self-harm behaviour. We present a model for risk stratification for repeated DSH describing low-risk (18%), median-risk (28% to 32%) and high-risk (47% to 72%). Our results might help caretakers to direct optimal resources to these groups.

School grades, parental education and suicide: A national register-based cohort study

Bjorkenstam C, Weitoft GR, Hjern A, Nordstrom P, Hallqvist J, Ljung R (Sweden)
Journal of Epidemiology and Community Health. Published online: 19 Ocotber 2010. doi:10.1136/jech.2010.117226, 2010

Background: To investigate whether school performance is a risk factor for suicide death later in life and, if so, to what extent this is explained by inter-generational effects of parental education.

Methods: This population-based cohort study comprises national birth cohorts between 1972 and 1981 in Sweden. We followed 898 342 students, graduating between 1988 and 1997 from the 9 years of compulsory school, equivalent to junior high school, until 31 December 2006, generating 11 148 758 person-years and 1490 suicides. Final school grades, in six categories, and risk of suicide were analysed with Poisson regression.

Results: The incidence rate ratio (RR) for suicide death for students with the lowest grades was 4.57 (95% CI 2.82 to 7.40) for men and 2.67 (1.42 to 5.01) for women compared to those with highest grades after adjustment for a number of sociodemographic and parental morbidity variables, such as year of graduation, parental education, lone parenthood, household receiving social welfare or disability pension, place of schooling, adoption, maternal age and parent's mental illness. Students with grades in the middle categories had RRs in between. These relationships were not modified by parental education.

Conclusions: The strong association between low school grades and suicide in youth and young adulthood emphasises the importance of both primary and secondary prevention in schools.

Population-attributable fractions of Axis I and Axis II Mental disorders for suicide attempts: Findings from a representative sample of the adult, noninstitutionalized US population

Bolton JM, Robinson J (USA)

American Journal of Public Health 100, 2473-2480, 2010

Objectives: We aimed to determine the percentage of suicide attempts attributable to individual Axis I and Axis II mental disorders by studying population-attributable fractions (PAFs) in a nationally representative sample.

Methods: Data were from the National Epidemiologic Survey on Alcohol and Related Conditions Wave 2 (NESARC; 2004–2005), a large (N = 34 653) survey of mental illness in the United States. We used multivariate logistic regression to compare individuals with and without a history of suicide attempt across Diagnostic and Statistical Manual of Mental Disorders, Fourth Edition, Axis I disorders (anxiety, mood, psychotic, alcohol, and drug disorders) and all 10 Axis II personality disorders. PAFs were calculated for each disorder.

Results: Of the 25 disorders we examined in the model, 4 disorders had notably high PAF values: major depressive disorder (PAF = 26.6%; 95% confidence interval [CI] = 20.1, 33.2), borderline personality disorder (PAF = 18.1%; 95% CI = 13.4, 23.5), nicotine dependence (PAF = 8.4%; 95% CI = 3.4, 13.7), and posttraumatic stress disorder (PAF = 6.3%; 95% CI = 3.2, 10.0).

Conclusions: Our results provide new insight into the relationships between mental disorders and suicide attempts in the general population. Although many mental illnesses were associated with an increased likelihood of suicide attempt, elevated rates of suicide attempts were mostly attributed to the presence of 4 disorders.

Sexual orientation and its relation to mental disorders and suicide attempts: Findings from a nationally representative sample

Bolton S-L, Sareen J (Canada)

Canadian Journal of Psychiatry 56, 35-43, 2011

Objective: To compare the rates of all Axis I and II mental disorders and suicide attempts in sexual orientation minorities with rates in heterosexuals using a nationally representative sample.

Method: Data used were from the National Epidemiologic Survey on Alcohol and Related Conditions Wave 2 (*n* = 34 653, response rate = 70.2%). Cross-tabulations and multivariate logistic regression analyses were performed to determine differences in rates of mental disorders and suicide attempts by sexual orientation. All analyses were stratified by sex.

Results: Compared with their heterosexual counterparts, lesbians and bisexual women demonstrated a 3-fold increased likelihood of substance use disorders, and gay and bisexual men showed twice the rate of anxiety disorders and schizophrenia and (or) psychotic illness, even after accounting for mental disorder comorbidity. Suicide attempts were independently associated with bisexuality, with odds 3 times higher than in heterosexuals.

Conclusion: Findings from our study emphasise the fact that sexual orientation minorities are vulnerable to poor mental health outcomes, including suicide attempts. Clinicians need to be aware of these specific negative mental health consequences when assessing sexual orientation minorities.

The associations between early alcohol use and suicide attempts among adolescents with a history of major depression

Bossarte RM, Swahn MH (USA)
Addictive Behaviors 175, 703-704, 2010

Objective: Previous studies have identified significant associations between alcohol initiation before the age of 13 years and risk for suicide attempts. However, these associations have not been extensively tested using data obtained from populations with clinically significant psychopathology. The current study seeks to extend knowledge of the associations between early alcohol initiation and risk for suicide by identifying the associations between age of first alcohol use and suicide attempts among a sample of youth age 13 to 15years with a history of major depression.

Methodology: Data were obtained from the National Study of Drug Use and Health (NSDUH), a household-based survey of U.S. adolescents and adults age 12 years and older.

Results: Results from these analyses confirm previous reports of significant associations between age of first alcohol use and suicide attempts and extend previous understanding of risk by using data obtained from a household-based survey and from adolescents with clinically relevant psychopathology.

Conclusions: These findings provide further support for the implementation, enforcement, and continued support of both targeted and universal prevention strategies designed to reduce underage drinking.

Prescription sleeping pills, insomnia, and suicidality in the National Comorbidity Survey Replication

Brower KJ, McCammon RJ, Wojnar M, Ilgen MA, Wojnar J, Valenstein M (USA)
Journal of Clinical Psychiatry. Published online: 21 September 2010. doi:10.4088/JCP.09m05484gry, 2010

Background: Sedative-hypnotics have been associated with suicide attempts and completed suicides in a number of toxicologic, epidemiologic, and clinical studies. Most studies, however, inadequately address confounding by insomnia, which not only is a component of many mental health disorders that increase suicidal risk, but also is independently associated with suicidality. Moreover, the association of nonbenzodiazepine benzodiazepine receptor agonists (NBRAs) with suicidality has not been specifically studied in the US general population.

Objective: The purpose of this study was to assess the independent contribution of prescription sedative-hypnotic use, particularly the NBRAs, to suicidal ideas, plans, and suicide attempts in the general US population, after adjusting for insomnia and other confounding variables.

Method: Secondary analyses of National Comorbidity Survey Replication data for 5,692 household respondents interviewed between 2001 and 2003 assessed the cross-sectional relationships between prescription sedative-hypnotic use and suicidality in the previous 12 months. Multivariate, hierarchical logistic regression analyses controlled for symptoms of insomnia, past-year mental disorders, lifetime chronic physical illnesses, and demographic variables.

Results: Prescription sedative-hypnotic use in the past year was significantly associated with suicidal thoughts (adjusted odds ratio [AOR] = 2.2; $P < .001$), suicide plans (AOR = 1.9; $P < .01$), and suicide attempts (AOR = 3.4; $P < .01$). It was a stronger predictor than insomnia for both suicidal thoughts and suicide attempts and significantly improved the fit of these regression models (suicidal thoughts, $P < .01$; suicide attempts, $P < .05$).

Conclusions: Prescription sleeping pills, as exemplified by zolpidem and zaleplon, are associated with suicidal thoughts and suicide attempts during the past 12 months, but no evidence of causality was provided by this study. Clinical practitioners should recognize that patients taking similar types of sedative-hypnotics have a marker of increased risk for suicidality.

Mortality and suicide after self-harm: Community cohort study in Taiwan

Chen VC, Tan HK, Chen CY, Chen TH, Liao LR, Lee CT, Dewey M, Stewart R, Prince M, Cheng AT (Taiwan)
British Journal of Psychiatry 198, 31-36, 2011

Background: Little is known about outcomes after self-harm in East Asia.

Aims: To investigate mortality after self-harm in a Taiwanese population.

Method: Between 2000 and 2003, 1083 individuals who self-harmed were identified through a population self-harm register in Nantou County, Taiwan, and followed until 2007 for date and cause of death on a national mortality database.

Results: In total, 145 individuals died, 48 through suicide. The risks of all-cause and suicide mortality in the first year were 4.7% and 2.1% respectively, representing 8- and 131-fold age- and gender-standardised increases. Male gender and older age were independent risk factors for both suicide and non-suicide mortality. Use of more lethal methods in the index episode was associated with higher mortality but this was accounted for by gender.

Conclusions: Results in this sample support the recommendation that people with a history of recent self-harm should be a major target for suicide prevention programs.

Economic fluctuations and suicide: A comparison of Taiwan and Hong Kong

Chen Y-Y, Yip PS, Lee C, Fan H-F, Fu K-W (Taiwan, Hong Kong)
Social Science and Medicine 71, 2083-2090, 2010

This study examines the impact of unemployment on suicide rates in Taiwan and Hong Kong during the period of rising unemployment (1997–2003) and its subsequent decline (2003–2007), with 2003 as the turning point. During these initial years of high unemployment, suicide rates increased markedly in Hong Kong and Taiwan; however, as employment conditions improved, suicide rates fell in Hong Kong but continued to increase in Taiwan. ARMAX time-series models with appropriate time lags were used to assess the impact of unemployment on suicide rates for both periods. It was found that for Taiwan, the unemployment rate was positively related with the suicide rate for both males and females during the period of high unemployment, whereas a negative relationship was observed as the rate of unemployment decreased. On the other hand, the reduction in suicide rates since 2003 was not statistically significantly related to the improvement of employment conditions for Hong Kong; whereas the suicide rate in Taiwan still remained at a high level due to the increasing number of charcoal burning suicide deaths despite improvements in employment conditions. In conclusion, lower unemployment was not necessarily associated with lower suicide rates. Exogenous factors other than economic ones have been suggested to be important for understanding differences in suicide patterns in Hong Kong and Taiwan. The impact of employment conditions on suicide across different countries deserves further investigation.

Lifetime suicidal ideation and suicide attempts in Asian Americans

Cheng JK, Fancher TL, Ratanasen M, Conner KR, Duberstein PR, Sue S, Takeuchi D (USA)
Asian American Journal of Psychology 1, 18-30, 2010

Few studies have examined the role of culturally relevant factors in suicidal behavior among Asian Americans. Using the National Latino and Asian American Study (NLAAS) (Alegria et al., 2004; Heeringa et al., 2004), the current study examined the role of culturally related variables (family conflict, perceived discrimination, and ethnic identity) on suicidal ideation and suicide attempts in a nationally representative sample of 2,095 Asian Americans. Important covariates were sociodemographic characteristics (gender, age, marital status, years of education, household poverty, and nativity status), depressive and anxiety disorders, and number of chronic conditions. Gender related correlates were also explored. The lifetime prevalence of suicidal ideation and attempts was 8.8% and 2.5%, respectively. Female gender, family conflict, perceived discrimination, and the presence of lifetime depressive or anxiety disorders were positively correlated with suicidal ideation and attempts. A high level of identification with one's ethnic group was associated with lower rates of suicide attempts. Among Asian men, but not women, the presence of chronic medical conditions was associated with suicidal ideation. Findings highlight the contributions to suicide risk of cultural factors and gender differences in Asian Americans.

Resilience and suicidality among homeless youth

Cleverley K, Kidd SA (Canada)

Journal of Adolescence. Published online: 3 December 2010. doi:10.1016/j.adolescence.2010.11.003, 2010

Homeless and street-involved youth are considered an extremely high risk group, with many studies highlighting trajectories characterised by abusive, neglectful, and unstable family histories, victimization and criminal involvement while on the streets, high rates of physical and mental illness, and extremely high rates of mortality. While there exists a substantial body of knowledge regarding risk, in recent years attention has been increasingly shifting to the examination of resilience, intervention, and service delivery models for these young people. The present study describes the findings from a quantitative examination of personal and street-related demographics, psychological distress, self-esteem, resilience, and suicidality among 47 homeless and street-involved youth. Key findings indicate that the apparent erosion of mental health variables, including resilience, occurs as a function of how long the youths have been without stable housing. Finally, those youths' perceived resilience was associated with less suicidal ideation whereas higher psychological distress was associated with higher suicidal ideation, even when accounting for resiliency.

'Well it's like someone at the other end cares about you.' A qualitative study exploring the views of users and providers of care of contact-based interventions following self-harm

Cooper J, Hunter C, Owen-Smith A, Gunnell D, Donovan J, Hawton K, Kapur N (UK)

General Hospital Psychiatry. Published online: 2 March 2011. doi:10.1016/j.genhosppsych.2011.01.009, 2011

Objective: We investigated the views of service users and staff regarding contact-based interventions (e.g., letters, telephone calls or crisis cards) following self-harm.

Method: Self-harm patients recently discharged from an emergency department were selected using purposive sampling ($n = 11$). Clinical staff from relevant service areas and voluntary staff took part in a focus group and individual interviews ($n = 10$). Interviews were transcribed and thematic analyses were conducted using methods of constant comparison to ensure that emergent themes remained grounded in the data.

Results: Most service users and staff participants identified the period of time directly after discharge as the time of greatest need. A contact-based intervention was viewed by service users as a gesture of caring, which counteracted feelings of loneliness. Delivery by mental health specialists was preferred, initially by phone, but letters were considered helpful later. The intervention should be both genuine in delivery and linked to current services. Potential barriers included means of accessing the service and threats to privacy.

Conclusion: The findings suggest that an appropriate design for an intervention might be the provision of an information leaflet, telephone calls (soon after discharge), then letters (offering continuity of contact). Aspects of value and concern expressed by service users should be helpful to clinicians and service providers.

Queensland Aboriginis, multiple realities and the social sources of suffering, Part 2: suicide, spirits and symbolism

Cox L (Australia)
Oceania 80, 241-262, 2010

This is the second part of a paper that explores a range of magico-religious experiences such as immaterial voices and visions, in terms of local cultural, moral and socio-political circumstances in an Aboriginal town in rural Queensland. This part of the paper explores the political and cultural symbolism and meaning of suicide. It charts the saliency of suicide amongst two groups of kin and cohorts and the social meaningfulness and problematic of the voices and visions in relation to suicide, to identity and family forms and to funerals and a heavily drinking lifestyle. I argue that voices and visions are used to reinterpret social experience and to establish meaning and that tragically suicide evokes connectivity rather than anomie and here cannot be understood merely as an individualistic act or evidence of individual pathology. Rather it is about transformation and crossing a threshold to join an enduring domain of Aboriginality. In this life world, where family is the highest social value and where a relational view of persons holds sway, the individualistic practice of psychiatric and other helping professions, is a considerable problem.

The effect of participating in suicide research: Does participating in a research protocol on suicide and psychiatric symptoms increase suicide ideation and attempts?

Cukrowicz K, Smith P, Poindexter E (USA)
Suicide and Life-Threatening Behavior 40, 535-543, 2010

The effect of engaging in an intensive research protocol that inquired extensively about psychiatric and suicide symptoms and exposed participants to a number of images, including suicide-related content was explored. Individuals experiencing a major depressive episode were called at 1 and 3 months after the initial protocol. Participants were asked about changes in suicide ideation and the occurrence of self-harm or suicide attempts following participation. Participants reported experiencing reductions in suicide ideation at the first follow-up and no changes at the second follow-up. No participant reported having engaged in self-harm or having attempted suicide at either follow-up. Results suggest that basic science/nontreatment research can be conducted safely with suicidal participants and in a manner that does not increase suicide symptoms or suicide risk.

Youth perceptions of suicide and help-seeking: 'They'd think I was weak or "mental"'

Curtis C (New Zealand)
Journal of Youth Studies 13, 699-715, 2010

Youth suicide is an issue of international concern and the college population may have a considerably higher rate of suicidal behaviour than the general population, yet seeking help for suicidality is uncommon. This research sought to understand college students' knowledge of suicidal behaviour and attitudes to help-seeking, in a New Zealand university. A mixed-method approach comprising a survey and interviews was utilised. Approximately one-fifth of participants had been suicidal, were aware of another student's suicide and/or had supported a suicidal student. Some participants expressed willingness to seek help for another, but far fewer were willing to seek help for themselves. Key reasons for the latter include stigma and a perceived need for self-reliance. Participants expressed greater willingness to seek help for another if they were not a close friend.

The effectiveness of middle and high school-based suicide prevention programs for adolescents: A systematic review

Cusimano MD, Sameem M (Canada)

Injury Prevention 17, 43-49, 2011

Objective: To assess the effectiveness of middle and high school-based suicide prevention curricula.

Data sources: The following were searched: Ovid MEDLINE(R) in-process and other non-indexed citations and Ovid MEDLINE(R), Ovid Healthstar, CINAHL, PsycINFO, all EBM reviews — Cochrane DSR, ACP Journal Club, DARE, CCTR, CMR, HTA, and NHSEED, and the ISI Web of Science, until October 2009; government web pages for statistics and other demographic data in countries where they were available; citation lists of relevant articles.

Review methods: Randomised controlled studies, interrupted time series analyses with a concurrent comparison group, studies with follow-up examinations (post-test questionnaires and monitoring suicide rates), and middle to high school-based curriculum studies, including both male and female participants, were included.

Results: 36 potentially relevant studies were identified, eight of which met the inclusion criteria. Overall, statistically significant improvements were noted in knowledge, attitude, and help-seeking behaviour. A decrease in self reported ideation was reported in two studies. None reported on suicide rates.

Conclusion: Although evidence exists that school-based programmes to prevent suicide among adolescents improve knowledge, attitudes, and help-seeking behaviours, no evidence yet exists that these prevention programmes reduce suicide rates. Further well designed, controlled research is required before such programs are instituted broadly to populations at risk.

The impact of psychiatric symptoms, interpersonal style, and coercion on aggression and self-harm during psychiatric hospitalisation

Daffern M, Thomas S, Ferguson M, Podubinski T, Hollander Y, Kulkhani J, DeCastella A, Foley F (Australia)

Psychiatry 73, 365-381, 2010

Interpersonal style, a key component of personality and personality disorder, has emerged as an important characteristic that is relevant to aggressive behavior by patients in psychiatric hospitals. However, studies examining the relationship between interpersonal style and aggression have thus far only been conducted with patients with personality disorder and/or mild and stable symptoms of mental illness. This study explored the relative importance of patients' interpersonal style, psychiatric symptoms, and perceptions of staff coercion on aggression and self-harm during acute psychiatric hospitalization. One hundred and fifty-two patients (M = 38.32 years, SD = 12.06; 56.8% males and 43.2% females) admitted for short-term assessment and treatment to the acute units of a civil and a forensic psychiatric hospital were administered the Brief Psychiatric Rating Scale, Impact Message Inventory, and MacArthur Admission Experience Survey. Participants' files were reviewed and nursing staff were interviewed at the end of each patient's hospital stay to determine whether participants had self-harmed or acted aggressively towards others. Initial univariate analyses showed that thought disorder and dominant and hostile-dominant interpersonal styles predicted aggression. Using multiple regression and controlling for gender and age, only a hostile-dominant interpersonal style predicted aggression (β = .258, $p < .05$). No factors were significantly related to self-harm. These results suggest that measures of interpersonal style are sensitive to those aspects of interpersonal functioning that are critical to patient's responses to the demands of psychiatric in-patient treatment. Procedures to assess risk and engage and manage potentially aggressive patients, including limit-setting styles and de-escalation strategies, should take into account the interpersonal style of patients and the interpersonal behavior of staff.

'And then one day he'd shot himself. Then I was really shocked': General practitioners' reaction to patient suicide

Davidsen AS (Denamark)

Patient Education and Counseling. Published online: 27 September 2010. doi:10.1016/j.pec.2010.08.020, 2010

Objective: Patients who commit suicide have often seen their GP shortly before the suicide. This study explored the emotional effect of patients' suicides on GPs, and whether this effect was linked to the GPs' propensity to explore suicide risk.

Methods: Semi-structured interviews were carried out with 14 GPs sampled purposively aiming at maximum variation. Analysis by Interpretative Phenomenological Analysis.

Results: Patients' suicides had a substantial emotional effect on all GPs. Some developed a feeling of guilt and of having failed. If patients had contacted the GP about physical symptoms and the suicide ideation had not been diagnosed, this led to considerable self-scrutiny. GPs differed in their propensity to explore suicide ideation, but all were emotionally shaken and struck by guilt, failure, and self-scrutiny if a patient committed suicide.

Conclusion: A patient's suicide can be experienced as a 'critical case' that greatly affects all GPs irrespective of other differences among the GPs. The feeling of insufficiency was linked to not having realized during the visit that the patient may have had suicidal thoughts.

Practice implications: GPs' need for support in emotionally stressful situations should be investigated, and training should be directed towards discovering suicide ideation masked by vague physical symptoms.

Suicide risk assessment and content of VA health care contacts before suicide completion by veterans in Oregon

Denneson LM, Basham C, Dickinson KC, Crutchfield MC, Millet L, Shen X, Dobscha SK (USA)

Psychiatric Services 61, 1192-1197, 2010

Objective: This study described health care contacts at a Department of Veterans Affairs (VA) medical center in Oregon in the year before death of veterans who completed suicide.

Methods: Oregon Violent Death Reporting System (OVDRS) data and VA administrative data were linked to identify the 112 veterans who completed suicide in Oregon between 2000 and 2005 and who had contact with a single VA medical center in the year before death. Medical records were reviewed to collect data on clinician assessment of suicide risk and reasons for the last contact.

Results: In the year before death, 54 veterans (48%) had one or more mental health contacts and 71 (63%) had one or more primary care contacts. The mean age was 57; common diagnoses included mood disorders (38%) and cardiovascular disease (38%). The median number of days between the last contact and date of death was 42 (range = 0–358). Thirty-six last contacts (32%) were patient initiated for new or exacerbated medical concerns, and 76 (68%) were follow-ups for ongoing problems. Clinicians noted that 41 patients (37%) were experiencing emotional distress at the last contact. Thirteen of the 18 patients (72%) who were assessed for suicidal ideation at their last contact denied such thoughts.

Conclusions: During their last contact, most veterans were seen for routine medical care and few endorsed thoughts of suicide. Results underscore challenges that clinicians face in identifying and caring for veterans at risk of suicide in health care settings. Additional research is indicated to identify better ways to facilitate communication of suicidal thoughts when they are present.

Intensive case management for severe mental illness

Dieterich M, Irving CB, Park B, Marshall M (Italy)

Cochrane Database of Systematic Reviews 10, CD007906, 2010

Background: Intensive Case Management (ICM) is a community based package of care, aiming to provide long term care for severely mentally ill people who do not require immediate admission. ICM evolved from two original community models of care, Assertive Community Treatment (ACT) and Case Management (CM), where ICM emphasises the importance of small caseload (less than 20) and high intensity input.

Objectives: To assess the effects of Intensive Case Management (caseload < 20) in comparison with non-Intensive Case Management (caseload > 20) and with standard community care in people with severe mental illness. To evaluate whether the effect of ICM on hospitalisation depends on its fidelity to the ACT model and on the setting.

Search strategy: For the current update of this review we searched the Cochrane Schizophrenia Group Trials Register (February 2009), which is compiled by systematic searches of major databases, hand searches and conference proceedings.

Selection criteria: All relevant randomised clinical trials focusing on people with severe mental illness, aged 18 to 65 years and treated in the community-care setting, where Intensive Case Management, non-Intensive Case Management or standard care were compared. Outcomes such as service use, adverse effects, global state, social functioning, mental state, behaviour, quality of life, satisfaction and costs were sought.

Data collection and analysis: We extracted data independently. For binary outcomes we calculated relative risk (RR) and its 95% confidence interval (CI), on an intention-to-treat basis. For continuous data we estimated mean difference (MD) between groups and its 95% confidence interval (CI). We employed a random-effects model for analyses.We performed a random-effects meta-regression analysis to examine the association of the intervention's fidelity to the ACT model and the rate of hospital use in the setting where the trial was conducted with the treatment effect.

Main results: We included 38 trials (7328 participants) in this review. The trials provided data for two comparisons: (1) ICM versus standard care, (2) ICM versus non-ICM. (1) ICM versus standard care: Twenty-four trials provided data on length of hospitalisation, and results favoured Intensive Case Management ($n = 3595$, 24 RCTs, MD -0.86 CI -1.37 to -0.34). There was a high level of heterogeneity, but this significance still remained when the outlier studies were excluded from the analysis ($n = 3143$, 20 RCTs, MD -0.62 CI -1.00 to -0.23). Nine studies found participants in the ICM group were less likely to be lost to psychiatric services ($n = 1633$, 9 RCTs, RR 0.43 CI 0.30 to 0.61, I = 49%, $p = .05$). One global state scale did show an Improvement in global state for those receiving ICM, the GAF scale ($n = 818$, 5 RCTs, MD 3.41 CI 1.66 to 5.16). Results for mental state as measured through various rating scales, however, were equivocal, with no compelling evidence that ICM was really any better than standard care in improving mental state. No differences in mortality between ICM and standard care groups occurred, either due to 'all causes' ($n = 1456$, 9 RCTs, RR 0.84 CI 0.48 to 1.47) or to 'suicide' ($n = 1456$, 9 RCTs, RR 0.68 CI 0.31 to 1.51). Social functioning results varied, no differences were found in terms of contact with the legal system and with employment status, whereas significant improvement in accommodation status was found, as was the incidence of not living independently, which was lower in the ICM group ($n = 1185$, 4 RCTs, RR 0.65 CI 0.49 to 0.88). Quality of life data found no significant difference between groups, but data were weak. CSQ scores showed a greater participant satisfaction in the ICM group ($n = 423$, 2 RCTs, MD 3.23

CI 2.31 to 4.14). (2) ICM versus non-ICM: The included studies failed to show a significant advantage of ICM in reducing the average length of hospitalisation (n = 2220, 21 RCTs, MD -0.08 CI -0.37 to 0.21). They did find ICM to be more advantageous than non-ICM in reducing rate of lost to follow-up (n = 2195, 9 RCTs, RR 0.72 CI 0.52 to 0.99), although data showed a substantial level of heterogeneity (I = 59%, p = .01). Overall, no significant differences were found in the effects of ICM compared to non-ICM for broad outcomes such as service use, mortality, social functioning, mental state, behaviour, quality of life, satisfaction and costs. (3) Fidelity to ACT: Within the meta-regression we found that i. the more ICM is adherent to the ACT model, the better it is at decreasing time in hospital ('organisation fidelity' variable coefficient —0.36 CI -0.66 to -0.07); and ii. the higher the baseline hospital use in the population, the better ICM is at decreasing time in hospital ('baseline hospital use' variable coefficient -0.20 CI -0.32 to -0.10). Combining both these variables within the model, 'organisation fidelity' is no longer significant, but 'baseline hospital use' result is still significantly influencing time in hospital (regression coefficient -0.18 CI -0.29 to -0.07, p = .0027).

Authors conclusions: ICM was found effective in ameliorating many outcomes relevant to people with severe mental illnesses. Compared to standard care ICM was shown to reduce hospitalisation and increase retention in care. It also globally improved social functioning, although ICM's effect on mental state and quality of life remains unclear. ICM is of value at least to people with severe mental illnesses who are in the subgroup of those with a high level of hospitalisation (about 4 days/month in past 2 years) and the intervention should be performed close to the original model.It is not clear, however, what gain ICM provides on top of a less formal non-ICM approach. We do not think that more trials comparing current ICM with standard care or non-ICM are justified, but currently we know of no review comparing non-ICM with standard care and this should be undertaken.

Substance misuse, suicidal ideation, and suicide attempts among a national sample of homeless

Dietz TL (USA)

Journal of Social Service Research 37, 1-18, 2010

This study's purpose was to identify the relationship between the annual incidence of drug and alcohol misuse among a national probability sample of 2,974 homeless individuals and self-reports of suicidal ideation and attempts while considering the predictors of both drug and alcohol misuse and suicidal ideation and attempts. By using a national dataset, the National Survey of Homeless Assistance Providers and Clients (NSHAPC), and testing a series of logistic models, this study allows for the development of empirically-driven prevention and treatment programs designed to appropriately and effectively target suicidal ideation and attempts among homeless substance misusers.

Evidence for an emotion-cognition interaction in the statistical prediction of suicide attempts

Dour HJ, Cha CB, Nock MK (USA)

Behaviour Research and Therapy 49, 294-298, 2011

Suicidal behavior is a prevalent problem among adolescents and young adults. Although most theoretical models of suicide suggest that this behavior results from the interaction of different risk factors, most prior studies have tested only bivariate associations between individual risk factors and suicidal behaviors. The current study was designed to address this limitation by testing the effect of an emotion–cognition interaction on suicide attempts among youth. Specifically, we hypothesised that the interaction of emotion reactivity and problem-solving skills would statistically predict the probability of a recent suicide attempt among 87 adolescents and young adults. Results revealed a significant interaction, such that emotion reactivity was strongly associated with the probability of a suicide attempt among those with poor problem-solving skills, moderately associated among those with average problem-solving skills, and not significantly associated among those with good problem-solving skills. The next generation of studies on suicidal behavior should continue to examine how risk factors interact to predict this dangerous outcome.

Early risk factors for suicide in an epidemiological first episode psychosis cohort

Dutta R, Murray RM, Allardyce J, Jones PB, Boydell J (UK)

Schizophrenia Research 126, 11-19, 2011

Background: Much remains unknown about whether there are early risk factors for suicide in psychosis.

Aim: The aim of the study was to determine whether there are any identifiable early symptom clusters, aetiological factors or illness course markers for suicide in first episode psychosis.

Method: A total of 2132 patients with first episode psychosis presenting to secondary care services in London (1965-2004; $n = 1474$), Nottingham (1997-1999; $n = 195$) and Dumfries and Galloway (1979-1998; $n = 463$) were traced after up to 40 years (mean 13 years) following first presentation. Risk factors were identified from the Operational Checklist for Psychotic Disorders rated for the first year following presentation.

Results: Overall, there were 51 suicides and 373 deaths from other causes. Male gender (RR 2.84, 95% CI 1.20-6.69, $p = .02$) and a cumulative threshold effect of symptoms early in the illness (RR 6.81, 95% CI 2.33-19.85, $p < .001$) were associated with a higher propensity for later completed suicide. There was also a suggestion that early manic symptoms might increase the risk of later suicide irrespective of initial diagnosis.

Conclusion: Suicide risk was associated with a cumulative threshold effect of symptoms and manic symptoms. As suicide is a relatively rare event in psychotic disorders, general population-based prevention strategies may have more impact in this vulnerable group as well as the wider population.

Reassessing the long-term risk of suicide after a first episode of psychosis

Dutta R, Murray RM, Hotopf M, Allardyce J, Jones PB, Boydell J (UK)
Archives of General Psychiatry 67, 1230-1237, 2010

Context: The long-term risk of suicide after a first episode of psychosis is unknown because previous studies often have been based on prevalence cohorts, been biased to more severely ill hospitalised patients, extrapolated from a short follow-up time, and have made a distinction between schizophrenia and other psychoses.

Objective: To determine the epidemiology of suicide in a clinically representative cohort of patients experiencing their first episode of psychosis.

Design: Retrospective inception cohort.

Setting: Geographic catchment areas in London, England (between January 1, 1965, and December 31, 2004; $n = 2056$); Nottingham, England (between September 1, 1997, and August 31, 1999; $n = 203$); and Dumfries and Galloway, Scotland (between January 1, 1979, and December 31, 1998; $n = 464$).

Participants: All 2723 patients who presented for the first time to secondary care services with psychosis in the 3 defined catchment areas were traced after a mean follow-up period of 11.5 years. Main Outcome Measure Deaths by suicide and open verdicts according to the International Classification of Diseases (seventh through tenth editions).

Results: The case fatality from suicide was considerably lower than expected from previous studies (1.9% [53/2723]); the proportionate mortality was 11.9% (53/444). Although the rate of suicide was highest in the first year after presentation, risk persisted late into follow-up, with a median time to suicide of 5.6 years. Suicide occurred approximately 12 times more than expected from the general population of England and Wales (standardised mortality ratio, 11.65; 95% confidence interval, 8.73–15.24), and 49 of the 53 suicides were excess deaths. Even a decade after first presentation-a time when there may be less intense clinical monitoring of risk-suicide risk remained almost 4 times higher than in the general population (standardised mortality ratio, 3.92; 95% confidence interval, 2.22–6.89).

Conclusions: The highest risk of suicide after a psychotic episode occurs soon after presentation, yet physicians should still be vigilant in assessing risk a decade or longer after first contact. The widely held view that 10% to 15% die of suicide is misleading because it refers to proportionate mortality, not lifetime risk. Nevertheless, there is a substantial increase in risk of suicide compared with the general population.

Perceived burdensomeness, familism, and suicidal ideation among Mexican women: Enhancing understanding of risk and protective factors

Garza MJ, Pettit JW (USA)

Suicide & Life-Threatening Behavior 40, 561-573, 2010

The interpersonal-psychological theory of suicide and a culturally-relevant construct, familism, was used to examine predictors of suicidal ideation among Mexican and Mexican American women in the United States. A sense of perceived burdensomeness toward others was expected to significantly predict suicidal ideation, especially among women who endorsed high levels of familism. Mexican and Mexican American outpatient women (N = 73) completed self-report measures and an interview measure of suicidal ideation. Main and interactive effects of perceived burdensomeness and familism were examined. Perceived burdensomeness, but not familism, significantly predicted suicidal ideation. The interaction hypothesis was not supported. These findings highlight perceived burdensomeness as a risk factor for suicidal behavior in Mexican and Mexican American women.

Parental psychopathology and the risk of suicidal behavior in their offspring: results from the World Mental Health surveys

Gureje O, Oladeji B, Hwang I, Chiu WT, Kessler RC, Sampson NA, Alonso J, Andrade LH, Beautrais A, Borges G, Bromet E, Bruffaerts R, de Girolamo G, de Graaf R, Gal G, He Y, Hu C, Iwata N, Karam EG, Kovess-Masféty V, Matschinger H, Moldovan MV, Posada-Villa J, Sagar R, Scocco P, Seedat S, Tomov T, Nock MK (USA)

Molecular Psychiatry. Published online: 16 November 2010. doi:10.1038/mp.2010.111, 2010

Previous research suggests that parental psychopathology predicts suicidal behavior among offspring; however, the more fine-grained associations between specific parental disorders and distinct stages of the pathway to suicide are not well understood. We set out to test the hypothesis that parental disorders associated with negative mood would predict offspring suicide ideation, whereas disorders characterized by impulsive aggression (for example, antisocial personality) and anxiety/agitation (for example, panic disorder) would predict which offspring act on their suicide ideation and make a suicide attempt. Data were collected during face-to-face interviews conducted on nationally representative samples (N = 55,299; age 18+) from 21 countries around the world. We tested the associations between a range of parental disorders and the onset and persistence over time (that is, time since most recent episode controlling for age of onset and time since onset) of subsequent suicidal behavior (suicide ideation, plans and attempts) among offspring. Analyses tested bivariate and multivariate associations between each parental disorder and distinct forms of suicidal behavior. Results revealed that each parental disorder examined increased the risk of suicide ideation among offspring, parental generalised anxiety and depression emerged as the only predictors of the onset and persistence (respectively) of suicide plans among offspring with ideation, whereas parental antisocial personality and anxiety disorders emerged as the only predictors of the onset and persistence of suicide attempts among ideators. A dose-response relation between parental disorders and respondent risk of suicide ideation and attempt was also found. Parental death by suicide was a particularly strong predictor of persistence of suicide attempts among offspring. These associations remained significant after controlling for comorbidity of parental disorders and for the presence of mental disorders among offspring. These findings should inform future explorations of the mechanisms of intergenerational transmission of suicidal behaviour.

Compensation for workplace injury leading to suicide in Australia

Guthrie R, Westaway J (Australia)
Journal of Law and Medicine 18, 333-343, 2011

Workplace-related death by suicide raises a number of difficult issues in the context of workers compensation. On first reading, workers compensation statutes usually prevent recovery of compensation where an injury is self-inflicted, suggesting that compensation for suicide will be excluded. Additionally, compensation is usually denied when the nexus between employment and injury is broken which is frequently the defence to any claim by the dependants of workers who takes their own life following a work injury. This article examines the Australian landscape in relation to the evolution of principles that apply to consideration of workers compensation claims where suicide is an element.

Adolescent help-seeking and the yellow ribbon suicide prevention program: An evaluation

Freedenthal S (USA)
Suicide and Life-Threatening Behavior 40, 628-639, 2010

The Yellow Ribbon Suicide Prevention Program has gained national and international recognition for its school- and community-based activities. After the introduction of Yellow Ribbon to a Denver-area high school, staff and adolescents were surveyed to determine if help-seeking behavior had increased. Using a pre-post intervention design, staff at an experimental school and comparison school were surveyed about their experiences with student help-seeking. Additionally, 146 students at the experimental high school were surveyed. Staff did not report any increase in student help-seeking, and students' reports of help-seeking from 11 of 12 different types of helpers did not increase; the exception was help-seeking from a crisis hotline, which increased from 2.1% to 6.9%. Further research with larger, more inclusive samples is needed to determine whether Yellow Ribbon is effective in other locations.

Parental bonding in severely suicidal adolescent inpatients

Freudenstein O, Zohar A, Apter A, Shoval G, Weizman A, Zalsman G (Israel)
European Psychiatry. Published online: 11 March 2011. doi: 10.1016/j.eurpsy.2011.01.006, 2011

Family environment has a clear role in suicidal behavior of adolescents. We assessed the relationship between parental bonding and suicidal behavior in suicidal ($n = 53$) and non-suicidal ($n = 47$) adolescent inpatients. Two dimensions of parental bonding: care and overprotection, were assessed with the Parental Bonding Instrument. Results showed that adolescents with severe suicidal behavior tended to perceive their mothers as less caring and more overprotective compared to those with mild or no suicidal behavior. A discriminant analysis distinguished significantly between adolescents with high suicidality and those with low suicidality, $\chi^2(5)=15.54$; $p = .01$, in 71% of the cases. The perception of the quality of maternal bonding may be an important correlate of suicidal behavior in adolescence and may guide therapeutic strategies and prevention.

Newspaper reporting of suicides in Hong Kong, Taiwan and Guangzhou: Compliance with WHO media guidelines and epidemiological comparisons

Fu KW, Chan YY, Yip PS (Hong Kong, Taiwan, China)
Journal of Epidemiology and Community Health. Published online: 1 October 2010. doi:10.1136/jech.2009.105650, 2010

Background: Media guidelines for suicide reporting are available in many countries. However, to what extent the mass media comply with the guidelines is unknown. Few studies are available that investigate systematically whether the mass media reflect the epidemiological reality of suicide deaths in their articles.

Methods: Based on the WHO media guidelines, this study investigated the characteristics of newspaper articles of suicides in three Chinese communities, namely Hong Kong, Taiwan and Guangzhou. Epidemiological comparisons were conducted to identify the age and gender differences between the suicide victims as reported in the newspapers and the official records of suicide deaths in all three places.

Results: The results found that one media characteristic complied with the WHO media guidelines (i.e., only about 2% of the articles were printed on the front page), but there were a number of instances of non-compliance (ie, only 4-14% provided sources for help-seeking and 27-90% printed with photos). The epidemiological comparisons revealed an over-representation of younger suicides and an under-representation of late-life suicides in the newspapers of all three places. Furthermore, female suicides were found to be under-reported in Taiwan and Guangzhou newspapers, but not in Hong Kong papers.

Conclusion: Non-compliant suicide articles are prevalent in the newspapers of these three Chinese settings. The observed media misrepresentations may potentially mislead the public and the policy makers about the actual risk for suicide in some demographic groups.

Suicidal ideation among individuals whose parents have divorced: Findings from a representative Canadian community survey

Fuller-Thomson E, Dalton AD (Canada)
Psychiatry Research. Published online: 5 January 2011. doi:10.1016/j.psychres.2010.12.004, 2011

This study used a large, nationally representative sample to examine the gender-specific association between parental divorce and the cumulative lifetime incidence of suicidal ideation. Known risk factors for suicidal ideation, such as childhood stressors, socioeconomic factors, adult health behaviors and stressors, marital status, and any history of mood and/or anxiety disorders were controlled. Gender-specific analyses revealed that for men, the parental divorce-suicidal ideation relationship remained statistically significant even when the above-listed cluster of risk factors were included in the analyses (odds ratio (OR) = 2.36, 95% confidence interval (CI) = 1.56, 3.58). For women, the association between parental divorce and suicidal ideation was reduced to non-significance when other adverse childhood experiences were included in the analyses (full adjustment OR = 1.04, 95% CI = 0.72, 1.50). These findings indicate a need for screening of suicidal ideation among individuals, particularly men and those with mood and/or anxiety disorders, who have experienced parental divorce. Future research should focus on the mechanisms linking parental divorce and suicidal ideation.

Prevalence and correlates of suicidal ideation during pregnancy

Gavin AR, Tabb KM, Melville JL, Guo Y, Katon W (USA)
Archives of Women's Mental Health. Published online: 17 February 2011. doi:10.1007/s00737-011-0207-5, 2011

Data are scarce regarding the prevalence and risk factors for antenatal suicidal ideation because systematic screening for suicidal ideation during pregnancy is rare. This study reports the prevalence and correlates of suicidal ideation during pregnancy. We performed cross-sectional analysis of data from an ongoing registry. Study participants were 2,159 women receiving prenatal care at a university obstetric clinic from January 2004 through March 2010. Multiple logistic regression identified factors associated with antenatal suicidal ideation as measured by the Patient Health Questionnaire. Overall, 2.7% of the sample reported antenatal suicidal ideation. Over 50% of women who reported antenatal suicidal ideation also reported major depression. In the fully adjusted model antenatal major depression (OR = 11.50; 95% CI 5.40, 24.48) and antenatal psychosocial stress (OR = 3.19; 95% CI 1.44, 7.05) were positively associated with an increased risk of antenatal suicidal ideation. We found that being non-Hispanic White was associated with a decreased risk of antenatal suicidal ideation (OR = 0.51; 95% CI 0.26-0.99). The prevalence of antenatal suicidal ideation in the present study was similar to rates reported in nationally representative non-pregnant samples. In other words, pregnancy is not a protective factor against suicidal ideation. Given the high comorbidity of antenatal suicidal ideation with major depression, efforts should be made to identify those women at risk for antenatal suicidal ideation through universal screening.

Do local landmark bridges increase the suicide rate? An alternative test of the likely effect of means restriction at suicide-jumping sites

Glasgow G (USA)

Social Science & Medicine. Published online: 1 February 2011. doi:10.1016/j.socscimed.2011.01.001, 2011

A number of recent studies have examined the effect of installing physical barriers or otherwise restricting access to public sites that are frequently used for suicides by jumping. While these studies demonstrate that barriers lead to a reduction in the number of suicides by jumping at the site where they are installed, thus far no study has found a statistically significant reduction in the local suicide rate attributable to a barrier. All previous studies are case studies of particular sites, and thus have limited statistical power and ability to control for confounding factors, which may obscure the true relationship between barriers and the suicide rate. This study addresses these concerns by examining the relationship between large, well-known bridges ('local landmark' bridges) of the type that are often used as suicide-jumping sites and the local suicide rate, an approach that yields many more cases for analysis. If barriers at suicide-jumping sites decrease the local suicide rate, then this implies that the presence of an unsecured suicide-jumping site will lead to a higher local suicide rate in comparison to areas without such a site. The relationship between suicides and local landmark bridges is examined across 3,116 US counties or county equivalents with negative binomial regression models. I found that while exposure to local landmark bridges was associated with an increased number of suicides by jumping, no positive relationship between these bridges and the overall number of suicides was detected. It may be impossible to conclusively determine if barriers at suicide-jumping sites reduce the local suicide rate with currently available data. However, the method introduced in this paper offers the possibility that better data, or an improved understanding of which potential jumping sites attract suicidal individuals, may eventually allow researchers to determine if means restriction at suicide-jumping sites reduces total suicides.

Relationship duration and mental health outcomes: Findings from a 30-year longitudinal study

Gibb SJ, Fergusson DM, Horwood LJ (New Zealand)
British Journal of Psychiatry 198, 24-30, 2011

Background: Marriage is known to be associated with improved mental health, but little research has examined whether the duration of a cohabiting relationship is associated with mental health.

Aims: To examine the associations between relationship duration and mental health problems in a birth cohort of 30-year-olds.

Method: Associations between relationship duration and mental health were examined using a generalised estimating equation approach. Associations were adjusted for covariates, including prior mental health problems.

Results: Longer relationship duration was significantly associated with lower rates of depression, suicidal behaviour and substance abuse/dependence, even after adjustment for covariates. In most cases the associations did not vary with gender. Legal relationship status (legally or de facto married) was not significantly related to mental health once due allowance was made for relationship duration.

Conclusions: Increasing relationship duration, but not legal relationship status, has a protective effect on mental health for men and women.

Relationship separation and mental health problems: findings from a 30-year longitudinal study

Gibb SJ, Fergusson DM, Horwood LJ (New Zealand)
Australian & New Zealand Journal of Psychiatry 45, 163-169, 2011

Objective: To examine the associations between relationship separation and a range of mental health problems including depression, anxiety disorders, alcohol abuse/dependence, cannabis abuse/dependence, and total number of mental health problems.

Method: Data were drawn from a 30-year longitudinal study of a birth cohort of individuals born in Christchurch, New Zealand. Associations between separation and mental health problems were examined using two types of regression models: population-averaged generalized estimating equation models and fixed effects models. Associations were adjusted for a wide range of fixed and time-dynamic potential covariate factors.

Results: After due allowance was made for confounding, separation was associated with depression, suicidal behaviour, and the total number of mental health problems (rate ratios range 1.7–3.4, median 3.2). These associations were apparent both when separation was used as the dependent variable and when the mental health problems were used as the dependent variables. In contrast, separation was not significantly associated with anxiety disorders, alcohol abuse/dependence, or illicit drug abuse/dependence when due allowance was made for confounding. Associations between separation and mental health problems were not significantly different for men and women.

Conclusions: Separation of a cohabiting relationship is associated with increased rates of depression, suicidal behaviour, and total mental health problems. However, it was not possible to determine the causal direction of the relationship between separation and mental health problems. Future studies may need to employ approaches other than observational research designs in order to address issues of causality.

The impact of the 2009 Red River flood on interpersonal risk factors for suicide

Gordon KH, Bresin K, Dombeck J, Routledge C, Wonderlich JA (USA)
Crisis 32, 52-55, 2011

Background: Natural disasters are frequently associated with increases in risk factors for suicide, yet research indicates that suicide rates tend to stay the same or decrease in the wake of disasters.

Aims: The present research sought to shed light on this counterintuitive phenomenon by testing hypotheses derived from interpersonal-psychological theory of suicidal behavior, which proposes that the desire to die by suicide is the result of feeling like one does not belong and feeling like one is a burden on others. During natural disasters, community members often pull together in volunteering efforts, and it was predicted that such behaviors would boost feelings of belonging and reduce feelings that one is a burden.

Methods: The present study tested these predictions in a sample of 210 undergraduate students in Fargo, North Dakota, following the 2009 Red River Flood.

Results: Consistent with prediction, greater amounts of time spent volunteering in flood efforts were associated with increased feelings of belongingness and decreased feelings of burdensomeness.

Conclusions: The findings in the current study are consistent with the notion that communities pulling together during a natural disaster can reduce interpersonal risk factors associated with the desire for suicide.

Feasibility of screening patients with nonpsychiatric complaints for suicide risk in a pediatric emergency department: A good time to talk?

Horowitz L, Ballard E, Teach SJ, Bosk A, Rosenstein DL, Joshi P, Dalton ME, Pao M (USA)

Pediatric Emergency Care 26, 787-792, 2010

Objective: Screening children for suicide risk when they present to the emergency department (ED) with nonpsychiatric complaints could lead to better identification and treatment of high-risk youth. Before suicide screening protocols can be implemented for nonpsychiatric patients in pediatric EDs, it is essential to determine whether such efforts are feasible.

Methods: As part of an instrument validation study, ED patients (10-21 years old) with both psychiatric and nonpsychiatric presenting complaints were recruited to take part in suicide screening. Clinically significant suicidal thoughts, as measured by the Suicidal Ideation Questionnaire, and suicidal behaviors were assessed, as well as patient opinions about suicide screening. Recruitment rates for the study as well as impact on length of stay were assessed.

Results: Of the 266 patients and parents approached for the study, 159 (60%) agreed to participate. For patients entering the ED for nonpsychiatric reasons ($n = 106$), 5.7% ($n = 6$) reported previous suicidal behavior, and 5.7% ($n = 6$) reported clinically significant suicidal ideation. There were no significant differences for mean length of stay in the ED for nonpsychiatric patients with positive triggers and those who screened negative (means, 382 [SD, 198] and 393 [SD, 166] minutes, respectively; $P = 0.80$). Ninety-six per cent of participants agreed that suicide screening should occur in the ED.

Conclusions: Suicide screening of nonpsychiatric patients in the ED is feasible in terms of acceptability to parents, prevalence of suicidal thoughts and behaviors, practicality to ED flow, and patient opinion. Future endeavors should address brief screening tools validated on nonpsychiatric populations.

Intervention studies in suicide prevention research

Huisman A, Pirkis J, Robinson J (The Netherlands)

Crisis 31, 281-284, 2010

Background: Despite the growing strength of the field of suicidology, various commentators have recently noted that insufficient effort is being put into intervention research, and that this is limiting our knowledge of which suicide prevention strategies might be the most effective.

Aims: To profile the types of studies currently being undertaken by suicide prevention researchers from around the world, in order to examine the relative balance between intervention studies and other types of research.

Methods: We searched the abstract books from the 22nd, 23rd, and 24th Congresses of the International Association for Suicide Prevention and the 10th, 11th, and 12th European Symposia on Suicide and Suicidal Behavior (held between 2003 and 2008), and classified the abstracts in them according to a modified version of an existing taxonomy.

Results: We screened 1,209 abstracts and found that only 12% described intervention studies.

Conclusions: We need to redouble our efforts and make intervention studies our priority if we are to combat the global problem of suicide.

Separation as an important risk factor for suicide: A systematic review

Ide N, Wyder M, Kolves K, De Leo D (Australia)
Journal of Family Issues 31, 1689-1716, 2010

Examining how different phases of relationship separation effects the development of suicidal behaviors has been largely ignored in suicide studies. The few studies conducted suggest that individuals experiencing the acute phase of marital/de facto separation may be at greater risk of suicide compared with those experiencing long-term separation (divorce). To clarify the effects of these factors on detection and prevention of suicidal behaviors, a critical review of the English-language literature on this topic from 1966 to 2008 was undertaken. No studies reliably indicate the impacts of acute separation versus long-term divorce on suicidality. Moreover, research has not specifically addressed the interaction between the psychosocial factors influencing suicidal behaviors in the context of a marital/de facto separation. Considering the large proportion of suicides that occur in the context of marital/de facto separation, our limited understanding of the factors involved in the development of these suicidal behaviours is of concern.

Psychiatric diagnoses and risk of suicide in veterans

Ilgen MA, Bohnert ASB, Ignacio RV, McCarthy JF, Valenstein MM, Kim HM, Blow FC (USA)
Archives of General Psychiatry 67, 1152-1158, 2010

Context: Although numerous studies have documented the clear link between psychiatric conditions and suicide, few have allowed for the comparison between the strength of association between different psychiatric diagnoses and suicide.

Objective: To examine the strength of association between different types of psychiatric diagnoses and the risk of suicide in patients receiving health care services from the Department of Veterans Affairs in fiscal year (FY) 1999.

Design: This project examined National Death Index data and Veterans Health Administration patient treatment records.

Setting: Department of Veterans Affairs, Veterans Health Administration.

Participants: All veterans who used Veterans Health Administration services during FY 1999 ($N = 3,291,891$) who were alive at the start of FY 2000.

Main Outcome Measures: Psychiatric diagnoses were obtained from patient treatment records in FY 1998 and 1999 and used to predict subsequent death by suicide during the following 7 years in sex-stratified survival analyses controlling for age.

Results: In the 7 years after FY 1999, 7684 veterans died by suicide. In diagnosis-specific analyses, patients with bipolar disorder had the greatest estimated risk of suicide among men (hazard ratio, 2.98; 95% confidence interval, 2.73-3.25), and patients with substance use disorders had the greatest risk among women (6.62; 4.72-9.29).

Conclusions: Although all the examined psychiatric diagnoses were associated with elevated risk of suicide in veterans, results indicate that men with bipolar disorder and women with substance use disorders are at particularly elevated risk for suicide.

Antidepressant medication prevents suicide in depression

Isacsson G, Reutfors J, Papadopoulos FC, Ösby U, Ahlner J (Sweden)

Acta Psychiatrica Scandinavica 122, 454-460, 2010

Objective: Ecological studies have demonstrated a substantial decrease in suicide in parallel with an increasing use of antidepressants. To investigate on the individual level the hypothesis that antidepressant medication was a causal factor.

Method: Data on the toxicological detection of antidepressants in 18 922 suicides in Sweden 1992-2003 were linked to registers of psychiatric hospitalization as well as registers with sociodemographic data.

Results: The probability for the toxicological detection of an antidepressant was lowest in the non-suicide controls, higher in suicides, and even higher in suicides that had been psychiatric in-patients but excluding those who had been in-patients for the treatment of depression.

Conclusion: The finding that in-patient care for depression did not increase the probability of the detection of antidepressants in suicides is difficult to explain other than by the assumption that a substantial number of depressed individuals were saved from suicide by postdischarge treatment with antidepressant medication.

Young people's risk of suicide attempts in relation to parental death: A population-based register study

Jakobsen IS, Christiansen E (Denmark)
Journal of Child Psychology and Psychiatry 52, 176-183, 2011

Background: The objective of this study was to examine the association between the death of a biological parent and subsequent suicide attempts by young people (aged 10-22 years), and to explore sociodemographic factors as modifying factors in the process.

Methods: The study used a nested case-control design. The full study population was obtained from the Danish longitudinal registers and included all individuals born between 1983 and 1989 (n = 403,431 individuals). The 3,465 registered suicide attempters from that group were matched with 75,300 population-based control subjects. Potentially confounding variables including age and gender were controlled for by conditional logistic regression analyses.

Results: The findings indicated that young people who had lost one biological parent showed a significantly increased risk of attempting suicide (relative risk = 1.71, 95% confidence interval = 1.49-1.96). Losing the remaining parent nearly doubled the risk (relative risk = 2.7, 95% confidence interval = 1.48-5.06).

Conclusion: Experiencing the death of one or both biological parents increased the risk of suicide attempts in young people. Relative risk was moderated by high income of the father.

Unplanned versus planned suicide attempters, precipitants, methods, and an association with mental disorders in a Korea-based community sample

Jeon HJ, Lee JY, Lee YM, Hong JP, Won SH, Cho SJ, Kim JY, Chang SM, Lee HW, Cho MJ (Korea)
Journal of Affective Disorders 127, 274-280, 2010

Background: Studies have consistently reported that a considerable proportion of suicidal attempts are unplanned. We have performed the first direct comparison between planned and unplanned attempts including associated methods and precipitants.

Method: A total of 6510 adults, who had been randomly selected through a one-person-per-household method, completed interviews (response rate 81.7%). All were interviewed using the K-CIDI and a questionnaire for suicide.

Results: Two hundred and eight subjects reported a suicide attempt in their lifetime, one-third of which had been unplanned. These individuals exhibited a lower level of education; however, no significant differences were found with regard to age, gender, marital and economic status. Further, 84.0% of unplanned attempters experienced previous suicidal ideation, experiencing their first attempt 1.9 years before ideation. Additionally, 94.4% of unplanned attempters had precipitants for attempts such as familial conflict and it was also found that methods such as the use of chemical agents or falling were three times more common in unplanned than planned attempters. With respect to unplanned attempters, they exhibited a significant association with alcohol use disorder, major depressive disorder, posttraumatic stress disorder, and bipolar disorder. In particular, bipolar disorder was found to be 3.5 times higher in these individuals.

Conclusions: Results have revealed that unplanned suicide attempters experience suicidal ideation and precipitants prior to their attempt. Further, attempts were associated with affective and alcohol use disorders. Therefore, in order to reduce the number of suicidal attempts, it may be useful to evaluate suicidal ideation concurrent to the treatment of existing mental disorders.

Chain of care for patients who have attempted suicide: A follow-up study from Baerum, Norway

Johannessen HA, Dieserud G, De Leo D, Claussen B, Zahl PH (Norway)

BMC Public Health 11, 81, 2011

Background: Individuals who have attempted suicide are at increased risk of subsequent suicidal behavior. Since 1983, a community-based suicide prevention team has been operating in the municipality of Baerum, Norway. This study aimed to test the effectiveness of the team's interventions in preventing repeated suicide attempts and suicide deaths, as part of a chain of care model for all general hospital treated suicide attempters.

Methods: Data has been collected consecutively since 1984 and a follow-up was conducted on all individuals admitted to the general hospital after a suicide attempt. The risk of repeated suicide attempt and suicide were comparatively examined in subjects who received assistance from the suicide prevention team in addition to treatment as usual versus those who received treatment as usual only. Logistic regression and Cox regression were used to analyze the data.

Results: Between January 1984 and December 2007, 1,616 subjects were registered as having attempted suicide; 197 of them (12%) made another attempt within 12 months. Compared to subjects who did not receive assistance from the suicide prevention team, individuals involved in the prevention program did not have a significantly different risk of repeated attempt within 6 months (adjusted OR = 1.08; 95% CI = 0.66-1.74), 12 months (adjusted OR = 0.86; 95% CI = 0.57-1.30), or 5 years (adjusted RR = 0.90; 95 % CI = 0.67-1.22) after their first recorded attempt. There was also no difference in risk of suicide (adjusted RR = 0.85; 95% CI = 0.46-1.57). Previous suicide attempts, marital status, and employment status were significantly associated with a repeated suicide attempt within 6 and 12 months ($p < .05$). Alcohol misuse, employment status, and previous suicide attempts were significantly associated with a repeated attempt within 5 years ($p < .05$) while marital status became non-significant ($p > .05$). With each year of age, the risk of suicide increased by 3% ($p < .05$).

Conclusions: The present study did not find any differences in the risk of fatal and non-fatal suicidal behavior between subjects who received treatment as usual combined with community assistance versus subjects who received only treatment as usual. However, assistance from the community team was mainly offered to attempters who were not receiving sufficient support from treatment as usual and was accepted by 50-60% of those deemed eligible. Thus, obtaining similar outcomes for individuals, all of whom were clinically judged to have different needs, could in itself be considered a desirable result.

Resilience to suicidality: The buffering hypothesis

Johnson J, Wood AM, Gooding P, Taylor P, Tarrier N (UK)
Clinical Psychology Review. Published online: 21 December 2010. doi:10.1016/j.cpr.2010.12.007, 2010

Recent years have seen a growing interest into resilience to suicidality, which has been described as a perception or set of beliefs which buffer individuals from suicidality in the face of stressors. The current review extends this research by introducing the buffering hypothesis, a framework for the investigation of resilience to suicidality. The key proposal of this is that psychological resilience factors should be viewed as existing on a separate dimension to risk which acts to moderate the impact of risk on suicidality. Furthermore, like risk factors, resilience factors are bipolar, with their positive pole conferring resilience and their negative pole acting to amplify suicidality. Seventy-seven studies were identified which investigated (a) whether psychological moderators of risk exist and (b) the particular psychological constructs which may act as moderators. The review found strong support for the existence of psychological moderators and indicated a moderating impact of attributional style, perfectionism, agency and hopelessness. These findings support the buffering hypothesis and suggest that a range of psychological factors may confer resilience to suicidality. These results suggest that the identification of moderators may improve estimates of suicide risk and that the development of buffering factors could be a key focus of suicide interventions.

Peak window of suicides occurs within the first month of diagnosis: implications for clinical oncology

Johnson TV, Garlow SJ, Brawley OW, Master VA (USA)
Psychooncology. Published online: 24 January 2011. doi:10.1002/pon.1905, 2011

Objective: A diagnosis of cancer can provoke painful emotional reactions and possibly suicidal thoughts in a patient. Consequently, cancer patients carry a twofold increased lifetime risk of suicide. This risk is much higher within 1 year of diagnosis. However, it remains largely unknown whether suicide frequency remains constant within the first year. Therefore, we sought to characterize the distribution of suicides in order to potentially identify a clinically important window of peak suicide risk.

Methods: We queried the Surveillance, Epidemiology, and End Results (SEER) database for cancer patients 20+ years old with diagnosed with a single malignancy from 1973 to 2005 and known cause of death, including whether a patient committed suicide. Initial frequency analysis was performed to identify the period of maximum suicide risk. One-way ANOVA was performed to assess the relationship between year of diagnosis and suicide completions within 1 month of diagnosis.

Results: The cohort consisted of 3,678,868 patients. Of the total cohort, 0.2% (5875 patients) committed suicide, 36% (2,111 patients) within 1 year of diagnosis. One in three (701 of the patients) who committed suicide in the first year did so within 1 month of diagnosis. No change in this distribution occurred over time.

Conclusions: Cancer patients carry an increased risk of suicide. However, this risk peaks with the month following diagnosis. Clinicians should be aware of this increased risk and include assessments of mood state and suicidality at the time of initial diagnosis of the malignancy and be prepared to provide referral to mental health treatment providers.

The profile of suicide: changing or changeable?

Judd F, Jackson H, Komiti A, Bell R, Fraser C (Australia)

Social Psychiatry & Psychiatric Epidemiology. Published online: 30 October 2010. doi:10.1007/s00127-010-0306-z, 2010

Purpose: The aims of this study were to: (1) examine the role of psychosocial factors, physical and mental health in suicide; (2) to examine gender differences on those variables; and (3) determine whether there was a group who died by suicide who did not have a history of mental illness.

Method: Data were obtained from The Australian National Coroners Information System (NCIS) for all deaths classified as suicides from 2000 to 2004 in all Australian states. The NCIS is an internet-based system for storing and retrieving data on coronial cases.

Results: The overall results from the total sample reinforces many previous findings but also found some differences; importantly, psychiatric morbidity was less than generally reported, and comparable proportions of males and females used violent means to suicide. Using latent class analysis the study identified four clusters of people who had suicided. In two of those clusters mental illness appeared to be a significant factor; in one of those two clusters the mental illness was compounded by additional drug and alcohol and relationship problems whilst the other was without such levels of comorbidity. The third group was predominantly male, older and physical illness seemed to be a significant factor.

The final group was characterised by low rates of mental illness and treatment for the same, but marked by relationship and financial difficulties.

Conclusions: These data may suggest that the profile of suicide is changing or changeable. Certainly there has been a shift in the gender profile with comparable proportions of women and men. Whilst mental illness remains a major risk factor, perhaps greater emphasis needs to be placed on the broader psychosocial issues which may initiate or hasten the pathway to suicide. In addition, it may be that the relative contribution of mental illness and other factors is fluid in relation to both life stage and life circumstances. Suicide prevention programmes might usefully define a range of discrete areas of work.

Subjective quality of life and suicidal behavior among Taiwanese schizophrenia patients

Kao YC, Liu YP, Cheng TH, Chou MK (Taiwan)

Social Psychiatry & Psychiatric Epidemiology. Published online: 10 March 2011. Doi: 10.1007/s00127-011-0361-0, 2011

Purpose: Research of suicidal behavior in individuals with schizophrenia has often suggested that clinical characteristics and symptoms likely influence a patient's suicidal risk. However, there is a lack of research describing the link between patients' subjective quality of life (SQOL) and suicidal behavior in non-Western countries. Therefore, the current study attempts to explore how schizophrenia patients' SQOL and their suicidal behavior are related in a Taiwanese sample.

Methods: In this study, 102 schizophrenia outpatients were investigated using the Taiwanese World Health Organization Quality of Life Schedule-Brief Version (WHO-QOL-BREF-TW), several Beck-Related symptom rating scales, and the Positive and Negative Syndrome Scale (PANSS) for psychopathology. These patients were also evaluated for suicidal risk using the critical items of the Scale for Suicide Ideation (SSI) and lifetime suicide attempts.

Results: Statistical analyses, including independent sample *t* tests, analysis of covariance (ANCOVA) and logistic stepwise regression models were completed. Compared with the non-suicidal group, suicidal patients had significantly lower scores in SQOL domains. The differences in social domain remained significant after adjusting for depressive symptoms. In multiple logistic regression analyses, level of depressive and psychotic symptoms increased and poor social and psychological SQOL were significant contributors to suicidal behavior. Having removed depressive symptoms from the model, only dissatisfaction with social SQOL was associated with heightened suicidal risk.

Conclusions: Schizophrenia is associated with a high suicidal risk, of which depressive and psychotic symptoms are the major correlates. Again, the present study confirms and extends previous research showing that dissatisfied SQOL, particularly dissatisfaction with social relationships, should be considered in the assessment of suicidal risk in outpatients with schizophrenia, even when accounting other possible confounding factor such as depression.

Availability of mental health service providers and suicide rates in Austria: A nationwide study

Kapusta ND, Posch M, Niederkrotenthaler T, Fischer-Kern M, Etzersdorfer E, Sonneck G (Austria)

Psychiatric Services 61, 1198-1203, 2010

Objective: Evidence shows that access to mental health services may have an impact on mental health outcomes such as suicide rates. This small-area analysis examined whether the availability of professionals providing mental health treatment in Austria had an effect on regional suicide rates.

Methods: A hierarchical Bayesian model accounting for spatially correlated random effects using an intrinsic conditional autoregressive prior that incorporated the neighborhood structure of districts and that assumed a Poisson distribution for the observed number of suicides was used to estimate the effects of access to mental health care (population density of general practitioners, psychiatrists, and psychotherapists) in Austria.

Results: Regional socioeconomic factors were correlated with the density of psychiatrists and psychotherapists. Only the number of psychotherapists per 10,000 population had a significant effect on suicide rates (relative risk [RR] = .97, 95% confidence interval [CI]=.94-.997, and absolute risk reduction [ARR] = -.62, CI = -1.20 to -.11); however, after adjustment for socioeconomic factors (in particular urbanicity as indicated by population density, average income, and proportion of non-Catholics), the observed effects were no longer significant. In the final model, only the socioeconomic component remained significant (RR = .94, CI=.88-.99), and ARR = -1.17, CI = -2.34 to -.05).

Conclusions: The availability of specialized mental health service providers was associated with regional socioeconomic factors, and these factors appeared to be stronger predictors of suicide rates than the availability of providers. Therefore, suicide prevention efforts need to acknowledge that availability of services is only one aspect of access to care; a more influential factor is whether availability satisfies local demand.

The judgment of future suicide-related behaviour

Karver MS, Tarquini SJ, Caporino NE (USA)

Crisis 31, 272-280, 2010

Background: Judging whether a youth is at risk for suicide-related behavior (SRB) is considered an extremely challenging task. There are only few studies of helpline counselors, and little is known about their ability to accurately determine the level of risk for SRB.

Aims: To examine whether helpline counselors can agree on judgments of risk for SRB, and whether their judgments are consistent with youths' actual behavior in a 6-month period following intake.

Methods: 34 helpline counselors, recruited from three helplines, were studied. Information was collected on their judgments of risk for SRB for each of 45 youths over a 6-month period following initial intake.

Results: Contrary to expectations, the counselors had a high rate of agreement (k = .56), and their risk judgments could be used quite successfully (80.0% correct classification) in identifying youths who later engaged in SRB.

Conclusions: Unlike most other groups represented in the decision-making literature, helpline counselors agree and are accurate in their judgments of risk for SRB. Our findings suggest that it might be beneficial to apply some of the procedures used to train helpline clinicians to other types of clinicians. Further studies of helpline clinicians are suggested.

Development of 2-hour suicide intervention program among medical residents: First pilot trial

Kato TA, Suzuki Y, Sato R, Fujisawa D, Uehara K, Hashimoto N, Sawayama Y, Hayashi J, Kanba S, Otsuka K (Japan)
Psychiatry and Clinical Neurosciences 64, 531-540, 2010

Aim: Suicide is associated not only with primary psychiatric disorders but also with physical disorders. Physicians' education on suicide prevention contributes to reducing suicide. Therefore, medical residents, who contact patients daily and who eventually become primary physicians in each specialty, might be the most appropriate candidates for intervention. In this article, we introduce our newly developed suicide intervention program among medical residents.

Methods: We developed a 2-hour suicide intervention program among medical residents, based on the Mental Health First Aid (MHFA), which had originally been developed for the public. The program contains a 1-hour lecture and a 1-hour role-play session. As the first pilot trial, we conducted the program among 44 first-year medical residents at a university hospital and evaluated its effectiveness. Changes in confidence, attitudes and behavior toward suicidal people were evaluated using self-reported questionnaires before, immediately after, and 6 months after the program.

Results: Participants' confidence and attitudes significantly improved after the program. The total mean score (standard deviation) of the Suicide Intervention Response Inventory improved from 18.4 (2.0) before the intervention to 19.4 (2.0) immediately after the intervention. However, the effectiveness was limited after 6 months. In the course of 6 months, the participants learned to apply the MHFA principles in their daily clinical practice.

Conclusion: Our newly developed brief suicide intervention program demonstrating its effectiveness among medical residents should be modified in order to be more effective in the long term. The next trial with a control group ought to be conducted to evaluate our developed program.

Comparative epidemiology of suicide in South Korea and Japan: Effects of age, gender and suicide methods

Kim SY, Kim MH, Kawachi I, Cho Y (South Korea, Japan)

Crisis 32, 5-14, 2011

Background: Suicide is one of the leading causes of mortality in both South Korea and Japan. Aims: The study aims to compare the descriptive epidemiology of suicide over the last two decades (1985-2006) and to explore the conditions associated with the different distribution of suicides in both countries.

Methods: Age-standardised suicide rates were obtained from the OECD Health Data 2009. Age-specific suicide rates for the age groups were calculated from the WHO Mortality Database. Suicide methods were identified based on ICD-10.

Results: Through 1980-2000, Japan showed consistently higher suicide rates compared to Korea. However, from the mid-1990s, Korea showed an acute increase of suicides and finally surpassed Japan; the age-standardised suicide rate of Korea increased from 10.2 (per 100,000) in 1985 to 21.5 in 2006, while it slightly increased from 18.4 to 19.1 in Japan. The highest age-specific suicide rate was observed among Japanese men aged 45-64 years and Korean men aged over 64 years. The increase of elderly suicides among Korean women was notable. The gender ratio increased in Japan and decreased in Korea, respectively. The preferred suicide methods were hanging and pesticide poisoning in Korea and hanging in Japan. Because of the limited number of observations, hypothesis testing of specific risk factors was not possible.

Conclusions: Age and gender distribution of suicide rates differed considerably between the two countries. Welfare protection throughout the life course in both countries, and pesticide regulation in Korea would be helpful in reducing the burden of suicide mortality in both countries, even if the social values could not be changed in a short time.

Non-suicidal self-injury in United States adults: Prevalence, sociodemographics, topography and functions

Klonsky ED (USA)

Psychological Medicine. Published online: 5 January 2011. doi:10.1017/S0033291710002497, 2011

Background: Non-suicidal self-injury (NSSI) has received increased attention in the mental health literature and has been proposed as a diagnostic entity for DSM-5. However, data on NSSI in the United States adult population are lacking.

Method: The prevalence and nature of NSSI were examined in a random-digit dialing sample of 439 adults in the United States. Participants were recruited during July and August of 2008.

Results: Lifetime prevalence of NSSI was 5.9%, including 2.7% who had self-injured five or more times. The 12-month prevalence was 0.9%. Methods of NSSI reported included cutting/carving, burning, biting, scraping/scratching skin, hitting, interfering with wound healing and skin picking. Half of self-injurers reported multiple methods. The average age of onset was 16 years (median 14 years). Instances of NSSI infrequently co-occurred with suicidal thoughts and with use of alcohol or drugs and rarely required medical treatment. Most injurers reported that NSSI functioned to alleviate negative emotions. Fewer reported that they self-injured to punish themselves, to communicate with others/get attention or to escape a situation or responsibility. NSSI was associated with younger age, being unmarried and a history of mental health treatment, but not with gender, ethnicity, educational history or household income.

Conclusions: Results are largely consistent with previous research in adolescent and young adult samples. Study limitations notwithstanding, this study provides the most definitive and detailed information to date regarding the prevalence and characteristics of NSSI in US adults. In the future, it will be important for large-scale epidemiological studies of psychopathology to include questions about NSSI.

Rethinking impulsivity in suicide

Klonsky ED, May A (USA)
Suicide & Life-Threatening Behavior 40, 612-619, 2010

Elevated impulsivity is thought to facilitate the transition from suicidal thoughts to suicidal behavior. Therefore, impulsivity should distinguish those who have attempted suicide (attempters) from those who have only considered suicide (ideators-only). This hypothesis was examined in three large non-clinical samples: (1) 2,011 military recruits, (2) 1,296 college students, and (3) 399 high school students. In sample 1, contrary to traditional models of suicide risk, a unidimensional measure of impulsivity failed to distinguish attempters from ideators-only. In samples 2 and 3, which were administered a multidimensional measure of impulsivity (i.e., the UPPS impulsive behavior scale; Whiteside & Lynam, 2001), different impulsivity-related traits characterized attempters and ideators-only. Whereas both attempters and ideators-only exhibited high urgency (the tendency to act impulsive in the face of negative emotions), only attempters exhibited poor premeditation (a diminished ability to think through the consequences of one's actions). Neither attempters nor ideators-only exhibited high sensation seeking or lack of perseverance. Future research should continue to distinguish impulsivity-related traits that predict suicide ideation from those that predict suicide attempts, and models of suicide risk should be revised accordingly.

Unikkaartuit: Meanings of well-being, unhappiness, health, and community change among Inuit in Nunavut, Canada

Kral MJ, Idlout L, Minore JB, Dyck RJ, Kirmayer LJ (Canada)
American Journal of Community Psychology. Published online: 13 March 2011. doi:10.1007/s10464-011-9431-4, 2011

Suicide among young Inuit in the Canadian Arctic is at an epidemic level. In order to understand the distress and well-being experienced in Inuit communities, a first step in understanding collective suicide, this qualitative study was designed. Fifty Inuit were interviewed in two Inuit communities in Nunavut, Canada, and questionnaires asking the same questions were given to 66 high school and college students. The areas of life investigated here were happiness and wellbeing, unhappiness, healing, and community and personal change. Three themes emerged as central to well-being: the family, talking/communication, and traditional Inuit cultural values and practices. The absence of these factors were most closely associated with unhappiness. Narratives about community and personal change were primarily about family, intergenerational segregation, an increasing population, more trouble in romantic relationships among youth, drug use, and poverty. Change over time was viewed primarily as negative. Discontinuity of kinship structure and function appears to be the most harmful effect of the internal colonialism imposed by the Canadian government in the 1950s and 1960s. Directions toward community control and action are encouraging, and are highlighted. Inuit community action toward suicide prevention and community wellness is part of a larger movement of Indigenous self-determination.

On-line support and resources for people bereaved through suicide: What is available?

Krysinska K, Andriessen K (Belgium)
Suicide and Life-Threatening Behavior 40, 640-650, 2010

The Internet is a potentially valuable source of information for the bereaved, but the current knowledge regarding the type and quality of online material on suicide bereavement is very limited. This study was designed to explore the types of online information and support available for people bereaved by suicide and the quality of such resources. Four popular Internet search engines were searched using terms related to suicide bereavement and support. Although a wide range of Internet resources exist for people bereaved by suicide, these resources may not meet basic quality standards. It is unknown who uses these sites, how such material is used, and whether it helps people to cope effectively with grief after suicide.

Maternal or paternal suicide and offspring's psychiatric and suicide-attempt hospitalisation risk

Kuramoto SJ, Stuart EA, Runeson B, Lichtenstein P, Langstrom N, Wilcox HC (Sweden)

Pediatrics 126, 1026-1032, 2010

Objective: We examined whether the risk for psychiatric morbidity requiring inpatient care was higher for offspring who experienced parental suicide, compared with offspring of fatal accident decedents, and whether the association varied according to the deceased parent's gender.

Methods: Children and adolescents (0-17 years of age) who experienced maternal ($N = 5600$) or paternal ($N = 17,847$) suicide in 1973-2003 in Sweden were identified by using national, longitudinal, population-based registries. Cox regression modeling was used to compare psychiatric hospitalization risks among offspring of suicide decedents and propensity score-matched offspring of accident decedents.

Results: Offspring of maternal suicide decedents had increased risk of suicide-attempt hospitalisation, after controlling for psychiatric hospitalisation for decedents and surviving parents, compared with offspring of maternal accidental decedents. Offspring of paternal suicide decedents had similar risk of suicide-attempt hospitalisation, compared with offspring of accident decedents, but had increased risk of hospitalisation attributable to depressive and anxiety disorders. The magnitude of risks for offspring suicide-attempt hospitalization was greater for those who experienced maternal versus paternal suicide, compared with their respective control offspring (interaction $P = .05$; offspring of maternal decedents, adjusted hazard ratio: 1.80 [95% confidence interval: 1.19-2.74]; offspring of paternal decedents, adjusted hazard ratio: 1.14 [95% confidence interval: 0.96-1.35]).

Conclusions: Maternal suicide is associated with increased risk of suicide-attempt hospitalization for offspring, beyond the risk associated with maternal accidental death. However, paternal suicide is not associated with suicide-attempt hospitalisation. Future studies should examine factors that might differ between offspring who experience maternal versus paternal suicide, including genetic or early environmental determinants.

Systematic review and meta-analysis of the clinical factors associated with the suicide of psychiatric in-patients

Large M, Smith G, Sharma S, Nielssen O, Singh SP (Australia)

Acta Psychiatrica Scandinavica. Published online: 25 January 2011. doi:10.1111/
j.1600-0447.2010.01672.x, 2011

Objective: To estimate the strength of the associations between the suicide of psychiatric in-patients and demographic, historical, symptomatic, diagnostic and treatment factors.

Method: A systematic review and meta-analysis of controlled studies of the suicide of psychiatric in-patients including suicides while on approved or unapproved leave.

Results: Factors that were significantly associated with in-patient suicide included a history of deliberate self-harm, hopelessness, feelings of guilt or inadequacy, depressed mood, suicidal ideas and a family history of suicide. Patients suffering from both schizophrenia and depressed mood appeared to be at particular risk. The association between suicidal ideas and in-patient suicide was weak and did not reach statistical significance after a quantitative correction for publication bias. A high-risk categorisation as defined by a combination of retrospectively determined individual risk factors was strongly statistically associated with in-patient suicide (OR = 10.9), with a sensitivity of 64% and a specificity of 85%.

Conclusion: Despite the apparently strong association between high-risk categorisation and subsequent suicide, the low base rate of in-patient suicide means that predictive value of a high-risk categorisation is below 2%. The development of safer hospital environments and improved systems of care are more likely to reduce the suicide of psychiatric in-patients than risk assessment.

Daytime versus night time intentional drug overdose: The outcome is different

Lee KL, Ng HW, Tse ML, Lau FL (Hong Kong)
Hong Kong Journal of Emergency Medicine 17, 347-351, 2010

Introduction: In drug overdose, it is generally perceived that the dosage can predict the clinical outcome. Are the dosages of intentional drug overdosing the same between day and night? If so, are these overdoses followed by similar clinical outcomes? Answers to these two questions might affect resource allocation and clinical judgment. The present study was performed to establish whether daytime patients and night time patients report similar drug doses, and see which group of patients would have a higher incidence of severe outcomes.

Method: A retrospective observational study on intentional drug overdose was performed. The reported numbers of total tablets ingested and the incidences of major outcomes, in terms of death and intensive care unit admissions, were compared between daytime and night time.

Results: A total of 400 patients were included. The reported number of ingested tablets in daytime had no statistical difference with that at night time. The numbers of severe outcomes had no differences between the patients presenting to the emergency department at daytime or night time. Yet overdosing at night time was more likely associated with severe outcomes.

Conclusions: We advise a higher index of suspicion at the emergency department on the reliability of the dosages reported by patients who overdose during night time. The larger number of severe outcomes may also be related to more toxic drug exposures in the night time. More resources in the community could be allocated to self-harm prevention at night time.

Attributable risk of psychiatric and socio-economic factors for suicide from individual-level, population-based studies: A systematic review

Li Z, Page A, Martin G, Taylor R (Australia)
Social Science and Medicine 72, 608-616, 2011

The overall importance of a risk factor for suicide in a population is determined not only by the relative risk (RR) of suicide but also the prevalence of the risk factor in the population, which can be combined with the RR to calculate the population attributable risk (PAR). This study compares risk factors from two well studied domains of suicide research — socio-economic deprivation (relatively low RR, but high population prevalence) and mental disorders (relatively high RR risk, but low population prevalence). RR and PAR associated with suicide was estimated for high prevalence ICD-10/DSM-IV psychiatric disorders and measures of socio-economic status (SES) from individual-level, population-based studies. A systematic review and meta-analysis was conducted of population-based case-control and cohort studies of suicide where relative risk estimates for males and females could be extracted. RR for any mental disorder was 7.5 (6.2–9.0) for males and 11.7 (9.7–14.1) for females, compared to RR for the lowest SES groups of 2.1 (1.5–2.8) for males and 1.5 (1.2–1.9) for females. PAR in males for low educational achievement (41%, range 19–47%) and low occupational status (33%, range 21–42%) was of a similar magnitude to affective disorders (26%, range 7–45%) and substance use disorders (9%, range 5–24%). Similarly in females the PAR for low educational achievement (20%, range 19–22%) was of a similar magnitude to affective disorders (32%, range 19–67%), substance use disorder (25%, range 5–32%) and anxiety disorder (12%, range 6–22%). The findings of the present study suggest that prevention strategies which focus on lower socio-economic strata (more distal risk factors) have the potential to have similar population-level effects as strategies which target more proximal psychiatric risk factors in the prevention and control of suicide.

Treatment engagement: a neglected aspect in the psychiatric care of suicidal patients

Lizardi D, Stanley B (USA)

Psychiatric Services 61, 1183-1191, 2010

Objective: Suicide remains a serious health problem in the United States and worldwide. Despite changing distributions in sex, race-ethnicity, and age and considerable efforts to reduce the incidence rate, the number of suicides has remained relatively stable. The transition from emergency services to outpatient services is a crucial but often neglected step in treating suicidal individuals. Up to 50% of attempters refuse recommended treatment, and up to 60% drop out after only one session. This point of intervention is crucial for patients at elevated risk of suicide to reduce imminent danger and to increase the chances that patients will follow up on recommended treatment.

Methods: PubMed, MEDLINE, and PsycINFO databases were searched for empirical investigations of treatment engagement of suicide attempters. Keywords searched included treatment, intervention, engagement, adherence, compliance, utilization, participation, and suicide attempt. Mapped terms were also included. Thirteen articles were selected.

Results: Studies that have examined the effectiveness of postdischarge contact with suicide attempters (phone, letter, and in-person visits) to increase treatment adherence have found some immediate effects after substantial contact that were not sustained. Simple referrals to outpatient care were not effective. Family group interventions for adolescents have improved adherence, as have brief interventions in the emergency department.

Conclusions: Despite greater public awareness of suicide, heightened prevention effort, and increased efficacy of treatment interventions, success in reducing suicidal behavior has been limited. Developing brief interventions for use in emergency settings that can reduce suicide risk and enhance treatment follow-up has been a neglected aspect of suicide prevention and may help to reduce suicidal behavior.

Decrease in suicide rates after a change of policy reducing access to firearms in adolescents: A naturalistic epidemiological study

Lubin G, Werbeloff N, Halperin D, Shmushkevitch M, Weiser M, Knobler HY (Israel)

Suicide & Life-Threatening Behaviour 40, 421-424, 2010

The use of firearms is a common means of suicide. We examined the effect of a policy change in the Israeli Defense Forces reducing adolescents' access to firearms on rates of suicide. Following the policy change, suicide rates decreased significantly by 40%. Most of this decrease was due to decrease in suicide using firearms over the weekend. There were no significant changes in rates of suicide during weekdays. Decreasing access to firearms significantly decreases rates of suicide among adolescents. The results of this study illustrate the ability of a relatively simple change in policy to have a major impact on suicide rates.

Sexual attraction, depression, self-harm, suicidality and help-seeking behaviour in New Zealand secondary school students

Lucassen MF, Merry SN, Robinson EM, Denny S, Clark T, Ameratunga S, Crengle S, Rossen FV (New Zealand)

The Australian and New Zealand Journal of Psychiatry. Published online: 2 March 2011. doi: 10.3109/00048674.2011.559635, 2011

Objective: To describe the sexual attractions of New Zealand secondary school students and investigate the associations between sexual attraction and self-reported depression, self-harm, suicidality and help-seeking behaviour.

Method: Multiple logistic regression was used to examine the associations between sexual attraction and depressive symptoms, suicidality, self-harming and help-seeking behaviours in a nationally representative secondary school health and wellbeing survey, undertaken in 2007.

Results: Of the students surveyed, 92% were attracted to the opposite sex, 1% to the same sex, 3% to both sexes, 2% were not sure and 2% were attracted to neither sex. Students who were attracted to the same or to both sexes consistently had higher prevalence estimates of depression ($p \leq 0.0001$), suicidality ($p \leq 0.0001$) and self-harming ($p \leq .0001$). Odds ratios were highest for students who reported they were attracted to both sexes for depressive symptoms (OR 3.7, 95%CI 2.8–4.7), self-harm (OR 5.8, 95%CI 4.4?7.6) and attempted suicide (OR 7.0, 95%CI 5.2–9.4). Students not exclusively attracted to the opposite sex were more likely to report having seen a health professional for an emotional worry and were more likely to have difficulty accessing help for emotional concerns.

Conclusions: The study findings highlight significant mental health disparities faced by students attracted to the same or both sexes, with those attracted to both sexes appearing particularly vulnerable. There is a vital need to ensure primary care and mental health services have the capacity and capability to screen and provide appropriate responsive care for youth who are attracted to the same or both sexes.

A register-based study on excess suicide mortality among unemployed men and women during different levels of unemployment in Finland

Mäki N, Martikainen P (Finland)

Journal of Epidemiology & Community Health. Published online: 21 October 2010.
doi:10.1136/jech.2009.105908, 2010

Background: Suicide mortality is high among the unemployed, but the role of causation and selection models in producing employment status differences remains to be understood. This study analyses the association between unemployment and suicide during different levels of national unemployment adjusting for several factors that might explain or mediate the relationship.

Methods: The data comprised annual population-register and death-register information on 25- to 64-year-old Finns at the beginning of each year in the period 1988-2003; thus forming 16 separate follow-up cohorts. Experience of unemployment was measured at baseline and during the previous year for each cohort. Suicide was followed for 12 months after each baseline giving a total of 7388 suicides.

Results: Overall, age-adjusted suicide mortality was two to three times higher among the unstably employed and almost fourfold among the long-term unemployed. Adjustment for social class and living arrangements had small effect on the HRs, but adjustment for household income per consumption unit decreased the differences by 13% and 31% among the long-term unemployed women and men, respectively. When the national unemployment level was high, excess suicide mortality among the unstably employed was lower than during low unemployment when those becoming unemployed might be more selected. No such differences were found among the long-term unemployed.

Conclusion: Long-term unemployment seems to have causal effects on suicide, which may be partly mediated by low income. As the effect of unstable employment is lower during the recessionary stage of the economic cycle some part of the excess suicide among the unstably employed is likely to be attributable to selection into unemployment.

Suicide fantasy as a life-sustaining recourse

Maltsberger JT, Ronningstam E, Weinberg I, Schechter M, Goldblatt MJ (USA)

Journal of the American Academy of Psychoanalysis and Dynamic Psychiatry 38, 611-624, 2010

The suicide literature tends to lump all suicidal ideation together, thereby implying that it is all functionally equivalent. However obvious the claim that suicidal ideation is usually a prelude to suicidal action, some suicidal daydreaming tends to inhibit suicidal action. How are we to distinguish between those daydreams that augur an impending attempt from those that help patients calm down?

The role of child sexual abuse in the etiology of suicide and non-suicidal self-injury

Maniglio R (Italy)

Acta Psychiatrica Scandinavica. Published online: 11 October 2010. doi:10.1111/j.1600-0447.2010.01612.x

Objective: To address the best available scientific evidence on the role of child sexual abuse in the etiology of suicide and non-suicidal self-injury.

Method: Seven databases were searched, supplemented with hand-search of reference lists from retrieved papers. The author and a psychiatrist independently evaluated the eligibility of all studies identified, abstracted data, and assessed study quality. Disagreements were resolved by consensus.

Results: Four reviews, including about 65,851 subjects from 177 studies, were analysed. There is evidence that child sexual abuse is a statistically significant, although general and non-specific, risk factor for suicide and non-suicidal self-injury. The relationship ranges from small to medium in magnitude and is moderated by sample source and size. Certain biological and psychosocial variables, such as serotonin hypoactivity and genes, family dysfunction, other forms of maltreatment, and some personality traits and psychiatric disorders, may either act independently or interact with child sexual abuse to promote suicide and non-suicidal self-injury in abuse victims, with child sexual abuse conferring additional risk, either as a 'distal' and indirect cause or as a 'proximal' and direct cause.

Conclusion: Child sexual abuse should be considered one of the several risk factors for suicide and non-suicidal self-injury and included in multifactorial etiological models.

The association between income and distress, mental disorders, and suicidal ideation and attempts: Findings from the collaborative psychiatric epidemiology surveys

McMillan KA, Enns MW, Asmundson GJG, Sareen J (USA)

Journal of Clinical Psychiatry 71, 116-175, 2010

Objective: To examine the relationship between household income and psychological distress, suicidal ideation and attempts, and mood, anxiety, and substance use disorders.

Method: Data came from the Collaborative Psychiatric Epidemiology Surveys, a collection of 3 nationally representative surveys of American adults conducted between 2001 and 2003. Psychological distress, suicidal ideation, suicide attempts, and mood, anxiety, and substance use disorders were examined in relation to household income after adjusting for sex, marital status, race, age, and employment status.

Results: Analyses revealed an inverse association between income and psychological distress as measured by the Kessler Psychological Distress Scale, with those in the lowest income quartile demonstrating significantly more distress than any of the remaining 3 income quartiles ($P < .05$). Subsequent analysis of DSM-IV-diagnosed psychological disorders revealed a similar pattern of results, which were particularly strong for substance use disorders (adjusted odds ratio [AOR] = 1.74; 95% CI, 1.39-2.18), suicidal ideation (AOR = 1.77; 95% CI, 1.46-2.13), and suicide attempts (AOR = 2.15; 95% CI, 1.55-2.98). The association between income and mood and anxiety disorders was less consistent, and the relationship between income and suicidal ideation differed among the 5 race categories (non-Hispanic white, Hispanic, Asian American, black, and other). Non-Hispanic white persons showed a strong, negative relationship between income and suicidal ideation (AOR = 2.15; 95% CI, 1.66-2.80), while the association was considerably weaker or nonexistent for the other races.

Conclusions: Although conclusions cannot be drawn concerning causation, the strength of associations between income, suicidal ideation, suicide attempts, and substance abuse points to the need for secondary prevention strategies among low-income, high-risk populations.

Antecedents of hospital admission for deliberate self-harm from a 14-year follow-up study using data-linkage

Mitrou F, Gaudie J, Lawrence D, Silburn SR, Stanley FJ, Zubrick SR (Australia)
BMC Psychiatry 10, 82, 2010

Background: A prior episode of deliberate self-harm (DSH) is one of the strongest predictors of future completed suicide. Identifying antecedents of DSH may inform strategies designed to reduce suicide rates. This study aimed to determine whether individual and socio-ecological factors collected in childhood and adolescence were associated with later hospitalisation for DSH.

Methods: Longitudinal follow-up of a Western Australian population-wide random sample of 2,736 children aged 4-16 years, and their carers, from 1993 until 2007 using administrative record linkage. Children were aged between 18 and 31 years at end of follow-up. Proportional hazards regression was used to examine the relationship between child, parent, family, school and community factors measured in 1993, and subsequent hospitalisation for DSH.

Results: There were six factors measured in 1993 that increased a child's risk of future hospitalisation with DSH: female sex; primary carer being a smoker; being in a step/blended family; having more emotional or behavioural problems than other children; living in a family with inconsistent parenting style; and having a teenage mother. Factors found to be not significant included birth weight, combined carer income, carer's lifetime treatment for a mental health problem, and carer education.

Conclusions: The persistence of carer smoking as an independent risk factor for later DSH, after adjusting for child, carer, family, school and community level socio-ecological factors, adds to the known risk domains for DSH, and invites further investigation into the underlying mechanisms of this relationship. This study has also confirmed the association of five previously known risk factors for DSH.

CSF 5-HIAA and exposure to and expression of interpersonal violence in suicide attempters

Moberg T, Nordström P, Forslund K, Kristiansson M, Asberg M, Jokinen J (Sweden)
Journal of Affective Disorders. Published online: 26 February 2011. doi: 10.1016/j.jad.2011.01.018, 2011

Background: Serotonin is implicated in impaired impulse control, aggression and suicidal behaviour. Low cerebrospinal fluid (CSF) concentrations of the serotonin metabolite 5-hydroxyindoleacetic acid (5-HIAA) have been found in violent suicide attempters, suicide victims and in violent offenders. CSF 5-HIAA concentrations have both genetic and environmental determinants. Childhood trauma may have an effect on central monoamine function as an adult.

Aim: The aim of this study was to assess the relationship of CSF 5-HIAA and the exposure to and the expression of violence in childhood and during adult life measured with the Karolinska Interpersonal Violence Scale (KIVS).

Method: 42 medication free suicide attempters underwent lumbar puncture and were assessed with the Karolinska Interpersonal Violence Scale (KIVS) to assess history of childhood exposure to violence and lifetime expressed violent behaviour.

Results: In women, but not in men, CSF 5-HIAA showed a significant negative correlation to exposure to violence during childhood. Furthermore, suicide attempters with low CSF 5-HIAA were more prone to commit violent acts as an adult if exposed to violence as a child compared to suicide attempters with high CSF 5-HIAA. In the non-traumatised group, CSF 5-HIAA showed a significant negative correlation to expressed violent behaviour in childhood.

Conclusions: Although central serotonergic function has important genetic determinants, exposure to childhood trauma may also affect serotonergic function. Low serotonergic function may facilitate impaired aggression control in traumatized suicide attempters.

The psychoactive effects of antidepressants and their association with suicidality

Moncrieff J, Goldsmith L (USA)

Current Drug Safety. Published online: 4 March 2011

Although antidepressants are known to produce some adverse mental effects, their full range of psychoactive effects has not been systematically described. It has been suggested that some antidepressants are associated with increased suicidal thoughts and actions, but the issue remains controversial, and the mechanism of association, if any, is unclear. In the current study we examined descriptions of the major psychoactive and physical effects experienced by users of two commonly used antidepressants, fluoxetine and venlafaxine, as reported on a patient-oriented web site. We categorised responses into common psychoactive effects and explored associations among those effects, including reported increases in suicidal ideation. In the 468 descriptions we examined, the most commonly reported drug-induced psychoactive effects were sedation, impaired cognition, reduced libido, emotional blunting, activation (feelings of arousal, insomnia and agitation) and emotional instability. There were no differences between the two drugs in the prevalence of reporting of these effects. Activation effects were associated with involuntary movements, suggesting a physical basis. Emotional blunting was associated with cognitive impairment, reduced libido and sedation. Emotional instability, which included the reported side effects of increased anxiety, anger, aggression and mood swings, was related to activation effects and was more commonly reported by younger respondents. Increased suicidal thoughts were rare but were associated with both types of emotional effect. The effects identified are consistent with other data, and suggest that some antidepressants may induce emotional effects that are experienced as unpleasant, may impact on the symptoms of mental disorders, and may account for the suggested occurrence of increased suicidal impulses in some users.

Doing qualitative research on suicide in a developing country

Mugisha J, Knizek BL, Kinyanda E, Hjelmeland H (Uganda)

Crisis 32, 15-23, 2011

Background: This article describes and discusses the challenges faced by researchers who conducted a qualitative interview study on attitudes toward suicide among the Baganda, Uganda. Many of the challenges addressed in this article have not been described earlier in suicide research conducted in the developing world.

Aims: The aim of this study was to explore attitudes and cultural responses toward suicide among the Baganda, Uganda.

Methods: Data were collected and analysed using grounded theory. A total of 28 focus group discussions and 30 key informant interviews were conducted.

Results: The findings of this study are organised under two broad categories: community access challenges and expectation challenges. Community access challenges entailed cultural, legal, rapport, informed consent, language, and other research process related issues that could hinder effective access to the study respondents. Expectation challenges concerned how to deal with the immediate and strategic needs of the study communities.

Conclusions: This study demonstrates that culturally sensitive approaches to data collection can reduce ethical challenges and, through innovative approaches, practical challenges faced during data collection can be minimized.

Mental health disorders, psychological distress, and suicidality in a diverse sample of lesbian, gay, bisexual, and transgender youths

Mustanski BS, Garofalo R, Emerson EM (USA)
American Journal of Public Health 100, 2426-2432, 2010

Objectives: We examined associations of race/ethnicity, gender, and sexual orientation with mental disorders among lesbian, gay, bisexual, and transgender (LGBT) youths.

Methods: We assessed mental disorders by administering a structured diagnostic interview to a community sample of 246 LGBT youths aged 16 to 20 years. Participants also completed the Brief Symptom Inventory 18 (BSI 18).

Results: One third of participants met criteria for any mental disorder, 17% for conduct disorder, 15% for major depression, and 9% for posttraumatic stress disorder. Anorexia and bulimia were rare. Lifetime suicide attempts were frequent (31%) but less so in the prior 12 months (7%). Few racial/ethnic and gender differences were statistically significant. Bisexually identified youths had lower prevalences of every diagnosis. The BSI 18 had high negative predictive power (90%) and low positive predictive power (25%) for major depression.

Conclusions: LGBT youths had higher prevalences of mental disorder diagnoses than youths in national samples, but were similar to representative samples of urban, racial/ethnic minority youths. Suicide behaviors were similar to those among representative youth samples in the same geographic area. Questionnaires measuring psychological distress may overestimate depression prevalence among this population.

Risk assessment following self-harm: Comparison of mental health nurses and psychiatrists

Murphy E, Kapur N, Webb R, Cooper J (UK)
Journal of Advanced Nursing 67, 127-139, 2010

Aim: This paper is a report of a study conducted to compare risk assessments by psychiatrists and mental health nurses following an episode of self-harm.

Background: Self-harm assessments by nurses and psychiatrists are similar in terms of overall content, but risk assessment may vary by professional discipline. To our knowledge previous researchers have not compared the positive predictive value of risk assessments by nurses and psychiatrists, the factors that inform those assessments in clinical practice or the management of people assessed as being at high risk.

Methods: We conducted a prospective cohort study (2002-2006) of 3491 individuals presenting with self-harm to three hospitals in the North West of England. A standard assessment form including detailed demographic and clinical data was completed by the assessing psychiatrist or nurse.

Results: The positive predictive value of risk assessments for self-harm repetition was 25% (95% CI: 20-31) among nurses and 23% (95% CI: 13-37) among psychiatrists. There was strong agreement on factors associated with high risk assessment by both professions. Following assessment of high risk, psychiatrists were much more likely than nurses to admit people for inpatient treatment (RR = 5·6, 95% CI: 3·2-9·7). This difference remained highly statistically significant after controlling for case-mix differences (RR = 4·3, 95% CI: 2·4-7·7).

Conclusion: Our finding that risk assessments were comparable by profession supports the provision of nurse-led assessment services. However, inpatient admission was influenced largely by assessor type rather than patient characteristics. This has important implications for equity of care and may reflect professional differences in referral practices.

The anxiety disorders and suicidal ideation: Accounting for co-morbidity via underlying personality traits

Naragon-Gainey K, Watson D (USA)
Psychological Medicine. Published online: 8 November 2010. doi:10.1017/S0033291710002096, 2010

Background: The anxiety disorders are robust correlates/predictors of suicidal ideation, but it is unclear whether (a) the anxiety disorders are specifically associated with suicidal ideation or (b) the association is due to comorbidity with depression and other disorders. One means of modeling comorbidity is through the personality traits neuroticism/negative emotionality (N/NE) and extraversion/positive emotionality (E/PE), which account for substantial shared variance among the internalizing disorders. The current study examines the association between the internalising disorders and suicidal ideation, after controlling for co-morbidity via N/NE and E/PE.MethodThe sample consisted of 327 psychiatric out-patients. Multiple self-report and interview measures were collected for internalising disorders [depression, generalised anxiety disorder (GAD), post-traumatic stress disorder (PTSD), social anxiety, panic and specific phobia] and suicidal ideation, as well as self-report measures for N/NE and E/PE. A model was hypothesised in which each disorder and suicidal ideation was regressed on N/NE, and depression and social anxiety were regressed on E/PE. Structural equation modeling (SEM) was used to examine the unique association of suicidality with each disorder, beyond shared variance with N/NE and E/PE.

Results: The hypothesized model was an acceptable fit to the data. Although zero-order analyses indicated that suicidal ideation was moderately to strongly correlated with all of the disorders, only depression and PTSD remained significantly associated with suicidal ideation in the SEM analyses.

Conclusions: In a latent variable model that accounts for measurement error and a broad source of comorbidity, only depression and PTSD were uniquely associated with suicidal ideation; panic, GAD, social anxiety and specific phobia were not.

Improving risk assessment with suicidal patients

Nelson C, Johnston M, Shrivastava A (Canada)
Crisis 31, 231-237, 2010

Background: Although a number of suicide-risk assessment tools are available to clinicians, the high levels of suicide still evident in society suggest a clear need for new strategies in order to facilitate the prevention of suicidal behaviours.

Aims: The present study examined the utilisation of a new structured clinical interview called the Scale for Impact of Suicidality Management, Assessment, and Planning of Care (SIS-MAP).

Methods: SIS-MAP ratings were obtained from a group of incoming psychiatric patients over a 6-month period at Regional Mental Health Care, St. Thomas, Canada.

Results: A canonical discriminant function analysis resulted in a total 74.0% of original grouped cases correctly classified based on admission status (admitted or not; Wilks $\lambda = .749, p < .001$). The specificity of the scale was 78.1%, while the sensitivity of the scale was 66.7%. Additionally, mean total scores on the scale were used to establish clinical cutoffs to facilitate future level of care decisions.

Conclusions: Preliminary analysis suggests the SIS-MAP is a valid and reliable tool for determining the level of psychiatric care needed for adults with suicidal ideation.

Revisiting the association of aggression and suicidal behaviour in schizophrenic inpatients

Neuner T, Hübner-Liebermann B, Hausner H, Hajak G, Wolfersdorf M, Spießl H (Germany)

Suicide and Life-Threatening Behaviors. Published online: 22 February 2011. doi:10.1111/j.1943-278X.2011.00018.x, 2011

Our study investigated the association of aggression and suicidal behavior in schizophrenic inpatients. Eight thousand nine hundred one admissions for schizophrenia (1998–2007) to a psychiatric university hospital were included. Schizophrenic suicides ($n = 7$)/suicide attempters ($n = 40$) were compared to suicides ($n = 30$)/suicide attempters ($n = 186$) with other diagnoses and to schizophrenic non-attempters regarding aggression. Logistic regression analysis was performed to explore risk factors for attempted suicide. Schizophrenic suicides/suicide attempters did not differ from other suicides/suicide attempters or from schizophrenic non-attempters with regard to aggression. Risk of inpatient suicide attempt was increased for patients with attempted suicide at admission, high school graduation, and disorganized subtype. Aggression could not be found to be a predictor of attempted suicide. Aggression seems to have a minor role for suicidal behavior in schizophrenia.

Perceptions of suicide and their impact on policy, discourse and welfare

Nuttman-Shwartz O, Lebel U, Avrami S, Volk N (Israel)

European Journal of Social Work 13, 375-392, 2010

In recent years, there has been an increase in suicide rates throughout the Western world. However, psycho-social responses to the problem are limited, as is public awareness of suicide and its consequences. This article presents findings from a survey on public attitudes toward suicide in Israel. The survey was conducted among a representative sample, and examined the extent to which the problem is a public priority for developing interventions aimed at preventing and reducing the rates of suicide. The findings revealed that despite the prevalence of suicide in Israel, and even though many of the participants had been personally acquainted with the families of suicide victims, suicide still ranks low on the hierarchy of bereavement. The Israeli public is ignorant about suicide, and does not consider it a problem that calls for government intervention and accountability. The study highlights the need for social workers to play an active role as social agents in an attempt to change the social 'bereavement pyramid' perception and effect on government policy toward suicide.

What can post-mortem studies tell us about the pathoetiology of suicide?

Pandey GN, Dwivedi Y (USA)

Future Neurology 5, 701-720, 2010

Suicide is a major public health concern; however, its neurobiology is unclear. Post-mortem brain tissue obtained from suicide victims and normal controls offers a useful method for studying the neurobiology of suicide. Despite several limitations, these studies have offered important leads in the neurobiology of suicide. In this article, we discuss some important findings resulting from these studies, focusing on serotonergic mechanisms, signal transduction systems, neuroendocrine studies and immune function abnormalities in suicide. These studies suggest that abnormalities of certain receptor subtypes, components of signaling systems such as protein kinase C and protein kinase A, transcription factors such as cyclic AMP response element-binding protein and neurotrophins may play an important role in the pathophysiology of suicide. These studies also suggest abnormalities of hypothalamic-pituitary-adrenal axis system components, feedback mechanisms and cytokines, which are chemical mediators of the immune functions. Post-mortem brain tissue offers an opportunity for future studies, such as genetic and epigenetic studies.

Identification of hospitalizations for intentional self-harm when E-codes are incompletely recorded

Patrick AR, Miller M, Barber CW, Wang PS, Canning CF, Schneeweiss S (USA)

Pharmacoepidemiology & Drug Safety 19, 1263-1275, 2010

Context: Suicidal behavior has gained attention as an adverse outcome of prescription drug use. Hospitalizations for intentional self-harm, including suicide, can be identified in administrative claims databases using external cause of injury codes (E-codes). However, rates of E-code completeness in US government and commercial claims databases are low due to issues with hospital billing software.

Objective: To develop an algorithm to identify intentional self-harm hospitalizations using recorded injury and psychiatric diagnosis codes in the absence of E-code reporting.

Methods: We sampled hospitalisations with an injury diagnosis (ICD-9 800-995) from two databases with high rates of E-coding completeness: 1999-2001 British Columbia, Canada data and the 2004 US Nationwide Inpatient Sample. Our gold standard for intentional self-harm was a diagnosis of E950-E958. We constructed algorithms to identify these hospitalizations using information on type of injury and presence of specific psychiatric diagnoses.

Results: The algorithm that identified intentional self-harm hospitalizations with high sensitivity and specificity was a diagnosis of poisoning, toxic effects, open wound to elbow, wrist, or forearm, or asphyxiation; plus a diagnosis of depression, mania, personality disorder, psychotic disorder, or adjustment reaction. This had a sensitivity of 63%, specificity of 99% and positive predictive value (PPV) of 86% in the Canadian database. Values in the US data were 74, 98, and 73%. PPV was highest (80%) in patients under 25 and lowest those over 65 (44%).

Conclusions: The proposed algorithm may be useful for researchers attempting to study intentional self-harm in claims databases with incomplete E-code reporting, especially among younger populations.

A closer look at self-reported suicide attempts: False positives and false negatives

Ploderl M, Kralovec K, Yazdi K, Fartacek R (Austria)
Suicide and Life–Threatening Behavior 41, 1-5, 2011

The validity of self-reported suicide attempt information is undermined by false positives (e.g., incidences without intent to die), or by unreported suicide attempts, referred to as false negatives. In a sample of 1,385 Austrian adults, we explored the occurrence of false positives and false negatives with detailed, probing questions. Removing false positives decreased the rate of suicide attempters from 4.3% to 2.7%. Probing questions also revealed 0.8% false negatives. We recommend using probing questions with both those who report a suicide attempt and those who do not report a suicide attempt to increase the validity of self-reported suicide-related information.

Life events as precipitants of suicide attempts among first-time suicide attempters, repeaters, and non-attempters

Pompili M, Innamorati M, Szanto K, Di Vittorio C, Conwell Y, Lester D, Tatarelli R, Girardi P, Amore M (Italy)
Psychiatry Research 186, 300-305, 2010

The aims of this study were to investigate risk factors for suicide attempts and propose a model explaining the associations among life events and suicide status. We assessed 263 subjects admitted following a suicide attempt to the Division of Psychiatry of the Department of Neurosciences of the University of Parma and compared them with 263 non-attempter clinical control subjects. Attempters reported significantly more adverse life events both in the last 6 months, and between the ages of 0–15 years than non-attempters. A multinomial logistic regression analysis with stepwise forward entry indicated that the best model to explain suicide status was one which included life events in the last 6 months, life events during age 0–15 years, and their interaction. First-time attempter status (vs. non-attempters) was more likely to be linked to life events in the last 6 months, the interaction between life events in the last 6 months and life events during age 0–15 years, and low social support. Those attempters with one or more prior attempts (repeat attempters) were more likely than non-attempters to be linked to the interaction between life events in the last 6 months and life events during age 0–15 years, and to higher rates of psychopharmacological treatment before the index admission. Guided by these findings, monitoring the impact of early-life and recent events in vulnerable individuals should be part of risk assessment and treatment.

A comprehensive meta-analysis of the risk of suicide in eating disorders

Preti A, Rocchi MB, Sisti D, Camboni MV, Miotto P (Italy)
Acta Psychiatrica Scandinavica. Published online: 24 November 2010. doi:10.1111/j.1600-0447.2010.01641.x, 2010

Objective: Past meta-analyses on suicide in eating disorders included few available studies.

Method: PubMed / Medline search for papers including sample n ‡ 40 and follow-up ‡5 years: 40 studies on anorexia nervosa (AN), 16 studies on bulimia nervosa (BN), and three studies on binge eating disorder (BED) were included.

Results: Of 16 342 patients with AN, 245 suicides occurred over a mean follow-up of 11.1 years (suicide rate = 0.124 per 100 personyears). Standardized mortality ratio (SMR) was 31.0 (Poisson 95% CI = 21.0–44.0); a clear decrease in suicide risk over time was observed in recent decades. Of 1768 patients with BN, four suicides occurred over a mean follow-up of 7.5 years (suicide rate = 0.030 per 100 person-years): SMR was 7.5 (1.6–11.6). No suicide occurred among 246 patients with BED (mean follow-up = 5.3 years).

Conclusion: AN and BN share many risk factors for suicide: the factors causing lower suicide rates per person-year in BN compared to AN should be investigated.

Spatial distribution of suicide in Queensland, Australia

Qi X, Tong S, Hu W (Australia)
BMC Psychiatry 10, 106, 2010

Background: There has been a lack of investigation into the spatial distribution and clustering of suicide in Australia, where the population density is lower than many countries and varies dramatically among urban, rural and remote areas. This study aims to examine the spatial distribution of suicide at a Local Governmental Area (LGA) level and identify the LGAs with a high relative risk of suicide in Queensland, Australia, using geographical information system (GIS) techniques.

Methods: Data on suicide and demographic variables in each LGA between 1999 and 2003 were acquired from the Australian Bureau of Statistics. An age stan-dardised mortality (ASM) rate for suicide was calculated at the LGA level. GIS techniques were used to examine the geographical difference of suicide across different areas.

Results: Far north and north-eastern Queensland (i.e., Cook and Mornington Shires) had the highest suicide incidence in both genders, while the south-western areas (i.e., Barcoo and Bauhinia Shires) had the lowest incidence in both genders. In different age groups ([less than or equal to]24 years, 25 to 44 years, 45 to 64 years, and [greater than or equal to]65 years), ASM rates of suicide varied with gender at the LGA level. Mornington and six other LGAs with low socioeconomic status in the upper Southeast had significant spatial clusters of high suicide risk.

Conclusions: There was a notable difference in ASM rates of suicide at the LGA level in Queensland. Some LGAs had significant spatial clusters of high suicide risk. The determinants of the geographical difference of suicide should be addressed in future research. Key words: suicide, Queensland, spatial, cluster.

The effectiveness of electroconvulsive therapy: A literature review

Read J, Bentall R (New Zealand)
Epidemiologia e Psichiatria Sociale 19, 333-347, 2010

Aim: To review the literature on the efficacy of electroconvulsive therapy [ECT], with a particular focus on depression, its primary target group.

Methods: PsycINFO, Medline, previous reviews and the eight identified meta-analyses were searched in an attempt to identify all studies comparing ECT with simulated-ECT [SECT].

Results: These placebo controlled studies show minimal support for effective-ness with either depression or 'schizophrenia' during the course of treatment (only for some patients, on some measures, sometimes perceived only by psy-chiatrists and not by other raters), and no evidence, for either diagnostic group, of any benefits beyond the treatment period. There are no placebo-con-trolled studies evaluating the hypothesis that ECT prevents suicide, and no robust evidence from other kinds of studies to support the hypothesis.

Conclusions: Given the strong evidence (summarised here) of persistent and, for some, permanent brain dysfunction, primarily evidenced in the form of retrograde and anterograde amnesia. and the evidence of a slight but signifi-cant increased risk of death, the cost-benefit analysis for ECT is so poor that its use cannot be scientifically justified.

The reliability of suicide rates: An analysis of railway suicides from two sources in fifteen European countries

Reynders A, Scheerder G, Van Audenhove C (Belgium)
Journal of Affective Disorders. Published online: 1 December 2010. doi:10.1016/j.jad.2010.11.003, 2010

Background: National suicide data are an underestimation of the actual number of suicides but are often assumed to be reliable and useful for scientific research. The aim of this study is to contribute to the discussion of the reliability of suicide mortality data by comparing railway suicides from two data sources.

Methods: Data for the railway suicides and the concurrent causes of death of fifteen European countries were collected from the European Detailed Mortality Database and the European Railway Agency (ERA). Suicide rates, odds ratios and confidence intervals were calculated.

Results: The suicide data from the ERA were significantly higher than the national data for six out of fifteen countries. In three countries, the ERA registered significantly more railway suicides compared to the sum of the national suicides and undetermined deaths. In Italy and France, the ERA statistics recorded significantly more railway related fatalities than the national statistical offices. In total the ERA statistics registered 34% more suicides and 9% more railway fatalities compared with the national statistics.

Limitations: The findings of this study concern railway suicides and they cannot be extrapolated to all types of suicides. Further, the national suicide statistics and the ERA data are not perfectly comparable, due to the different categorisations of the causes of death.

Conclusions: Based on the data for railway suicides, it seems that the underestimation of suicide rates is significant for some countries, and that the degree of underestimation differs substantially among countries. Caution is needed when comparing national suicide rates. There is a need for standardisation of national death registration procedures at the European level.

Overweight of adolescent girls is associated with self-mutilative behaviour

Riala K, Juutinen J, Hakko H, Räsänen P (Finland)
Psychopathology 44, 147-151, 2011

Background: The purpose of the present study was to examine the association of overweight with suicide ideation, self-mutilative behavior (SMB) and suicide attempts among underage psychiatric inpatient adolescents.

Sampling and Methods: Data were collected from 439 adolescents (age = 12-17 years) admitted to psychiatric hospitalization between April 2001 and March 2006. Information on adolescents' suicidal behavior and psychiatric

DSM-IV diagnoses was obtained by using the Schedule for Affective Disorder and Schizophrenia for School-Age Children. An adolescent was defined as overweight if his/her BMI exceeded the 85th percentile BMI in the age- and sex-matched Finnish population. Results: Compared to adolescents without overweight, a 2.5-fold likelihood for SMB was found among overweight girls, but not among boys.

Conclusions: Low self-esteem, depression or dysfunctional emotion regulation may be possible mediating factors between overweight and SMB.

Psychiatric disorders in male prisoners who made near-lethal suicide attempts: Case-control study

Rivlin A, Hawton K, Marzano L, Fazel S (UK)

British Journal of Psychiatry 197, 313-319, 2010

Background: Although male prisoners are five times more likely to die by suicide than men of a similar age in the general population, the contribution of psychiatric disorders is not known. Aims: To investigate the association of psychiatric disorders with near-lethal suicide attempts in male prisoners.

Method: A matched case-control study of 60 male prisoners who made near-lethal suicide attempts (cases) and 60 prisoners who had never carried out near-lethal suicide attempts in prison (controls) was conducted. Psychiatric disorders were identified with the Mini International Neuropsychiatric Interview (MINI), and information on sociodemographic characteristics and criminal history was gathered using a semi-structured interview.

Results: Psychiatric disorders were present in all cases and 62% of controls. Most current psychiatric disorders were associated with near-lethal suicide attempts, including major depression (odds ratio (OR) = 42.0, 95% CI 5.8-305), psychosis (OR = 15.0, 95% CI 2.0-113), anxiety disorders (OR = 6.0, 95% CI 2.3-15.5) and drug misuse (OR = 2.9, 95% CI 1.3-6.4). Lifetime psychiatric disorders associated with near-lethal attempts included recurrent depression and psychoses. Although cases were more likely than controls to meet criteria for antisocial personality disorder, the difference was not statistically significant. Comorbidity was also significantly more common among cases than controls for both current and lifetime disorders.

Conclusions: In male prisoners, psychiatric disorders, especially depression, psychosis, anxiety and drug misuse, are associated with near-lethal suicide attempts, and hence probably with suicide.

Suicide risk and its relationship to change in marital status

Roskar S, Podlesek A, Kuzmanic M, Demsar LO, Zaletel M, Marusic A (Slovenia)

Crisis 32, 24-30, 2011

Background: Different types of marital status are associated with different levels of suicidal risk. Aims: To study marital status change and the effect of its recency in relation to suicidal behavior.

Methods: Suicide victims (1614) in Slovenia and matched controls (4617) were compared for incidence and recency of marital status change during the last 5 years of their lives.

Results: A higher percentage of suicide victims (10.7%) had a marital status change in the last 5 years compared with the controls (5.6%). All types of marital status changes (becoming widowed, getting divorced, getting married) proved to be risk factors for suicidal behavior. Almost half of all marital status changes in suicide victims occurred in the year prior to suicide, whereas marital status changes in the control group were equally distributed over the last 5 years. For recently married and divorced people, the increase in suicide risk depended on age: The risk was higher in older people.

Conclusions: Marital status change represents a risk factor for suicidal behavior. The first year after the change is critical for elevated suicidal risk, in particular for older people.

Effects of training program on recognition and management of depression and suicide risk evaluation for Slovenian primary-care physicians: Follow-up study

Roskar S, Podlesek A, Zorko M, Tavcar R, Dernovsek ZM, Groleger U, Mirjanic M, Konec N, Janet E, Marusic A (Slovenia)

Croatian Medical Journal 51, 237-242, 2010

Aim: To implement and evaluate an educational program for primary care physicians on recognition and treatment of depression and suicide prevention.

Method: The study was conducted in 3 Slovenian neighboring regions (Celje, Ravne na Koroskem, and Podravska) with similar suicide rates and other health indicators. All primary care physicians from Celje ($N = 155$) and Ravne na Koroskem ($N = 35$) were invited to participate in the educational program on depression treatment and suicide risk recognition. From January to March 2003, approximately half of them (82 out of 190; educational group) attended the program, whereas the other half (108 out of 190; control group 1) and physicians from the Podravska region ($N = 164$; control group 2) did not attend the program. The prescription rates of antidepressants and anxiolytics before and after the intervention were compared between the studied regions. Also, suicide rates three-years before and after the intervention were compared.

Results: From 2002 to 2003, there was a 2.33-fold increase in the rate of antide-pressant prescriptions in the educational group ($P < .05$) and only 1.28-fold (P .05) and 1.34-fold ($P < .05$) increase in control groups 1 and 2, respectively. However, the 12% decrease in suicide rate in the intervention regions was not significantly greater than the 4% decrease in the non-intervention region ($P > .05$).

Conclusion: Our training program was beneficial for primary care physicians' ability to recognise and manage depression. However, there was no significant decrease in local suicide rates.

Does state spending on mental health lower suicide rates?

Ross JM, Yakovlev PA, Carson F (USA)

Journal of Socio-Economics 37, 237-261, 2010

Using recently released data on public mental health expenditures by U.S. states from 1997 to 2005, this study is the first to examine the effect of state mental health spending on suicide rates. We find the effect of per capita public mental health expenditures on the suicide rate to be qualitatively small and lacking statistical significance. This finding holds across different estimation techniques, gender, and age groups. The estimates suggest that policies aimed at income growth, divorce prevention or support, and assistance to low income individuals could be more effective at suicide prevention than state mental health expenditures.

Clinical decisions in psychiatry should not be based on risk assessment

Ryan C, Nielssen O, Paton M, Large M (Australia)

Australasian Psychiatry 18, 398-403, 2010

Objective: Risk assessments that place patients in high or low risk categories have been widely adopted by mental health services in an attempt to reduce the harms associated with psychiatric disorders. This paper examines the effects of categorisation based on the results of a risk assessment.

Methods: The violence prediction instrument derived from the MacArthur Study of Mental Disorder and Violence was used to illustrate the nature and effects of risk assessment and the consequent categorisation of patients.

Results: The majority of patients categorized as being at high risk will not commit any harmful acts.

Conclusions: Patients who are classified as high risk share the cost of efforts to reduce harm in the form of additional treatment and restrictions, although the majority will not go on to commit a harmful act. Clinical decisions made on the basis of risk assessment also divert resources away from patients classified as low risk, even though a significant proportion do go on to a commit harmful act. We argue that psychiatric professionals should discuss the risks of treatment and of non-treatment with patients (or with their substitute decision-makers) and should maintain a duty to warn about the consequences of not having treatment. However, assessment of risk of harm should not form the basis for clinical decision-making. We should aim to provide optimal care according to the treatment needs of each patient, regardless of the perceived risk of adverse events.

Suicide prevention in primary care: General practitioners' views on service availability

Saini P, Windfuhr K, Pearson A, Da Cruz D, Miles C, Cordingley L, While D, Swinson N, Williams A, Shaw J, Appleby L, Kapur N (UK)
BMC Research Notes 3, 246, 2010

Background: Primary care may be a key setting for suicide prevention. However, comparatively little is known about the services available in primary care for suicide prevention. The aims of the current study were to describe services available in general practices for the management of suicidal patients and to examine GPs views on these services. We carried out a questionnaire and interview study in the North West of England. We collected data on GPs views of suicide prevention generally as well as local mental health service provision.

Findings: During the study period (2003-2005) we used the National Confidential Inquiry Suicide database to identify 286 general practitioners (GPs) who had registered patients who had died by suicide. Data were collected from GPs and practice managers in 167 practices. Responses suggested that there was greater availability of services and training for general mental health issues than for suicide prevention specifically. The three key themes which emerged from GP interviews were: barriers accessing primary or secondary mental health services; obstacles faced when referring a patient to mental health services; managing change within mental health care services

Conclusions: Health professionals have an important role to play in preventing suicide. However, GPs expressed concerns about the quality of primary care mental health service provision and difficulties with access to secondary mental health services. Addressing these issues could facilitate future suicide prevention in primary care.

Suicide and gambling: Psychopathology and treatment-seeking

Seguin M, Boyer R, Lesage A, McGirr A, Suissa A, Tousignant M, Turecki G (Canada)
Psychology of Addictive Behaviors 24, 541-547, 2010

The aim of this study was to evaluate suicides with a history of problem gambling (PG) and others with no such history (NPG) and to compare the two on mental health problems and service utilisation. Data on a sample of 49 PG suicides and 73 NPG suicides were obtained from informants and hospital records. Psychopathology was prevalent in both groups, but problem gamblers were twice as likely to have a personality disorder. Moreover, PG suicides were less in contact with mental health services in their last month, their last year, and their lifetime. NPG suicides consulted specialised services from 3 (last month and last year) to 13 times (lifetime) as often as their PG counterparts. Lower service utilization associated with PG suicides argues in favor of stepping up detection, engagement in care and treatment with respect to problem gambling, especially when comorbidity is present.

Persistent suicide risk in clinically improved schizophrenia patients: Challenge of the suicidal dimension

Shrivastava A, Johnston ME, Shah N, Innamorati M, Stitt L, Thakar M, Lester D, Pompili M (India)

Neuropsychiatric Disease and Treatment 6, 633-638, 2010

Background: Suicide is a major problem in schizophrenia, estimated to affect 9%-13% of patients. About 25% of schizophrenic patients make at least one suicide attempt in their lifetime. Current outcome measures do not address this problem, even though it affects quality of life and patient safety. The aim of this study was to assess suicidality in long-term clinically improved schizophrenia patients who were treated in a nongovernmental psychiatric treatment centre in Mumbai, India.

Method: Participants were 61 patients out of 200 consecutive hospitalized first-episode patients with schizophrenia diagnosed according to the Diagnostic and Statistical Manual of Mental Disorders who were much improved on the Clinical Global Impression Scale-Improvement (CGI-I) scale at the endpoint of a 10-year follow-up. Clinical assessment tools included the Positive and Negative Syndrome Scale for Schizophrenia, CGI-I, Global Assessment of Functioning, and suicidality.

Results: Many of the patients, although clinically improved, experienced emerging suicidality during the 10-year follow-up period. All of the patients reported significant suicidality (i.e., suicide attempts, suicidal crises, or suicidal ideation) at the end of the study, whereas only 83% had reported previous significant suicidality at baseline. No sociodemographic and clinical variables at baseline were predictive of suicidal status at the end of the 10-year follow-up.

Conclusion: Schizophrenia is a complex neurobehavioral disorder that appears to be closely associated with suicidal behavior. Adequate assessment and management of suicidality needs to be a continual process, even in patients who respond well to treatment.

Association of suicide attempts with acne and treatment with isotretinoin: retrospective Swedish cohort study

Sundström A, Alfredsson L, Sjölin-Forsberg G, Gerdén B, Bergman U, Jokinen J (Sweden)

British Medical Journal 341, c5812, 2010

Objective: To assess the risk of attempted suicide before, during, and after treatment with isotretinoin for severe acne.

Design: Retrospective cohort study linking a named patient register of isotretinoin users (1980–9) to hospital discharge and cause of death registers (1980–2001).

Setting: Sweden, 1980–2001. Population 5756 patients aged 15 to 49 years prescribed isotretinoin for severe acne observed for 17,197 person years before, 2905 person years during, and 87,120 person years after treatment.

Main Outcome Measures: Standardised incidence ratio (observed number divided by expected number of suicide attempts standardised by sex, age, and calendar year), calculated up to three years before, during, and up to 15 years after end of treatment.

Results: 128 patients were admitted to hospital for attempted suicide. During the year before treatment, the standardised incidence ratio for attempted suicide was raised: 1.57 (95% confidence interval 0.86 to 2.63) for all (including repeat) attempts and 1.36 (0.65 to 2.50) counting only first attempts. The standardised incidence ratio during and up to six months after treatment was 1.78 (1.04 to 2.85) for all attempts and 1.93 (1.08 to 3.18) for first attempts. Three years after treatment stopped, the observed number of attempts was close to the expected number and remained so during the 15 years of follow-up: standardised incidence ratio 1.04 (0.74 to 1.43) for all attempts and 0.97 (0.64 to 1.40) for first attempts. Twelve (38%) of 32 patients who made their first suicide attempt before treatment made a new attempt or committed suicide thereafter. In contrast, 10 (71%) of the 14 who made their first suicide attempt within six months after treatment stopped made a new attempt or committed suicide during follow-up (two sample test of proportions, P=0.034). The number needed to harm was 2300 new 6-month treatments per year for one additional first suicide attempt to occur and 5000 per year for one additional repeat attempt.

Conclusions: An increased risk of attempted suicide was apparent up to six months after the end of treatment with isotretinoin, which motivates a close monitoring of patients for suicidal behaviour for up to a year after treatment has ended. However, the risk of attempted suicide was already rising before treatment, so an additional risk due to the isotretinoin treatment cannot be established. As patients with a history of suicide attempts before treatment made new attempts to a lesser extent than did patients who started such behaviour in connection with treatment, patients with severe acne should not automatically have isotretinoin treatment withheld because of a history of attempted suicide.

Alcohol and suicide in Russia, 1870–1894 and 1956–2005: Evidence for the continuation of a harmful drinking culture across time?

Stickley A, Jukkala T, Norström T (Russia)
Journal of Studies on Alcohol and Drugs 72, 341-347, 2010

Objective: Previous research suggests that a strong relation exists between alcohol consumption and suicide in Soviet and post-Soviet Russia. This study extends this analysis across a much longer historical time frame by examining the relationship between heavy drinking and suicide in tsarist and post-World War II Russia.

Method: Using alcohol poisoning mortality data as a proxy for heavy drinking, time-series analytical modeling techniques were used to examine the strength of the alcohol-suicide relation in the provinces of European Russia in the period 1870-1894 and for Russia in 1956-2005.

Results: During 1870-1894, a decreasing trend was recorded in heavy drinking in Russia that contrasted with the sharp increase observed in this phenomenon in the post-World War II period. A rising trend in suicide was recorded in both study periods, although the increase was much greater in the latter period. The strength of the heavy drinking-suicide relation nevertheless remained unchanged across time, with a 10% increase in heavy drinking resulting in a 3.5% increase in suicide in tsarist Russia and a 3.8% increase in post-World War II Russia.

Conclusions: Despite the innumerable societal changes that have occurred in Russia across the two study periods and the growth in the level of heavy drinking, the strength of the heavy drinking-suicide relation has remained unchanged across time. This suggests the continuation of a highly detrimental drinking culture where the heavy episodic drinking of distilled spirits (vodka) is an essential element in the alcohol-suicide association.

The contribution of psychological distress to socio-economic differences in cause-specific mortality: A population-based follow-up of 28 years

Talala KM, Huurre TM, Laatikainen TK, Martelin TP, Ostamo AI, Prattala RS (Finland)
BMC Public Health 28, 138, 2011

Background: Psychological factors associated with low social status have been proposed as one possible explanation for the socio-economic gradient in health. The aim of this study is to explore whether different indicators of psychological distress contribute to socio-economic differences in cause-specific mortality.

Methods: The data source is a nationally representative, repeated cross-sectional survey, 'Health Behaviour and Health among the Finnish Adult Population' (AVTK). The survey results were linked with socio-economic register data from Statistics Finland (from the years 1979-2002) and mortality follow-up data up to 2006 from the Finnish National Cause of Death Register. The data included 32451 men and 35420 women (response rate 73.5%). Self-reported measures of depression, insomnia and stress were used as indicators of psychological distress. Socio-economic factors included education, employment status and household income. Mortality data consisted of unnatural causes of death (suicide, accidents and violence, and alcohol-related mortality) and coronary heart disease (CHD) mortality. Adjusted hazard ratios were calculated using the Cox regression model.

Results: In unnatural mortality, psychological distress accounted for some of the employment status (11–31%) and income level (4–16%) differences among both men and women, and for the differences related to the educational level (5–12%) among men; the educational level was associated statistically significantly with unnatural mortality only among men. Psychological distress had minor or no contribution to socio-economic differences in CHD mortality.

Conclusions: Psychological distress partly accounted for socio-economic disparities in unnatural mortality. Further studies are needed to explore the role and mechanisms of psychological distress associated with socio-economic differences in cause-specific mortality.

The impact of inpatient suicide on psychiatric nurses and their need for support

Takahashi C, Chida F, Nakamura H, Akasaka H, Yagi J, Koeda A, Tagusari E, Otsuka K, Sakai A (Japan)
BMC Psychiatry 11, 38, 2011

Background: The nurses working in psychiatric hospitals and wards are prone to encounter completed suicides. The research was conducted to examine post-suicide stress in nurses and the availability of suicide-related mental health care services and education.

Methods: Experiences with inpatient suicide were investigated using an anonymous, self-reported questionnaire, which was, along with the Impact of Event Scale-Revised, administered to 531 psychiatric nurses.

Results: The rate of nurses who had encountered patient suicide was 55.0%. The mean Impact of Event Scale-Revised (IES-R) score was 11.4. The proportion of respondents at a high risk ([greater than or equal to] 25 on the 88-point IES-R score) for post-traumatic stress disorder (PTSD) was 13.7%. However, only 15.8% of respondents indicated that they had access to post-suicide mental health care programmes. The survey also revealed a low rate of nurses who reported attending in-hospital seminars on suicide prevention or mental health care for nurses (26.4% and 12.8%, respectively).

Conclusions: These results indicated that nurses exposed to inpatient suicide suffer significant mental distress. However, the low availability of systematic post-suicide mental health care programs for such nurses and the lack of suicide-related education initiatives and mental health care for nurses are problematic. The situation is likely related to the fact that there are no formal systems in place for identifying and evaluating the psychological effects of patient suicide in nurses and to the pressures stemming from the public perception of nurses as suppliers rather than recipients of health care.

The suicidal process and self-esteem

Thompson AH (Canada)
Crisis 31, 311-316, 2010

Background: It has not been made clear whether self-esteem is associated with the severity of suicidal behavior.

Aims: To test the association between responses to a self-esteem inventory and levels of suicidal behavior as conceptualized in the notion of the suicide process.

Methods: Questions on the severity of suicidal behavior over the lifespan (death wishes, ideation, plans, and attempts), as well as a self-esteem inventory, were administered to 227 university undergraduates.

Results: A negative relationship was found between the level of suicidality and self-esteem. As hypothesised, there were fewer cases in each succeeding level of seriousness of suicidal behavior. However, nearly all cases from any particular level were contained in the cohort of individuals who had displayed suicidal behavior at a less serious level.

Conclusions: This suggests a possible progression through each of the stages of suicidal behavior, with very few cases showing a level of suicidal behavior that was not associated with a previous, less serious, form. It was hypothesized that early entry into the suicidal process may be indicated by low self-esteem, thus, allowing for a more timely preventive intervention.

Why do people choose charcoal burning as a method of suicide? An interview based study of survivors in Taiwan

Tsai C-W, Gunnell D, Chou Y-H, Kuo C-J, Lee M-B, Chen Y-Y (Taiwan)
Journal of Affective Disorders. Published online: 12 January 2011. doi:10.1016/j.jad.2010.12.013, 2010

Background: Marked increases in the incidence of charcoal burning suicide have contributed to Taiwan's rising suicide rate in the past decade. To assess possible opportunities for intervention, we have compared survivors of suicide attempts by charcoal burning with people who ingested poisons.

Methods: We interviewed a consecutive series of suicide attempters by charcoal burning ($n = 37$) and self-poisoning ($n = 38$) admitted to Taipei Veterans General Hospital (TVGH) between January 2009 and March 2010. Interviews included the Structured Clinical Interview of DSMIV (SCID) and Beck Suicide Intent Scale.

Results: Compared to people who ingested medicines/poisons, charcoal burning suicide attempters were less likely to have a pre-existing physical illness or contact with psychiatric services prior to the attempt and more likely to be employed. Charcoal burning suicide attempters had higher levels of suicide intent (mean score 20.1) compared to people ingesting poisons (mean score 13.5) ($p < .001$) and were considerably more likely to report that their choice of method was influenced by the media (87% vs. 8%), particularly the portrayal of the method as a peaceful way of dying. Charcoal burning suicides were less impulsive.

Limitations: The study sample was limited to a single hospital.

Conclusions: Survivors of suicide attempts by charcoal burning have high levels of intent and low levels of psychiatric contact indicating they may be more difficult to prevent than suicides by self-poisoning. Encouraging responsible media reporting of suicide and restricting the availability of charcoal may be the most promising approaches to preventing these deaths.

Assessment of self harm in an accident and emergency service: The development of a proforma to assess suicide intent and mental state in those presenting to the emergency department with self harm

Ul Haq S, Subramanyam D, Agius M (UK)
Psychiatria Danubina 22, 1, 2010

Introduction: The UK has one of the highest rates of self harm in Europe, around 400 per 100,000 people (Horrocks et al. 2002). It accounts for 150,000 attendances to the Emergency department each year and is one of the top five causes of acute medical admissions in the UK (NICE 2002).

Aims: Objectives included to explore the method of self harm and the demographic factors of those presenting the Emergency department with self harm.

In addition we wanted to review the exploration of suicide risk factors and suicide intent by the Emergency department doctor and ascertain whether a psychiatric assessment with full mental state examination had been conducted with referral to psychiatric services if deemed necessary. We wanted to explore the current practice around self harm presentations in the Emergency department accordance with NICE guidelines.

Methods: Data was collected retrospectively from February to August 2009. Twenty-five sets of medical notes were collated at random for patients who had presented with self harm to the Emergency department. Notes were reviewed for evidence of exploration of the event, psychiatric assessment, risk factors for suicide and further referral.

Results: 14 of the 25 patients presented having taken an overdose. 9 had inflicted some other form of self injury, namely lacerations to self. In 2 cases a mixed presentation was found. Previous psychiatric history was documented in 16 cases. 11 had a previous history of depression or anxiety disorder; 1 was known to have bipolar affective disorder; 1 was diagnosed in the past with borderline personality disorder; and 3 patients had no previous history. In 9 cases previous history was not documented.

Discussion: Twenty-five sets of medical notes were reviewed from February to August 2009 for individuals presenting to the Emergency department with self harm. Of those, 12 fell into the over 25 age group. 17 were female and 8 were male. The majority of patients were of white British ethnicity. 14 had taken an overdose; 9 had inflicted some other form of self-injury; and 2 had a mixed presentation. Suicide risk factors and suicidal intent was poorly documented with mental state examination found not to be documented in all 25 cases reviewed. 18 were deemed medically fit in the Emergency department and were referred for psychiatric review. These unfortunate findings may be a reflection on the time pressures faced by Emergency department doctors, namely the four hour targets, and perhaps lack of adequate training in psychosocial risk assessment. With such poor documentation made by the Emergency department doctors, a proforma was produced which incorporates suicide risk factors and assessment of suicide intent in addition to a brief version of the mental state examination.

Conclusion: Concerns have been raised by the recent Royal College of Psychiatrists report on self harm, that current level of care provided to service users fall short of the standards set out in policies and guidelines, with poor assessments, unskilled staff and insufficient care pathways (Royal College of Psychiatrists. Report CR 158. 2010). Indeed evidence suggest that appropriate training and intervention given to A&E staff can lead to improvements in the quality of psychosocial assessment of patients with deliberate self harm (Crawford et al. 1998).

ALGOS: The development of a randomised controlled trial testing a case management algorithm designed to reduce suicide risk among suicide attempters

Vaiva G, Walter M, Al Arab AS, Courtet P, Bellivier F, Demarty AL, Duhem S, Ducrocq F, Goldstein P, Libersa C (France)
BMC Psychiatry 11, 1, 2011

Background: Suicide attempts (SA) constitute a serious clinical problem. People who attempt suicide are at high risk of further repetition. However, no interventions have been shown to be effective in reducing repetition in this group of patients.

Methods/Design: Multicentre randomized controlled trial. We examine the effectiveness of 'ALGOS algorithm': an intervention based in a decisional tree of contact type which aims at reducing the incidence of repeated suicide attempt during 6 months. This algorithm of case management comprises the two strategies of intervention that showed a significant reduction in the number of SA repeaters: systematic telephone contact (ineffective in first-attempters) and Crisis card (effective only in first-attempters). Participants who are lost from contact and those refusing healthcare, can then benefit from 'short letters' or 'postcards'.

Discussion: ALGOS algorithm is easily reproducible and inexpensive intervention that will supply the guidelines for assessment and management of a population sometimes in difficulties with healthcare compliance. Furthermore, it will target some of these subgroups of patients by providing specific interventions for optimising the benefits of case management strategy.

Drug suicide: A sex-equal cause of death in 16 European countries

Värnik A, Sisask M, Värnik P, Wu J, Kõlves K, Arensman E, Maxwell M, Reisch T, Gusmäo R, Van Audenhove C, Scheerder G, van der Feltz-Cornelis CM, Coffey C, Kopp M, Szekely A, Roskar S, Hegerl U (Estonia)
BMC Public Health 11, 61, 2010

Background: There is a lack of international research on suicide by drug overdose as a preventable suicide method. Sex- and age-specific rates of suicide by drug self-poisoning (ICD-10, X60-64) and the distribution of drug types used in 16 European countries were studied, and compared with other self-poisoning methods (X65-69) and intentional self-injury (X70-84).

Methods: Data for 2000-04/05 were collected from national statistical offices. Age-adjusted suicide rates, and age and sex distributions, were calculated.

Results: No pronounced sex differences in drug self-poisoning rates were found, either in the aggregate data (males 1.6 and females 1.5 per 100,000) or within individual countries. Among the 16 countries, the range (from some 0.3 in Portugal to 5.0 in Finland) was wide. 'Other and unspecified drugs' (X64) were recorded most frequently, with a range of 0.2-1.9, and accounted for more than 70% of deaths by drug overdose in France, Luxembourg, Portugal and Spain. Psychotropic drugs (X61) ranked second. The X63 category ('other drugs acting on the autonomic nervous system') was least frequently used. Finland showed low X64 and high X61 figures, Scotland had high levels of X62 ('narcotics and hallucinogens, not elsewhere classified') for both sexes, while England exceeded other countries in category X60. Risk was highest among the middle-aged everywhere except in Switzerland, where the elderly were most at risk.

Conclusions: Suicide by drug overdose is preventable. Intentional self-poisoning with drugs kills as many males as females. The considerable differences in patterns of self-poisoning found in the various European countries are relevant to national efforts to improve diagnostics of suicide and appropriate specific prevention. The fact that vast majority of drug-overdose suicides came under the category X64 refers to the need of more detailed ICD coding system for overdose suicides is needed to permit better design of suicide-prevention strategies at national level.

Suicide or undetermined? A national assessment of police suicide death classification

Violanti JM (USA)

International Journal of Emergency Mental Health 12, 89-94, 2010

The validity of police suicide rates is questionable. The objective of this paper is to compare national police suicide rates with 'undetermined' death rates and compare across occupations similar in exposure. An additional objective is to compare police suicide and undetermined rates in female and minority officers. Results indicated that male police officer deaths had a 17% increased risk of being misclassified as undetermined (Proportionate Mortality Ratio (PMR) = 117, 95% CI = 110,123, significant at $p < .01$). The risk was higher than both firefighter and military occupations (PMR = 101 (1% risk), 95% CI = 89, 114; PMR = 108 (8% risk), 95% CI = 104,113 respectively). A high risk of misclassification was also seen in female and African American officer deaths (PMR = 198 (98% risk), 95% CI = 151-255, sig. $p < .01$ and PMR = 344 (344% risk), 95% CI = 178-601, sig. $p < .01$ respectively). The significantly higher ratio of police deaths classified as undetermined is interesting, given the high profile of law enforcement in society and the generally thorough investigations of police officer deaths. Also of interest is the suggestion that police misclassification risk is higher for police than other similar occupations. Future research should suggest possible ways to increase the validity of police suicide rates through methods such as post-suicide psychological autopsies.

Suicide in later life: A comparison between cases with early-onset and late-onset depression

Voshaar RC, Kapur N, Bickley H, Williams A, Purandare N (The Netherlands)

Journal of Affective Disorders. Published online: 18 March 2011. Doi: 10.1016/j.jad.2011.02.008, 2011

Background: Suicide rates are high in elderly people with depressive disorder. We compared behavioural, clinical and care characteristics of depressed elderly patients, aged 60years and over at the time of death by suicide, with an early-onset depression (EOD, onset before 60years) with those patients with a late age of onset (LOD).

Method: From a 10-year national clinical survey of all suicides in England and Wales ($n = 13,066$) we identified 549 LOD cases, and 290 EOD cases. EOD and LOD cases were compared by logistic regression adjusted for age at suicide.

Results: Method of suicide did not differ by age of onset of depression. LOD cases were significantly less likely to have a history of psychiatric admissions (OR = 0.2 [0.1-0.3]), alcohol misuse (OR=0.6 [0.4-0.9]) and self-harm (0.6 [0.4-0.8]). LOD cases also had a lower prevalence of a psychiatric co-morbid diagnosis (0.6 [0.4-0.7]) and a lower prescription rate for psychotropic drugs other than antidepressants. Furthermore, the number of recent life-events was significantly higher (OR = 1.4 [1.0-1.9]) in LOD while the frequency of recent self-harm was similar to EOD.

Conclusion: Although our study suggests that psychopathology of suicide among elderly depressed patients differs between EOD and LOD, the final pathway (via recent self-harm) to suicide may be similar in up to a quarter of patients in both groups. Our results suggest that strategies to enhance coping abilities and provision of support to negate the effects of life-events might be especially important in the prevention of suicide in LOD.

Latent class analysis of comorbidity in the Adult Psychiatric Morbidity Survey in England 2007: Implications for DSM-5 and ICD-11

Weich S, McBride O, Hussey D, Exeter D, Brugha T, McManus S (UK)
Psychological Medicine. Published online: 4 March 2011. Doi: 10.1017/S0033291711000249, 2011

Background: Psychiatric co-morbidity is complex and ubiquitous. Our aim was to describe the extent, nature and patterning of psychiatric co-morbidity within a representative sample of the adult population of England, using latent class analysis.

Method: Data were used from the 2007 Adult Psychiatric Morbidity Survey, a two-phase national household survey undertaken in 2007 comprising 7325 participants aged 16 years and older living in private households in England. The presence of 15 common mental health and behavioural problems was ascertained using standardised clinical and validated self-report measures, including three anxiety disorders, depressive episode, mixed anxiety depressive disorder, psychosis, antisocial and borderline personality disorders, eating disorders, post-traumatic stress disorder, attention deficit disorder, alcohol and drug dependencies, problem gambling and attempted suicide.

Results: A four-class model provided the most parsimonious and informative explanation of the data. Most participants (81.6%) were assigned to a non-symptomatic or 'Unaffected' class. The remainder were classified into three qualitatively different symptomatic classes: 'Co-thymia' (12.4%), 'Highly Co-morbid' (5.0%) and 'Addictions' (1.0%). Classes differed in mean numbers of conditions and impairments in social functioning, and these dimensions were correlated.

Conclusions: Our findings confirm that mental disorders typically co-occur and are concentrated in a relatively small number of individuals. Conditions associated with the highest levels of disability, mortality and cost — psychosis, suicidality and personality disorders — are often comorbid with more common conditions. This needs to be recognised when planning services and when considering aetiology.

Precarious spaces: Risk, responsibility and uncertainty in school-based suicide prevention programs

White J, Morris J (USA)

Social Science and Medicine 71, 2187-2194, 2010

We report on findings from an in-depth qualitative case study designed to closely examine the social practices of planning and implementing a four-part (6-hour) classroom-based suicide prevention program within two classrooms in one secondary school in Vancouver, British Columbia. Representing a departure from traditional evaluation research studies in suicidology, we examine how school-based youth suicide prevention programs get brought into being in 'real world' contexts. Using a discursive, critical constructionist methodology, we aim to illuminate the complexities of this work. Based on our analysis, we suggest that suicide (and its prevention), in all its complex and culturally situated forms, simply cannot be conceptualised through singular, stable or universalising terms that transcend time and context. Implications for (re)- conceptualising suicide prevention education are discussed.

Sleep problems, suicidal ideation, and self-harm behaviors in adolescence

Wong MM, Brower KJ, Zucker RA (USA)

Journal of Psychiatric Research 45, 505-511, 2010

Objective: Previous research has found an association between sleep problems and suicidal behavior. However, it is still unclear whether the association can be largely explained by depression. In this study, we prospectively examined relationships between sleep problems when participants were 12–14 years old and subsequent suicidal thoughts and self-harm behaviors-including suicide attempts-at ages 15–17 while controlling for depressive symptoms at baseline.

Methods: Study participants were 280 boys and 112 girls from a community sample of high-risk alcoholic families and controls in an ongoing longitudinal study.

Results: Controlling for gender, parental alcoholism and parental suicidal thoughts, and prior suicidal thoughts or self-harm behaviors when participants were 12–14 years old, having trouble sleeping at 12–14 significantly predicted suicidal thoughts and self-harm behaviors at ages 15–17. Depressive symptoms, nightmares, aggressive behavior, and substance-related problems at ages 12–14 were not significant predictors when other variables were in the model.

Conclusions: Having trouble sleeping was a strong predictor of subsequent suicidal thoughts and self-harm behaviors in adolescence. Sleep problems may be an early and important marker for suicidal behavior in adolescence. Parents and primary care physicians are encouraged to be vigilant and screen for sleep problems in young adolescents. Future research should determine if early intervention with sleep disturbances reduces the risk for suicidality in adolescents.

The impact of quality and quantity of social support on help-seeking behavior prior to deliberate self-harm

Wu CY, Stewart R, Huang HC, Prince M, Liu SI (Taiwan)
General Hospital Psychiatry 33, 37-44, 2010

Objective: Little is known about use of formal or informal help-seeking resources prior to deliberate self-harm (DSH) outside Western settings. The aim of the study was to investigate help-seeking behavior and correlates of this prior to self-harm in an East Asian setting.

Methods: Over a year period, consecutive attendees at a general hospital emergency room in Taiwan with DSH were asked about prior medical contact and informal help-seeking in the month prior to DSH. Self-reported social support/network was measured using the Close Persons Questionnaire.

Results: The mean age of the 209 participants was 35.2 years (*SD* = 13.3), with three times more women (75.6%) than men. Nearly half had made medical contact (47.1%) or sought informal help (54.1%) within the month prior to DSH. After adjustment, higher level of confiding and practical support were associated with seeking informal help (odds ratio [OR] 1.14, 95% confidence interval [CI] 1.06–1.23; OR 1.17, 95% CI 1.04–1.32, respectively). Prior medical contact was negatively associated with higher social network outside the home (OR 0.91, 95% CI 0.85–0.98).

Conclusion: Social support/network potentially modifies help-seeking behavior prior to DSH. Quality rather than quantity of social support was associated with seeking informal support, with the reverse pattern associated with prior medical contact.

Youth suicide: An insight into previous hospitalisation for injury and sociodemographic conditions from a nationwide cohort study

Zambon F, Laflamme L, Spolaore P, Visentin C, Hasselberg M (Sweden)
Injury Prevention. Published online: 5 December 2010. doi:10.1136/ip.2010.030080, 2010

Background: This study investigates the degree to which a previous hospitalization for injury of any intent is a risk of subsequent youth suicide and whether this
association is influenced by family socioeconomic status or economic stress.

Methods: A nationwide register-based cohort study was conducted covering all
Swedish subjects born between January 1977 and December 1991 (*N* = 1,616,342,
male/female ratio = 1.05). The cohort subjects were followed-up from January
1998 to December 2003, when aged 7–26 years. Poisson regression and the likelihood ratio test (95% CI) were used to assess the age-adjusted effect of hospitalisation for injuries of various intent on youth suicide and its effect once adjusted
for family sociodemographic and social circumstances.

Results: Each set of exposures was associated independently and significantly with
suicide mortality. Being hospitalised for self-inflicted injuries or injuries of undetermined intent was associated with a risk of suicide 36 to 47 times, respectively,
that of subjects never hospitalised in the period under study (95% CI 28.36 to
45.58 and 26.67 to 83.87 for self-inflicted injuries and for events of undetermined
intent, respectively; overall *p* < .01). Similarly, previous events of unintentional
injury markedly increased the risk of suicide (RR 3.08; 95% CI 2.26 to 4.19).
These effects were solid and not substantially altered after adjustment for family
demographic and socioeconomic circumstances.

Conclusion: A strong association exists between previous hospitalisation for
injury of any intent and youth suicide. The association is robust and unaltered by
family socioeconomic circumstances.

Citation List

FATAL SUICIDAL BEHAVIOUR

Epidemiology

Aasland OG, Hem E, Haldorsen T, Ekeberg O (2011). Mortality among Norwegian medical doctors 1960-2000. *BMC Public Health* 11, 173.

Aggarwal KK, Kumar R, Tayal M (2010). Epidemiological trends in the fatal poisoning cases in the Malwa region of Punjab. *Medico-Legal Update* 10, 28-29.

Andres AR, Halicioglu F (2010). Testing the hypothesis of the natural suicide rates: Further evidence from OECD data. *Economic Modelling* 28, 22-26.

Anonymous (2010). Suicides in national parks - United States, 2003-2009. *Morbidity and Mortality Weekly Report* 59, 1546-1549.

Arensman E, McAuliffe C, Reulbach U (2010). Trends in suicide and other external causes of death in Ireland, 1980-2005. *Irish Journal of Medical Science* 179, 432-433.

Austin A, Winskog C, van den Heuvel C, Byard RW (2011). Recent trends in suicides utilizing helium. *Journal of Forensic Sciences*. Published online: 1 March 2011. doi:10.1111/j.1556-4029.2011.01723.x.

Babladi PI, Vijayanath V, Vijayamahantesh SN (2010). A five year (1998-2002) study of burns at Gulberga, Karnataka. *Medico-Legal Update* 10, 121-123.

Babu GR, Babu BV (2011). Dowry deaths: a neglected public health issue in India. *International Health* 3, 35-43.

Baldacchino A, Walls S (2011). A comparison of accidental and intentional fatal drug overdoses within the drug death population in Scotland: A case of comortality? *Mental Health and Substance Use: Dual Diagnosis* 4, 5-21.

Baralic I, Savic S, Alempijevic DM, Jecmenica DS, Sbutega-Milosevic G, Obradovic M (2010). Child homicide on the territory of Belgrade. *Child Abuse and Neglect* 34, 935-942.

Barber C, Hemenway D (2010). Too many or too few unintentional firearm deaths in official U.S. mortality data? *Accident Analysis and Prevention* 74, 724-731.

Barth A, Sögner L, Gnambs T, Kundi M, Reiner A, Winker R (2011). Socioeconomic factors and suicide: an analysis of 18 industrialized countries for the years 1983 through 2007. *Journal of Occupational & Environmental Medicine* 53, 313-317.

Bhupinder S, Kumara TK, Syed AM (2010). Completed suicides in the district of Timur Laut, Penang Island - A preliminary investigation of 3 years (2007-2009) prospective data. *Medical Journal of Malaysia* 65, 123-126.

Biswas S, Mondal KK, Som D, Roy SB, Haldar S (2010). Study of victims of organophosphorus compound poisoning: Evaluation after medicolegal autopsy. *Journal of the Indian Medical Association* 108, 568-570.

Boffin N, Bossuyt N, Vanthomme K, Van Casteren V (2011). Declining rates of suicidal behavior among general practice patients in Belgium: results from sentinel surveillance between 1993 and 2008. *Archives of Suicide Research* 15, 68-74.

Brenner B, Cheng D, Clark S, Camargo CA (2011). Positive association between altitude and suicide in 2584 U.S. Counties. *High Altitude Medicine & Biology*. Published online: 7 January 2011. doi:10.1089/ham.2010.1058.

Brooker C, Flynn J, Fox C (2010). Trends in self-inflicted deaths in prisons in England and Wales (2001-2008): towards targeted interventions. *Journal of Aggression, Conflict and Peace Research* 2, 34-43.

Brown D, Leyland AH (2010). Scottish mortality rates 2000-2002 by deprivation and small area population mobility. *Social Science and Medicine* 71, 1951-1957.

Bushe CJ, Taylor M, Haukka J (2010). Mortality in schizophrenia: A measurable clinical endpoint. *Journal of Psychopharmacology* 24, 17-25.

Byard R, Austin AE, Van Den Heuval C (2011). Suicide in forensic practice - an Australian perspective. *Australian Journal of Forensic Sciences* 43, 65-76.

Byard RW, Austin A, van den Heuvel C (2010). Suicide in Australia: Meta-analysis of rates and methods of suicide between 1988 and 2007. *The Medical Journal of Australia* 193, 432.

Canturk G, Canturk N, Teke HY, Erkol Z, Yavuz MS (2011). Suicidal deaths among children and adolescents in Ankara between 2001 and 2006. *Turkiye Klinikleri Journal of Medical Sciences* 30, 474-481.

Chan YC, Tse ML, Lau FL (2010). Hong Kong Poison Information Centre: Annual report 2008. *Hong Kong Journal of Emergency Medicine* 17, 395-405.

Chang SS, Sterne JA, Wheeler BW, Lu TH, Lin JJ, Gunnell D (2011). Geography of suicide in Taiwan: Spatial patterning and socioeconomic correlates. *Health Place*. Published online: 14 January 2011. doi:10.1016/j.healthplace.2011.01.003.

Chen J, Choi YJ, Sawada Y (2010). Joint liability borrowing and suicide: The case of Japan. *Economics Letters* 109, 69-71.

Chuang HL, Huang WC (2010). A re-examination of the suicide rates in Taiwan. *Social Indicators Research* 83, 465-485.

Cimino PJ, Williams TL, Fusaro A, Harruff R (2010). Case series of completed suicides by burning over a 13-year period. *Journal of Forensic Sciences* 56, 109-111.

Dieserud G, Gerhardsen RM, Van den Weghe H, Corbett K (2010). Adolescent suicide attempts in Baerum, Norway, 1984-2006. *Crisis* 31, 255-264.

El-Sayed AM, Tracy M, Scarborough P, Galea S (2011). Suicide among Arab-Americans. *PLoS ONE* 6, e14704.

Farzaneh E, Sayadrezai I, Mostafazadeh B, Seraji FN (2010). The epidemiologyic study of suicide in North West of Iran. *Drug Metabolism Reviews* 42, 128-129.

Fawcett K, Magee M, Timoney N, Mageean K, Yazid NH, Meehan J, Roche E, Hoey H, Doody B, Farrell C, Murphy AM (2010). Is child suicide on the increase in Ireland? *Acta Paediatrica* 99, 50-50.

Gal G, Goldberger N, Kabaha A, Haklai Z, Geraisy N, Gross R, Levav I (2011). Suicidal behavior among Muslim Arabs in Israel. *Social Psychiatry & Psychiatric Epidemiology*. Published online: 9 February 2011. doi:10.1007/s00127-010-0307-y.

Garrib A, Herbst AJ, Hosegood V, Newell ML (2011). Injury mortality in rural South Africa 2000 - 2007: Rates and associated factors. *Tropical Medicine & International Health*. Published online: 1 February 2011. doi:10.1111/j.1365-3156.2011.02730.x.

Goda NJW (2010). Suicide in Nazi Germany. *Journal of Contemporary History* 45, 883-885.

Gomperts E, Holtz J, Baker J, Geraghty S, Hudson M, Karp S, Osip J, Presley R (2010). Suicide among males with hemophilia in the US, 1998-2007. *Haemophilia* 16, 132-132.

Gonzalez-Andrade F, Lopez-Pulles R, Gascon S, Garcia Campayo J (2010). Epidemiological issues regarding suicides in Ecuador: an 8-year report. *Journal of Public Health*. Published online: 15 October 2010. doi:10.1007/s10389-010-0372-4.

Gunnell D, Wheeler B, Chang SS, Thomas B, Sterne JAC, Dorling D (2010). Changes in the geography of suicide in young men: England and Wales 1981-2005. *Journal of Epidemiology and Community Health*. Published online: 3 December 2010. doi:10.1136/jech.2009. 104000.

Gupta P, Gouda H, Honnungar R (2010). Profile of poisoning cases in north Karnataka. *Medico-Legal Update* 10, 61-63.

Hami H, Soulaymani A, Windy M, Mokhtari A, Soulaymani R (2011). Young men and suicide in Morocco. *Journal of Mens Health* 7, 327-327.

Hatcher S (2011). Young black females in three UK cities have higher rates of self-harm than other ethnic groups but are less likely to be referred for psychiatric care. *Evidence Based Mental Health* 14, 6.

Hawton K, Bergen H, Mahadevan S, Casey D, Simkin S (2010). Suicide and deliberate self-harm in Oxford University students over a 30-year period. *Social Psychiatry and Psychiatric Epidemiology.* Published online: 13 November 2010. doi:10.1007/s00127-010-0310-3.

Howard MO, Hall MT, Edwards JD, Vaughn MG, Perron BE, Winecker RE (2011). Suicide by asphyxiation due to helium inhalation. *American Journal of Forensic Medicine and Pathology* 32, 61-70.

Howell E, Decker S, Hogan S, Yemane S, Foster J (2010). Declining child mortality and continuing racial disparities in the era of the Medicaid and SCHIP insurance coverage expansions. *American Journal of Public Health* 100, 2500-2506.

Hugar BS, Harish S, Girish Chandra YP (2010). Pattern of homicidal deaths in children in Bangalore (2003-2009). *Indian Journal of Forensic Medicine and Toxicology* 4, 28-30.

Inoue K, Tanii H, Maeda A, Ishiguri T, Hosokawa K, Hagiwara K, Mori T, Ono Y (2010). The increase in suicide as a cause of death in men aged 40 to 59 years in Japan: A comparison between 1958 and 1998. *West Indian Medical Journal* 59, 115-116.

Jia CX, Zhang J (2011). Characteristics of young suicides by violent methods in rural China. *Journal of Forensic Sciences.* Published online: 3 February 2011. doi:10.1111/j.1556-4029.2010.01695.x.

Kapusta ND, Posch M, Niederkrotenthaler T, Fischer-Kern M, Etzersdorfer E, Sonneck G (2010). Availability of mental health service providers and suicide rates in Austria: a nationwide study. *Psychiatric Services* 61, 1198-1203.

Kar SM, Timsinha S, Agrawal P (2010). An epidemiological study of organophosphorus poisoning at Manipal Teaching Hospital, Pokhara, Nepal. *Journal of Indian Academy of Forensic Medicine* 32, 108-109.

Kim SY, Kim MH, Kawachi I, Cho Y (2011). Comparative epidemiology of suicide in South Korea and Japan: Effects of age, gender and suicide methods. *Crisis* 32, 5-14.

Klein S, Bischoff C, Schweitzer W (2010). Suicides in the Canton of Zurich. *Swiss Medical Weekly* 140, 35.

Krzyzaniak SM, Betz ME, Lowenstein SR, Hedegaard H (2010). Suicide epidemiology in Colorado: Comparison of Hispanic and Non-Hispanic populations. *Annals of Emergency Medicine* 56, 54-55.

Kumar S, Ragavan S, Baskar D, Revathy S (2011). A multidimensional and retrospective analysis of female suicide deaths in Chennai. *Indian Journal of Forensic Medicine and Toxicology* 4, 96-99.

Kwon C, Liu M, Quan H, Thoo V, Wiebe S, Jette N (2011). Motor vehicle accidents, suicides, and assaults in epilepsy: A population-based study. *Neurology* 76, 801-806.

Laberke PJ, Bartsch C (2010). Trends in methadone-related deaths in Zurich. *International Journal of Legal Medicine* 124, 381-385.

Ladouceur R (2011). Suicide among men. *Canadian Family Physician* 57, 148-148.

Lahti A, Rasanen P, Riala K, Keränen S, Hakko H (2011). Youth suicide trends in Finland, 1969-2008. *Journal of Child Psychology and Psychiatry,* Published online: 5 February 2011. doi:10.1111/j.1469-7610.2011.02369.x.

Lee WJ, Cha ES, Moon EK (2011). Disease prevalence and mortality among agricultural workers in Korea. *Journal of Korean Medical Science* 25, 112-118.

Lubin G, Werbeloff N, Halperin D, Shmushkevitch M, Weiser M, Knobler HY (2010). Decrease in suicide rates after a change of policy reducing access to firearms in adolescents: a naturalistic epidemiological study. *Suicide and Life-Threatening Behaviour* 40, 421-424.

Madden ME, Shapiro SL (2010). The methadone epidemic: Methadone-related deaths on the rise in Vermont. *The American Journal of Forensic Medicine and Pathology.* Published online: 27 October 2010. doi:10.1097/PAF.0b013e3181e8af3d.

Meel B (2011). Trends of suicide in the Transkei region of South Africa. *South African Journal of Psychiatry* 16, 109-110.

Lustenberger T, Inaba K, Schnüriger B, Barmparas G, Eberle BM, Lam L, Talving P, Demetriades D (2011). Gunshot injuries in the elderly: Patterns and outcomes. A national trauma databank analysis. *World Journal of Surgery* 35, 528-534.

Mäki N, Martikainen P (2010). A register-based study on excess suicide mortality among unemployed men and women during different levels of unemployment in Finland. *Journal of Epidemiology & Community Health.* Published online: 21 October 2010. doi:10.1136/jech.2009.105908.

Makhlouf F, Alvarez J-C, de la Grandmaison GL (2011). Suicidal and criminal immolations: An 18-year study and review of the literature. *Legal Medicine* 13, 98-102.

McFarland BH, Kaplan MS, Huguet N (2010). Datapoints: Self-inflicted deaths among women with U.S. Military service: A hidden epidemic? *Psychiatric Services* 61, 1177.

Meshram R, Adhya S, Sukul B (2010). Seasonal trends in suicide - A retrospective study. *Medico-Legal Update* 10, 78-79.

Milner A, McClure R, De Leo D (2010). Socio-economic determinants of suicide: an ecological analysis of 35 countries. *Social Psychiatry & Psychiatric Epidemiology.* Published online: 17 November 2010. doi:10.1007/s00127-010-0316-x.

Morii D, Miyagatani Y, Nakamae N, Murao M, Taniyama K (2010). Japanese experience of hydrogen sulfide: The suicide craze in 2008. *Journal of Occupational Medicine and Toxicology* 5, 28.

Muazzam S, Nasrullah M (2010). Macro determinants of cause-specific injury mortality in the OECD countries: an exploration of the importance of GDP and unemployment. *Journal of Community Health.* Published online: 30 November 2010. doi:10.1007/s10900-010-9343-5.

Murphy SM, Kieran I, Shaughnessy MO (2011). The trauma of a recession. *Irish Journal of Medical Science.* Published online: 23 March 2011. Doi: 10.1007/s11845-011-0705-5.

Nader IW, Pietschnig J, Niederkrotenthaler T, Kapusta ND, Sonneck G, Voracek M (2011). Suicide seasonality: Complex demodulation as a novel approach in epidemiologic analysis. *Plos One* 6, e17413.

Petersen L, Sorensen TIA, Mortensen EL, Andersen PK (2010). Excess mortality rate during adulthood among Danish adoptees. *PLoS One* 5, 12.

Pilgrim JL, Gerostamoulos D, Drummer OH (2010). Deaths involving contraindicated and inappropriate combinations of serotonergic drugs. *International Journal of Legal Medicine.* Published online: 1 December 2010. doi:10.1007/s00414-010-0536-3.

Qi X, Tong S, Hu W (2010). Spatial distribution of suicide in Queensland, Australia. *BMC Psychiatry* 10, 106.

Reynders A, Scheerder G, Van Audenhove C (2010). The reliability of suicide rates: An analysis of railway suicides from two sources in fifteen European countries. *Journal of Affective Disorders.* Published online: 1 December 2010. doi:10.1016/j.jad.2010.11.003.

Rintoul AC, Dobbin MD, Drummer OH, Ozanne-Smith J (2010). Increasing deaths involving oxycodone, Victoria, Australia, 2000-09. *Injury Prevention.* Published online: 16 December 2010. doi:10.1136/ip.2010.029611.

Rockett IR (2010). Counting suicides and making suicide count as a public health problem. *Crisis* 31, 227-230.

Rockett IR, Hobbs GR, De Leo D, Stack S, Frost JL, Ducatman AM, Kapusta ND, Walker RL (2010). Suicide and unintentional poisoning mortality trends in the United States, 1987-2006: Two unrelated phenomena? *BMC Public Health* 10, 705.

Sancho FM, Ruiz CN (2011). Risk of suicide amongst dentists: Myth or reality? *International Dental Journal* 60, 411-418.

Schmitt MW, Williams TL, Woodard KR, Harruff RC (2011). Trends in suicide by carbon monoxide inhalation in King County, Washington: 1996-2009. *Journal of Forensic Sciences.* Published online: 3 February 2010. doi:10.1111/j.1556-4029.2010.01688.x.

Selvakumar V, Srinivasa RN, Baskar D, Revathy S (2010). Female suicide deaths - A multidimensional retrospective analysis. *Indian Journal of Forensic Medicine and Toxicology* 4, 47-52.

Shang TF, Chen PC, Wang JD (2010). Mortality of doctors in Taiwan. *Occupational Medicine* 61, 29-32.

Sheikhazadi A, Saberi Anary SH, Ghadyani MH (2010). Nonfire carbon monoxide-related deaths: A survey in Tehran, Iran (2002-2006). *American Journal of Forensic Medicine and Pathology* 31, 359-363.

Sheppard G, Quinlivan L, Guerandel A, Farrell B, Malone K (2010). Suicide, statistics and the state: A study of Dublin city suicide deaths 2006-2007. *Irish Journal of Medical Science* 179, 2.

Shen J, Liu M, Zhou M, Li W (2011). Causes of death among active leprosy patients in China. *International Journal of Dermatology* 50, 57-60.

Shrivastava P, Som D, Nandy S, Saha I, Pal PB, Ray TG, Haldar S (2010). Profile of post-mortem cases conducted at a morgue of a tertiary care hospital in Kolkata. *Journal of the Indian Medical Association* 108, 730-733.

Sobnach S, Castillo F, Blanco Vinent R, Kahn D, Bhyat A (2011). Penetrating cardiac injury following sewing needle ingestion. *Heart, Lung and Circulation.* Published online: 9 February 2011. doi:10.1016/j.hlc.2011.01.006.

Sonar V (2010). A retrospective study of prison deaths in western Maharashtra (2001-2008). *Medico-Legal Update* 10, 112-114.

Stefulj J, Mokrovic G, Hranilovic D, Bordukalo-Niksic T, Bakula M, Kubat M, Jernej B (2011). Functional promoter polymorphism of the neuronal isoform of tryptophan hydroxylase (Tph2) in suicide. *Psychiatry Research* 186, 446-447.

Stickley A, Jukkala T, Norström T (2011). Alcohol and suicide in Russia, 1870-1894 and 1956-2005: evidence for the continuation of a harmful drinking culture across time? *Journal of Studies on Alcohol and Drugs* 72, 341-347.

Strand LA, Martinsen JI, Koefoed VF, Sommerfelt-Pettersen J, Grimsrud TK (2011). Cause-specific mortality and cancer incidence among 28 300 Royal Norwegian Navy servicemen followed for more than 50 years. *Scandinavian Journal of Work Environment & Health.* Published online: 5 January 2011.

Sumelahti M-L, Hakama M, Elovaara I, Pukkala E (2010). Causes of death among patients with multiple sclerosis. *Multiple Sclerosis* 16, 1437-1442.

Taghaddosinejad F, Sheikhazadi A, Behnoush B, Reshadati J, Anary SHS (2010). A survey of suicide by burning in Tehran, Iran. *Acta Medica Iranica* 48, 266-272.

Teoh SH, Ang SB, Tan BY, Lim PH, Tan CY (2009). An overview of the status of men's health in Singapore. *Journal of Men's Health* 6, 307-316.

Turillazzi E, Vacchiano G, Luna-Maldonado A, Neri M, Pomara C, Rabozzi R, Riezzo I, Fineschi V (2010). Tryptase, CD15 and IL-15 as reliable markers for the determination of soft and hard ligature marks vitality. *Histology and Histopathology* 25, 1539-1546.

Värnik A, Sisask M, Värnik P, Wu J, Kõlves K, Arensman E, Maxwell M, Reisch T, Gusmäo R, Van Audenhove C, Scheerder G, van der Feltz-Cornelis CM, Coffey C, Kopp M, Szekely A, Roskar S, Hegerl U (2011). Drug suicide: A sex-equal cause of death in 16 European countries. *BMC Public Health* 11, 61.

Wasserman I, Stack S (2011). Race, urban context, and Russian roulette: findings from the national violent death reporting system, 2003-2006. *Suicide and Life-Threatening Behavior* 41, 33-40.

Yeh C, Lester D (2010). Suicides from the Golden Gate Bridge: Have they changed over time? *Psychological Reports* 107, 491-492.

Yip PSF, Caine ED (2010). Employment status and suicide: The complex relationships between changing unemployment rates and death rates. *Journal of Epidemiology and Community Health.* Published online: 28 November 2011. doi:10.1136/jech.2010.110726.

Yood MU, DeLorenze G, Quesenberry CP, Tsai AL, Phillips S, Willey VJ, Niemcryk SJ, Wells K, Skovron ML, Cziraky MJ, Carson W, Oliveria SA (2010). Epidemiologic study of aripiprazole use and the incidence of suicide events. *Pharmacoepidemiology and Drug Safety* 19, 1124-1130.

Yoshida K, Noguchi M, Mine T, Komatsu N, Yutani S, Ueno T, Yanagimoto H, Kawano K, Itoh K, Yamada A (2011). Characteristics of severe adverse events after peptide vaccination for advanced cancer patients: Analysis of 500 cases. *Oncology Reports* 25, 57-62.

Yur'yev A, Värnik A, Värnik P, Sisask M, Leppik L (2010). Employment status influences suicide mortality in Europe. *International Journal of Social Psychiatry.* Published online: November 18, 2010. doi:10.1177/0020764010387059.

Zariwala RC, Mehta TJ, Bhise RS (2010). A retrospective study of Aluminium Phosphide poisoning cases in Ahmadabad region. *Medico-Legal Update* 10, 80-81.

Zhou L, Liu L, Chang L, Li L (2011). Poisoning deaths in central China (Hubei): A 10-year retrospective study of forensic autopsy cases. *Journal of Forensic Sciences* 56, 234-237.

Risk and protective factors

Abdel-Baki A, Lesage A, Nicole L, Cossette M, Salvat E, Lalonde P (2011). Schizophrenia, an illness with bad outcome: Myth or reality? *Canadian Journal of Psychiatry* 56, 92-101.

Adinkrah M (2010). Better dead than dishonored: Masculinity and male suicidal behavior in contemporary Ghana. *Social Science & Medicine.* Published online: 29 October 2010. doi:10.1016/j.socscimed.2010.10.011.

Asscheman H, Giltay EJ, Megens JA, de Ronde W, Van Trotsenburg M, Gooren LJ (2011). A long-term follow-up study of mortality in transsexuals receiving treatment with cross-sex hormones. *European Journal of Endocrinology.* Published onle: 25 January 2011. doi:10.1530/EJE-10-1038.

Atilola GO, Akpa OM, Komolafe IO (2010). HIV/AIDS and the long-distance truck drivers in south-west Nigeria: A cross-sectional survey on the knowledge, attitude, risk behaviour and beliefs of truckers. *Journal of Infection and Public Health* 3, 166-178.

Baller RD, Levchak P, Schultz M (2010). "The great transformation" and suicide: Local and long-lasting effects of 1930 bank suspensions. *Suicide and Life-Threatening Behavior* 40, 574-586.

Barnes AJ (2011). Attachment-based family therapy reduces suicidal ideation in adolescents. *Evidence-Based Mental Health* 14, 8.

Bennett MR (2011). The prefrontal-limbic network in depression: modulation by hypothalamus, basal ganglia and midbrain. *Progress in Neurobiology* 93, 468-487.

Bern-Klug M (2011). Psychosocial concerns in the context of geriatric palliative care in nursing homes: enlisting the skills of social workers. *Topics in Geriatric Rehabilitation* 27, 62-70.

Bhugra D (2010). Commentary: Religion, religious attitudes and suicide. *International Journal of Epidemiology* 39, 1496-1498.

Bhui K (2010). Commentary: Religious, cultural and social influences on suicidal behaviour. *International Journal of Epidemiology* 39, 1495-1496.

Bjorkenstam C, Weitoft GR, Hjern A, Nordstrom P, Hallqvist J, Ljung R (2010). School grades, parental education and suicide - A national register-based cohort study. *Journal of Epidemiology and Community Health*. Published online: 19 October 2010. doi:10.1136/jech.2010.117226.

Black DW, Gunter T, Loveless P, Allen J, Sieleni B (2010). Antisocial personality disorder in incarcerated offenders: Psychiatric comorbidity and quality of life. *Annals of Clinical Psychiatry* 22, 113-120.

Bossarte RM, Claassen CA, Knox KL (2010). Evaluating evidence of risk for suicide among veterans. *Military Medicine* 175, 703-704.

Braswell H, Kushner HI (2010). Suicide, social integration, and masculinity in the US military. *Social Science & Medicine*. Published online: 8 October 2010. doi:10.1016/j.socscimed.2010.07.031.

Brownell MD, Derksen SA, Jutte DP, Roos NP, Ekuma O, Yallop L (2010). Socio-economic inequities in children's injury rates: has the gradient changed over time? *Canadian Journal of Public Health* 101 (Suppl 3), 28-31.

Butler AW, Breen G, Tozzi F, Craddock N, Gill M, Korszun A, Maier W, Middleton LT, Mors O, Owen MJ, Perry J, Preisig M, Rice JP, Rietschel M, Jones L, Farmer AE, Lewis CM, McGuffin P (2010). A genomewide linkage study on suicidality in major depressive disorder confirms evidence for linkage to 2p12. *American Journal of Medical Genetics. Part B, Neuropsychiatric Genetics* 153B, 1465-1473.

Byard RW, Austin AE, van den Heuvel C (2011). Characteristics of asphyxial deaths in adolescence. *Journal of Forensic and Legal Medicine*. Published online: 8 February 2011. doi:10.1016/j.jflm.2011.01.011.

Ceskova E, Prikryl R, Kasparek T (2011). Suicides in males after the first episode of schizophrenia. *Journal of Nervous and Mental Disease* 199, 62-64.

Chan ACY, Beh PSL, Broadhurst RG (2010). To flee or not: Postkilling responses among intimate partner homicide offenders in Hong Kong. *Homicide Studies* 14, 400-418.

Chen CK, Tsai YC, Hsu HJ, Wu IW, Sun CY, Chou CC, Lee CC, Tsai CR, Wu MS, Wang LJ (2010). Depression and suicide risk in hemodialysis patients with chronic renal failure. *Psychosomatics* 51, 528.

Chen VC, Tan HK, Chen CY, Chen TH, Liao LR, Lee CT, Dewey M, Stewart R, Prince M, Cheng AT (2011). Mortality and suicide after self-harm: Community cohort study in Taiwan. *British Journal of Psychiatry* 198, 31-36.

Chen YY, Chen F, Yip PS (2010). The impact of media reporting of suicide on actual suicides in Taiwan, 2002-05. *Journal of Epidemiology and Community Health.* Published online: 5 December 2010. doi:10.1136/jech.2010.117903.

Chen Y-Y, Yip PSF, Lee C, Fan H-F, Fu K-W (2011). Economic fluctuations and suicide: A comparison of Taiwan and Hong Kong. *Social Science and Medicine* 71, 2083-2090.

Cheng H-T, Yeh C-C, Hsieh C-H (2011). Acute gastric perforation after butane ingestion. *American Surgeon* 76, 165-167.

Church MK, Maurer M, Simons FE, Bindslev-Jensen C, van Cauwenberge P, Bousquet J, Holgate ST, Zuberbier T (2011). Risk of first-generation H(1)-antihistamines: a GA(2)LEN position paper. *Allergy* 65, 459-466.

Classen TJ, Dunn RA (2011). The effect of job loss and unemployment duration on suicide risk in the United States: a new look using mass-layoffs and unemployment duration. *Health Economics.* Published online: 14 February 2011. doi:10.1002/hec.1719.

Cornaggia CM, Beghi M, Pavone F, Barale F (2011). Aggression in psychiatry wards: A systematic review. *Psychiatry Research.* Published online: 13 January 2011. doi:10.1016/j.psychres.2010.12.024.

Cousteaux AS, Pan Ké Shon JL (2010). Is Ill-being gendered? Suicide, risk for suicide, depression and alcohol dependence. *Revue Française de Sociologie: An annual English Selection* 51, 3-40.

Cox L (2010). Queensland Aborigines, multiple realities and the social sources of suffering, Part 2: suicide, spirits and symbolism. *Oceania* 80, 241-262.

Crocq MA, Naber D, Lader MH, Thibaut F, Drici M, Everitt B, Hall GC, Le Jeunne C, Mittoux A, Peuskens J, Priori S, Sturkenboom M, Thomas SHL, Tanghoj P, Toumi M, Mann R, Moore ND (2010). Suicide attempts in a prospective cohort of patients with schizophrenia treated with sertindole or risperidone. *European Neuropsychopharmacology* 20, 829-838.

Cryan J, Cathiin N, Curtis M, Cassidy M, Brett FM (2011). The contribution of alcohol to fatal traumatic head injuries in the forensic setting. *Irish Medical Journal* 103, 1-2.

Davila G, Berthier ML, Kulisevsky J, Chacon SJ (2010). Suicide and attempted suicide in Tourette's syndrome: A case series with literature review. *Journal of Clinical Psychiatry* 71, 1401-1402.

Davis R (2010). Domestic violence-related deaths. *Journal of Aggression, Conflict and Peace Research* 2, 44-52.

Davis SJ, Koch DS, Mbugua A, Johnson A (2011). Recognizing suicide risk in consumers with HIV/AIDS. *Journal of Rehabilitation* 77, 14-19.

Denneson LM, Basham C, Dickinson KC, Crutchfield MC, Millet L, Shen X, Dobscha SK (2010). Suicide risk assessment and content of VA health care contacts before suicide completion by veterans in Oregon. *Psychiatric Services* 61, 1192-1197.

Desmyter S, Van Heeringen C, Audenaert K (2011). Structural and functional neuroimaging studies of the suicidal brain. *Progress in Neuro-Psychopharmacology and Biological Psychiatry.* Published online: 6 January 2011. doi:10.1016/j.pnpbp.2010.12.026.

Dhejne C, Lichtenstein P, Boman M, Johansson, ALV, Langstrom N, Landen M (2011). Long-term follow-up of transsexual persons undergoing sex reassignment surgery: cohort study in Sweden. *Plos One* 6, e16885.

Dombrovski AY, Szanto K, Siegle GJ, Wallace ML, Forman SD, Sahakian B, Reynolds CF 3rd, Clark L (2011). Lethal forethought: delayed reward discounting differentiates high- and low-lethality suicide attempts in old age. *Biological Psychiatry.* Published online: 15 February 2011. doi:10.1016/j.biopsych.2010.12.025.

Drazkowski JF, Sirven JI (2011). Motor vehicle crashes, suicides, and assaults: The dangers of epilepsy? *Neurology* 76, 770-771.

Dreyer L, Kendall S, Danneskiold-Samsoe B, Bartels EM, Bliddal H (2010). Mortality in a cohort of Danish patients with fibromyalgia: Increased frequency of suicide. *Arthritis Rheumatism* 62, 3101-3108.

Duggan M, Hjalmarsson R, Jacob BA (2010). The short-term and localized effect of gun shows: Evidence from California and Texas. *The Review of Economics and Statistics*. Published online: 9 September 2010. doi:10.1162/REST_a_00120.

Dutta R, Murray RM, Allardyce J, Jones PB, Boydell J (2011). Early risk factors for suicide in an epidemiological first episode psychosis cohort. *Schizophrenia Research* 126, 11-19.

Dutta R, Murray RM, Hotopf M, Allardyce J, Jones PB, Boydell J (2010). Reassessing the long-term risk of suicide after a first episode of psychosis. *Archives of General Psychiatry* 67, 1230-1237.

Eichelman B (2010). Borderline personality disorder, PTSD, and suicide. *American Journal of Psychiatry* 167, 1152-1154.

Eliason M (2011). Introduction to special issue on suicide, mental health, and youth development. *Journal of Homosexuality* 58, 4-9.

El Naggar ARM, El Mahdy MN (2011). Zinc phosphide toxicity with a trial of tranexamic acid in its management. *Journal of Advanced Research*. Published online: 10 February 2011. doi:10.1016/j.jare.2011.01.001.

Emerging Risk Factors Collaboration: Seshasai SR, Kaptoge S, Thompson A, Di Angelantonio E, Gao P, Sarwar N, Whincup PH, Mukamal KJ, Gillum RF, Holme I, Njølstad I, Fletcher A, Nilsson P, Lewington S, Collins R, Gudnason V, Thompson SG, Sattar N, Selvin E, Hu FB, Danesh J (2011). Diabetes mellitus, fasting glucose, and risk of cause-specific death. *The New England Journal of Medicine* 364, 829-841.

Exeter DJ, Boyle PJ, Norman P (2010). Deprivation (im)mobility and cause-specific premature mortality in Scotland. *Social Science & Medicine* 72, 389-397.

Eytan A (2011). Religion and mental health during incarceration: a systematic literature review. *Psychiatric Quarterly* 1, 9.

Fazel S, Baillargeon J (2010). The health of prisoners. *The Lancet*. Published online: 19 November 2010. doi:10.1016/S0140-6736(10)61053-7.

Fiori LM, Bureau A, Labbe A, Croteau J, Noël S, Mérette C, Turecki G (2011). Global gene expression profiling of the polyamine system in suicide completers. *International Journal of Neuropsychopharmacology*. Published online: 5 January 2011. doi:10.1017/S1461145710 001574.

Fishbain DA, Bruns D, Lewis JE, Disorbio JM, Gao J, Meyer LJ (2010). Predictors of homicide-suicide affirmation in acute and chronic pain patients. *Pain Medicine* 12, 127–137.

Foster EM (2011). Deployment and the citizen soldier: Need and resilience. *Medical Care* 49, 301-312.

Foster T (2011). Adverse life events proximal to adult suicide: a synthesis of findings from psychological autopsy studies. *Archives of Suicide Research* 15, 1–15.

Fountoulakis KN, Vieta E, Schmidt F (2010). Aripiprazole monotherapy in the treatment of bipolar disorder: A meta-analysis. *Journal of Affective Disorders*. Published online: 30 October 2010. doi:10.1016/j.jad.2010.10.018.

Fudalej S, Ilgen M, Fudalej M, Kostrzewa G, Barry K, Wojnar M, Krajewski P, Blow F, Ploski R (2011). Association between tryptophan hydroxylase 2 gene polymorphism and completed suicide. *Suicide and Life-Threatening Behavior* 40, 553-560.

Garcia-Sevilla JA, Alvaro-Bartolome M, Diez-Alarcia R, Ramos-Miguel A, Puigdemont D, Perez V, Alvarez E, Meana JJ (2010). Reduced platelet G protein-coupled receptor kinase 2 in major depressive disorder: Antidepressant treatment-induced upregulation of GRK2 protein discriminates between responder and non-responder patients. *European Neuropsychopharmacology* 20, 721-730.

Gaygisiz E (2010). National income, life satisfaction, and male-female suicide ratio in industrialised countries. *Perceptual and Motor Skills* 2, 433-436.

Glatt SJ, Cohen OS, Faraone SV, Tsuang MT (2011). Dysfunctional gene splicing as a potential contributor to neuropsychiatric disorders. *American Journal of Medical Genetics Part B: Neuropsychiatric Genetics*. Published online: 22 March 2011. doi: 10.1002/ajmg.b.31181.

Goeschel C (2010). Suicide in Nazi concentration camps, 1933-9. *Journal of Contemporary History* 45, 628-648.

Goldblatt MJ, Maltsberger JT (2011). Self-harming behavior and suicidality: suicide risk assessment. *Suicide and Life-Threatening Behaviour*. Published online: 10 February 2011. doi:10.1111/j.1943-278X.2011.00004.x.

Gradus JL, Qin P, Lincoln AK, Miller M, Lawler E, Sorensen HT, Lash TL (2011). Corrigendum: Acute stress reaction and completed suicide. *International Journal of Epidemiology* 40, 266-266.

Graham J, Banaschewski T, Buitelaar J, Coghill D, Danckaerts M, Dittmann RW, Döpfner M, Hamilton R, Hollis C, Holtmann M, Hulpke-Wette M, Lecendreux M, Rosenthal E, Rothenberger A, Santosh P, Sergeant J, Simonoff E, Sonuga-Barke E, Wong IC, Zuddas A, Steinhausen HC, Taylor E; European Guidelines Group (2011). European guidelines on managing adverse effects of medication for ADHD. *European Child and Adolescent Psychiatry* 20, 17-37.

Gruere G, Sengupta D (2011). Bt cotton and farmer suicides in India: An evidence-based assessment. *Journal of Development Studies* 47, 316-337.

Gunnell D, Löfving S, Gustafsson JE, Allebeck P (2011). School performance and risk of suicide in early adulthood: Follow-up of two national cohorts of Swedish schoolchildren. *Journal of Affective Disorder*. Published online: 4 February 2011. doi:10.1016/j.jad.2011.01.002,

Haas AP, Eliason M, Mays VM, Mathy RM, Cochran SD, D'Augelli AR, Silverman MM, Fisher PW, Hughes T, Rosario M, Russell ST, Malley E, Reed J, Litts DA, Haller E, Sell RL, Remafedi G, Bradford J, Beautrais AL, Brown GK, Diamond GM, Friedman MS, Garofalo R, Turner MS, Hollibaugh A, Clayton PJ (2011). Suicide and suicide risk in lesbian, gay, bisexual, and transgender populations: review and recommendations. *Journal of Homosexuality* 58, 10-51.

Haffner WH (2010). Veteran suicide. *Military Medicine* 175, 1.

Haines J, Williams CL, Lester D (2010). Completed suicides: Is there method in their madness? Correlates of choice of method for suicide in an Australian sample of suicides. *Clinical Neuropsychiatry* 7, 133-140.

Haliburn J (2010). Adolescent suicide and SSRI antidepressants. *Australasian Psychiatry* 18, 587-587.

Hamid H, Devinsky O, Vickrey BG, Berg AT, Bazil CW, Langfitt JT, Walczak TS, Sperling MR, Shinnar S, Spencer SS (2011). Suicide outcomes after resective epilepsy surgery. *Epilepsy Behaviour*. Published online: 19 February 2011. doi:10.1016/j.yebeh.2010.12.031.

Hardt J, Johnson JG (2010). Suicidality, depression, major and minor negative life events: a mediator model. *Psychosocial Medicine* 7, 5.

Hays JT, Ebbert JO (2010). Adverse effects and tolerability of medications for the treatment of tobacco use and dependence. *Drugs* 70, 2357-2372.

Henderson M, Hotopf M, Shah I, Hayes RD, Kuh D (2011). Psychiatric disorder in early adulthood and risk of premature mortality in the 1946 British Birth Cohort. *BMC Psychiatry* 11, 37.

Hesdorffer DC, Berg AT, Kanner AM (2010). An update on antiepileptic drugs and suicide: Are there definitive answers yet? *Epilepsy Currents* 10, 137-145.

Hicks MH-R, Dardagan H, Serdan G, Bagnall PM, Sloboda JA, Spagat M (2011). Violent deaths of Iraqi civilians, 2003-2008: Analysis by perpetrator, weapon, time, and location. *PLoS Medicine* 8, 2.

Hoffer TA, Shelton JLE, Behnke S, Erdberg P (2010). Exploring the impact of child sex offender suicide. *Journal of Family Violence* 25, 777-786.

Holm JS, Brixen K, Andries A, Hørder K, Støving RK (2011). Reflections on involuntary treatment in the prevention of fatal anorexia nervosa: A review of five cases. *International Journal of Eating Disorders*. Published online: 22 February 2011. doi:10.1002/eat.20915.

Hor K, Taylor M (2010). Suicide and schizophrenia: A systematic review of rates and risk factors. *Journal of Psychopharmacology* 24, 81-90.

Huas C, Caille A, Godart N, Foulon C, Pham-Scottez A, Divac S, Dechartres A, Lavoisy G, Guelfi JD, Rouillon F, Falissard B (2010). Factors predictive of ten-year mortality in severe anorexia nervosa patients. *Acta Psychiatrica Scandinavica* 123, 62-70.

Hundekari IA, Suryakar AN, Rathi DB (2010). Biochemical changes in acute organophosphorus pesticide poisoning in Bijapur, Karnataka. *Indian Journal of Forensic Medicine and Toxicology* 4, 65-67.

Hunt IM, Windfuhr K, Swinson N, Shaw J, Appleby L, Kapur N (2011). Electroconvulsive therapy and suicide among the mentally ill in England: A national clinical survey. *Psychiatry Research*. Published online: 4 January 2011. doi: 10.1016/j.psychres.2010.12.014.

Ide N, Wyder M, Kolves K, De Leo D (2010). Separation as an important risk factor for suicide: a systematic review. *Journal of Family Issues* 31, 1689-1716.

Ilgen MA, Bohnert ASB, Ignacio RV, McCarthy JF, Valenstein MM, Kim HM, Blow FC (2010). Psychiatric diagnoses and risk of suicide in veterans. *Archives of General Psychiatry* 67, 1152-1158.

Ilgen MA, Zivin K, Austin KL, Bohnert ASB, Czyz EK, Valenstein M, Kilbourne AM (2010). Severe pain predicts greater likelihood of subsequent suicide. *Suicide and Life-Threatening Behavior* 40, 597-608.

Inelmen EM, Gazerro M, Inelmen E, Sergi G, Manzato E (2010). Alcohol consumption and suicide: A country-level study. *Italian Journal of Public Health* 7, 226-234.

Inoue K, Fukunaga T, Okazaki Y, Fujita Y, Abe S, Ono Y (2011). Causes of suicide in middle-aged men in prefectures in Japan during the recent spike in suicides. *West Indian Medical Journal* 59, 342-343.

Johnson RM, Barber C, Azrael D, Clark DE, Hemenway D (2011). Who are the owners of firearms used in adolescent suicides? *Suicide and Life-Threatening Behavior* 40, 609-611.

Johnson TV, Garlow SJ, Brawley OW, Master VA (2011). Peak window of suicides occurs within the first month of diagnosis: implications for clinical oncology. *Psychooncology*. Published online: 24 January 2011. doi:10.1002/pon.1905.

Jollant F, Lawrence NL, Olié E, Guillaume S, Courtet P (2011). The suicidal mind and brain: A review of neuropsychological and neuroimaging studies. *World Journal of Biological and Psychiatry*. Published online: 6 March 2011. doi:10.3109/15622975.2011.556200.

Judd F, Jackson H, Komiti A, Bell R, Fraser C (2010). The profile of suicide: changing or changeable? *Social Psychiatry & Psychiatric Epidemiology.* Published online: 30 October 2010. doi:10.1007/s00127-010-0306-z.

Kale NM, Mankar DM (2010). Socio-economic dimensions of suicidal and non-suicidal farmers of Western Vidarbha region. *Journal of Rural Development* 29, 425-433.

Kalkman HO (2011). Circumstantial evidence for a role of glutamine-synthetase in suicide. *Medical Hypotheses.* Published online: 22 March 2011. doi:10.1016/j.mehy.2011.03.005.

Kaniecki RG (2010). Anticonvulsant medications and the risk of suicide, attempted suicide, or violent death: Comments. *Headache* 50, 1621-1622.

Kapusta ND, Voracek M, Etzersdorfer E, Niederkrotenthaler T, Dervic K, Plener PL, Schneider E, Stein C, Sonneck G (2010). Characteristics of police officer suicides in the federal Austrian police corps. *Crisis* 31, 265-271.

Karch D, Nunn KC (2011). Characteristics of elderly and other vulnerable adult victims of homicide by a caregiver: national violent death reporting system - 17 US States, 2003-2007. *Journal of Interpersonal Violence* 26, 137-157.

Karege F, Perroud N, Burkhardt S, Fernandez R, Ballmann E, La Harpe R, Malafosse A (2011). Alterations in phosphatidylinositol 3-kinase activity and PTEN phosphatase in the prefrontal cortex of depressed suicide victims. *Neuropsychobiology* 63, 224-231.

Khan MM (2010). Commentary: When the cameras disappear: acute stress and suicide. *International Journal of Epidemiology* 39, 1484-1485.

Kittirattanapaiboon P, Mahatnirunkul S, Booncharoen H, Thummawomg P, Dumrongchai U, Chutha W (2010). Long-term outcomes in methamphetamine psychosis patients after first hospitalisation. *Drug and Alcohol Review* 29, 456-461.

Kjølseth I, Ekeberg O, Steihaug S (2010). Elderly people who committed suicide — their contact with the health service: What did they expect, and what did they get? *Aging & Mental Health* 14, 938-946.

Kohler IV, Preston SH (2011). Ethnic and religious differentials in Bulgarian mortality, 1993-98. *Population Studies* 2, 23.

Kohyama J (2011). Sleep, serotonin, and suicide in Japan. *Journal of Physiological Anthropology* 30, 1-8.

Kohyama J (2011). Sleep debt and serotonin. A response to a comment on my hypothesis. *Medical Hypotheses* 76, 304.

Kraft TL, Jobes DA, Lineberry TW, Conrad A, Kung S (2010). Why suicide? Perceptions of suicidal inpatients and reflections of clinical researchers. *Archives of Suicide Research* 14, 375-382.

Kral MJ, Idlout L, Minore JB, Dyck RJ, Kirmayer LJ (2011). Unikkaartuit: Meanings of well-being, unhappiness, health, and community change among Inuit in Nunavut, Canada. *American Journal of Community Psychology.* Published online: 13 March 2011. doi:10.1007/s10464-011-9431-4.

Kristensen P, Gravseth HM, Bjerkedal T (2010). Influence of early life factors on social inequalities in psychiatric outcomes among young adult Norwegian men. *European Journal of Public Health* 20, 517-523.

Kunrath S, Baumert J, Ladwig KH (2010). Increasing railway suicide acts after media coverage of a fatal railway accident? An ecological study of 747 suicidal acts. *Journal of Epidemiology and Community Health.* Published online: 19 October 2010. doi:10.1136/jech.2009.098293.

Labonté B, Turecki G (2010). The epigenetics of suicide: explaining the biological effects of early life environmental adversity. *Archives of Suicide Research* 14, 291-310.

LaPorta LD (2010). Occupational stress in oral and maxillofacial surgeons: tendencies, traits, and triggers. *Oral and Maxillofacial Surgery Clinics of North America* 22, 495-502.

Large M, Smith G, Sharma S, Nielssen O, Singh SP (2011). Systematic review and meta-analysis of the clinical factors associated with the suicide of psychiatric in-patients. *Acta Psychiatrica Scandinavica*. Published online: 25 January 2011. doi:10.1111/j.1600-0447.2010.01672.x.

Larsen KK, Agerbo E, Christensen B, Søndergaard J, Vestergaard M (2010). Myocardial infarction and risk of suicide: A population-based case-control study. *Circulation* 122, 2388-2393.

Leigh A, Neill C (2010). Do gun buybacks save lives? Evidence from panel data. *American Law and Economics Review* 12, 509-557.

Lemogne C, Fossati P, Limosin F, Nabi H, Encrenaz G, Bonenfant S, Consoli SM (2010). Cognitive hostility and suicide. *Acta Psychiatrica Scandinavica*. Published online: 28 December 2010. doi:10.1111/j.1600-0447.2010.01658.x.

Lester D (2010). Brain parasites and suicide. *Psychological Report* 107, 424.

Lester D (2010). Predicting European suicide rates with physiological indices. *Psychological Reports* 107, 713-714.

Lettau LA (2011). Sleep, depression and suicide. *Sleep Medicine* 12, 198.

Li Z, Page A, Martin G, Taylor R (2011). Attributable risk of psychiatric and socio-economic factors for suicide from individual-level, population-based studies: A systematic review. *Social Science and Medicine* 72, 608-616.

Lord VB, Sloop MW (2010). Suicide by cop: Police shooting as a method of self-harming. *Journal of Criminal Justice* 38, 889-895.

Löfman S, Rasanen P, Hakko H, Mainio A (2011). Suicide among persons with back pain: A population-based study of 2,310 suicide victims in Northern Finland. *Spine*. Published online: 5 January 2011. doi:10.1097/BRS.0b013e3181f2f08a.

Ludvigsson JF, Sellgren C, Runeson B, Langstrom N, Lichtenstein P (2011). Increased suicide risk in coeliac disease - A Swedish nationwide cohort study. *Digestive and Liver Disease*. Published online: 16 March 2011. Doi: 10.1016/j.dld.2011.02.009.

Machado RA, Espinosa AG, Melendrez D, Gonzalez YR, Garcia VF, Rodriguez YQ (2011). Suicidal risk and suicide attempts in people treated with antiepileptic drugs for epilepsy. *Seizure*. Published online: 26 January 2011. doi:10.1016/j.seizure.2010.12.010.

Maier C, Gockel H-H, Gruhn K, Krumova EK, Edel M-A (2011). Increased risk of suicide under intrathecal ziconotide treatment? - A warning. *Pain* 152, 235-237.

Maimon D, Browning CR, Brooks-Gunn J (2010). Collective efficacy, family attachment, and urban adolescent suicide attempts. *Journal of Health and Social Behavior* 51, 307-324.

Maltsberger JT, Ronningstam E, Weinberg I, Schechter M, Goldblatt MJ (2010). Suicide fantasy as a life-sustaining recourse. *Journal of the American Academy of Psychoanalysis and Dynamic Psychiatry* 38, 611-624.

McCann SJ (2010). Suicide, big five personality factors, and depression at the American state level. *Archives for Suicide Research* 14, 368-374.

McCrory P (2011). Sports concussion and the risk of chronic neurological impairment. *Clinical Journal of Sport Medicine* 21, 6-12.

McKee GR, Bramante A (2010). Maternal filicide and mental illness in Italy: A comparative study. *Journal of Psychiatry and Law* 38, 271-282.

McLean LM, Hales S (2010). Childhood trauma, attachment style, and a couple's experience of terminal cancer: Case study. *Palliative & Supportive Care* 8, 227-233.

Melkane AE, Matar NE, Haddad AC, Zoghbi AC (2010). Suicidal hanging attempt: Poor symptoms for a potentially lethal injury. *The Journal of Trauma* 69, 36.

Mills PD, Huber SJ, Vince Watts B, Bagian JP (2011). Systemic vulnerabilities to suicide among veterans from the iraq and afghanistan conflicts: review of case reports from a National Veterans Affairs Database. *Suicide and Life-Threatening Behaviour* 41, 21-32.

Miranda D, Magno A, Neves F, Pimenta G, Mello M, De Marco L, Correa H, Romano-Silva M (2010). Association of akt1 but not aktip genetic variants with increased risk for suicidal behavior in bipolar patients. *International Journal of Neuropsychopharmacology* 13, 170-170.

Mula M, Sander JW (2010). Antiepileptic drugs and suicide risk: could stopping medications pose a greater hazard? *Expert Review of Neurotherapeutics* 10, 1775-1776.

Mulder RT (2010). Antidepressants and suicide: population benefit vs. individual risk. *Acta Psychiatrica Scandinavica* 122, 442-443.

Mustak MS, Hegde ML, Dinesh A, Britton GB, Berrocal R, Rao KS, Shamasundar NM, Rao KSJ, Rao TSS (2010). Evidence of altered DNA integrity in the brain regions of suicidal victims of Bipolar Depression. *Indian Journal of Psychiatry* 52, 220-228.

Nasseri K, Moulton LH (2011). Patterns of death in the first and second generation immigrants from selected Middle Eastern countries in California. *Journal of Immigrant and Minority Health* 13, 361-370.

Nell R, Salvatore T (2011). Suicide factors: unsafe or safer? *Current Psychiatry* 10, 35-36.

Nikfar S, Rahimi R, Abdollahi M (2010). A meta-analysis of the efficacy and tolerability of interferon- in multiple sclerosis, overall and by drug and disease type. *Clinical Therapeutics* 32, 1871-1888.

Nyhlen A, Fridell M, Hesse M, Krantz P (2011). Causes of premature mortality in Swedish drug abusers: A prospective longitudinal study 1970-2006. *Journal of Forensic and Legal Medicine* 18, 66-72

Oates M, Cantwell R (2011). Centre for Maternal and Child Enquiries: Deaths from psychiatric causes. *International Journal of Obstetrics and Gynaecology* 118, 132-142.

Olivier JDA, Blom T, Arentsen T, Homberg JR (2010). The age-dependent effects of selective serotonin reuptake inhibitors in humans and rodents: A review. *Progress in Neuro-Psychopharmacology and Biological Psychiatry*. Published online: 25 September 2010. doi:10.1016/j.pnpbp.2010.09.013.

Ouda J, Jokinen J, Nordstrom P (2010). CSF MHPG and dexamethasone test as predictors of suicide risk. *International Journal of Neuropsychopharmacology* 13, 159-159.

Pae CU, Koh JS, Lee SJ, Han C, Patkar AA, Masand PS (2011). Association of sedative-hypnotic medications with suicidality. Expert Review of Neurotherapeutics 11, 345-349.

Panagioti M, Gooding PA, Dunn G, Tarrier N (2011). Pathways to suicidal behavior in post-traumatic stress disorder. *Journal of Trauma & Stress*. Published online: 24 March 2011. doi: 10.1002/jts.20627.

Pandey GN (2011). Neurobiology of adult and teenage suicide. *Asian Journal of Psychiatry* 4, 2-13.

Pandey GN, Dwivedi Y (2010). What can post-mortem studies tell us about the pathoetiology of suicide? *Future Neurology* 5, 701-720.

Paraschakis A, Douzenis A, Michopoulos I, Christodoulou C, Vassilopoulou K, Koutsaftis F, Lykouras L (2011). Late onset suicide: Distinction between 'young-old' vs. 'old-old' suicide victims. How different populations are they? *Archives of Gerontology and Geriatrics*. Published online: 10 March 2011. doi:10.1016/j.archger.2011.02.011.

Parry J (2010). Medicine and the media: Can media depictions of suicide influence copycat acts? *BMJ* 341, c5067.

Patil AM, Vaz WF (2010). Pattern of fatal blunt head injury: A two year retrospective/prospective medicolegal autopsy study. *Journal of Indian Academy of Forensic Medicine* 32, 144-149.

Pharoah F, Mari J, Rathbone J, Wong W (2010). Family intervention for schizophrenia. *Cochrane Database of Systematic Reviews* 12, 88.

Pigeon WR, Caine ED (2011). Response to L.A. Lettau's "Sleep, Depression and Suicide". *Sleep Medicine* 12, 198-199.

Platt B, Hawton K, Simkin S, Mellanby RJ (2010). Suicidal behaviour and psychosocial problems in veterinary surgeons: a systematic review. *Social Psychiatry and Psychiatric Epidemiology*. Published online: 23 December 2010. doi:10.1007/s00127-010-0328-6.

Pompili M, Baldessarini RJ (2010). Epilepsy: Risk of suicidal behavior with antiepileptic drugs. *Nature Reviews Neurology* 6, 651-653.

Pompili M, Serafini G, Innamorati M, Ambrosi E, Giordano G, Girardi P, Tatarelli R, Lester D (2010). Antidepressants and suicide risk: A comprehensive overview. *Pharmaceuticals* 3, 2861-2883.

Poudel-Tandukar K, Nanri A, Mizoue T, Matsushita Y, Takahashi Y, Noda M, Inoue M, Tsugane S (2010). Differences in suicide risk according to living arrangements in Japanese men and women — The Japan Public Health Center-based (JPHC) prospective study. *Journal of Affective Disorders*. Published online: 17 December 2010. doi:10.1016/j.jad.2010.11.027.

Prakash O, Prasad GC (2011). Deliberate self-harm and domestic violence: Some answers needed. *Indian Journal of Psychiatry* 53, 77.

Preti A (2011). Animal model and neurobiology of suicide. *Progress in Neuropsychopharmacology and Biological Psychiatry*. Published online: 24 February 2011. doi: 10.1016/j.pnpbp.2010.10.027.

Preti A, Rocchi MB, Sisti D, Camboni MV, Miotto P (2010). A comprehensive meta-analysis of the risk of suicide in eating disorders. *Acta Psychiatrica Scandinavica*. Published online: 24 November 2010. doi:10.1111/j.1600-0447.2010.01641.x.

Pridmore S (2011). Suicide risk factors for NSW. *Australian and New Zealand Journal of Psychiatry*. Published online: 4 March 2011. doi:10.1080/00048674.2011.561481.

Procopio M (2010). New users of the anticonvulsants gabapentin, lamotrigine, oxcarbazepine or tiagabine are at increased risk of suicidal acts compared with new users of topiramate. *Evidence-Based Mental Health* 13, 102.

Putkonen H, Amon S, Eronen M, Klier CM, Almiron MP, Cederwall JY, Weizmann-Henelius G (2010). Child murder and gender differences - a nationwide register-based study of filicide offenders in two European countries. *Journal of Forensic Psychiatry and Psychology* 21, 637-648.

Qin P, Mortensen PB, Waltoft BL, Postolache TT (2010). Allergy is associated with suicide completion with a possible mediating role of mood disorder - a population-based study. *Allergy*. Published online: 8 December 2010. doi:10.1111/j.1398-9995.2010.02523.x.

Quan VM, Minh NL, Ha TV, Ngoc NP, Vu PT, Celentano DD, Mo TT, Go VF (2011). Mortality and HIV transmission among male Vietnamese injection drug users. *Addiction* 106, 583-589.

Queinec R, Beitz C, Contrand B, Jougla E, Leffondré K, Lagarde E, Encrenaz G (2010). Research Letter: Copycat effect after celebrity suicides: Results from the French national death register. *Psychological Medicine* 41, 668-671.

Rastogi P, Kochar S (2010). A study of suicide in Jaipur, Rajasthan (2002-2007). *Medico-Legal Update* 10, 99-101.

Ratnaparkhi M, Mohanta GP, Upadhyay L (2010). A typical antipsychotic: A review. *International Journal of Drug Development and Research* 2, 879-885.

Rebholz CM, Gu D, Yang W, Chen J, Wu X, Huang JF, Chen JC, Chen CS, Kelly TN, Duan X, Bazzano LA, He J (2011). Mortality from suicide and other external cause injuries in China: a prospective cohort study. *BMC Public Health* 11, 56.

Redden L, Pritchett Y, Robieson W, Kovacs X, Garofalo M, Tracy K, Saltarelli M (2011). Suicidality and divalproex sodium: Analysis of controlled studies in multiple indications. *Annals of General Psychiatry*. Published online: 18 January 2011. doi:10.1186/1744-859X-10-1.

Renaud J, Berlim MT, Turecki G (2010). Sexual orientation and suicide: A comment on Renaud et al. Response. *Canadian Journal of Psychiatry* 55, 747-747.

Rod NH, Vahtera J, Westerlund H, Kivimaki M, Zins M, Goldberg M, Lange T (2011). Sleep disturbances and cause-specific mortality: Results from the GAZEL cohort study. *American Journal of Epidemiology* 173, 300-309.

Roskar S, Podlesek A, Kuzmanic M, Demsar LO, Zaletel M, Marusic A (2011). Suicide risk and its relationship to change in marital status. *Crisis* 32, 24-30.

Ross JM, Yakovlev PA, Carson F (2010). Does state spending on mental health lower suicide rates? *Journal of Socio-Economics* 37, 237-261.

Ross L, Shuker DM, Pen I (2011). The evolution and suppression of male suicide under paternal genome elimination. *Evolution* 65, 554-563.

Satar K, Koroush S, Khairollah A (2010). Study of process and causes related to suicide in Ham province during 1992-2005. *Research Journal of Medical Sciences* 4, 217-221.

Schaffer CB, Schaffer LC, Miller AR, Hang E, Nordahl TE (2011). Efficacy and safety of non-benzodiazepine hypnotics for chronic insomnia in patients with bipolar disorder. *Journal of Affective Disorders* 128, 305-308.

Scorza FA, Cavalheiro EA, Albuquerque MD, Albuquerque JD, Cysneiros RM, Terra VC, Arida RM (2011). Thyroid gland and cerebella lesions: New risk factors for sudden cardiac death in schizophrenia? *Medical Hypotheses* 76, 251-253.

Seguin M, Boyer R, Lesage A, McGirr A, Suissa A, Tousignant M, Turecki G (2010). Suicide and gambling: Psychopathology and treatment-seeking. *Psychology of Addictive Behaviors* 24, 541-547.

Shah A (2011). Is there any additional evidence for the epidemiological transition hypothesis of elderly suicides? *International Psychogeriatrics* 23, 331-333.

Shah A, Bhandarkar R (2011). Does adversity early in life affect general population suicide rates? A cross-national study. *Journal of Injury and Violence Research* 3, 25-27.

Sharkey L (2010). Does overcrowding in prisons exacerbate the risk of suicide among women prisoners? *The Howard Journal of Criminal Justice* 49, 111-124.

Sher L (2010). Brain-derived neurotrophic factor and suicidal behaviour. *Quarterly Journal of Medicine*. Published online: 4 November 2010. doi:10.1093/qjmed/hcq207.

Sher L (2011). Is it possible to predict suicide? *Australian and New Zealand Journal of Psychiatry*. Published online: 9 February 2011. doi:10.3109/00048674.2011.560136.

Smith EG, Craig TJ, Ganoczy D, Walters HM, Valenstein M (2010). Treatment of veterans with depression who died by suicide: Timing and quality of care at last Veterans Health Administration visit. *Journal of Clinical Psychiatry*. Published online: 7 September 2010. doi:10.4088/JCP.09m05608blu.

Son CH, Topyan K (2011). The effect of alcoholic beverage excise tax on alcohol-attributable injury mortalities. *The European Journal of Health Economics* 12, 103-113.

Spaulding AC, Seals RM, McCallum VA, Perez SD, Brzozowski AK, Steenland NK (2011). Prisoner survival inside and outside of the institution: implications for health-care planning. *The American Journal of Epidemiology* 173, 479-487.

Suissa AJ (2011). Vulnerability and gambling addiction: psychosocial benchmarks and avenues for intervention. *International Journal of Mental Health and Addiction* 9, 12-23.

Sun W, Schooling CM, Chan WM, Ho KS, Lam TH (2010). The association between depressive symptoms and mortality among chinese elderly: A Hong Kong cohort study. *The Journals of Gerontology: Series A, Biological Sciences and Medical Sciences*. Published online: 24 November 2010. doi:10.1093/gerona/glq206.

Sun WJ, Xu L, Chan WM, Lam TH, Schooling CM (2011). Depressive symptoms and suicide in 56,000 older Chinese: a Hong Kong cohort study. *Social Psychiatry and Psychiatric Epidemiology*. Published online: 8 March 2011. doi:10.1007/s00127-011-0362-z.

Supriyanto I, Sasada T, Fukutake M, Asano M, Ueno Y, Nagasaki Y, Shirakawa O, Hishimoto A (2011). Association of FKBP5 gene haplotypes with completed suicide in the Japanese population. *Progress in Neuro-Psychopharmacology and Biological Psychiatry* 35, 252-256.

Stefulj J, Bordukalo-Niksic T (2010). Neuronal tryptophan hydroxylase (TPH2) in suicidal behaviour. *Translational Neuroscience* 1, 207-213.

Stübner S, Grohmann R, von Stralendorff I, Rüther E, Möller HJ, Müller-Oerlinghausen B, Engel RR, Horvath A, Greil W (2010). Suicidality as rare adverse event of antidepressant medication: report from the AMSP multicenter drug safety surveillance project. *Journal of Clinical Psychiatry* 71, 1293-1307.

Talala KM, Huurre TM, Laatikainen TK, Martelin TP, Ostamo AI, Prattala RS (2011). The contribution of psychological distress to socio-economic differences in cause-specific mortality: A population-based follow-up of 28 years. *BMC Public Health* 28, 138.

Tang TC, Yen CF, Cheng CP, Yang P, Chen CS, Yang RC, Huang MS, Jong YJ, Yu HS (2010). Suicide risk and its correlate in adolescents who experienced typhoon-induced mudslides: a structural equation model. *Depression & Anxiety* 27, 1143-1148.

Taylor FR (2010). Anticonvulsant medications and the risk of suicide, attempted suicide, or violent death: Comments. *Headache* 50, 1619-1621.

Theodorou P, Phan VT, Weinand C, Maegele M, Maurer CA, Perbix W, Leitsch S, Lefering R, Spilker G (2011). Suicide by burning: epidemiological and clinical profile. *Annals of Plastic Surgery* 66, 339-343.

Tousignant M, Pouliot L, Routhier D, Vrakas G, McGirr A, Turecki G (2011). Suicide, schizophrenia, and schizoid-type psychosis: role of life events and childhood factors. *Suicide and Life--Threatening Behavior* 41, 66-78.

Trujillo AJ, Hyder AA, Ruiz F (2010). Association between economic growth and injury mortality among seniors in Colombia. *Injury Prevention* 16, 383-388.

Tsai C-W, Gunnell D, Chou Y-H, Kuo C-J, Lee M-B, Chen Y-Y (2011). Why do people choose charcoal burning as a method of suicide? An interview based study of survivors in Taiwan. *Journal of Affective Disorders*. Published online: 12 January 2011. doi:10.1016/j.jad.2010.12.013.

Tse R, Sims N, Byard RW (2011). Alcohol ingestion and age of death in hanging suicides. *Journal of Forensic Sciences*. Published online: 21 March 2011. Doi: 10.1111/j.1556-4029.2011.01751.x.

Ulcickas Yood M, Delorenze G, Quesenberry CP Jr, Tsai AL, Phillips S, Willey VJ, Niemcryk SJ, Wells K, Skovron ML, Cziraky MJ, Carson W, Oliveria SA (2010). Epidemiologic study of aripiprazole use and the incidence of suicide events. *Pharmacoepidemiology and Drug Safety* 19, 1124–1130.

Valdizan EM, Diez-Alarcia R, Gonzalez-Maeso J, Pilar-Cuellar F, Garcia-Sevilla JA, Meana JJ, Pazos A (2010). (2)-adrenoceptor functionality in postmortem frontal cortex of depressed suicide victims. *Biological Psychiatry* 68, 869-872.

Van Heeringen K (2010). Functional brain imaging in suicidal patients. *Psychiatria Danubina* 22, 1.

Van Orden K, Conwell Y (2011). Suicides in late life. *Current Psychiatry Reports.* Published online: 3 March 2011. doi:10.1007/s11920-011-0193-3O.

Vento AE, Pompili M, Schifano F, Corkery JM, Innamorati M, Girardi P, Ghodse H (2011). Distinguishing between suicides and accidental deaths in substance-related deaths (UK, 2001-2007). *Progress in Neuropsychopharmacology and Biological Psychiatry.* Published online: 24 February 2011. doi: 10.1016/j.pnpbp.2011.02.014.

Vijayakumar L, Kumar MS, Vijayakumar V (2011). Substance use and suicide. *Current Opinion in Psychiatry.* Published online: 22 March 2011. Doi: 10.1097/YCO.0b013e32834 59242.

Vijayakumar S, Fareedullah Md, Ashok Kumar E, Mohan Rao K (2011). A prospective study on electrocardiographic findings of patients with organophosphorus poisoning. *Cardiovascular Toxicology.* Published online: 20 February 2011. doi:10.1007/s12012-011-9104-4.

Voshaar RC, Kapur N, Bickley H, Williams A, Purandare N (2011). Suicide in later life: A comparison between cases with early-onset and late-onset depression. *Journal of Affective Disorders.* Published online: 18 March 2011. Doi: 10.1016/j.jad.2011.02.008.

Wagner G, Koch K, Schachtzabel C, Schultz CC, Sauer H, Schlosser RG (2010). Structural brain alterations in patients with major depressive disorder and high risk for suicide: Evidence for a distinct neurobiological entity? *NeuroImage* 54, 1607-1614.

Waider J, Araragi N, Gutknecht L, Lesch K-P (2011). Tryptophan hydroxylase-2 (TPH2) in disorders of cognitive control and emotion regulation: A perspective. *Psychoneuroendocrinology* 36, 393-405.

Walsh PC (2010). Immediate risk of suicide and cardiovascular death after a prostate cancer diagnosis: Cohort study in the United States Editorial Comment. *Journal of Urology* 184, 1356-1356.

Webb RT, Qin P, Stevens H, Mortensen PB, Appleby L, Shaw J (2011). National study of suicide in all people with a criminal justice history. *Archives of General Psychiatry.* Published online: 7 February 2011. doi:10.1001/archgenpsychiatry.2011.7.

Webb RT, Marshall CE, Abel KM (2011). Teenage motherhood and risk of premature death: long-term follow-up in the ONS Longitudinal Study. *Psychological Medicine.* Published online: 28 January 2011. doi:10.1017/S0033291711000055.

Wichman CL (2011). The safety of antipsychotic drugs in pregnancy: Recent controversy. *Current Women's Health Reviews* 7, 35-36.

Wide J, Mok H, McKenna M, Ogrodniczuk JS (2011). Effect of gender socialization on the presentation of depression among men. A pilot study. *Canadian Family Physician* 57, 74-78.

Wightman DS, Foster VJ, Krishen A, Richard NE, Modell JG (2010). Meta-analysis of suicidality in placebo-controlled clinical trials of adults taking bupropion. *Primary Care Companion to the Journal of Clinical Psychiatry* 12, 1-8.

Wijeratne C, Reutens S, Draper B, Sachdev P (2011). Psychiatric disorders in ageing. *Current Topics in Behavioral Neurosciences*. Published online: 18 March 2011. doi: 10.1007/7854_2011_124.

Wilcox HC (2011). Method used in an unsuccessful suicide attempt predicts likelihood of future completed suicide. *Evidence Based Mental Health* 14, 16.

Wildgust HJ, Hodgson R, Beary M (2010). The paradox of premature mortality in schizophrenia: new research questions. *Journal of Psychopharmacology* 24, 9-15.

Williams RB (2010). Myocardial infarction and risk of suicide: Another reason to develop and test ways to reduce distress in postmyocardial-infarction patients? *Circulation* 122, 2356-2358.

Wong PWC, Cheung DYT, Conner KR, Conwell Y, Yip PSF (2010). Gambling and completed suicide in Hong Kong: A review of coroner court files. *Primary Care Companion to the Journal of Clinical Psychiatry* 12, 6.

Wong SY, Leung JC, Woo J (2011). The relationship between worthlessness and mortality in a large cohort of Chinese elderly men. *International Psychogeriatrics* 23, 609-615.

Yang AC, Tsai SJ, Huang NE, Peng CK (2011). Association of Internet search trends with suicide death in Taipei City, Taiwan, 2004-2009. *Journal of Affective Disorders*. Published online: 1 March 2011. doi: 10.1016/j.jad.2011.019.

Yoon Y-H, Chen CM, Yi H-Y, Moss HB (2010). Effect of comorbid alcohol and drug use disorders on premature death among unipolar and bipolar disorder decedents in the United States, 1999 to 2006. *Comprehensive Psychiatry*. Published online: 10 December 2010. doi:10.1016/j.comppsych.2010.10.005.

Yu NW, Chen CY (2011). Significant higher depression rate and suicidal ideation among underweight male adult population: results from a general population study in Taiwan. *Journal of Mens Health* 6, 237.

Zalsman G, Patya M, Frisch A, Ofek H, Schapir L, Blum I, Harell D, Apter A, Weizman A, Tyano S (2010). Association of polymorphisms of the serotonergic pathways with clinical traits of impulsive-aggression and suicidality in adolescents: A multi-center study. *World Journal of Biological Psychiatry* 12, 33-41.

Zambon F, Laflamme L, Spolaore P, Visentin C, Hasselberg M (2010). Youth suicide: An insight into previous hospitalisation for injury and sociodemographic conditions from a nationwide cohort study. *Injury Prevention*. Published online: 5 December 2010. doi:10.1136/ip.2010.030080.

Zebley BD, Ferrando SJ, Striano P, Zara F, Minetti C, Arana A, Ayuso-mateos JL, Arellano FM (2010). Suicide-related events in patients treated with antiepileptic drugs. *The New England Journal of Medicine* 363, 1873-1874.

Zhang J (2011). Marriage and suicide among Chinese rural young women. *Social Forces* 89, 311-326.

Zhang J, Li N, Tu XM, Xiao S, Jia C (2010). Risk factors for rural young suicide in China: A case-control study. *Journal of Affective Disorders* 129, 244-251.

Zhao Y, Montoro R, Igartua K; Thombs BD (2010). Sexual orientation and suicide: A comment on Renaud et al. *Canadian Journal of Psychiatry* 55, 746-747.

Zill P, Vielsmeier V, Büttner A, Eisenmenger W, Siedler F, Scheffer B, Möller HJ, Bondy B (2011). Postmortem proteomic analysis in human amygdala of drug addicts: Possible impact of tubulin on drug-abusing behavior. *European Archives of Psychiatry and Clinical Neuroscience* 261, 121-131.

Zupanc T, Pregelj P, Tomori M, Komel R, Paska AV (2010). No association between polymorphisms in four serotonin receptor genes, serotonin transporter gene and alcohol-related suicide. *Psychiatria Danubina* 22, 522-527.

Zupanc T, Pregelj P, Tomori M, Komel R, Paska AV (2010). TPH2 polymorphisms and alcohol-related suicide. *Neuroscience Letters* 490, 78-81.

Prevention

Anestis MD, Bagge CL, Tull MT, Joiner TE (2010). Clarifying the role of emotion dysregulation in the interpersonal-psychological theory of suicidal behavior in an undergraduate sample. *Journal of Psychiatric Research*. Published online: 17 November 2010. doi:10.1016/j.jpsychires.2010.10.013.

Annonymous (2010). A follow-up report on preventing suicide: focus on medical/surgical units and the emergency department. *Sentinel event alert* 17, 1-4.

Argyle N (2010). Suicide trends in an expanding mental health service in Auckland. *Australasian Psychiatry* 18, 437-440.

Badiadka KK, Vasu S, Dsouza DH (2010). Victim profile and influencing factors in traumatic deaths on railway tracks in Calicut, Kerala. *Medico-Legal Update* 10, 25-27.

Bartlett JM (2011). Raising awareness of elderly suicide risk in Sandpoint, Idaho. *Journal of Investigative Medicine* 59, 428-428.

Basic J, Mihic J, Novak M (2010). Risk analysis in the period of growing-up of children and youth: starting point for effective prevention. *Journal of Public Health*. Published online: 2 November 2010. doi:10.1007/s10389-010-0362-6.

Bean G, Baber KM (2011). Connect: an effective community-based youth suicide prevention program. *Suicide and Life-Threatening Behaviour* 41, 87-97.

Biddle L, Donovan J, Owen-Smith A, Potokar J, Longson D, Hawton K, Kapur N, Gunnell D (2010). Factors influencing the decision to use hanging as a method of suicide: Qualitative study. *British Journal of Psychiatry* 197, 320-325.

Blumenthal DS (2011). Physician education: a promising strategy to prevent adolescent suicide - commentary. *Academic Medicine* 86, 349.

Boeke M, Griffin T, Reidenberg DJ (2011). The physician's role in suicide prevention: lessons learned from a public awareness campaign. *Minnesota Medicine* 94, 44-46.

Boyce N (2010). Pilots of the future: Suicide prevention and the internet. *The Lancet* 376, 1889-1890.

Bruce ML (2010). Suicide risk and prevention in veteran populations. *Annals of New York Academy of Sciences* 120, 98-103.

Bryan CJ, Kanzler KE, Durham TL, West CL, Greene E (2010). Challenges and considerations for managing suicide risk in combat zones. *Military Medicine* 175, 713-718.

Caine ED (2010). Preventing suicide is hard to do! *Psychiatric Services* 61, 1171.

Caine ED (2011). Societal stigma and suicide prevention—in reply. *Psychiatric Services* 62, 223.

Chen C-Y (2010). Meeting the challenges of eldercare in Taiwan's aging society. *Journal of Clinical Gerontology and Geriatrics* 1, 2-4.

Clark TR, Matthieu MM, Ross A, Knox KL (2010). Training outcomes from the Samaritans of New York suicide awareness and prevention programme among community- and school-based staff. *British Journal of Social Work* 40, 2223-2238.

Cliquennois G (2010). Preventing suicide in French prisons. *British Journal of Criminology* 50, 1023-1040.

Coverdale JH, Roberts LW, Balon R (2011). The public health priority to address the accessibility and safety of firearms: recommendations for training. *Academic Psychiatry* 34, 405-408.

Cusimano MD, Sameem M (2011). The effectiveness of middle and high school-based suicide prevention programmes for adolescents: A systematic review. *Injury Prevention* 17, 43-49.

Demircin S, Akkoyun M, Yilmaz R, Gokdogan MR (2011). Suicide of elderly persons: Towards a framework for prevention. *Geriatrics and Gerontology International* 11, 107-113.

Dudley S (2011). Lessons from Randy. Subtle clues from your patients can help you head off regret. *Medical Economics* 87, 64-66.

Eddleston M, Bateman DN (2010). Major reductions in global suicide numbers can be made rapidly through pesticide regulation without the need for psychosocial interventions. *Social Science & Medicine* 72, 1-2.

Edwards SJ, Sachmann MD (2010). No-suicide contracts, no-suicide agreements, and no-suicide assurances. *Crisis* 31, 290-302.

Erickson J, Aughey D, Moeller A, Finkelstein M (2011). Mental health and suicide screening in adolescent primary care. *Journal of Adolescent Health* 48, 95-96.

Espitia-Hardeman V, Borse NN, Dellinger AM, Betancourt CE, Villareal AN, Caicedo LD, Portillo C (2011). The burden of childhood injuries and evidence based strategies developed using the injury surveillance system in Pasto, Colombia. *Injury Prevention* 17(Suppl 1), 38-44.

Florentine JB, Crane C (2010). Corrigendum to: "Suicide prevention by limiting access to methods: A review of theory and practice". *Social Science and Medicine* 70, 1626-1632.

Florentine JB, Crane C (2010). Pesticides, paracetamol and psychosocial interventions: A reply to a commentary on Florentine and Crane. *Social Science and Medicine* 72, 3-5.

Foreman M, Saenz M (2010). Preventing teen suicide. *NCSL Legisbrief* 18, 1-2.

Freedenthal S (2010). Adolescent help-seeking and the yellow ribbon suicide prevention program: An evaluation. *Suicide and Life-Threatening Behavior* 40, 628-639.

Fu KW, Chan YY, Yip PS (2010). Newspaper reporting of suicides in Hong Kong, Taiwan and Guangzhou: Compliance with WHO media guidelines and epidemiological comparisons. *Journal of Epidemiology and Community Health*. Published online: 1 October 2010. doi:10.1136/jech.2009.105650.

Gallicchio VS (2011). Lithium - still interesting after all these years. *Trace Elements and Electrolytes* 28, 56-69.

Glasgow G (2011). Do local landmark bridges increase the suicide rate? An alternative test of the likely effect of means restriction at suicide-jumping sites. *Social Science & Medicine*. Published online: 1 February 2011. doi:10.1016/j.socscimed.2011.01.001.

Gottman JM, Gottman JS, Atkins CL (2011). The comprehensive soldier fitness program family skills component. *American Psychologist* 66, 52-57.

Greden JF, Valenstein M, Spinner J, Blow A, Gorman LA, Dalack GW, Marcus S, Kees M (2010). Buddy-to-Buddy, a citizen soldier peer support program to counteract stigma, PTSD, depression, and suicide. *Annals of the New York Academy of Sciences* 1208, 90-97.

Hassanian-Moghaddam H, Sarjami S, Kolahi AA, Carter GL (2011). Postcards in Persia: randomised controlled trial to reduce suicidal behaviours 12 months after hospital-treated self-poisoning. *British Journal of Psychiatry*. Published online: 22 February 2011. doi:10.1192/bjp.bp.109.067199.

Hensley MA, Matthieu MM (2011). Educational needs assessment for homeless service providers on preventing suicide. *Social Work in Mental Health* 9, 92-106.

Ho WW, Chen WJ, Ho CK, Lee MB, Chen CC, Chou FH (2010). Evaluation of the suicide prevention program in Kaohsiung city, Taiwan, using the CIPP evaluation model. *Community Mental Health Journal*. Published online: 4 December 2010. doi:10.1007/s10597-010-9364-7.

Hovens JE, van der Ploeg GJ (2011). Societal stigma and suicide prevention. *Psychiatric Services* 62, 222-223.

Huisman A, Pirkis J, Robinson J (2010). Intervention studies in suicide prevention research. *Crisis* 31, 281-284.

Inman DD, Van Bakergem KM, Larosa AC, Garr DR (2011). Evidence-based health promotion programs for schools and communities. *American Journal of Preventive Medicine* 40, 207-219.

Inoue K, Fukunaga T, Fujita Y, Iida T, Okazaki Y, Ono Y (2011). Urgent importance of various suicide prevention measures among the elderly in South Korea. *West Indian Medical Journal* 59, 344-344.

Inoue K, Fukunaga T, Okazaki Y, Masaki M, Nishimura Y, Nishida A; Hagiwara K, Ono Y (2010). Necessity of comprehensive suicide prevention measures among women in Japan: a comparison between Japan and France in age-classified suicide rates. *West Indian Medical Journal* 59, 231-232.

Jaiprakash H, Sarala N, Venkatarathnamma PN, Kumar TN (2010). Analysis of different types of poisoning in a tertiary care hospital in rural south India. *Food and Chemical Toxicology* 49, 248-250.

Jayaram G, Sporney H, Perticone P (2010). The utility and effectiveness of 15-minute checks in inpatient settings. *Psychiatry (Edgmont)* 7, 46-49.

Jenkins R, Mussa M, Haji SA, Haji MS, Salim A, Suleiman S, Riyami AS, Wakil A, Mbatia J (2011). Developing and implementing mental health policy in Zanzibar, a low income country off the coast of East Africa. *International Journal of Mental Health Systems* 5, 1-6.

Kasckow J, Felmet K, Zisook S (2011). Managing suicide risk in patients with schizophrenia. *CNS Drugs* 25, 129-143.

Kaufman KR, Struck PJ (2010). Psychogenic nonepileptic seizures and suicidal behavior on a video/EEG telemetry unit: The need for psychiatric assessment and screening for suicide risk. *Epilepsy and Behavior* 19, 656-659.

Klimes-Dougan B, Lee CY (2010). Suicide prevention public service announcements. *Crisis* 31, 247-254.

Knizek BL, Kinyanda E, Owens V, Hjelmeland H (2011). Ugandan men's perceptions of what causes and what prevents suicide. *Journal of Men, Masculinities and Spirituality* 5, 4-21.

Lee J, Park S, Choi K, Kwon SM (2010). The association between the supply of primary care physicians and population health outcomes in Korea. *Family Medicine* 42, 628-635.

Levenson Jr RL, O'Hara AF, Clark Sr R (2010). The badge of life psychological survival for police officers program. *International Journal of Emergency Mental Health* 12, 95-102.

Little C (2010). Reducing the suicide rate in the profession. *Veterinary Record* 167, 879-880.

Luxton DD, June JD, Kinn JT (2011). Technology-based suicide prevention: current applications and future directions. *Telemedicine and e-Health* 17, 50-55.

Madhusoodanan S, Ibrahim FA, Malik A (2011). Primary prevention in geriatric psychiatry. *Annals of Clinical Psychiatry* 22, 249-261.

Malpass A, Kessler D, Sharp D, Shaw A (2011). 'I didn't want her to panic': Unvoiced patient agendas in primary care consultations when consulting about antidepressants. *British Journal of General Practice* 61, 63-71.

Manthorpe J, Iliffe S (2011). Social work with older people - Reducing suicide risk: A critical review of practice and prevention. *British Journal of Social Work* 41, 131-147.

McCay E, Langley J, Beanlands H, Cooper L, Mudachi N, Harris A, Blidner R, Bach K, Dart C, Howes C, Miner S (2010). Mental health challenges and strengths of street-involved youth: The need for a multi-determined approach. *Canadian Journal of Nursing Research* 42, 30-49.

Miller M, Bhalla K (2010). An urgent need to restrict access to pesticides based on human lethality. *PLoS Medicine* 7, e1000358.

Milner A, De Leo D (2010). Suicide research and prevention in developing countries in Asia and the Pacific. *Bulletin of the World Health Organization* 88, 795-796.

Niederkrotenthaler T, Voracek M, Herberth A, Till B, Strauss M, Etzersdorfer E, Eisenwort B, Sonneck G (2010). Media and suicide. Papageno v Werther effect. *British Medical Journal* 341, c5841.

Nordentoft M (2010). Crucial elements in suicide prevention strategies. *Progress in Neuro-Psychopharmacology and Biological Psychiatry*. Published online: 2 December 2010. doi:10.1016/j.pnpbp.2010.11.038.

Nuttman-Shwartz O, Lebel U, Avrami S, Volk N (2010). Perceptions of suicide and their impact on policy, discourse and welfare. *European Journal of Social Work* 13, 375-392.

Ogburn KM, Messias E, Buckley PF (2011). New-age patient communications through social networks. *General Hospital Psychiatry*. Published online: 13 January 2011. doi:10.1016/j.genhosppsych.2010.08.006.

Olden M, Cukor J, Rizzo AS, Rothbaum B, Difede JA (2010). House calls revisited: Leveraging technology to overcome obstacles to veteran psychiatric care and improve treatment outcomes. *Annals of the New York Academy of Sciences* 120, 133-141.

Opler M, Sodhi D, Zaveri D, Madhusoodanan S (2011). Primary psychiatric prevention in children and adolescents. *Annals of Clinical Psychiatry* 22, 220-234.

Ougrin D, Banarsee R, Dunn-Toroosian V, Majeed A (2010). Suicide survey in a London borough: primary care and public health perspectives. *Journal of Public Health*. Published online: 8 November 2010. doi:10.1093/pubmed/fdq094.

Parry J (2010). Can media depictions of suicide influence copycat acts? *British Medical Journal* 341, c5067.

Patel V (2010). Building social capital and improving mental health care to prevent suicide. *International Journal of Epidemiology* 39, 1411-1412.

Pompili M (2010). Suicide on my mind. A look back and ahead at suicide prevention in Italy. *Minerva Medica* 101, 353-362.

Pompili M (2010). Suicide prevention: A long-lasting Italian tradition. Toward understanding the suicidal mind. *Italian Journal of Psychopathology* 16, 231-238.

Prabhu SL, Molinari V, Bowers T, Lomax J (2010). Role of the family in suicide prevention: An attachment and family systems perspective. *Bulletin of the Menninger Clinic* 74, 301-327.

Price M, Norris DM (2010). Firearm laws: A primer for psychiatrists. *Harvard Review of Psychiatry* 18, 326-335.

Read J, Bentall R (2010). The effectiveness of electroconvulsive therapy: A literature review. *Epidemiologia e Psichiatria Sociale* 19, 333-347.

Reynolds DVD (2011). Preventing Bullycides. *National Association of School Nurses* 26, 31-34.

Ritter C, Teller JL, Marcussen K, Munetz MR, Teasdale B (2010). Crisis intervention team officer dispatch, assessment, and disposition: Interactions with individuals with severe mental illness. *International Journal of Law and Psychiatry* 34, 30-38.

Robinson J, Hetrick SE, Martin C (2011). Preventing suicide in young people: systematic review. *Australian & New Zealand Journal of Psychiatry* 45, 3-26.

Roskar S, Podlesek A, Zorko M, Tavcar R, Dernovsek ZM, Groleger U, Mirjanic M, Konec N, Janet E, Marusic A (2010). Effects of training program on recognition and management of depression and suicide risk evaluation for Slovenian primary-care physicians: Follow-up study. *Croatian Medical Journal* 51, 237-242.

Saini P, Windfuhr K, Pearson A, Da Cruz D, Miles C, Cordingley L, While D, Swinson N, Williams A, Shaw J, Appleby L, Kapur N (2010). Suicide prevention in primary care: General practitioners' views on service availability. *BMC Research Notes* 3, 246.

Salvatore T (2011). Peer specialists can prevent suicides. *Behavioral Healthcare* 30, 10.

Sanaei-Zadeh H, Valian Z, Zamani N, Farajidana H, Mostafazadeh B (2011). Clinical features and successful management of suicidal digoxin toxicity without use of digoxin-specific antibody (Fab) fragments - is it possible? *Tropical Doctor*. Published online: 24 January 2011. doi:10.1258/td.2010.100195.

Serhan N (2010). Adolescent health risk screening in primary care setting. *Bahrain Medical Bulletin* 32, 1-12.

Shantz J (2010). 'The foundation of our community': Cultural restoration, reclaiming children and youth in an indigenous community. *Journal of Social Welfare and Family Law* 32, 229-236.

Sher L, Mindes J, Novakovic V (2010). Transcranial magnetic stimulation and the treatment of suicidality. *Expert Review of Neurotherapeutics* 10, 1781-1784.

Simm R, Roen K, Daiches A (2010). Primary school children and self harm: The emotional impact upon education professionals, and their understandings of why children self harm and how this is managed. *Oxford Review of Education* 36, 677-692.

Spiegel BM, Khanna D, Bolus R, Agarwal N, Khanna P, Chang L (2011). Understanding gastrointestinal distress: a framework for clinical practice. *American Journal of Gastroenterology* 106, 280-385.

Sun FK, Long A, Huang XY, Chiang CY (2011). A quasi-experimental investigation into the efficacy of a suicide education programme for second-year student nurses in Taiwan. *Journal of Clinical Nursing* 20, 837-846.

Takeuchi T (2010). Matrix analysis and risk management to avert depression and suicide among workers. *BioPsychoSocial Medicine* 4, 15.

Tompkins TL, Witt J, Abraibesh N (2010). Does a gatekeeper suicide prevention program work in a school setting? Evaluating training outcome and moderators of effectiveness. *Suicide and Life-Threatening Behaviour* 40, 506-515.

Tucker R (2011). Suicide watch. *Mental Health Practice* 14, 9.

Vaiva G, Walter M, Al Arab AS, Courtet P, Bellivier F, Demarty AL, Duhem S, Ducrocq F, Goldstein P, Libersa C (2011). ALGOS: The development of a randomized controlled trial testing a case management algorithm designed to reduce suicide risk among suicide attempters. *BMC Psychiatry* 11, 1.

van Dusseldorp LR, van Meijel BK, Derksen JJ (2011). Emotional intelligence of mental health nurses. *Journal of Clinical Nursing* 20, 555-562.

Verwey B, van Waarde JA, Bozda MA, van Rooij I, de Beurs E, Zitman FG (2011). Reassessment of suicide attempters at home, shortly after discharge from hospital. *Crisis* 31, 303-310.

Vogel L (2010). Canada suicide prevention efforts lagging, experts say. *Canadian Medical Association Journal*. Published online: 11 January 2011. doi:10.1503/cmaj.109-3724.

Weinberg I, Maltsberger JT, Ronningstam E, Goldblatt MJ, Schechter M, Olivardia R, Gold-blatt MJ, Maltsberger JT (2011). Treatment following a near fatal suicide attempt. *Suicide and Life-Threatening Behavaviour*. Published online: 10 Februar 2011. doi:10.1111/j.1943-278X.2010.00010.x.

White J, Morris J (2010). Precarious spaces: Risk, responsibility and uncertainty in school-based suicide prevention programs. *Social Science & Medicine* 71, 2187-2194.

Whitney SD, Renner LM, Pate CM, Jacobs KA (2011). Principals' perceptions of benefits and barriers to school-based suicide prevention programs. *Children and Youth Services Review*. Published online: 9 January 2011. doi:10.1016/j.childyouth.2010.12.015.

Wilkinson P, Kelvin R, Roberts C, Dubicka B, Goodyer I (2011). Clinical and psychosocial predictors of suicide attempts and nonsuicidal self-injury in the Adolescent Depression Antidepressants and Psychotherapy Trial (ADAPT). *American Journal of Psychiatry*. Published online: 1 February 2011. doi:10.1176/appi.ajp.2010.10050718.

Wurz KA (2011). Adolescent suicide prevention in Dayton, Washington. *Journal of Investigative Medicine* 59, 57.

Zigmond J (2010). Prevention through intervention. Programs use training, patient education to help head off suicide attempts. *Modern Healthcare* 40, 39.

Young J, Eisendrath S (2011). Enhancing patient safety and resident education during the academic year-end transfer of outpatients: Lessons from the suicide of a psychiatric patient. *Academic Psychiatry* 35, 54-57.

Postvention and bereavement

Agnew A, Manktelow R, Haynes T, Jones L (2011). Bereavement assessment practice in hospice settings: Challenges for palliative care social workers. *British Journal of Social Work* 41, 111-130.

Akhtar S (2011). Editor's introduction: The aftermath of suicide. *International Journal of Applied Psychoanalytic Studies* 8, 95-96.

Barlow CA, Waegemakers Schiff J, Chugh U, Rawlinson D, Hides E, Leith J (2010). An evaluation of a suicide bereavement peer support program. *Death Studies* 34, 915.

Berman AL (2011). Estimating the population of survivors of suicide: Seeking an evidence base. *Suicide and Life-Threatening Behaviour* 41, 110-116.

Berman J (2010). In her wake: a child psychiatrist explores the mystery of her mother's suicide. *Death Studies* 34, 947-955.

Chapple A, Ziebland S (2010). How the Internet is changing the experience of bereavement by suicide: A qualitative study in the UK. *Health (London)*. Published online: 22 December 2010. doi:10.1177/1363459309360792.

Davidsen AS (2010). 'And then one day he'd shot himself. Then I was really shocked': General practitioners' reaction to patient suicide. *Patient Education and Counseling*. Published online: 27 September 2010. doi:10.1016/j.pec.2010.08.020.

Dyregrov K, Dieserud G, Straiton M, Rasmussen M, Hjelmeland H, Knizek B, Leenaars A (2011). Motivation for research participation among people bereaved by suicide. *Omega: Journal of Death and Dying* 62, 149-168.

Feigelman B, Feigelman W (2011). Suicide survivor support groups: Comings and goings, part I. *Illness Crisis and Loss* 19, 57-71.

de Groot M, Neeleman J, van der Meer K, Burger H (2010). The effectiveness of family-based cognitive-behavior grief therapy to prevent complicated grief in relatives of suicide victims: The mediating role of suicide ideation. *Suicide and Life-Threatening Behavior* 40, 425-437.

Gaffney M, Hannigan B (2010). Suicide bereavement and coping: A descriptive and interpretative analysis of the coping process. *Procedia — Social and Behavioral Sciences* 5, 526-535.

Harper M, O'Connor R, Dickson A, O'Carroll R (2011). Mothers continuing bonds and ambivalence to personal mortality after the death of their child - An interpretative phenomenological analysis. *Psychology, Health and Medicine* 16, 203-214.

Hibberd R, Elwood LS, Galovski TE (2010). Risk and protective factors for posttraumatic stress disorder, prolonged grief, and depression in survivors of the violent death of a loved one. *Journal of Loss & Trauma* 15, 426-447.

Krysinska K, Andriessen K (2010). On-line support and resources for people bereaved through suicide: What is available? *Suicide and Life-Threatening Behavior* 40, 640-650.

Takahashi C, Chida F, Nakamura H, Akasaka H, Yagi J, Koeda A, Tagusari E, Otsuka K, Sakai A (2011). The impact of inpatient suicide on psychiatric nurses and their need for support. *BMC Psychiatry* 11, 38.

Youngblut JM, Brooten D, Blais K, Hannan J, Niyonsenga T (2010). Grandparent's health and functioning after a grandchild's death. *Journal of Pediatric Nursing* 25, 352-359.

NON-FATAL SUICIDAL BEHAVIOUR

Epidemiology

Adams-Fryatt A (2010). Acknowledging, recognizing, and treating depression in elderly long-term care residents. *Annals of Long-Term Care* 18, 30-32.

Appelbaum KL, Savageau JA, Trestman RL, Metzner JL, Baillargeon J (2011). A national survey of self-injurious behavior in American prisons. *Psychiatric Services* 62, 285-290.

Asad N, Karmaliani R, Sullaiman N, Bann CM, McClure EM, Pasha O, Wright LL, Golden-berg RL (2010). Prevalence of suicidal thoughts and attempts among pregnant Pakistani women. *Acta Obstetricia et Gynecologica Scandinavica* 89, 1545-1551.

Baca-Garcia E, Perez-Rodriguez MM, Keyes KM, Oquendo MA, Hasin DS, Grant BF, Blanco C (2010). Suicidal ideation and suicide attempts among Hispanic subgroups in the United States: 1991-1992 and 2001-2002. *Journal of Psychiatric Research*. Published online: 9 October 2010. doi:10.1016/j.jpsychires.2010.09.004.

Baetens I, Claes L, Muehlenkamp J, Grietens H, Onghena P (2011). Non-suicidal and suicidal self-injurious behavior among Flemish adolescents: a web-survey. *Archives of Suicide Research* 15, 56-67.

Basha VC, Mohiyuddin SS, Reddy SR, Kumar LA (2010). A retrospective study of organo phosphrous compound poisonings in tertiary hospital in Hyderabad region. *Indian Journal of Forensic Medicine and Toxicology* 4, 6-8.

Belik SL, Stein MB, Asmundson GJ, Sareen J (2010). Are Canadian soldiers more likely to have suicidal ideation and suicide attempts than Canadian civilians? *American Journal of Epidemiology*. Published online: 26 October 2010. doi:10.1093/aje/kwq290.

Bentur Y, Obchinikov ND, Cahana A, Kovler N, Bloom-Krasik A, Lavon O, Gurevych B, Lurie Y (2010). Pediatric poisonings in Israel: National poison center data. *Israel Medical Association Journal* 12, 554-559.

Bergen H, Hawton K, Waters K, Cooper J, Kapur N (2010). Epidemiology and trends in non-fatal self-harm in three centres in England: 2000-2007. *British Journal of Psychiatry* 197, 493-498.

Berntsen E, Starling J, Durheim E, Hainsworth C, de Kloet L, Chapman L, Hancock K (2011). Temporal trends in self harm and aggression on a paediatric mental health ward. *Australasian Psychiatry* 19, 64-69.

Bursztein Lipsicas C, Makinen IH, Apter A, De Leo D, Kerkhof A, Lonnqvist J, Michel K, Salander Renberg E, Sayil I, Schmidtke A, van Heeringen C, Varnik A, Wasserman D (2010). Attempted suicide among immigrants in European countries: An international perspective. *Social Psychiatry and Psychiatric Epidemiology*. Published online: 1 January 2011. doi:10.1007/s00127-010-0336-6.

Chakraborty S, Bisoi S, Chattopadhyay D, Mishra R, Bhattacharya N, Biswas B (2010). A study on demographic and clinical profile of burn patients in an Apex Institute of West Bengal. *Indian Journal of Public Health* 54, 27-29.

Cheng JK, Fancher TL, Ratanasen M, Conner KR, Duberstein PR, Sue S, Takeuchi D (2010). Lifetime suicidal ideation and suicide attempts in Asian Americans. *Asian American Journal of Psychology* 1, 18-30.

Coentrao L, Moura D (2011). Acute cyanide poisoning among jewelry and textile industry workers. *American Journal of Emergency Medicine* 29, 78-81.

Cooper J (2011). Young black females in three UK cities have higher rates of self-harm than other ethnic groups but are less likely to be referred for psychiatric care. *Evidence-Based Mental Health* 14, 6.

Cox S, Kuo C, Jamieson DJ, Kourtis AP, McPheeters ML, Meikle SF, Posner SF (2011). Poisoning hospitalisations among reproductive-aged women in the USA, 1998-2006. *Injury Prevention*. Published online: 4 February 2011. doi:10.1136/ip.2010.029793.

Craig DG, Bates CM, Davidson JS, Martin KG, Hayes PC, Simpson KJ (2011). Overdose pattern and outcome in paracetamol-induced acute severe hepatotoxicity. *British Journal of Clinical Pharmacology* 71, 273-282.

Dai J, Chiu HFK, Conner KR, Chan SSM, Hou ZJ, Yu X, Caine ED (2010). Suicidal ideation and attempts among rural Chinese aged 16-34 years - Socio-demographic correlates in the context of a transforming China. *Journal of Affective Disorders*. doi:10.1016/j.jad.2010.10.042.

Darke S, Torok M, Kaye S, Ross J (2011). Attempted suicide, self-harm, and violent victimization among regular illicit drug users. *Suicide and Life-Threatening Behavior* 40, 587-596.

Daw R, Malzfeldt A (2010). Self-harm. *Mental Health Today* (Brighton, England), October 2010, 16-18.

Fein JA, Pailler ME, Barg FK, Wintersteen MB, Hayes K, Tien AY, Diamond GS (2010). Feasibility and effects of a web-based adolescent psychiatric assessment administered by clinical staff in the Pediatric Emergency Department. *Archives of Pediatrics and Adolescent Medicine* 164, 1112-1117.

Güloglu C, Orak M, Ustündag M, Altunci YA (2010). Analysis of amitriptyline overdose in emergency medicine. *Emergency Medicine Journal*. Published online: 5 October 2010. doi:10.1136/emj.2009.076596.

Gwashavanhu C (2010). Demographics of people who self-harm deliberately. *Emergency Nurse* 18, 28-32.

Joshi SC, Joshi A, Nigam P, Joshi G, Prakash C (2010). Pattern of poisoning cases admitted at a tertiary care centre in the Kumaon region of Uttarakhand. *Indian Journal of Forensic Medicine and Toxicology* 4, 4-5.

Khalil AH, Rabie MA, Abd-El-Aziz MF, Abdou TA, El-Rasheed AH, Sabry WM (2010). Clinical characteristics of depression among adolescent females: A cross-sectional study. *Child and Adolescent Psychiatry and Mental Health* 4, 6.

Kim JY, Lee JK (2010). Relationship of social support and meaning of life to suicidal thoughts in cancer patients. *Journal of Korean Academy of Nursing* 40, 524-532.

Kinyanda E, Kizza R, Levin J, Ndyanabangi S, Abbo C (2011). Adolescent suicidality as seen in rural northeastern Uganda. *Crisis* 32, 43-51.

Klonsky ED (2011). Non-suicidal self-injury in United States adults: Prevalence, sociodemographics, topography and functions. *Psychological Medicine*. Published online: 5 January 2011. doi:10.1017/S0033291710002497.

Krakowiak A, Kotwica M, Sliwkiewicz K (2011). Poisonings with street drugs: A review of 1993-2008 data from the toxicology unit in Poland. *International Journal of Occupational Medicine and Environmental Health* 23, 357-365.

Kuehn BM (2010). Military probes epidemic of suicide: Mental health issues remain prevalent. *Journal of American Medical Association* 304, 1427.

Lawler K, Mosepele M, Seloilwe E, Ratcliffe S, Steele K, Nthobatsang R, Steenhoff A (2011). Depression among HIV-positive individuals in Botswana: A behavioral surveillance. *AIDS and Behavior* 15, 204-208.

Lundh LG, Wångby-Lundh M, Paaske M, Ingesson S, Bjärehed J (2011). Depressive symptoms and deliberate self-harm in a community sample of adolescents: A prospective study. *Depression Research and Treatment* 2011, 935871.

Mahgoub N, Klimstra S, Kotbi N, Docherty JP (2011). Self-injurious behavior in the nursing home setting. *International Journal of Geriatric Psychiatry* 26, 27-30.

Manthripragada AD, Zhou EH, Budnitz DS, Lovegrove MC, Willy ME (2011). Characterization of acetaminophen overdose-related emergency department visits and hospitalizations in the United States. *Pharmacoepidemiology and Drug Safety*. Published online: 3 February 2011. doi:10.1002/pds.2090.

Martin G, Swannell SV, Hazell PL, Harrison JE, Taylor AW (2010). Self-injury in Australia: A community survey. *Medical Journal Australia* 193, 506-510.

Martin TC, Rocque MA (2011). Accidental and non-accidental ingestion of methadone and buprenorphine in childhood: A single center experience, 1999-2009. *Current Drug Safety* 6, 12-16.

McNicholas F, Adamson N, O'Sullivan M, Lennon R, Tobin B, Doherty M (2010). Children and adolescents presenting with deliberate self-harm (DSH): An eleven-year retrospective study. *Irish Journal of Medical Science* 179, 230-230.

Moberg T, Nordström P, Forslund K, Kristiansson M, Asberg M, Jokinen J (2011). CSF 5-HIAA and exposure to and expression of interpersonal violence in suicide attempters. *Journal of Affective Disorders*. Published online: 26 February 2011. doi: 10.1016/j.jad.2011.01.018.

Moniz P, Casal D, Mavioso C, Videira-Castro J, Angelica-Almeida M (2010). The self-inflicted burns-Typology and its prognostic relevance in a 14-year review of self-inflicted burns in a tertiary referral centre. *Burns* 37, 322-327.

Obeidat NM, Abutayeh RF, Hadidi KA (2010). Poisoning in Jordan: Analysis of three year data from Jordan National Drug and Poison Information Center. *Jordan Medical Journal* 44, 298-304.

Oprescu F, Peek-Asa C, Wallis A, Young T, Nour D, RM (2011). Pediatric poisonings and risk markers for hospital admission in a major emergency department in Romania. *Maternal and Child Health Journal*. Published online: 3 February 2011. doi:10.1007/s10995-011-0742-8.

Page RM, West JH (2011). Suicide ideation and psychosocial distress in sub-Saharan African youth. *American Journal of Health Behaviour* 35, 129-141.

Patrick AR, Miller M, Barber CW, Wang PS, Canning CF, Schneeweiss S (2010). Identification of hospitalizations for intentional self-harm when E-codes are incompletely recorded. *Pharmacoepidemiology and Drug Safety* 19, 1263-1275.

Pena JB, Matthieu MM, Zayas LH, Masyn K, Caine ED (2010). Co-occurring risk behaviors among White, Black, and Hispanic US high school adolescents with suicide attempts requiring medical attention, 1999-2007: Implications for future prevention initiatives. *Social Psychiatry and Psychiatric Epidemiology*. Published online: 9 December 2010. doi:10.1007/s00127-010-0322-z.

Peñas-Lledó EM, Dorado P, Agüera Z, Gratacós M, Estivill X, Fernández-Aranda F, Llerena A (2011). High risk of lifetime history of suicide attempts among CYP2D6 ultrarapid metabolizers with eating disorders. *Molecular Psychiatry*. Published online: 15 February 2011. doi:10.1038/mp.2011.5.

Ploderl M, Kralovec K, Yazdi K, Fartacek R (2011). A closer look at self-reported suicide attempts: false positives and false negatives. *Suicide and Life-Threatening Behavior* 41, 1-5.

Rafiei M, Seyfi A (2010). Epidemiologic study of suicide attempt referred to Hospitals of University of Medical Sciences in Markazi-Province from 2002 to 2006. *Iran Journal of Epidemiology* 4, 59-69.

Roos RAC (2011). Huntington's disease: a clinical review. *Orphanet Journal of Rare Diseases* 5, 40.

Sam-angsri N, Assanangkornchai S, Pattanasattayawong U, Muekthong A (2010). Health-risk behaviors among high-school students in southern Thailand. *Journal of the Medical Association of Thailand* 93, 1075-1083.

Scivoletto S, Boarati MA, Turkiewicz G (2010). Psychiatric emergencies in childhood and adolescence. *Revista Brasileira De Psiquiatria* 32, 112-120.

Shirkhoda M, Kaviani Far K, Narouie B, Shikhzadeh A, Ghasemi Rad M, Hanfi Bojd H (2011). Epidemiology and evaluation of 1073 burn patients in the southeast of Iran. *Shiraz E-Medical Journal* 12, 11-21.

Smith HP, Kaminski RJ (2010). Self-injurious behaviors in state prisons. *Criminal Justice Behaviour* 38, 26-41.

Snarr JD, Heyman RE, Slep AM (2011). Recent suicidal ideation and suicide attempts in a large-scale survey of the U.S. Air Force: Prevalences and demographic risk factors. *Suicide and Life-Threatening Behavior* 40, 544-552.

Sorodoc V, Jaba IM, Lionte C, Mungiu OC, Sorodoc L (2011). Epidemiology of acute drug poisoning in a tertiary center from Iasi county, Romania. *Human & Experimental Toxicology*. Published online: 26 March 2011. doi: 10.1177/0960327111403172.

Suokas JT, Perala J, Suominen K, Saarni S, Lonnqvist J, Suvisaari JM (2010). Epidemiology of suicide attempts among persons with psychotic disorder in the general population. *Schizophrenia Research* 124, 22-28.

Taylor AW, Martin G, Dal Grande E, Swannell S, Fullerton S, Hazell P, Harrison JE (2011). Methodological issues associated with collecting sensitive information over the telephone - experience from an Australian non-suicidal self-injury (NSSI) prevalence study. *BMC Medical Research Methodology* 11, 20.

Topal AE, Eren MN (2010). Gradually increasing predominance of self-mutilation in upper extremity arterial injuries: less morbidity but with high threat to society. *Turkish Journal of Trauma & Emergency Surgery* 16, 527-531.

Toprak S, Cetin I, Guven T, Can G, Demircan C (2010). Self-harm, suicidal ideation and suicide attempts among college students. *Psychiatry Research*. Published online: 30 October 2010. doi:10.1016/j.psychres.2010.09.009.

Tsalkidis A, Vaos G, Gardikis S, Kambouri K, Tripsianis G, Mantadakis E, Paraskakis E, Chatzimicael A (2010). Acute poisoning among children admitted to a regional University Hospital in Northern Greece. *Central European Journal of Public Health* 18, 219-223.

Ul Haq S, Subramanyam D, Agius M (2010). Assessment of self harm in an accident and emergency service - The development of a proforma to assess suicide intent and mental state in those presenting to the emergency department with self harm. *Psychiatria Danubina* 22, 1.

Veale DJ, Wium CA, Muller GJ (2011). Amitraz poisoning in South Africa: A two year survey (2008-2009). *Clinical Toxicology* 49, 40-44.

Vos P, Cloete K, le Roux A, Kidd M, Jordaan G (2011). A retrospective review of trends and clinical characteristics of methamphetamine-related acute psychiatric admissions in a South African context. *African Journal of Psychiatry* 13, 390-394.

Vrouva I, Fonagy P, Fearon PR, Roussow T (2010). The risk-taking and self-harm inventory for adolescents: Development and psychometric evaluation. *Psychological Assessment* 22, 852-865.

Wani AA, Ramzan AU, Malik NK, Qayoom A, Nizami FA, Kirmani AR, Wani MA (2011). Missile injury to the pediatric brain in conflict zones. *Journal of Neurosurgery: Pediatrics* 7, 276-281.

Xiang Y, Zhao W, Xiang H, Smith GA (2011). ED visits for drug-related poisoning in the United States, 2007. *American Journal of Emergency Medicine*. Published online: 2 March 2011. doi: 10.1016/j.ajem.2010.11.031.

You J, Leung F, Fu K, Lai CM (2011). The prevalence of nonsuicidal self-injury and different subgroups of self-injurers in Chinese adolescents. *Archives in Suicide Research* 15, 75-86.

Risk and protective factors

Abasiubong F, Bassey EA, Ogunsemi OO, Udobang JA (2011). Assessing the psychological well-being of caregivers of people living with HIV/AIDS in Niger Delta region, Nigeria. *AIDS Care* 23, 494-500.

Adrian M, Zeman J, Erdley C, Lisa L, Sim L (2010). Emotional dysregulation and interpersonal difficulties as risk factors for nonsuicidal self-injury in adolescent girls. *Journal of Abnormal Child Psychology*. Published online: 16 October 2010. doi:10.1007/s10802-010-9465-3.

Ahmad NS, Nasir R (2010). Emotional reactions and behavior of incest victims. *Procedia - Social and Behavioral Sciences* 5, 1023-1027.

Al-Barraq A, Farahat F, Daffallah NI (2010). Pattern and determinants of poisoning in a teaching hospital in Riyadh, Saudi Arabia. *Saudi Pharmaceutical Journal* 19, 57-63.

Algorta GP, Youngstrom EA, Frazier TW, Freeman AJ, Youngstrom JK, Findling RL (2011). Suicidality in pediatric bipolar disorder: predictor or outcome of family processes and mixed mood presentation? *Bipolar Disorder* 13, 76-86.

Alvarez MJ, Roura P, Osés A, Foguet Q, Solà J, Arrufat FX (2011). Prevalence and clinical impact of childhood trauma in patients with severe mental disorders. *The Journal of Nervous and Mental Disease* 199, 156-161.

Amaral G, Geierstanger S, Soleimanpour S, Brindis C (2011). Mental health characteristics and health-seeking behaviors of adolescent school-based health center users and nonusers. *Journal of School Health* 81, 138-145.

Andriopoulos I, Ellul J, Skokou M, Beratis S (2011). Suicidality in the "prodromal" phase of schizophrenia. *Comprehensive Psychiatry*. Published online: 22 December 2010. doi:10.1016/j.comppsych.2010.10.011.

Aronne LJ, Finer N, Hollander PA, England RD, Klioze SS, Chew RD, Fountaine RJ, Powell CM, Obourn JD (2011). Efficacy and safety of CP-945,598, a selective Cannabinoid CB1 receptor antagonist, on weight loss and maintenance. *Obesity (Silver Spring)*. Published online: 3 February 2011. doi:10.1038/oby.2010.352.

Arron K, Oliver C, Moss J, Berg K, Burbidge C (2010). The prevalence and phenomenology of self-injurious and aggressive behaviour in genetic syndromes. *Journal of Intellectual Disability Research* 55, 109-120.

Asenjo Lobos C, Komossa K, Rummel-Kluge C, Hunger H, Schmid F, Schwarz S, Leucht S (2010). Clozapine versus other atypical antipsychotics for schizophrenia. *Cochrane Database Systematic Reviews* 11, CD006633.

Aschenbrenner DS (2011). New use for duloxetine. *The American Journal of Nursing* 111, 23.

Aubin HJ, Berlin I, Reynaud M (2011). Current smoking, hypoxia, and suicide. *American Journal of Psychiatry* 168, 326-327.

Auxemery Y, Fidelle G (2010). Internet and suicidality. A googling study about mediatic view of a suicidal pact. *Annales Médico-psychologiques* 168, 502-507.

Ayuso-Mateos JL (2011). Conventional antiepileptic drugs are not associated with an increased risk of suicidal behaviour or self-harm. *Evidence Based Mental Health* 14, 2.

Azorin JM, Kaladjian A, Adida M, Fakra E, Hantouche E, Lancrenon S (2011). Baseline and prodromal characteristics of first- versus multiple-episode mania in a French cohort of bipolar patients. *European Psychiatry*. Published online: 2 February 2011. doi:10.1016/j.eurpsy.2010.11.001.

Bae J, Park EY, Park SW (2011). Modifying effect of suicidal ideation on the relationship between asthma and cigarette use behaviours among Korean adolescents. *Journal of Adolescent Health* 48, S18-S19.

Baetens I, Claes L, Willem L, Muehlenkamp J, Bijttebier P (2010). The relationship between non-suicidal self-injury and temperament in male and female adolescents based on child- and parent-report. *Personality and Individual Differences* 50, 527-530.

Bagary M (2011). Epilepsy, antiepileptic drugs and suicidality. *Current Opinion in Neurology* 24, 177-182.

Bahk WM, Park S, Jon DI, Yoon BH, Min KJ, Hong JP (2011). Relationship between painful physical symptoms and severity of depressive symptomatology and suicidality. *Psychiatry Research*. Published online: 15 February 2011. doi:10.1016/j.psychres.2011.01.009.

Bakhshani NM, Bahareh B, Bakhshani S, Lashkaripour K (2010). Suicidal attempts among individuals seeking treatment for substance dependency. *Procedia - Social and Behavioral Sciences* 5, 1982-1985.

Balch CM, Shanafelt TD, Sloan J, Satele DV, Kuerer HM (2010). Burnout and career satisfaction among surgical oncologists compared with other surgical specialties. *Annals of Surgical Oncology* 18, 16-25.

Balfe M, Tantam D (2010). A descriptive social and health profile of a community sample of adults and adolescents with Asperger syndrome. *BMC Research Notes* 3, 300.

Balkin RS, Leicht DJ, Sartor T, Powell J (2011). Assessing the relationship between therapeutic goal attainment and psychosocial characteristics for adolescents in crisis residence. *Journal of Mental Health* 20, 32-42.

Barkacs LL, Barkacs CB (2010). Do you think I'm sexty? Minors and sexting: Teenage fad or child pornography? *Journal of Legal, Ethical and Regulatory Issues* 13, 23-31.

Barnes AJ (2011). Suicide attempts more common in offspring of depressed parents exposed to suicidal behaviour than unexposed offspring. *Evidence Based Mental Health* 14, 7.

Baumann AA, Kuhlberg JA, Zayas LH (2010). Familism, mother-daughter mutuality, and suicide attempts of adolescent Latinas. *Journal of Family Psychology* 24, 616-624.

Bergen H, Hawton K, Waters K, Cooper J, Kapur N (2010). Epidemiology and trends in non-fatal self-harm in three centres in England: 2000-2007. *British Journal of Psychiatry* 197, 493-498.

Bhoomikumar J, Kullgren G (2011). Gender difference in suicidal expressions and it's determinants among young people in Cambodia, a post-conflict country. *BMC Psychiatry* 11, 47.

Bilen K, Ottosson C, Castren M, Ponzer S, Ursing C, Ranta P, Ekdahl K, Pettersson H (2010). Deliberate self-harm patients in the emergency department: Factors associated with repeated self-harm among 1524 patients. *Emergency Medicine Journal*. Published online: 12 November 2010. doi:10.1136/emj.2010.102616.

Blasco-Fontecilla H, Baca-Garcia E, Duberstein P, Perez-Rodriguez MM, Dervic K, Saiz-Ruiz J, Courtet P, De Leon J, Oquendo MA (2010). An exploratory study of the relationship between diverse life events and specific personality disorders in a sample of suicide attempters. *Journal of Personality Disorders* 24, 773-784.

Blasco-Ros C, Sanchez-Lorente S, Martinez M (2010). Recovery from depressive symptoms, state anxiety and post-traumatic stress disorder in women exposed to physical and psychological, but not to psychological intimate partner violence alone: A longitudinal study. *BMC Psychiatry* 10, 98.

Boeninger DK, Masyn KE, Feldman BJ, Conger RD (2011). Sex differences in developmental trends of suicide ideation, plans, and attempts among European American adolescents. *Suicide and Life-Threatening Behavior* 40, 451-464.

Bohman H, Jonsson U, Von Knorring A-L, Von Knorring L, Paaren A, Olsson G (2010). Somatic symptoms as a marker for severity in adolescent depression. *Acta Paediatrica* 99, 1724-1730.

Bolton JM, Robinson J (2010). Population-attributable fractions of Axis I and Axis II mental disorders for suicide attempts: findings from a representative sample of the adult, noninstitutionalized US population. *American Journal of Public Health* 100, 2473-2480.

Bolton S-L, Sareen J (2011). Sexual orientation and its relation to mental disorders and suicide attempts: Findings from a nationally representative sample. *Canadian Journal of Psychiatry* 56, 35-43.

Borges G, Nock MK, Abad JMH, Hwang I, Sampson NA, Alonso J, Andrade LH, Angermeyer MC, Beautrais A, Bromet E, Bruffaerts R, De Girolamo G, Florescu S, Gureje O, Hu C, Karam EG, Kovess-Masfety V, Lee S, Levinson D, Medina-Mora ME (2010). Twelve-month prevalence of and risk factors for suicide attempts in the World Health Organization World Mental Health Surveys. *Journal of Clinical Psychiatry* 71, 1617-1628.

Borschmann R, Moran P (2011). Crisis management in borderline personality disorder. *International Journal of Social Psychiatry* 57, 18-20.

Bossarte RM, Swahn MH (2011). The associations between early alcohol use and suicide attempts among adolescents with a history of major depression. *Addictive Behaviors* 36, 532-535.

Bouris A, Guilamo-Ramos V, Pickard A, Shiu C, Loosier PS, Dittus P, Gloppen K, Michael Waldmiller j (2010). A systematic review of parental influences on the health and well-being of lesbian, gay, and bisexual youth: time for a new public health research and practice agenda. *Journal of Primary Prevention* 31, 273-309.

Botega NJ, Mitsuush GN, Azevedo RC, Lima DD, Fanger PC, Mauro ML, Gaspar KC, Silva VF (2010). Depression, alcohol use disorders and nicotine dependence among patients at a general hospital. *Revista Brasileira de Psiquiatria* 32, 250-256.

Bradvik L, Berglund M (2010). Depressive episodes with suicide attempts in severe depression: suicides and controls differ only in the later episodes of unipolar depression. *Archives of Suicide Research* 14, 363-367.

Bradvik L, Berglund M (2011). Repetition of suicide attempts across episodes of severe depression Behavioural sensitisation found in suicide group but not in controls. *BMC Psychiatry* 11, 5.

Brewin CR, Garnett R, Andrews B (2010). Trauma, identity and mental health in UK military veterans. *Psychological Medicine* 14, 1-8.

Briere J, Hodges M, Godbout N (2010). Traumatic stress, affect dysregulation, and dysfunctional avoidance: A structural equation model. *Journal of Trauma & Stress* 23, 767–774.

Brietzke E, Moreira CLR, Toniolo RA, Lafer B (2010). Clinical correlates of eating disorder comorbidity in women with bipolar disorder type I. *Journal of Affective Disorders*. Published online: 10 November 2010. doi:10.1016/j.jad.2010.10.020.

Brinkman T, Delaney B, Manley P, Muriel A, Chordas C, Liptak C (2011). Suicidal ideation in survivors of pediatric brain tumors. *Pediatric Blood & Cancer* 55, 957-958.

Britton JW, Shih JJ (2010). Antiepileptic drugs and suicidality. *Drug, Healthcare and Patient Safety* 2, 181-189.

Brower KJ, McCammon RJ, Wojnar M, Ilgen MA, Wojnar J, Valenstein M (2010). Prescription sleeping pills, insomnia, and suicidality in the National Comorbidity Survey Replication. *Journal of Clinical Psychiatry*. Published online: 21 September 2010. doi:10.4088/JCP.09m05484gry.

Burbidge C, Oliver C, Moss J, Arron K, Berg K, Furniss F, Hill L, Trusler K, Woodock K (2010). The association between repetitive behaviours, impulsivity and hyperactivity in people with intellectual disability. *Journal of Intellectual Disability Research* 54, 1078-1092.

Butler AW, Breen G, Tozzi F, Craddock N, Gill M, Korszun A, Maier W, Middleton LT, Mors O, Owen MJ, Perry J, Preisig M, Rice JP, Rietschel M, Jones L, Farmer AE, Lewis CM, McGuffin P (2010). A genomewide linkage study on suicidality in major depressive disorder confirms evidence for linkage to 2p12. *American Journal of Medical Genetics Part B: Neuropsychiatric Genetics* 153b, 1465-1473.

Cahill K, Stead LF, Lancaster T (2011). Nicotine receptor partial agonists for smoking cessation. *Cochrane Database of Systematic Reviews* 2, 006103.

Carpiniello B, Lai L, Pirarba S, Sardu C, Pinna F (2010). Impulsivity and aggressiveness in bipolar disorder with co-morbid borderline personality disorder. *Psychiatry Research*. Published online: 3 December 2010. doi: 10.1016/j.psychres.2010.10.026.

Cassidy F (2011). Risk factors of attempted suicide in bipolar disorder. *Suicide and Life-Threatening Behaviour* 41, 6-11.

Cavalcante GIT, Capistrano VLM, Cavalcante FSD, Vasconcelos SMM, Macedo DS, Sousa FCF; Woods DJ, Fonteles MMF (2010). Implications of efavirenz for neuropsychiatry: a review. *International Journal of Neuroscience* 120, 739-745.

Ceskova E, Prikryl R, Kasparek T (2011). Suicides in males after the first episode of schizophrenia. *Journal of Nervous and Mental Disease* 199, 62-64.

Cetin M, Turk YZ, Ozer M, Turker T, Bakir B (2010). Analysis of patients followed-up at the emergency internal medicine outpatients department of Gulhane Military Hospital in 2003 for suicide attempt. *Pakistan Journal of Medical Sciences* 26, 842-846.

Cha CB, Najmi S, Park JM, Finn CT, Nock MK (2010). Attentional bias toward suicide-related stimuli predicts suicidal behavior: Correction. *Journal of Abnormal Psychology* 119, 874.

Chakraborty A, McManus S, Brugha TS, Bebbington P, King M (2011). Mental health of the non-heterosexual population of England. *British Journal of Psychiatry* 198, 143-148.

Champion JD (2011). Context of sexual risk behaviour among abused ethnic minority adolescent women. *International Nursing Review* 58, 61-67

Chang WC, Tang JY, Hui CL, Chiu CP, Lam MM, Wong GH, Chung DW, Law CW, Tso S, Chan KP, Hung SF, Chen EY (2011). Gender differences in patients presenting with first-episode psychosis in Hong Kong: a three-year follow up study. *Australian and New Zealand Journal of Psychiatry* 45, 199-205.

Chapman AL, Dixon-Gordon KL, Walters KN (2011). Experiential avoidance and emotion regulation in borderline personality disorder. *Journal of Rational-Emotive & Cognitive-Behaviour Therapy* 29, 35-52.

Chatard A, Selimbegovi L (2011). When self-destructive thoughts flash through the mind: Failure to meet standards affects the accessibility of suicide-related thoughts. *Journal of Personality and Social Psychology*. Published online: 10 February 2011. doi:10.1037/a0022461.

Chaytor N, Ciechanowski P, Miller JW, Fraser R, Russo J, Unutzer J, Gilliam F (2011). Long-term outcomes from the PEARLS randomized trial for the treatment of depression in patients with epilepsy. *Epilepsy and Behavior*. Published online: 16 March 2011. doi: 10.1016/j.yebeh.2011.01.017.

Chen CK, Tsai YC, Hsu HJ, Wu IW, Sun CY, Chou CC, Lee CC, Tsai CR, Wu MS, Wang LJ (2010). Depression and suicide risk in hemodialysis patients with chronic renal failure. *Psychosomatics* 52, 528-528.

Chen VC, Tan HK, Chen CY, Chen TH, Liao LR, Lee CT, Dewey M, Stewart R, Prince M, Cheng AT (2011). Mortality and suicide after self-harm: Community cohort study in Taiwan. *British Journal of Psychiatry* 198, 31-36.

Chen YY, Chen F, Yip PS (2010). The impact of media reporting of suicide on actual suicides in Taiwan, 2002-05. *Journal of Epidemiology and Community Health*. Published online: 5 December 2010. doi:10.1136/jech.2010.117903.

Cheng Q, Fu KW, Yip PS (2010). A comparative study of online suicide-related information in Chinese and English. *Journal of Clinical Psychiatry*. Published online: 7 September 2010. doi:10.4088/JCP.09m05440blu.

Chesin MS, Jeglic EL, Stanley B (2010). Pathways to high-lethality suicide attempts in individuals with borderline personality disorder. *Archives of Suicide Research* 14, 342-362.

Chiesa M, Sharp R, Fonagy P (2010). Clinical associations of deliberate self-injury and its impact on the outcome of community-based and long-term inpatient treatment for personality disorder. *Psychotherapy and Psychosomatics* 80, 100-109.

Chin YR, Lee HY, So ES (2011). Suicidal ideation and associated factors by sex in Korean adults: a population-based cross-sectional survey. *International Journal of Public Health*. Published online: 23 March 2011. Doi: 0.1007/s00038-011-0245-9.

Chiu JF, Chokka PR (2011). Prevalence of bipolar disorder symptoms in primary care (ProBiD-PC). A Canadian study. *Canadian Family Physician* 57, 58-67.

Christiansen E, Stenager E (2010). Risk for attempted suicide in children and youths after contact with somatic hospitals: A Danish register based nested case-control study. *Journal of Epidemiology and Community Health*. Published online: 14 October 2010. doi:10.1136/jech.2009.103887.

Chronis-Tuscano A, Molina BSG, Pelham WE, Applegate B, Dahlke A, Overmyer M, Lahey BB (2010). Very early predictors of adolescent depression and suicide attempts in children with attention-deficit/hyperactivity disorder. *Archives of General Psychiatry* 67, 1044-1051.

Clarke M, Davies S, Hollin C, Duggan C (2011). Long-term suicide risk in forensic psychiatric patients. *Archives of Suicide Research* 15, 16-28.

Cleverley K, Kidd SA (2010). Resilience and suicidality among homeless youth. *Journal of Adolescence*. Published online: 3 December 2010. doi:10.1016/j.adolescence.2010.11.003.

Cluver L, Bowes L, Gardner F (2010). Risk and protective factors for bullying victimization among AIDS-affected and vulnerable children in South Africa. *Child Abuse & Neglect* 34, 793-803.

Cnattingius S, Svensson T, Granath F, Iliadou A (2011). Maternal smoking during pregnancy and risks of suicidal acts in young offspring. *European Journal of Epidemiology*. Published online: 18 February 2011. doi:10.1007/s10654-011-9556-7.

Coêlho BM, Andrade LH, Guarniero FB, Yuan-Pang W (2010). The influence of the comorbidity between depression and alcohol use disorder on suicidal behaviors in the São Paulo Epidemiologic Catchment Area Study, Brazil. *Revista Brasileira de Psiquiatria*. Published online: 15 October 2010. doi:10.1590/S1516-44462010005000027.

Cohen A, Chapman BP, Gilman SE, Delmerico AM, Wieczorek W, Duberstein PR, Lyness JM (2010). Social inequalities in the occurrence of suicidal ideation among older primary care patients. *American Journal of Geriatric Psychiatry* 18, 1146-1154.

Conner KR, Gunzler D, Tang W, Tu XM, Maisto SA (2010). Test of a clinical model of drinking and suicidal risk. *Alcoholism, Clinical and Experimental Research* 35, 60-68.

Conus P, Cotton S, Schimmelmann BG, McGorry PD, Lambert M (2010). Pretreatment and outcome correlates of sexual and physical trauma in an epidemiological cohort of first-episode psychosis patients. *Schizophrenia Bulletin* 36, 1105-1114.

Courtet P (2010). Suicidality: Risk factors and the effects of antidepressants. The example of parallel reduction of suicidality and other depressive symptoms during treatment with the SNRI, milnacipran. *Neuropsychiatric Disease and Treatment* 6, 3-8.

Coventry WL, James MR, Eaves LJ, Gordon SD, Gillespie NA, Ryan L, Heath AC, Montgomery GW, Martin NG, Wray NR (2011). Do 5HTTLPR and stress interact in risk for depression and suicidality? Item response analyses of a large sample. *American Journal of Medical Genetics Part B: Neuropsychiatric Genetics* 153B, 757-765.

Cox DW, Ghahramanlou-Holloway M, Szeto EH, Greene FN, Engel C, Wynn GH, Bradley J, Grammer G (2011). Gender differences on documented trauma histories: Inpatients admitted to a Military Psychiatric Unit for suicide-related thoughts or behaviors. *The Journal of Nervous and Mental Disease* 199, 183-190.

Crane C, Shah D, Barnhofer T, Holmes EA (2011). Suicidal imagery in a previously depressed community sample. *Clinical Psychology & Psychotherapy*. Published online: 21 January 2011. doi:10.1002/cpp.741.

Cui S, Cheng Y, Xu Z, Chen D, Wang Y (2010). Peer relationships and suicide ideation and attempts among Chinese adolescents. *Child: Care, Health and Development*. Published online: 28 December 2010. 10.1111/j.1365-2214.2010.01181.x.

Cukrowicz KC, Cheavens JS, Van Orden KA, Ragain RM, Cook RL (2011). Perceived burdensomeness and suicide ideation in older adults. *Psychology and Aging*. Published online: 19 March 2011. doi:10.1037/a0021836.

Cukrowicz K, Smith P, Poindexter E (2011). The effect of participating in suicide research: Does participating in a research protocol on suicide and psychiatric symptoms increase suicide ideation and attempts? *Suicide and Life-Threatening Behavior* 40, 535-543.

Curtis C (2010). Youth perceptions of suicide and help-seeking: 'They'd think I was weak or "mental"'. *Journal of Youth Studies* 13, 699-715.

Czeizel AE (2011). Attempted suicide and pregnancy. *Journal of Injury and Violence Research* 3, 45-54.

Dake JA, Price JH, Kolm-Valdivia N, Wielinski M (2010). Association of adolescent choking game activity with selected risk behaviors. *Academic Pediatrics* 10, 410-416.

Dalal PK, Saha R, Agarwal M (2010). Psychiatric aspects of burn. *Indian Journal of Plastic Surgery* 43, 136-142.

Dale R, Power K, Kane S, Stewart AM, Murray L (2010). The role of parental bonding and early maladaptive schemas in the risk of suicidal behavior repetition. *Archives of Suicide Research* 14, 311-328.

Daffern M, Thomas S, Ferguson M, Podubinski T, Hollander Y, Kulkhani J, DeCastella A, Foley F (2010). The impact of psychiatric symptoms, interpersonal style, and coercion on aggression and self-harm during psychiatric hospitalization. *Psychiatry* 73, 365-381.

Dalrymple KL, Zimmerman M (2011). Age of onset of social anxiety disorder in depressed outpatients. *Journal of Anxiety Disorders* 25, 131-137.

Daly EJ, Trivedi MH, Fava M, Shelton R, Wisniewski SR, Morris DW, Stegman D, Preskorn SH, Rush AJ (2011). The relationship between adverse events during selective serotonin reuptake inhibitor treatment for major depressive disorder and nonremission in the suicide assessment methodology study. *Journal of Clinical Psychopharmacology* 31, 31-38.

Darrow SM, Follette WC, Maragakis A, Dykstra T (2010). Reviewing risk for individuals with developmental disabilities. *Clinical Psychology Review* 31, 472-477.

Daryanavard A, Madani A, Mahmoodi MS, Rahimi S, Nourooziyan F, Hosseinpoor M (2011). Prevalence of depression among high school students and its relation to family structure. *American Journal of Applied Sciences* 8, 39-44.

Daudin M, Cohen D, Edel Y, Bonnet N, Bodeau N, Consoli A, Deniau E, Guile J-M (2010). Psychosocial and clinical correlates of substance use disorder in an adolescent inpatient psychiatric population. *Journal of the Canadian Academy of Child and Adolescent Psychiatry* 19, 264-273.

Davaji RBO, Valizadeh S, Nikamal M (2010). The relationship between attachment styles and suicide ideation: The study of Turkmen students, Iran. *Procedia - Social and Behavioral Sciences* 5, 1190-1194.

Davidson KM, Tyrer P, Norrie J, Palmer SJ, Tyrer H (2010). Cognitive therapy v. usual treatment for borderline personality disorder: prospective 6-year follow-up. *British Journal of Psychiatry* 197, 456-462.

Deasy C, Bray J, Smith K, Harriss LR, Bernard SA, Cameron P (2011). Paediatric hanging associated out of hospital cardiac arrest in Melbourne, Australia: characteristics and outcomes. *Emergency Medicine Journal*. Published online: 18 February 2011. doi:10.1136/emj.2010.105510.

Deeley ST, Love AW (2010). Does asking adolescents about suicidal ideation induce negative mood state? *Violence and Victims* 25, 677-688.

Deng F, Tao F-B, Wan Y-H, Hao J-H, Su P-Y, Cao Y-X (2011). Early menarche and psychopathological symptoms in young Chinese women. *Journal of Women's Health* 20, 207-213.

De Morais NA, Koller SH, Raffaelli M (2010). Stressful events and adjustment indicators among socially vulnerable Brazilian teenagers. *Universitas Psychologica* 9, 787-806.

de Portugal E, Martínez C, González N, Del Amo V, Haro JM, Cervilla JA (2011). Clinical and cognitive correlates of psychiatric comorbidity in delusional disorder outpatients. *Australian and New Zealand Journal of Psychiatry*. Published online: 21 March 2011. doi:10.3109/00048674.2010.551279.

Dietz TL (2010). Substance misuse, suicidal ideation, and suicide attempts among a national sample of homeless. *Journal of Social Service Research* 37, 1-18.

Diflorio A, Jones I (2010). Is sex important? Gender differences in bipolar disorder. *International Review of Psychiatry* 22, 437-452.

Doerfler LA, Moran PW, Hannigan KE (2010). Situations associated with admission to an acute care inpatient psychiatric unit. *Psychological Services* 7, 254-265.

Dogra AK, Basu S, Das S (2011). Impact of meaning in life and reasons for living to hope and suicidal ideation: a study among college students. *SIS Journal of Projective Psychology & Mental Health* 18, 89-102.

Dour HJ, Cha CB, Nock MK (2011). Evidence for an emotion-cognition interaction in the statistical prediction of suicide attempts. *Behaviour Research and Therapy* 49, 294-298.

Dube P, Kroenke K, Bair MJ, Theobald D, Williams LS (2010). The P4 screener: Evaluation of a brief measure for assessing potential suicide risk in 2 randomized effectiveness trials of primary care and oncology patients. *Primary Care Companion to the Journal of Clinical Psychiatry* 12, 6.

Dyrbye LN, Power DV, Massie FS, Eacker A, Harper W, Thomas MR, Szydlo DW, Sloan JA, Shanafelt TD (2010). Factors associated with resilience to and recovery from burnout: A prospective, multi-institutional study of US medical students. *Medical Education* 44, 1016-1026.

Ecker-Schlipf B (2011). Suicide risk among antiepileptic drugs depending on the disease. *Psychopharmakotherapie* 18, 43-44.

Elkins IJ (2011). Young children with ADHD are at increased risk of depression and suicidal behaviour in adolescence. *Evidence Based Mental Health* 14, 15.

Engedal K, Barca ML, Laks J, Selbaek G (2010). Depression in Alzheimer's disease: Specificity of depressive symptoms using three different clinical criteria. *International Journal of Geriatric Psychiatry*. Published online: 7 December 2010. doi:10.1002/gps.2631.

Enriquez M, Kelly PJ, Witt J, Rodriguez L, Lopez N, Smueles J, Romey T, Sweet D (2010). Silence is not golden: Invisible Latinas living with HIV in the Midwest. *Journal of Immigrant and Minority Health* 12, 932-939.

Evensen J, Røssberg JI, Haahr U, Ten Velden Hegelstad W, Joa I, Johannessen JO, Langeveld H, Larsen TK, Melle I, Opjordsmoen S, Rund BR, Simonsen E, Sundet K, Vaglum P, Friis S, McGlashan T (2011). Contrasting monosymptomatic patients with hallucinations and delusions in first-episode psychosis patients: a five-year longitudinal follow-up study. *Psychopathology* 44, 90-97.

Fan AP, Kosik RO, Su TP, Lee FY, Hou MC, Chen YA, Chen CH, Lee CH (2011). Factors associated with suicidal ideation in Taiwanese medical students. *Medical Teacher* 33, 256-257.

Farooq U, Nasrullah M, Bhatti JA, Majeed M, Hanif M, Khan JS, Khan MM (2010). Incidence of burns and factors associated with their hospitalisation in Rawalpindi, Pakistan. *Burns*. Published online: 7 December 2010. doi:10.1016/j.burns.2010.10.009.

Fergusson DM, Horwood LJ, Miller AL, Kennedy MA (2011). Life stress, 5-HTTLPR and mental disorder: Findings from a 30-year longitudinal study. *British Journal of Psychiatry* 198, 129-135.

Fernando K, Carter JD, Frampton CM, Luty SE, McKenzie J, Mulder RT, Joyce PR (2011). Childhood-, teenage-, and adult-onset depression: Diagnostic and individual characteristics in a clinical sample. *Comprehensive Psychiatry*. Published online: 3 March 2011. .

Fiori LM, Wanner B, Jomphe V, Croteau J, Vitaro F, Tremblay RE, Bureau A, Turecki G (2010). Association of polyaminergic loci with anxiety, mood disorders, and attempted suicide. *Plos One* 5, e15146.

Forcano L, Alvarez E, Santamaria JJ, Jimenez-Murcia S, Granero R, Penelo E, Alonso P, Sanchez I, Menchon JM, Ulman F, Bulik CM, Fernandez-Aranda F (2010). Suicide attempts in anorexia nervosa subtypes. *Comprehensive Psychiatry*. Published online: 30 October 2010. doi:10.1016/j.comppsych.2010.09.003.

Fragoso YD, Frota ERC, Lopes JS, Noal JS, Giacomo MC, Gomes S, Goncalves MVM, da Gama PD, Finkelsztejn A (2010). Severe depression, suicide attempts, and ideation during the use of interferon Beta by patients with multiple sclerosis. *Clinical Neuropharmacology* 33, 312-316.

Franklin JC, Hessel ET, Aaron RV, Arthur MS, Heilbron N, Prinstein MJ (2010). The functions of nonsuicidal self-injury: Support for cognitive-affective regulation and opponent processes from a novel psychophysiological paradigm. *Journal of Abnormal Psychology* 119, 850-862.

Freedenthal S, Lamis DA, Osman A, Kahlo D, Gutierrez PM (2011). Evaluation of the psychometric properties of the Interpersonal Needs Questionnaire-12 in samples of men and women. *Journal of Clinical Psychology*. Published online: 3 March 2011. doi:10.1002/jclp.20782.

Freudenstein O, Zohar A, Apter A, Shoval G, Weizman A, Zalsman G (2011). Parental bonding in severely suicidal adolescent inpatients. *European Psychiatry*. Published online: 11 March 2011. doi: 10.1016/j.eurpsy.2011.01.006.

Fruh SM, Fulkerson JA, Mulekar MS, Kendrick LAJ, Clanton C (2011). The surprising benefits of the family meal. *Journal for Nurse Practitioners* 7, 18-22.

Fuller-Thomson E, Dalton AD (2011). Suicidal ideation among individuals whose parents have divorced: Findings from a representative Canadian community survey. *Psychiatry Research*. Published online: 5 January 2011. doi:10.1016/j.psychres.2010.12.004.

Galligan SB, Barnett RV, Brennan MA, Israel GD (2010). Understanding the link between gender role conflict, resilience, and propensity for suicide in adolescent and emerging adult males. *International Journal of Men's Health* 9, 201-210.

Galione J, Zimmerman M (2010). A comparison of depressed patients with and without borderline personality disorder: Implications for interpreting studies of the validity of the bipolar spectrum. *Journal of Personality Disorders* 24, 763-772.

Gammelgard M, Koivisto AM, Eronen M, Kaltiala-Heino R (2010). Violence risk and psychopathology in institutionalised adolescents. *Journal of Forensic Psychiatry and Psychology* 21, 933-949.

Ganz D, Sher L (2010). Suicidal behavior in adolescents with post-traumatic stress disorder. *Minerva Pediatrica* 62, 363-370.

Garland EL, Howard MO (2010). Phenomenology of adolescent inhalant intoxication. *Experimental and Clinical Psychopharmacology* 18, 498-509.

Garrido EF, Culhane SE, Raviv T, Taussig HN (2010). Does community violence exposure predict trauma symptoms in a sample of maltreated youth in foster care? *Violence and Victims* 25, 755-769.

Garza D, Murphy M, Tseng L-J, Riordan HJ, Chatterjee A (2011). A double-blind randomized placebo-controlled pilot study of neuropsychiatric adverse events in abstinent smokers treated with varenicline or placebo. *Biological Psychiatry*. Published online: 2 February 2011. doi:10.1016/j.biopsych.2010.12.005.

Garza MJ, Pettit JW (2010). Perceived burdensomeness, familism, and suicidal ideation among Mexican women: Enhancing understanding of risk and protective factors. *Suicide and Life-Threatening Behavior* 40, 561-573.

Gavin AR, Tabb KM, Melville JL, Guo Y, Katon W (2011). Prevalence and correlates of suicidal ideation during pregnancy. *Archives of Women's Mental Health*. Published online: 17 February 2011. doi:10.1007/s00737-011-0207-5.

Gaviria SL, Rondon MB (2010). Some considerations on women's mental health in Latin America and the Caribbean. *International Review of Psychiatry* 22, 363-369.

Ghoreishi A, Rahmanpour H, Mousavinasab N (2010). Evaluation of psychological problems in teenagers suffering from polycystic ovary syndrome. *Journal of Zanjan University of Medical Sciences and Health Services* 18, 76-83.

Gibb SJ, Fergusson DM, Horwood LJ (2011). Relationship duration and mental health outcomes: Findings from a 30-year longitudinal study. *British Journal of Psychiatry* 198, 24-30.

Gibb SJ, Fergusson DM, Horwood LJ (2011). Relationship separation and mental health problems: findings from a 30-year longitudinal study. *Australian & New Zealand Journal of Psychiatry* 45, 163-169.

Gibbons RD, Hur K, Brown CH, Mann JJ (2010). Gabapentin and suicide attempts. *Pharmacoepidemiology and Drug Safety* 19, 1241–1247.

Gilzean T (2011). Communicating chaos, regaining control: The implications for social work of writing about self-injury. *Journal of Social Work Practice* 25, 31-46.

Giupponi G, Bizzarri J, Pycha R, Innamorati M, Lester D, Conca A, Girardi P, Tatarelli R, Pompili M (2010). Socioeconomic risk factors and depressive symptoms in alcohol use disorders among male suicides in South Tirol, Italy. *Journal of Addictive Disorders* 29, 466-474.

Gjersvik P (2010). Suicidal thoughts linked to acne severity, not treatment! *Forum for Nordic Dermato-Venerology* 15, 103.

Glass JE, Ilgen MA, Winters JJ, Murray RL, Perron BE, Chermack ST (2010). Inpatient hospitalization in addiction treatment for patients with a history of suicide attempt: a case of support for treatment performance measures. *Journal of Psychoactive Drugs* 42,315-325.

Glenn CR, Klonsky ED (2010). A multimethod analysis of impulsivity in nonsuicidal self-injury. *Personality Disorders: Theory, Research, and Treatment* 1, 67-75.

Goodwin RD (2011). Is COPD associated with suicide behavior? *Journal of Psychiatric Research*. Published online: 15 February 2011. doi:10.1016/j.jpsychires.2011.01.014.

Gordon KH, Selby EA, Anestis MD, Bender TW, Witte TK, Braithwaite S, Van Orden KA, Bresin K, Joiner TE (2010). The reinforcing properties of repeated deliberate self-harm. *Archives of Suicide Research* 14, 329-341.

Gordon KH, Bresin K, Dombeck J, Routledge C, Wonderlich JA (2011). The impact of the 2009 Red River flood on interpersonal risk factors for suicide. *Crisis* 32, 52-5.

Gos T, Krell D, Bielau H, Steiner J, Mawrin C, Trubner K, Brisch R, Bernstein HG, Jankowski Z, Bogerts B (2010). Demonstration of disturbed activity of the lateral amygdaloid nucleus projection neurons in depressed patients by the AgNOR staining method. *Journal of Affective Disorders* 126, 402-410.

Goy ER, Ganzini L (2010). Prevalence and natural history of neuropsychiatric syndromes in Veteran Hospice patients. *Journal of Pain and Symptom Management* 41, 394-401.

Greydanus D, Patel D, Pratt H (2010). Suicide risk in adolescents with chronic illness: Implications for primary care and specialty pediatric practice: A review. *Developmental Medicine and Child Neurology* 52, 1083-1087.

Gulec MY, Ozalmete OA, Ozturk M, Gulec H, Sayar K, Kose S (2010). Plasma neuropeptide Y levels in medication naive adolescents with major depressive disorder. *Bulletin of Clinical Psychopharmacology* 20, 132-138.

Gunter WD, Bakken NW (2011). Transitioning to middle school in the sixth grade: A Hierarchical Linear Modeling (HLM) analysis of substance use, violence, and suicidal thoughts. *The Journal of Early Adolescents* 30, 895-915.

Gureje O, Oladeji B, Hwang I, Chiu WT, Kessler RC, Sampson NA, Alonso J, Andrade LH, Beautrais A, Borges G, Bromet E, Bruffaerts R, de Girolamo G, de Graaf R, Gal G, He Y, Hu C, Iwata N, Karam EG, Kovess-Masféty V, Matschinger H, Moldovan MV, Posada-Villa J, Sagar R, Scocco P, Seedat S, Tomov T, Nock MK (2010). Parental psychopathology and the risk of suicidal behavior in their offspring: Results from the World Mental Health surveys. *Molecular Psychiatry*. Published online: 16 November 2010. doi:10.1038/mp. 2010.111.

Hadland S, Kerr T, Marshall B, Qi JZ, Montaner J, Wood E (2011). Suicide and history of childhood trauma among street youth. *Journal of Adolescent Health* 48, S87-S88.

Hagopian A, Barker K (2011). Should we end military recruiting in high schools as a matter of child protection and public health? *American Journal of Public Health* 101, 19-23.

Hall MT, Howard MO, McCabe SE (2010). Prescription drug misuse among antisocial youths. *Journal of Studies on Alcohol and Drugs* 71, 917-924.

Hantouche E, Angst J, Azorin JM (2010). Explained factors of suicide attempts in major depression. *Journal of Affective Disorders* 127, 305-308.

Hamdan S, Melhem N, Orbach I, Farbstein I, El-Haib M, Apter A, Brint D (2011). Risk factors for suicide attempt in an Arab kindred. *Journal of Affective Disorders*. Published online: 18 February 2011. doi:10.1016/j.jad.2011.01.012.

Hampshire A, Di Nicola K (2011). What's worrying young Australians and where do they go for advice and support? Policy and practice implications for their well-being. *Early Intervention in Psychiatry* 5, 12-16.

Hardt J, Dragan M, Schultz S, Schier K (2010). Comparison of childhood adversities and their possible consequences in Poland and Germany. *Journal of Public Health*. Published online: 4 October 2010. 10.1007/s10389-010-0375-1.

Hardt J, Herke M, Schier K (2010). Suicidal ideation, parent-child relationships, and adverse childhood experiences: A cross-validation study using a graphical Markov model. *Child Psychiatry and Human Development*. Published online: 16 October 2010. doi:10.1007/s10578-010-0203-4.

Härmark L, van Puijenbroek E, Straus S, van Grootheest K (2011). Intensive monitoring of pregabalin: results from an observational, web-based, prospective cohort study in the Netherlands using patients as a source of information. *Drug Safety* 34, 221-231.

Harold GT, Rice F, Hay DF, Boivin J, van den Bree M, Thapar A (2010). Familial transmission of depression and antisocial behavior symptoms: Disentangling the contribution of inherited and environmental factors and testing the mediating role of parenting. *Psychological Medicine*. Published online: 22 September 2010. doi:10.1017/S0033291710001753.

Hassiotis A, Tanzarella M, Bebbington P, Cooper C (2010). Prevalence and predictors of suicidal behaviour in a sample of adults with estimated borderline intellectual functioning: Results from a population survey. *Journal of Affective Disorders* 129, 380-384.

Hayashi N, Igarashi M, Imai A, Osawa Y, Utsumi K, Ishikawa Y, Tokunaga T, Ishimoto K, Harima H, Tatebayashi Y, Kumagai N, Nozu M, Ishii H, Okazaki Y (2010). Psychiatric disorders and clinical correlates of suicidal patients admitted to a psychiatric hospital in Tokyo. *BMC Psychiatry* 10, 109.

Heidmets L, Samm A, Sisask M, Kolves K, Aasvee K, Varnik A (2010). Sexual behavior, depressive feelings, and suicidality among Estonian school children aged 13 to 15 years. *Crisis* 31, 128-136.

Hicks BM, Vaidyanathan U, Patrick CJ (2010). Validating female psychopathy subtypes: Differences in personality, antisocial and violent behavior, substance abuse, trauma, and mental health. *Personality Disorders: Theory, Research, and Treatment* 1, 38-57.

Hirst KP, Moutier CY (2010). Postpartum major depression. *American Family Physician* 82, 926-933.

Hodgins S, De Brito SA, Chhabra P, Cote G (2010). Anxiety disorders among offenders with antisocial personality disorders: A distinct subtype? *Canadian Journal of Psychiatry* 55, 784-791.

Holma KM, Melartin TK, Holma IA, Paunio T, Isometsä ET (2011). Family history of psychiatric disorders and the outcome of psychiatric patients with DSM-IV major depressive

disorder. *Journal of Affective Disorders*. Published online: 25 January 2011. doi:10.1016/
j.jad.2010.12.016.

Hong J, Knapp M, Mcguire A (2011). Income-related inequalities in the prevalence of depression and suicidal behaviour: A 10-year trend following economic crisis. *World Psychiatry* 10, 40-44.

Hong JS, Espelage DL, Kral MJ (2011). Understanding suicide among sexual minority youth in America: An ecological systems analysis. *Journal of Adolescence*. Published online: 8 February 2011. doi:10.1016/j.adolescence.2011.01.002.

Hooley JM, Ho DT, Slater J, Lockshin A (2010). Pain perception and nonsuicidal self-injury: A laboratory investigation. *Personality Disorders: Theory, Research, and Treatment* 1, 170-179.

Horwitz AG, Hill RM, King CA (2010). Specific coping behaviors in relation to adolescent depression and suicidal ideation. *Journal of Adolescence*. Published online: 12 November 2010. doi:10.1016/j.adolescence.2010.10.004.

Hoshiai M, Matsumoto Y, Sato T, Ohnishi M, Okabe N, Kishimoto Y, Terada S, Kuroda S (2010). Psychiatric comorbidity among patients with gender identity disorder. *Psychiatry and Clinical Neurosciences* 64, 514-519.

Huas C, Godart N, Foulon C, Pham-Scottez A, Divac S, Fedorowicz V, Peyracque E, Dardennes R, Falissard B, Rouillon F (2011). Predictors of dropout from inpatient treatment for anorexia nervosa: Data from a large French sample. *Psychiatry Research* 185, 421-426.

Hulbert C, Thomas R (2010). Predicting self-injury in BPD: An investigation of the experiential avoidance model. *Journal of Personality Disorders* 24, 651-663.

Hung TC, Tang HS, Chiu CH, Chen YY, Chou KR, Chiou HC, Chang HJ (2010). Anxiety, depressive symptom and suicidal ideation of outpatients with obsessive compulsive disorders in Taiwan. *Journal of Clinical Nursing* 19, 3092-3101.

Hunter AM, Leuchter AF, Cook IA, Abrams M (2010). Brain functional changes (QEEG cordance) and worsening suicidal ideation and mood symptoms during antidepressant treatment. *Acta Psychiatrica Scandinavica* 122, 461-469.

Husler G, Werlen E (2010). Swiss and migrant adolescents - Similarities and differences. *Vulnerable Children and Youth Studies* 5, 244-255.

Hyldahl R, Richardson B (2010). Key considerations for using no-harm contracts with clients who self-injure. *Journal of Counselling and Development* 89, 121-127.

Ilgen M, Kleinberg F (2011). The link between substance abuse, violence, and suicide implications and interventions. *Psychiatric Times* 28, 25-27.

Izadinia N, Amiri M, Jahromi RG, Hamidi S (2010). A study of relationship between suicidal ideas, depression, anxiety, resiliency, daily stresses and mental health among Tehran university students. *Procedia - Social and Behavioral Sciences* 5, 1615-1619.

Jabben N, Penninx BWJH, Beekman ATF, Smit JH, Nolen WA (2011). Co-occurring manic symptomatology as a dimension which may help explaining heterogeneity of depression. *Journal of Affective Disorders*. Published online: 3 February 2011. doi:10.1016/j.jad.2010. 12.012.

Jackson DO, Mrug S, Cook F, Beidleman W, Cropsey KL (2011). Factors predicting substance dependence and psychotropic medication use among offenders in community corrections. *Addictive Behaviors*. Published online: 13 January 2011. doi:10.1016/j.addbeh.2010.12.033.

Jahn DR, Cukrowicz KC, Linton K, Prabhu F (2010). The mediating effect of perceived burdensomeness on the relation between depressive symptoms and suicide ideation in a community sample of older adults. *Aging & Mental Health* 15, 214-220.

Jakobsen IS, Christiansen E (2011). Young people's risk of suicide attempts in relation to parental death: A population-based register study. *Journal of Child Psychology and Psychiatry* 52, 176-183.

Jakupcak M, Vannoy S, Imel Z, Cook JW, Fontana A, Rosenheck R, McFall M (2010). Does PTSD moderate the relationship between social support and suicide risk in Iraq and Afghanistan War Veterans seeking mental health treatment? *Depression and Anxiety* 27, 1001-1005.

James AC, Winmill L, Anderson C, Alfoadari K (2011). A preliminary study of an extension of a community dialectic behaviour therapy (dbt) programme to adolescents in the looked after care system. *Child and Adolescent Mental Health* 16, 9-13.

Janelidze S, Mattei D, Westrin A, Traskman-Bendz L, Brundin L (2011). Cytokine levels in the blood may distinguish suicide attempters from depressed patients. *Brain, Behavior and Immunity* 25, 335-339.

Jansen K, Ores LD, Cardoso TD, Lima RD, Souza LD, Magalhães PV, Pinheiro RT, da Silva RA (2010). Prevalence of episodes of mania and hypomania and associated comorbidities among young adults. *Journal of Affective Disorders.* Published online: 3 November 2010. doi:10.1016/j.jad.2010.10.007.

Jarpa E, Babul M, Calderon J, Gonzalez M, Martinez ME, Bravo-Zehnder M, Henriquez C, Jacobelli S, Gonzalez A, Massardo L (2011). Common mental disorders and psychological distress in systemic lupus erythematosus are not associated with disease activity. *Lupus* 20, 58-66.

Javdani S, Sadeh N, Verona E (2011). Suicidality as a function of impulsivity, callous-unemotional traits, and depressive symptoms in youth. *Journal of Abnormal Psychology.* Published online: 31 January 2011. doi:10.1037/ a0021805.

Jha CK, Plummer D, Bowers R (2011). Coping with HIV and dealing with the threat of impending death in Nepal. *Mortality* 16, 20-34.

Jimenez-Treviño L, Blasco-Fontecilla H, Braquehais MD, Ceverino-Dominguez A, Baca-Garcia E (2011). Endophenotypes and suicide behaviour. *Actas Espanolas de Psiquiatria* 39, 61-69.

Jo KH, An GJ, Sohn KC (2010). Qualitative content analysis of suicidal ideation in Korean college students. *Collegian.* Published online: 20 December 2010. doi:10.1016/j.colegn. 2010.11.001.

Johnson J, Wood AM, Gooding P, Taylor P, Tarrier N (2011). Resilience to suicidality: The buffering hypothesis. *Clinical Psychology Review.* Published online: 21 December 2010. doi:10.1016/j.cpr.2010.12.007

Jonsson U, Bohman H, von Knorring L, Olsson G, Paaren A, von Knorring AL (2010). Mental health outcome of long-term and episodic adolescent depression: 15-year follow-up of a community sample. *Journal of Affective Disorders.* Published online: 26 November 2010. doi:10.1016/j.jad.2010.10.046.

Jonville-Bera AP, Guilmot J-L, Aspe G, Autret-Leca E, Magnant J (2011). Is exogenous administration of IL-1ra (anakinra) likely to induce severe depression? *European Journal of Clinical Pharmacology* 67, 213-214.

Joseph Z, Victor K, Rimona D (2011). "Ego-dystonic" delusions as a predictor of dangerous behaviour. *Psychiatric Quarterly.* Published online: 23 January 2011. doi:10.1007/s11126-010-9150-2.

Jutengren G, Kerr M, Stattin H (2010). Adolescents' deliberate self-harm, interpersonal stress, and the moderating effects of self-regulation: A two-wave longitudinal analysis. *Journal of School Psychology.* Published online: 31 December 2010. doi:10.1016/j.jsp.2010.11.001.

Kannan K, Pillai SK, Gill JS, Hui KO, Swami V (2010). Religious beliefs, coping skills and responsibility to family as factors protecting against deliberate self-harm. *South African Journal of Psychiatry* 16, 138-146.

Kao YC, Liu YP (2010). Suicidal behavior and insight into illness among patients with schizophrenia spectrum disorders. *Psychiatric Quarterly*. Published online: 26 October 2010. doi:10.1007/s11126-010-9161-z.

Kao YC, Liu YP, Cheng TH, Chou MK (2011). Subjective quality of life and suicidal behavior among Taiwanese schizophrenia patients. *Social Psychiatry & Psychiatric Epidemiology*. Published online: 10 March 2011.

Kar N (2010). Suicidality following a natural disaster. *American Journal of Disaster Medicine* 5, 361-368.

Karakus G, Tamam L (2010). Impulse control disorder comorbidity among patients with bipolar I disorder. *Comprehensive Psychiatry*. Published online: 30 October 2010. doi:10.1016/j.comppsych.2010.08.004.

Karver MS, Tarquini SJ, Caporino NE (2010). The judgment of future suicide-related behavior. *Crisis* 31, 272-280.

Kasen S, Cohen P, Chen H (2011). Developmental course of impulsivity and capability from age 10 to age 25 as related to trajectory of suicide attempt in a community cohort. *Suicide and Life-Threatening Behaviour*. Published online: 22 February 2011. doi:10.1111/j.1943-278X.2011.00017.x.

Kaufman KR, Struck PJ (2011). Activation of suicidal ideation with adjunctive rufinamide in bipolar disorder. *Epilepsy and Behavior* 20, 386-389.

Kazemi MS, Javid MM (2010). The relationship between mental health and women's tendency to suicide in Sardasht. *Procedia - Social and Behavioral Sciences* 5, 1381-1386.

Kesebir S, Simsek Y, Akbas S (2010). Temperament in suicide attempt: A mediator role of cortisol. *Anadolu Psikiyatri Dergisi-Anatolian Journal of Psychiatry* 11, 293-298.

Khamker N, Moola NM, Roos JL, Rheeder P (2010). Profile of mortality of patients admitted to Weskoppies Psychiatric Hospital in South Africa over a 5-year period (2001-2005). *African Journal of Psychiatry (Johannesburg)* 3, 211-217.

Khang Y-H, Kim H-R, Cho S-J (2010). Relationships of suicide ideation with cause-specific mortality in a longitudinal study of South Koreans. *Suicide and Life-Threatening Behavior* 40, 465-475.

Kim JM, Kim SW, Stewart R, Kim SY, Yoon JS, Jung SW, Lee MS, Yim HW, Jun TY (2011). Predictors of 12-week remission in a nationwide cohort of people with depressive disorders: the CRESCEND study. *Human Psychopharmacology*. Published online: 23 February 2011. doi:10.1002/hup.1168.

Kim JM, Stewart R, Kim SY, Kim SW, Bae KY, Yang SJ, Shin IS, Yoon JS (2010). Synergistic associations of depression and apolipoprotein E genotype with incidence of dementia. *International Journal of Geriatric Psychiatry*. Published online: 29 October 2010. doi:10.1002/gps.2621.

Kim K-H, Lee S-M, Paik J-W, Kim N-S (2011). The effects of continuous antidepressant treatment during the first 6 months on relapse or recurrence of depression. *Journal of Affective Disorders*. Published online: 12 March 2011. doi:10.1016/j.jad.2011.02.016.

Kim YR, Choi KH, Oh Y, Lee HK, Kweon YS, Lee CT, Lee KU (2011). Elderly suicide attempters by self-poisoning in Korea. *International Psychogeriatrics*. Published online: 1 March 2011. doi:10.1017/S1041610211000263.

Kimonis ER, Skeem JL, Edens JF, Douglas KS, Lilienfeld SO, Poythress NG (2010). Suicidal and criminal behavior among female offenders: The role of abuse and psychopathology. *Journal of Personality Disorders* 24, 581-609.

Kinley DJ, Walker JR, Mackenzie CS, Sareen J (2011). Panic attacks and panic disorder in a population-based sample of active Canadian military personnel. *Journal of Clinical Psychiatry* 72, 66-74.

Kliem S, Kroger C, Kosfelder J (2010). Dialectical behavior therapy for borderline personality disorder: A meta-analysis using mixed-effects modeling. *Journal of Consulting and Clinical Psychology* 78, 936-951.

Klonsky ED, May A (2011). Rethinking impulsivity in suicide. *Suicide and Life-Threatening Behavior* 40, 612-619.

Knops ELR, Lemmens GMD, van Heeringen C, Audenaert K, Deschepper E, de Bacquer D Investigation of early suicide-related symptoms in a non-suicidal depressed patient population after escitalopram administration: A pilot study. *Internet Journal of Mental Health* 6, 2.

Kokkevi A, Rotsika V, Arapaki A, Richardson C (2010). Changes in associations between psychosocial factors and suicide attempts by adolescents in Greece from 1984 to 2007. *European Journal of Public Health*. Pnblished online: 26 November 2010. doi:10.1093/eurpub/ckq160.

Kolla BP, O'Connor SS, Lineberry TW (2011). The base rates and factors associated with reported access to firearms in psychiatric inpatients. *General Hospital Psychiatry*. Published online: 26 February 2011. doi:10.1016/j.genhosppsych.2011.01.011.

Krakow B, Ribeiro JD, Ulibarri VA, Krakow J, Joiner TE Jr (2011). Sleep disturbances and suicidal ideation in sleep medical centre patients. *Journal of Affective Disorders*. Published online: 6 January 2011. doi:10.1016/j.jad.2010.12.001.

Kuramoto SJ, Stuart EA, Runeson B, Lichtenstein P, Langstrom N, Wilcox HC (2010). Maternal or paternal suicide and offspring's psychiatric and suicide-attempt hospitalization risk. *Pediatrics* 126, 1026-1032.

Kwok SYCL, Shek DTL (2011). Family processes and suicidal ideation among Chinese adolescents in Hong Kong. *The Scientific World Journal* 11, 27-41.

Lahey Dr B (2010). Young children with ADHD are at increased risk of depression and suicidal behaviour in adolescence. *Evidence-Based Mental Health* 14, 15.

Lala A, Bobirnac G, Tipa R (2011). Stress levels, alexithymia, type A and type C personality patterns in undergraduate students. *Journal of Medicine and Life* 3, 200-205.

Lam BCP, Bond MH, Chen SX, Wu WCH (2010). Worldviews and individual vulnerability to suicide: The role of social axioms. *European Journal of Personality* 24, 602-622.

Lang CM, Sharma-Patel K (2011). The relation between childhood maltreatment and self-injury: a review of the literature on conceptualization and intervention. *Trauma Violence & Abuse* 12, 23-37.

Langhinrichsen-Rohling J, Lamis DA, Malone PS (2011). Sexual attraction status and adolescent suicide proneness: the roles of hopelessness, depression, and social support. *Journal of Homosexuality* 58, 52-82.

Lasgaard M, Goossens L, Bramsen RH, Trillingsgaard T, Elklit A (2011). Different sources of loneliness are associated with different forms of psychopathology in adolescence. *Journal of Research in Personality*. Published online: 23 December 2010. doi:10.1016/j.jrp.2010.12.005.

Lavania S (2010). Life stressors in substance dependence syndrome patients who attempted deliberate self harm and who did not - a comparative study. *International Journal of Neuropsychopharmacology* 13, 52-52.

Le Y-CL, Behnken MP, Markham CM, Temple JR (2011). Alcohol use as a potential mediator of forced sexual intercourse and suicidality among African American, Caucasian, and Hispanic high school girls. *Journal of Adolescent Health*. Published online: doi:10.1016/j.jadohealth.2011.01.003.

Lee BH, Kim YK (2010). The roles of BDNF in the pathophysiology of major depression and in antidepressant treatment. *Psychiatry Investigation* 7, 231-235.

Lee H-J, Bagge CL, Schumacher JA, Coffey SF (2010). Does comorbid substance use disorder exacerbate borderline personality features? A comparison of borderline personality disorder individuals with vs. without current substance dependence. *Personality Disorders: Theory, Research, and Treatment* 1, 239-249.

Lee HY, Kim YK (2011). Gender effect of Catechol-O-Methyltransferase Val158Met Polymorphism on suicidal behavior. *Neuropsychobiology* 63, 177-182.

Lee KL, Ng HW, Tse ML, Lav FL (2010). Daytime versus night time intentional overdose: The outcome is different. *Hong Kong Journal of Emergency Medicine* 17, 347-351.

Lee S, Jun Sung Hong, Espelage DL (2010). An ecological understanding of youth suicide in South Korea. *School Psychology International* 31, 531-546.

Leichsenring F, Jaeger U, Masuhr O, Streeck U (2010). Complex mental disorders - comorbidity structures in in-patients. *Nervenheilkunde* 29, 843-849.

Lemaire CM, Graham DP (2010). Factors associated with suicidal ideation in OEF/OIF veterans. *Journal of Affective Disorders*. Published online: 4 November 2010. doi:10.1016/j.jad.2010.10.021.

Lentz V, Robinson J, Bolton JM (2010). Childhood adversity, mental disorder comorbidity, and suicidal behavior in schizotypal personality disorder. *Journal of Nervous and Mental Disorders* 198, 795-801.

Leone JM (2010). Suicidal behavior among low-income, African American female victims of intimate terrorism and situational couple violence. *Journal of Interpersonal Violence*. Published online: 13 December 2010. doi:10.1177/0886260510388280.

Lewis SP, Rosenrot SA, Santor DA (2011) An Integrated model of self-harm: identifying predictors of intent. *Canadian Journal of Behavioural Science* 43, 20-29.

Li LW, Conwell Y (2010). Pain and self-injury ideation in elderly men and women receiving home care. *Journal of American Geriatric Society* 58, 2160-2165.

Li SX, Lam SP, Yu MW, Zhang J, Wing YK (2010). Nocturnal sleep disturbances as a predictor of suicide attempts among psychiatric outpatients: a clinical, epidemiologic, prospective study. *Journal of Clinical Psychiatry* 71, 1440-1446.

Lin YR, Liu TH, Liu TA, Chang YJ, Chou CC, Wu HP (2011). Pharmaceutical poisoning exposure and outcome analysis in children admitted to the pediatric emergency department. *Pediatrics & Neonatology* 52, 11-17.

Lindqvist D, Janelidze S, Erhardt S, Traskman-Bendz L, Engström G, Brundin L (2011). CSF biomarkers in suicide attempters - A principal component analysis. *Acta Psychiatrica Scandinavica*. Published online: 28 December 2010. doi:10.1111/j.1600-0447.2010.01655.x.

Little J, Trauer T, Rouhan J, Haines M (2010). Borderline personality disorder and interagency response. *Australasian Psychiatry* 18, 441-444.

Loosier PS, Dittus PJ (2010). Group differences in risk across three domains using an expanded measure of sexual orientation. *Journal of Primary Prevention* 31, 261-272.

Lopez-Castroman J, Perez-Rodriguez MDLM, Jaussent I, Alegria AA, Artes-Rodriguez A, Freed P, Guillaume S, Jollant F, Leiva-Murillo JM, Malafosse A, Oquendo MA, de Prado-Cumplido M, Saiz-Ruiz J, Baca-Garcia E, Courtet P (2010). Distinguishing the relevant features of frequent suicide attempters. *Journal of Psychiatric Research*. Published online: 4 November 2010. doi:10.1016/j.jpsychires.2010.09.017.

Lowry R, Eaton DK, Brener ND, Kann L (2011). Prevalence of health-risk behaviors among Asian American and Pacific Islander high school students in the US, 2001-2007. *Public Health Reports* 126, 39-49.

Lucassen MF, Merry SN, Robinson EM, Denny S, Clark T, Ameratunga S, Crengle S, Rossen FV (2011). Sexual attraction, depression, self-harm, suicidality and help-seeking behaviour in New Zealand secondary school students. *The Australian and New Zealand Journal of Psychiatry*. Published online: 2 March 2011. doi:10.3109/00048674.2011.559635.

Machado RA, Espinosa AG, Montoto AP (2010). Cholesterol concentrations and clinical response to sertraline in patients with epilepsy: Preliminary results. *Epilepsy & Behavior* 19, 509-512.

Mackenzie CS, Pagura J, Sareen J (2010). Correlates of perceived need for and use of mental health services by older adults in the collaborative psychiatric epidemiology surveys. *American Journal of Geriatric Psychiatry* 18, 1103-1115.

Mackenzie S, Wiegel JR, Mundt M, Brown D, Saewyc E, Heiligenstein E, Harahan B, Fleming M (2011). Depression and suicide ideation among students accessing campus health care. *American Journal of Orthopsychiatry* 81, 101-107.

MacLean J, Kinley DJ, Jacobi F, Bolton JM, Sareen J (2010). The relationship between physical conditions and suicidal behavior among those with mood disorders. *Journal of Affective Disorders*. Published online: 10 November 2010. doi:10.1016/j.jad.2010.10.028.

Magin P, Sullivan J (2010). Suicide attempts in people taking isotretinoin for acne. *British Medical Journal* 341c, 5866.

Maguen S, Luxton DD, Skopp NA, Gahm GA, Reger MA, Metzler TJ, Marmar CR. (2011). Killing in combat, mental health symptoms, and suicidal ideation in Iraq war veterans. *Journal of Anxiety Disorders*. Published online: 22 January 2011. doi:10.1016/j.janxdis.2011.01.003.

Maimon D, Browning CR, Brooks-Gunn J (2010). Collective efficacy, family attachment, and urban adolescent suicide attempts. *Journal of Health and Social Behavior* 51, 307-324.

Makkos Z, Fejes L, Inczedy-Farkas G, Kassai-Farkas A, Faludi G, Lazary J (2010). Psychopharmacological comparison of schizophrenia spectrum disorder with and without cannabis dependency. *Progress in Neuro-Psychopharmacology and Biological Psychiatry* 35, 212-217.

Mandelli L, Carli V, Roy A, Serretti A, Sarchiapone M (2010). The influence of childhood trauma on the onset and repetition of suicidal behavior: An investigation in a high risk sample of male prisoners. *Journal of Psychiatric Research*. Published online: 27 November 2010. doi:10.1016/j.jpsychires.2010.11.005.

Maniglio R (2010). The role of child sexual abuse in the etiology of suicide and non-suicidal self-injury. *Acta Psychiatrica Scandinavica*. Published online: 11 October 2010. doi:10.1111/j.1600-0447.2010.01612.x.

Marmorstein NR (2011). Associations between subtypes of major depressive episodes and substance use disorders. *Psychiatry Research* 186, 248-253.

Martiny C, de Oliveira e Silva AC, Neto JPS, Nardi AE (2011). Factors associated with risk of suicide in patients with hemodialysis. *Comprehensive Psychiatry*. Published online: 28 December 2010. doi:10.1016/j.comppsych.2010.10.009.

Marty MA, Segal DL, Coolidge FL (2010). Relationships among dispositional coping strategies, suicidal ideation, and protective factors against suicide in older adults. *Aging and Mental Health* 14, 1015-1023.

Marsh PJ, Odlaug BL, Thomarios N, Davis AA, Buchanan SN, Meyer CS, Grant JE (2010). Paraphilias in adult psychiatric inpatients. *Annals of Clinical Psychiatry* 22, 129-134.

Marshall S, Faaborg-Andersen P (2011). Peer sexual harassment and deliberate self-harm: A longitudinal cross-lag investigation. *Journal of Adolescent Health* 48, 87-87.

Martin J, Bureau JF, Cloutier P, Lafontaine MF (2011). A comparison of invalidating family environment characteristics between university students engaging in self-injurious. Thoughts & actions and non-self-injuring university students. *Journal of Youth and Adolescent*. Published online: 2 March 2011. doi:10.1007/s10964-011-9643-9.

Marty MA, Segal DL, Coolidge FL (2010). Relationships among dispositional coping strategies, suicidal ideation, and protective factors against suicide in older adults. *Aging & Mental Health* 14, 1015-1023.

Marzano L, Hawton K, Rivlin A, Fazel S (2011). Psychosocial influences on prisoner suicide: A case-control study of near-lethal self-harm in women prisoners. *Social Science and Medicine*. Published online: 4 February 2011. doi:10.1016/j.socscimed.2010.12.028.

Matlin SL, Molock SD, Tebes JK (2011). Suicidality and depression among African American adolescents: the role of family and peer support and community connectedness. *American Journal of Orthopsychiatry* 81, 108-117.

McCauley E, Schloredt K, Gudmundsen G, Martell C, Dimidjian S (2011). Expanding behavioral activation to depressed adolescents: lessons learned in treatment development. *Cognitive and Behavioral Practice*. Published online: 10 February 2010. doi:10.1016/j.cbpra.2010.07.006.

McCauley-Elsom K, Barnfield J, O'Brien L, Harrison B, Moss C, Elsom S (2010). Perinatal Depression and Suicide (PDS): A study of midwives and MHCNs ability and confidence to assess the mental health of women. *International Journal of Mental Health Nursing* 19A, 28.

McClintock SM, Husain MM, Wisniewski SR, Nierenberg AA, Stewart JW, Trivedi MH, Cook I, Morris D, Warden D, Rush AJ (2011). Residual symptoms in depressed outpatients who respond by 50% but do not remit to antidepressant medication. *Journal of Clinical Psychopharmacology* 31, 180-186.

McCoy K, Fremouw W, McNeil DW (2010). Thresholds and tolerance of physical pain among young adults who self-injure. *Pain Research & Management* 15, 371-377.

McGirr A, Diaconu G, Berlim MT, Turecki G (2010). Personal and family history of suicidal behaviour is associated with lower peripheral cortisol in depressed outpatients. *Journal of Affective Disorders*. Published online: 18 November 2010. doi:10.1016/j.jad.2010.10.050.

McMillan KA, Enns MW, Asmundson GJG, Sareen J (2010). The association between income and distress, mental disorders, and suicidal ideation and attempts: Findings from the collaborative psychiatric epidemiology surveys. *Journal of Clinical Psychiatry* 71, 116-1175.

Mechri A, Kerkeni N, Touati I, Bacha M, Gassab L (2011). Association between cyclothymic temperament and clinical predictors of bipolarity in recurrent depressive patients. *Journal of Affective Disorders*. Published online: 3 March 2011. doi:10.1016/j.jad.2011.02.006.

Meeks TW, Vahia IV, Lavretsky H, Kulkarni G, Jeste DV (2010). A tune in "a minor" can "b major": A review of epidemiology, illness course, and public health implications of subthreshold depression in older adults. *Journal of Affective Disorders* 129, 126-142.

Melville JL, Gavin A, Guo Y, Fan MY, Katon WJ (2010). Depressive disorders during pregnancy: Prevalence and risk factors in a large urban sample. *Obstetrics & Gynecology* 116, 1064-1070.

Mellqvist M, Wiktorsson S, Joas E, Ostling S, Skoog I, Waern M (2011). Sense of coherence in elderly suicide attempters: The impact of social and health-related factors. *International Psychogeriatrics*. Published online: 1 March 2011. doi:10.1017/S1041610211000196.

Meltzer H, Vostanis P, Ford T, Bebbington P, Dennis MS (2011). Victims of bullying in childhood and suicide attempts in adulthood. *European Psychiatry*. Published online: 9 February 2011. doi:10.1016/j.eurpsy.2010.11.006.

Mentari MD (2011). Antiepileptic drugs and suicide attempts in patients with bipolar disorder (Archives of General Psychiatry (2010) 67, 12 (1326-1327)). *Archives of General Psychiatry* 68, 123.

Merikangas KR, Jin R, He J, Kessler RC, Lee S, Sampson NA, Viana MC, Andrade LH, Hu C, Karam EG, Mora MEM, Browne MO, Ono Y, Posada-Villa J, Sagar R, Zarkov Z (2011). Prevalence and correlates of bipolar spectrum disorder in the World Mental Health Survey Initiative. *Archives of General Psychiatry* 68, 241.

Milak MS, Keilp J, Parsey RV, Oquendo MA, Malone KM, Mann JJ (2010). Regional brain metabolic correlates of self-reported depression severity contrasted with clinician ratings. *Journal of Affective Disorders* 126, 113-124.

Miller TR, Teti LO, Lawrence BA, Weiss HB (2010). Alcohol involvement in hospital-admitted nonfatal suicide acts. *Suicide and Life-Threatening Behavior* 40, 492-499.

Misery L (2011). Consequences of psychological distress in adolescents with acne. *Journal of Investigative Dermatology* 131, 290-292.

Mitchell KJ, Finkelhor D, Wolak J, Ybarra ML, Turner H (2011). Youth internet victimization in a broader victimization context. *Journal of Adolescent Health* 48, 128-134.

Mitrou F, Gaudie J, Lawrence D, Silburn SR, Stanley FJ, Zubrick SR (2010). Antecedents of hospital admission for deliberate self-harm from a 14-year follow-up study using data-linkage. *BMC Psychiatry* 10, 82.

Moncrieff J, Goldsmith L (2011). The psychoactive effects of antidepressants and their association with suicidality. *Current Drug Safety*. Published online: 4 March 2011.

Moore E, Andargachew S, Taylor PJ (2010). Working with women prisoners who seriously harm themselves: Ratings of staff expressed emotion (EE). *Criminal Behaviour and Mental Health*. Published online: 2010. doi:10.1002/cbm.795.

Moreira L, Neves FS, Schlottfeldt CG, Abrantes SSC, de Moraes PHP, Romano-Silva MA, Correa H, Malloy-Diniz LF (2010). Visual and verbal memory in euthymic bipolar patients: Impacts of subtype, psychotic symptoms and suicide behaviour. *Clinical Neuropsychiatry* 7, 116-120.

Moscicki EK, West JC, Rae DS, Rubio-Stipec M, Wilk JE, Regier DA (2010). Suicidality is associated with medication access problems in publicly insured psychiatric patients. *Journal of Clinical Psychiatry* 71, 1657-1663.

Muehlenkamp JJ, Claes L, Smits D, Peat CM, Vandereycken W (2011). Non-suicidal self-injury in eating disordered patients: A test of a conceptual model. *Psychiatry Research*. Published online: 7 January 2011. doi:10.1016/j.psychres.2010.12.023.

Muehlmann AM, Wilkinson JA, Devine DP (2010). Individual differences in vulnerability for self-injurious behavior: Studies using an animal model. *Behavioral Brain Research* 217, 148-154.

Mula M, Bell GS, Sander JW (2010). Assessing suicidal risk with antiepileptic drugs. *Neuropsychiatric Disease and Treatment* 6, 613-618.

Mustanski BS, Garofalo R, Emerson EM (2010). Mental health disorders, psychological distress, and suicidality in a diverse sample of lesbian, gay, bisexual, and transgender youths. *American Journal of Public Health* 100, 2426-2432.

Mutschler J, Grosshans M, Herwig U, Heekeren K, Kawohl W, Bruhl A (2011). Pregabalin-Induced suicidal ideations. *Pharmacopsychiatry*. Published online: 11 February 2011. doi:10.1055/s-0031-1271689.

Nadorff MR, Nazem S, Fiske A (2011). Insomnia symptoms, nightmares, and suicidal ideation in a college student sample. *Sleep* 34, 93-98.

Nakagawa M, Kawanishi C, Yamada T, Sugiura K, Iwamoto Y, Sato R, Morita S, Odawara T, Hirayasu Y (2010). Comparison of characteristics of suicide attempters with schizophrenia spectrum disorders and those with mood disorders in Japan. *Psychiatry Research*. Published online: 15 October 2010. doi:10.1016/j.psychres.2010.09.008.

Naragon-Gainey K, Watson D (2010). The anxiety disorders and suicidal ideation: accounting for co-morbidity via underlying personality traits. *Psychological Medicine*. Published online: 8 November 2010. doi:10.1017/S0033291710002096.

Nenadic-Sviglin K, Nedic G, Nikolac M, Kozaric-Kovacic D, Stipcevic T, Muck Seler D, Pivac N (2010). Suicide attempt, smoking, comorbid depression, and platelet serotonin in alcohol dependence. *Alcohol*. Published online : 15 December 2010. doi:10.1016/j.alcohol.2010.11.004.

Neuner T, Hübner-Liebermann B, Hausner H, Hajak G, Wolfersdorf M, Spießl H (2011). Revisiting the association of aggression and suicidal behavior in schizophrenic inpatients. *Suicide and Life-Threatening Behaviours*. Published online: 22 February 2011. doi:10.1111/j.1943-278X.2011.00018.x.

Neves FS, Malloy-Diniz L, Romano-Silva MA, Campos SB, Miranda DM, De Marco L, Figueira PG, Krebs M-O, Correa H (2010). The role of BDNF genetic polymorphisms in bipolar disorder with psychiatric comorbidities. *Journal of Affective Disorders*. Published online: 16 December 2010. doi:10.1016/j.jad.2010.11.022.

Ng SM, Ran MS, Chan C (2010). Factors related to suicidal ideation among adolescents in Hong Kong. *Illness Crisis and Loss* 18, 341-354.

Niederkrotenthaler T, Floderus B, Alexanderson K, Rasmussen F, Mittendorfer-Rutz E (2010). Exposure to parental mortality and markers of morbidity, and the risks of attempted and completed suicide in offspring: An analysis of sensitive life periods. *Journal of Epidemiology & Community Health*. Published online: 5 October 2010. doi:10.1136/jech.2010.109595.

Nielssen OB, Large MM (2011). Potentially lethal suicide attempts using sharp objects during psychotic illness. *Crisis* 32, 37-42.

Norton CL (2011). Developing empathy: A case study exploring transference and countertransference with adolescent females who self-injure. *Journal of Social Work Practice* 25, 95-107.

Novara C, Lavanco G, Romano F, Messina C (2010). Educational styles, peers' approval and adolescent self-injurious behaviours. *Procedia - Social and Behavioral Sciences* 2, 4933-4937.

Odgers CL, Robins SJ, Russell MA (2010). Morbidity and mortality risk among the "forgotten few": why are girls in the justice system in such poor health? *Journal of Family Violence* 25, 777-786.

Oguzturk H, Turtay MG, Pamukcu E, Ciftci O (2010). Demographic features of acute drug poisoning admitted to Inonu University Hospital in Malatya, Turkey. *Scientific Research and Essays* 5, 2761-2767.

Oiesvold T, Bakkejord T, Hansen V, Nivison M, Sørgaard KW (2011). Suicidality related to first-time admissions to psychiatric hospital. *Social Psychiatry and Psychiatric Epidemiology*. Published online: 3 February 2011. doi:10.1007/s00127-011-0343-2.

Okusaga O, Yolken RH, Langenberg P, Lapidus M, Arling TA, Dickerson FB, Scrandis DA, Severance E, Cabassa JA, Balis T, Postolache TT (2010). Association of seropositivity for influenza and coronaviruses with history of mood disorders and suicide attempts. *Journal of Affective Disorders*. Published online: 26 October 2010. doi:10.1016/j.jad.2010.09.029.

O'Neil A, Hawkes AL, Chan BC, Sanderson K, Forbes A, Hollingsworth B, Atherton J, Hare DL, Jelinek M, Eadie K, Taylor CB, Oldenburg B (2011). A randomised, feasibility trial of a tele-health intervention for Acute Coronary Syndrome patients with depression ('Mood-Care'): Study protocol. *BMC Cardiovascular Disorders* 11, 8.

Orui M, Kawakami N, Iwata N, Takeshima T, Fukao A (2011). Lifetime prevalence of mental disorders and its relationship to suicidal ideation in a Japanese rural community with high suicide and alcohol consumption rates. *Environmental Health and Preventive Medicine*. Published online: 23 February 2011. doi:10.1007/s12199-011-0209-y.

Orth M (2010). Observing Huntington's Disease: The European Huntington's Disease Network's Registry. *PLoS Currents* 2, 1184.

Ortiz A, Bradler K, Slaney C, Garnham J, Ruzickova M, O'Donovan C, Hajek T, Alda M (2010). An admixture analysis of the age at index episodes in bipolar disorder. *Psychiatry Research*. Published online: 4 December 2010. doi:10.1016/j.psychres.2010.10.033.

Pae C-U, Drago A, Kim J-J, Patkar AA, Jun T-Y, De Ronchi D, Serretti A (2010). TAAR6 variations possibly associated with antidepressant response and suicidal behaviour. *Psychiatry Research* 180, 20-24.

Page RM, West JH, Hall PC (2010). Psychosocial distress and suicide ideation in Chinese and Philippine adolescents. *Asia Pacific Journal of Public Health*. Published online: 30 November 2010. doi:10.1177/1010539509353113.

Park MH, Kim TS, Yim HW, Jeong SH, Lee C, Lee CU, Kim JM, Jung SW, Lee MS, Jun TY (2010). Clinical characteristics of depressed patients with a history of suicide attempts: Results from the CRESCEND Study in South Korea. *The Journal of nervous and mental disease* 198, 748-754.

Paton SL, Fernando I, Lamon RF (2011). A comparison of sexual and reproductive health services provided by genitourinary and family planning clinics for adolescents. *International Journal of STD & AIDS* 21, 642-647.

Peebles R, Wilson JL, Lock JD (2011). Self-injury in adolescents with eating disorders: Correlates and provider bias. *Journal of Adolescent Health* 48, 310-313.

Penney A, Mazmanian D, Jamieson J, Black N (2010). Factors associated with recent suicide attempts in clients presenting for addiction treatment. *International Journal of Mental Health and Addiction*. Published online: 18 December 2010. doi:10.1007/s11469-010-9307-0.

Perez-Rodriguez MM, Weinstein S, New AS, Bevilacqua L, Yuan Q, Zhou Z, Hodgkinson C, Goodman M, Koenigsberg HW, Goldman D, Siever LJ (2010). Tryptophan-hydroxylase 2 haplotype association with borderline personality disorder and aggression in a sample of patients with personality disorders and healthy controls. *Journal of Psychiatric Research* 44, 1075-1081.

Perez-Rodriguez MM, Lopez-Castroman J, Martinez-Vigo M, Diaz-Sastre C, Ceverino A, Nunez-Beltran A, Saiz-Ruiz J, de Leon J, Baca-Garcia E (2010). Lack of association between testosterone and suicide attempts. *Neuropsychobiology* 63, 125-130.

Perez-Sales P (2010). Identity and trauma in adolescents within the context of political violence: a psychosocial and communitarian view. *Clinical Social Work Journal* 38, 408-417.

Perlis RH (2010). Genome-wide association study of suicide attempts in mood disorder patients. *American Journal of Psychiatry* 167, 1499-1507.

Perlis RH, Huang J, Purcell S, Fava M, Rush AJ, Sullivan PF, Hamilton SP, McMahon FJ, Schulze T, Potash JB, Zandi PP, Willour VL, Penninx BW, Boomsma DI, Vogelzangs N, Middeldorp CM, Rietschel M, Nöthen M, Cichon S, Gurling H, Bass N, McQuillin A, Hamshere M; Wellcome Trust Case Control Consortium Bipolar Disorder Group, Craddock N, Sklar P, Smoller JW (2010). Genome-wide association study of suicide attempts in mood disorder patients. *American Journal of Psychiatry* 12, 1499-1507.

Perren S, Dooley J, Shaw T, Cross D (2010). Bullying in school and cyberspace: Associations with depressive symptoms in Swiss and Australian adolescents. *Child and Adolescent Psychiatry and Mental Health* 4, 28.

Perroud N, Uher R, Ng MY, Guipponi M, Hauser J, Henigsberg N, Maier W, Mors O, Gennarelli M, Rietschel M, Souery D, Dernovsek MZ, Stamp AS, Lathrop M, Farmer A, Breen G, Aitchison KJ, Lewis CM, Craig IW, McGuffin P (2010). Genome-wide association study of increasing suicidal ideation during antidepressant treatment in the GENDEP project. *The Pharmacogenomics Journal*. Published online: 28 September 2010. doi:10.1038/tpj.2010.70.

Pietrzak RH, Goldstein RB, Southwick SM, Grant BF (2010). Prevalence and Axis I comorbidity of full and partial posttraumatic stress disorder in the United States: Results from Wave 2 of the National Epidemiologic Survey on Alcohol and Related Conditions. *Journal of Anxiety Disorders* 25, 456-465.

Pietrzak RH, Russo AR, Ling Q, Southwick SM (2010). Suicidal ideation in treatment-seeking Veterans of Operations Enduring Freedom and Iraqi Freedom: The role of coping strategies, resilience, and social support. *Journal of Psychiatric Research*. Published online: 22 December 2010. doi:10.1016/j.jpsychires.2010.11.015.

Pinto C, Souza RP, Lioult D, Semeralul M, Kennedy JL, Warsh JJ, Wong AH, De Luca V (2011). Parent of origin effect and allelic expression imbalance of the serotonin transporter in bipolar disorder and suicidal behaviour. *European Archives of Psychiatry and Clinical Neuroscience*. Published online: 3 February 2011. doi:10.1007/s00406-011-0192-8.

Plener PL, Singer H, Goldbeck L (2011). Traumatic events and suicidality in a German adolescent community sample. *Journal of Traumatic Stress* 24, 121–124.

Plosker GL (2011). Interferon-beta-1b: A review of its use in multiple sclerosis. *Cns Drugs* 25, 67-88.

Pompili M, Iliceto P, Luciano D, Innamorati M, Serafini G, Del Casale A, Tatarelli R, Girardi P, Lester D (2011). Higher hopelessness and suicide risk predict lower self-deception among psychiatric patients and non-clinical individuals. *Rivista di Psichiatria* 46, 24-30.

Pompili M, Innamorati M, Narciso V, Kotzalidis GD, Dominici G, Talamo A, Girardi P, Lester D, Tatarelli R (2010). Burnout, hopelessness and suicide risk in medical doctors. *Clinical Therapeutics* 161, 511-514.

Pompili M, Innamorati M, Serafini G, Forte A, Cittadini A, Mancinelli I, Calabró G, Dominici G, Lester D, Akiskal HS, Rihmer Z, Iacorossi G, Girardi N, Talamo A (2011). Suicide attempters in the emergency department before hospitalization in a psychiatric ward. *Perspectives in Psychiatric Care* 47, 23.

Pompili M, Innamorati M, Szanto K, Di Vittorio C, Conwell Y, Lester D, Tatarelli R, Girardi P, Amore M (2010). Life events as precipitants of suicide attempts among first-time suicide attempters, repeaters, and non-attempters. *Psychiatry Research* 186, 300-305.

Pratt D, Gooding P, Johnson J, Taylor P, Tarrier N (2010). Suicide schemas in non-affective psychosis: An empirical investigation. *Behaviour Research and Therapy* 48, 1211-1220.

Preuss UW, Ridinger M, Fehr C, Koller G, Soyka M, Bondy B, Wodarz N, Zill P (2010). Genetic and behavioural risk factors for suicidal behaviour in alcohol dependence. 34, 30-30.

Procopio M (2010). New users of the anticonvulsants gabapentin, lamotrigine, oxcarbazepine or tiagabine are at increased risk of suicidal acts compared with new users of topiramate. *Evidence Based Mental Health* 13, 102-102.

Puri M, Tamang J, Shah I (2011). Suffering in silence: consequences of sexual violence within marriage among young women in Nepal. *BMC Public Health* 11, 29.

Quevedo L, da Silva RA, Coelho F, Pinheiro KAT, Horta BL, Kapczinski F, Pinheiro RT (2011). Risk of suicide and mixed episode in men in the postpartum period. *Journal of Affective Disorders.* Published online: 28 January 2011. doi:10.1016/j.jad.2011.01.004.

Raison CL, Lowry CA, Rook GA (2010). Inflammation, sanitation, and consternation: Loss of contact with coevolved, tolerogenic microorganisms and the pathophysiology and treatment of major depression. *Archives of General Psychiatry* 67, 1211-1224.

Rasic D, Robinson JA, Bolton J, Bienvenu OJ, Sareen J (2011). Longitudinal relationships of religious worship attendance and spirituality with major depression, anxiety disorders, and suicidal ideation and attempts: Findings from the Baltimore epidemiologic catchment area study. *Journal of Psychiatric Research.* Published online: 7 January 2011. doi:10.1016/j.jpsychires.2010.11.014.

Reeves RR, Panguluri RL (2011). Neuropsychiatric complications of traumatic brain injury. *Journal of Psychosocial Nursing & Mental Health Services* 49, 42-50.

Ren X, Dwivedi Y, Mondal AC, Pandey GN (2011). Cyclic-AMP response element binding protein (CREB) in the neutrophils of depressed patients. *Psychiatry Research* 185, 108-112.

Riala K, Juutinen J, Hakko H, Räsänen P (2011). Overweight of adolescent girls is associated with self-mutilative behavior. *Psychopathology* 44, 147-151.

Rivlin A, Hawton K, Marzano L, Fazel S (2010). Psychiatric disorders in male prisoners who made near-lethal suicide attempts: Case-control study. *British Journal of Psychiatry* 19, 313-319.

Roeger L, Allison S, Korossy-Horwood R, Eckert KA, Goldney RD (2010). Is a history of school bullying victimization associated with adult suicidal ideation? A South Australian population-based observational study. *The Journal of Nervous and Mental Disease* 198, 728-733.

Roth KB, Borges G, Medina-Mora M-E, Orozco R, Oueda C, Wilcox HC (2010). Depressed mood and antisocial behavior problems as correlates for suicide-related behaviors in Mexico. *Journal of Psychiatric Research.* Published online: 4 November 2010. doi:10.1016/j.jpsychires.2010.10.009.

Roy A (2010). Combination of family history of suicidal behavior and childhood trauma may represent correlate of increased suicide risk. *Journal of Affective Disorders.* Published online: 12 October 2010. doi:10.1016/j.jad.2010.09.022.

Rucci P, Frank E, Scocco P, Calugi S, Miniati M, Fagiolini A, Cassano GB (2011). Treatment-emergent suicidal ideation during 4 months of acute management of unipolar major depression with SSRI pharmacotherapy or interpersonal psychotherapy in a randomized clinical trial. *Depression & Anxiety*. Published onlne: 9 February 2011. doi:10.1002/da.20758.

Ruljancic N, Mihanovic M., Cepelak I (2011). Thrombocyte serotonin and serum cholesterol concentration in suicidal and non-suicidal depressed patients. *Progress in Neuro-Psychopharmacology and Biological Psychiatry*. Published online: 19 February 2011. doi:10.1016/j.pnpbp.2011.02.007.

Ryan C, Russell ST, Huebner D, Diaz R, Sanchez J (2010). Family acceptance in adolescence and the health of LGBT young adults. *Journal of Child & Adolescent Psychiatric Nursing* 23, 205-213.

Rybakowski JK, Dudek D, Pawlowski T, Lojko D, Siwek M, Kiejna A (2011). Use of the Hypomania Checklist-32 and the Mood Disorder Questionnaire for detecting bipolarity in 1,051 patients with major depressive disorder. *European Psychiatry*. Published online: 10 February 2011. doi:10.1016/j.eurpsy.2010.12.001.

Sadeh N, Javdani S, Finy MS, Verona E (2011). Gender differences in emotional risk for self- and other-directed violence among externalizing adults. *Journal of Consulting and Clinical Psychology* 79, 106-117.

Sanchez YM, Lambert SF, Ialongo NS (2011). Adverse life events and depressive symptoms in African American youth: The role of control-related beliefs. *Depression Research and Treatment*. Published online: 15 December 2010. doi:10.1155/2011/871843.

Sansone RA, Edwards HC, Forbis JS (2010). Sleep quality and self-harm behaviors among internal medicine outpatients. *Psychiatry (Edgemont)* 7, 12-13.

Sansone RA, Lam C, Wiederman MW (2010). History of attempted suicide and reckless driving: a cross-sectional study in primary care. *Primary Care Companion to the Journal of Clinical Psychiatry* 12, 888.

Sansone RA, Lam C, Wiederman MW (2010). Self-harm behaviors in borderline personality: an analysis by gender. *Journal of Nervous & Mental Disorders* 198, 914-915.

Sansone RA, Lam C, Wiederman MW (2011). The abuse of prescription medications in borderline personality disorder: A gender comparison. *Primary Care Companion to the Journal of Clinical Psychiatry* 12, 6.

Santa Mina EE (2010). Self-harm intentions: can they be distinguished based upon a history of childhood physical and sexual abuse? *Canadian Journal of Nursing Research* 42, 122-143.

Sarkar M, Byrne P, Power L, Fitzpatrick C, Anglim M, Boylan C, Morgan S (2010). Are suicidal phenomena in children different to suicidal phenomena in adolescents? A six-year review. *Child and Adolescent Mental Health* 15, 197-203.

Sayem AM (2011). Violence, negligence and suicidal tendency among physically disabled street children. *Asian Social Work and Policy Review* 5, 44-59.

Schepis TS, McFetridge A, Chaplin TM, Sinha R, Krishnan-Sarin S (2011). A pilot examination of stress-related changes in impulsivity and risk taking as related to smoking status and cessation outcome in adolescents. *Nicotine & Tobacco Research*. Published online: 28 February 2011. doi:10.1093/ntr/ntr022.

Schlebusch L, Vawda N (2010). HIV-infection as a self-reported risk factor for attempted suicide in South Africa. *African Journal of Psychiatry (Johannesburg)* 13, 280-283.

Schroeder M, Krebs MO, Bleich S, Frieling H (2010). Epigenetics and depression: Current challenges and new therapeutic options. *Current Opinion in Psychiatry* 23, 588-592.

Seghatoleslam T, Rezaee Mirghaed O, Sajadfar F, Sadr S, Zahiroddine A (2010). A study on psycho-social factors related to children's suicide. *Iranian Red Crescent Medical Journal* 12, 660-663.

Selby EA, Bulik CM, Thornton L, Brandt HA, Crawford S, Fichter MM, Halmi KA, Jacoby GE, Johnson CL, Jones I, Kaplan AS, Mitchell JE, Nutzinger DO, Strober M, Treasure J, Woodside DB, Kaye WH, Joiner Jr. TE (2010). Refining behavioral dysregulation in borderline personality disorder using a sample of women with anorexia nervosa. *Personality Disorders: Theory, Research, and Treatment* 1, 250-257.

Selby EA, Connell LD, Joiner Jr. TE (2010). The pernicious blend of rumination and fearlessness in non-suicidal self-injury. *Cognitive Therapy and Research* 34, 421-428.

Selvaraj V, Ramaswamy S, Sharma A, Wilson D (2010). New-onset psychosis and emergence of suicidal ideation with aripiprazole. *The American Journal of Psychiatry* 167, 1535-1536.

Selvi Y, Aydin A, Boysan M, Atli A, Agargun MY, Besiroglu L (2010). Associations between chronotype, sleep quality, suicidality, and depressive symptoms in patients with major depression and healthy controls. *Chronobiology International* 27, 1813-1828.

Selvi Y, Aydin A, Atli A, Boysan M, Selvi F, Besiroglu L (2011). Chronotype differences in suicidal behavior and impulsivity among suicide attempters. *Chronobiology International* 28, 170-175.

Seo HJ, Jung YE, Kim TS, Kim JB, Lee MS, Kim JM, Lim HW, Jun TY (2011). Distinctive clinical characteristics and suicidal tendencies of patients with anxious depression. *The Journal of Nervous and Mental Disease* 199, 42-48.

Serafini G, Pompili M, Innamorati M, Iacorossi G, Cuomo I, Vista MD, Lester D, de Biase L, Girardi P, Tatarelli R (2011). The impact of anxiety, depression, and suicidality on quality of life and functional status of patients with congestive heart failure and hypertension: An observational cross-sectional study. *Primary Care Companion to the Journal of Clinical Psychiatry* 12, 6.

Shaikh IA, Shaikh MA (2011). Correlates of seriously considering attempting suicide among Jordanian students in grades 8 to 10. *East Mediterrenian Health Journal* 16, 1198-1199.

Shea M, Yang LH, Leong FTL (2010). Loss, psychosis, and chronic suicidality in a Korean American immigrant man: Integration of cultural formulation model and multicultural case conceptualization. *Asian American Journal of Psychology* 1, 212-223.

Shanafelt TD, Balch CM, Dyrbye L, Bechamps G, Russell T, Satele D, Rummans T, Swartz K, Novotny PJ, Sloan J, Oreskovich MR (2011). Suicidal ideation among American surgeons. *Archives of Surgery* 146, 54-62.

Sheppard K, Badger T (2010). The lived experience of depression among culturally deaf adults. *Journal of Psychiatric and Mental Health Nursing* 17, 783-789.

Sher L, Zambrano-Enriquez D, Arendt M (2010). Is disturbed sleep a clinically useful marker to determine the suicide risk in patients with post-traumatic stress disorder? *Israel Journal of Psychiatry and Related Sciences* 47, 63-64.

Shi Z, Taylor AW, Goldney R, Winefield H, Gill TK, Tuckerman J, Wittert G (2010). The use of a surveillance system to measure changes in mental health in Australian adults during the global financial crisis. *International Journal of Public Health.* Published online: 21 October 2010. doi:10.1007/s00038-010-0200-1.

Shidhaye R, Patel V (2010). Association of socio-economic, gender and health factors with common mental disorders in women: A population-based study of 5703 married rural women in India. *International Journal of Epidemiology.* Published online: 29 October 2010. doi:10.1093/ije/dyq179.

Shoval G, Feld-Olspanger J, Nahshoni E, Gothelf D, Misgav S, Manor I, Apter A, Zalsman G (2011). Suicidal behavior and related traits among inpatient adolescents with first-episode schizophrenia. *Comparative Psychiatry.* Published online: 7 March 2011. doi:10.1093/ije/dyq179.

Shrivastava A, Johnston ME, Shah N, Innamorati M, Stitt L, Thakar M, Lester D, Pompili M (2010). Persistent suicide risk in clinically improved schizophrenia patients: Challenge of the suicidal dimension. *Neuropsychiatric Disease and Treatment* 6, 633-638.

Siemieniuk RAC, Krentz HB, Gish JA, Gill MJ (2010). Domestic violence screening: prevalence and outcomes in a Canadian HIV population. *AIDS Patient Care* 24, 763-770.

Sit D, Seltman H, Wisner KL (2011). Seasonal effects on depression risk and suicidal symptoms in postpartum women. *Depression and Anxiety.* Published online: 4 March 2011. doi:10.1002/da.20807.

Skapinakis P, Bellos S, Gkatsa T, Magklara K, Lewis G, Araya R, Stylianidis S, Mavreas V (2011). The association between bullying and early stages of suicidal ideation in late adolescents in Greece. *BMC Psychiatry* 11, 22.

Sloneem J, Oliver C, Udwin O, Woodcock KA (2011). Prevalence, phenomenology, aetiology and predictors of challenging behaviour in Smith-Magenis syndrome. *Journal of Intellectual Disability Research* 55, 138-151.

Smith GW, Shevlin M, Murphy J, Houston JE (2010). An assessment of the demographic and clinical correlates of the dimensions of alcohol use behaviour. *Alcohol and Alcoholism* 45, 563-572.

Sockalingam S, Links PS, Abbey SE (2011). Suicide risk in hepatitis C and during interferon-alpha therapy: A review and clinical update. *Journal of Viral Hepatitis* 18, 153-160.

Somes J, Donatelli NS (2011). Accident or suicide attempt: Car versus tree? *Journal of Emergency Nursing* 37, 179-181.

Souza RP, De Luca V, Manchia M, Kennedy JL (2010). Are serotonin 3A and 3B receptor genes associated with suicidal behavior in schizophrenia subjects? *Neuroscience Letters* 489, 137-141.

Spoletini I, Piras F, Fagioli S, Rubino IA, Martinotti G, Siracusano A, Caltagirone C, Spalletta G (2010). Suicidal attempts and increased right amygdala volume in schizophrenia. *Schizophrenia Research* 125, 30-40.

Steiger H, Fichter M, Bruce KR, Joober R, Badawi G, Richardson J, Groleau P, Ramos C, Israel M, Bondy B, Quadflieg N, Bachetzky N (2010). Molecular-genetic correlates of self-harming behaviors in eating-disordered women: Findings from a combined Canadian-German sample. *Progress in Neuro-Psychopharmacology and Biological Psychiatry* 35, 102-106.

Strelitz B, Rees J, Thompson E, Walker L (2011). Suicide risk behaviours in Washington state adolescents with disabilities: Examining the role of depressive symptoms. *Journal of Adolescent Health* 48, S81-S82.

Striano P, Zara F, Minetti C (2010). Suicide-related events in patients treated with antiepileptic drugs. *New England Journal of Medicine* 363, 1873-1874.

Sundström A, Alfredsson L, Sjölin-Forsberg G, Gerdén B, Bergman U, Jokinen J (2010). Association of suicide attempts with acne and treatment with isotretinoin: retrospective Swedish cohort study. *British Medical Journal* 341, c5812.

Swahn MH, Gaylor E, Bossarte RM, Van Dulmen M (2010). Co-occurring suicide attempts and physical fighting: A comparison between Urban, Suburban, and Rural high school students. *Vulnerable Children and Youth Studies* 5, 353-362.

Symons FJ, Byiers BJ, Raspa M, Bishop E, Bailey DB (2010). Self-injurious behavior and Fragile X syndrome: Findings from the National Fragile X Survey. *American Journal on Intellectual and Developmental Disabilities* 115, 473-481.

Szyszkowicz M, Willey JB, Grafstein E, Rowe BH, Colman I (2010). Air pollution and emergency department visits for suicide attempts in Vancouver, Canada. *Environmental Health Insights* 4, 79-86.

Tang CS, Wong W, Leung P, Chen WQ, Lee A, Ling D (2011). Health compromising behaviours among Chinese adolescents: Role of physical abuse, school experience, and social support. *Journal of Health Psychology*. Published online: 11 January 2011. doi:10.1177/1359 105310384297.

Tarantino N, Kuperminc G (2011). Suicidal risk behaviour in emerging adult ED patients screened for substance use. *Journal of Adolescent Health* 48, 70-70.

Taylor L, Oliver C, Murphy G (2011). The chronicity of self-injurious behaviour: a long-term follow-up of a total population study. *Journal of Applied Research in Intellectual Disabilities* 24, 105-117.

Thomas SHL, Drici MD, Hall GC, Crocq MA, Everitt B, Lader MH, Jeunne CL, Naber D, Priori S, Sturkenboom M, Thibaut F, Peuskens J, Mittoux A, Tanghoj P, Toumi M, Moore ND, Mann RD (2010). Safety of sertindole versus risperidone in schizophrenia: Principal results of the sertindole cohort prospective study (SCoP). *Acta Psychiatrica Scandinavica* 122, 345-355.

Thompson AH (2010). The suicidal process and self-esteem. *Crisis* 31, 311-316.

Thompson MP, Light LS (2011). Examining gender differences in risk factors for suicide attempts made 1 and 7 years later in a nationally representative sample. *Journal of Adolescence Health* 48, 391-397.

Tobaiqy M, Stewart D, Helms PJ, Williams J, Crum J, Steer C, McLay J (2011). Parental reporting of adverse drug reactions associated with attention-deficit hyperactivity disorder (ADHD). Medications in children attending specialist paediatric clinics in the UK. *Drug Safety* 34, 211-219.

Torres AR, Ramos-Cerqueira ATA, Ferrao YA, Fontenelle LF, Do Rosario MC, Miguel EC (2011). Suicidality in obsessive-compulsive disorder: Prevalence and relation to symptom dimensions and comorbid conditions. *Journal of Clinical Psychiatry* 72, 17-26.

Tozzi F, Manchia M, Galwey NW, Severino G, Del Zompo M, Day R, Matthews K, Strauss J, Kennedy JL, McGuffin P, Vincent JB, Farmer A, Muglia P (2011). Admixture analysis of age at onset in bipolar disorder. *Psychiatry Research* 185, 27-32.

Uebelacker LA, Strong D, Weinstock LM, Miller IW (2011). Likelihood of suicidality at varying levels of depression severity: a re-analysis of NESARC data. *Suicide Life-Threatening Behavior* 40, 620-627.

Unikel C, Von Holle A, Bulik CM, Ocampo R (2011). Disordered eating and suicidal intent: The role of thin ideal internalisation, shame and family criticism. *European Eating Disorders Review*. Published online: 3 January 2011. doi:10.1002/erv.1070.

Vachher AS, Sharma AK (2010). Domestic violence against women and their mental health status in a colony in Delhi. *Indian Journal of Community Medicine* 35, 403-405.

van Leeuwen N, Rodgers R, Régner I, Chabrol H (2010). The role of acculturation in suicidal ideation among second-generation immigrant adolescents in France. *Transcultural Psychiatry* 47, 812-832.

van Noorden MS, Minkenberg SE, Giltay EJ, den Hollander-Gijsman ME, van Rood YR, van der Wee NJ, Zitman FG (2010). Pre-adult versus adult onset major depressive disorder in a naturalistic patient sample: the Leiden Routine Outcome Monitoring Study. *Psychological Medicine*. Published online: 16 November 2010. doi:10.1017/S0033291710002199.

Vasquez F, Ysela N, Falconi F, Vite V (2010). Problematic internet use and suicide attempt. *International Journal of Neuropsychopharmacology* 13, 57-57.

Verona E, Javdani S (2011). Dimensions of adolescent psychopathology and relationships to suicide risk indicators. *Journal of Youth Adolescence*. Published online: 28 January 2011. doi:10.1007/s10964-011-9630-1.

Verrocchio MC, Conti C, Fulcheri M (2010). Deliberate self-harm in substance-dependent patients and relationship with alexithymia and personality disorders: A case-control study. *Journal of Biological Regulators and Homeostatic Agents* 24, 461-469.

Vidourek RA, King KA, Knopf EE (2010). Non-medical prescription drug use among university students. *American Journal of Health Education* 41, 345-352.

Wada K, Yoshikawa T, Goto T, Hirai A, Matsushima E, Nakashima Y, Akaho R, Kido M, Hosaka T (2010). Association of depression and suicidal ideation with unreasonable patient demands and complaints among Japanese physicians: A national cross-sectional survey. *International Journal of Behavioural Medicine*. Published online: 2 December 2010. 10.1007/s12529-010-9132-7.

Warner CH, Appenzeller GN, Parker JR, Warner CM, Hoge CW (2011). Effectiveness of mental health screening and coordination of in-theater care prior to deployment to Iraq: A cohort study. *American Journal of Psychiatry*. Published online: 18 January 2011. doi:10.1176/appi.ajp.2010.10091303.

Warzocha D, Pawelczyk T, Gmitrowicz A (2010). Associations between deliberate self-harm episodes in psychiatrically hospitalised youth and the type of mental disorders and selected environmental factors. *Archives of Psychiatry and Psychotherapy* 12, 23-29.

Waseem M, Prasankumar R, Pagan K, Leber M (2011). A retrospective look at length of stay for pediatric psychiatric patients in an urban emergency department. *Pediatric Emergency Care* 127, 170-173.

Wasserman GA, McReynolds LS, Schwalbe CS, Keating JM, Jones SA (2010). Psychiatric disorder, comorbidity, and suicidal behavior in juvenile justice youth. *Criminal Justice and Behaviour* 37, 1361-1376.

Wen X, Meador KJ, Loring DW, Eisenschenk S, Segal R, Hartzema AG (2010). Is antiepileptic drug use related to depression and suicidal ideation among patients with epilepsy? *Epilepsy & Behavior* 19, 494-500.

West BA, Swahn MH, McCarty F (2010). Children at risk for suicide attempt and attempt-related injuries: Findings from the 2007 Youth Risk Behavior Survey. *Western Journal of Emergency Medicine* 11, 257-263.

Wester KL, Trepal HC (2010). Coping behaviors, abuse history, and counseling: Differentiating college students who self-injure. *Journal of College Counseling* 13, 141-154.

Whitlock J (2011). Non-suicidal self-injury in adolescents and young adults: General trends and gender differences. *Journal of Adolescent Health* 48, S90-S90.

Wieland D, Hursey M, Delgado D (2010). Operation Enduring Freedom (OEF) and Operation Iraqi Freedom (OIF) military mental health issues. Information on the wars' signature wounds: Posttraumatic stress disorder and traumatic brain injury. *The Pennsylvania Nurse* 65, 4-11.

Wiesemann C (2011). Is there a right not to know one's sex? The ethics of 'gender verification' in women's sports competition. *Journal of Medical Ethics*. Published online: 1 March 2011. doi:10.1136/jme.2010.039081.

Wilkinson P, Goodyer I (2011). Non-suicidal self-injury. *European Child and Adolescent Psychiatry* 20, 103-108.

Williams ST, Kores RC, Currier JM (2011). Survivors of self-inflicted gunshot wounds: a 20-year chart review. *Psychosomatics* 52, 34-40.

Wilkinson B (2010). Current trends in remediating adolescent self-injury: an integrative review. *Journal of School Nursing*. Published online: 10 November 2010. doi:10.1177/1059 840510388570.

Willour VL, Seifuddin F, Mahon PB, Jancic D, Pirooznia M, Steele J, Schweizer B, Goes FS, Mondimore FM, Mackinnon DF; The Bipolar Genome Study (BiGS) Consortium, Perlis RH, Lee PH, Huang J, Kelsoe JR, Shilling PD, Rietschel M, Nöthen M, Cichon S, Gurling H, Purcell S, Smoller JW, Craddock N, Depaulo JR Jr, Schulze TG, McMahon FJ, Zandi PP, Potash JB (2011). A genome-wide association study of attempted suicide. *Molecular Psychiatry*. Published online: 22 March 2011. doi:10.1038/mp.2011.4.

Wilson MP, Castillo EM, Batey AM, Sapyta J, Aronson S (2010). Hepatitis C and depressive symptoms: Psychological and social factors matter more than liver injury. *International Journal of Psychiatry in Medicine* 40, 199-215.

Windover AK, Merrell J, Ashton K, Heinberg LJ (2010). Prevalence and psychosocial correlates of self-reported past suicide attempts among bariatric surgery candidates. *Surgery for Obesity and Related Diseases* 6, 702-706.

Winterrowd E, Canetto SS, Chavez EL (2011). Friendship factors and suicidality: Common and unique patterns in Mexican American and European American youth. *Suicide and Life-Threatening Behavior* 41, 50-65.

Wohab MDA, Akhter S (2010). The effects of childhood sexual abuse on children's psychology and employment. *Procedia - Social and Behavioral Sciences* 5, 144-149.

Woldu H, Porta G, Goldstein T, Sakolsky D, Perel J, Emslie G, Mayes T, Clarke G, Ryan ND, Birmaher B, Wagner KD, Asarnow JR, Keller MB, Brent D (2011). Pharmacokinetically and Clinician-Determined Adherence to an Antidepressant Regimen and Clinical Outcome in the TORDIA Trial. *Journal of the American Academy of Child and Adolescent Psychiatry*. Published online: 10 March 2011. doi:10.1016/j.jaac.2011.01.018.

Wong H-M, Leung HC-M, Chow L-Y, Kam W-K, Tang AK-L (2010). Prevalence of borderline personality disorder and its clinical correlates in Chinese patients with recent deliberate self-harm. *Journal of Personality Disorders* 24, 800-811.

Wong MM, Brower KJ, Zucker RA (2010). Sleep problems, suicidal ideation, and self-harm behaviors in adolescence. *Journal of Psychiatric Research* 45, 505-511.

Wood RL, Williams C, Lewis R (2010). Role of alexithymia in suicide ideation after traumatic brain injury. 16, 1108-1114.

Wu CY, Stewart R, Huang HC, Prince M, Liu SI (2010). The impact of quality and quantity of social support on help-seeking behavior prior to deliberate self-harm. *General Hospital Psychiatry* 33, 37-44.

Yakunina ES, Rogers JR, Waehler CA, Werth JL (2010). College students' intentions to seek help for suicidal ideation: Accounting for the help-negation effect. *Suicide and Life-Threatening Behavior* 40, 438-450.

Yamokoski CA, Scheel KR, Rogers JR (2011). The role of affect in suicidal thoughts and behaviors. *Suicide and Life-Threatening Behaviour*. Published online: 22 February 2011. doi:10.1111/j.1943-278X.2011.00019.x.

Yazzie RA (2011). Availability of treatment to youth offenders: Comparison of public versus private programs from a national census. *Children and Youth Services Review*. Published online: 4 December 2010. doi:10.1016/j.childyouth.2010.11.026.

Yen S, Shea MT, Walsh Z, Edelen MO, Hopwood CJ, Markowitz JC, Ansell EB, Morey LC, Grilo CM, Sanislow CA, Skodol AE, Gunderson JG, Zanarini MC, McGlashan TH (2011). Self-harm subscale of the Schedule for Nonadaptive and Adaptive Personality (SNAP):

Predicting suicide attempts over 8 years of follow-up. *Journal of Clinical Psychiatry*. Published online: 25 January 2011. doi:10.4088/JCP.09m05583blu.

You S, Van Orden KA, Conner KR (2010). Social connections and suicidal thoughts and behavior. *Psychology of Addictive Behaviours*. Published online: 13 December 2010. doi:10.1037/a0020936.

Zakeri Z, Shakiba M, Narouie B, Mladkova N, Ghasemi-Rad M, Khosravi A (2011). Prevalence of depression and depressive symptoms in patients with systemic lupus erythematosus: Iranian experience. *Rheumatology International*. Published online: 21 January 2011. doi:10.1007/s00296-010-1791-9.

Zubrick SR, Mitrou F, Lawrence D, Silburn SR (2011). Maternal death and the onward psychosocial circumstances of Australian Aboriginal children and young people. *Psychological Medicine*. Published online: 5 January 2011. doi:10.1017/S0033291710002485.

Care & Support

Aho H, Kauppila T, Haanpaa M (2010). Patients referred from a multidisciplinary pain clinic to the social worker, their general health, pain condition, treatment and outcome. *Scandinavian Journal of Pain* 1, 220-226.

Anonymous (2010). Acute poisoning following ingestion of medicines: Initial management. *Prescrire International* 19, 111.

Anonymous (2011). Attachment-based family therapy reduces suicidal ideation in adolescents. *Evidence Based Mental Health* 14, 8.

Baker C (2011). Managing self-harm: psychological perspectives. *Mental Health Practice* 14, 10.

Benbow M, Deacon M (2011). Helping people who self-harm to care for their wounds. *Mental Health Practice* 14, 28-31.

Benger JR (2010). Advanced directives and suicidal behaviour: "If in doubt treat" is not as easy as it sounds. *British Medical Journal* 341, c5478.

Brendel RW, Wei MH, Edersheim JG (2010). An approach to the patient in crisis: Assessments of the risk of suicide and violence. *Medical Clinics of North America* 94, 1089-1102.

Brennan JM (2010). Understanding the impact of war zone experiences: a primer for civilian nurses. The *Pennsylvanian Nurse* 65, 4-11.

Borg T, Holstad M, Larsson S (2010). Quality of life in patients operated for pelvic fractures caused by suicide attempt by jumping. *Scandinavian Journal of Surgery* 99, 180-186.

Bruffaerts R, Demyttenaere K, Hwang I, Chiu WT, Sampson N, Kessler RC, Alonso J, Borges G, de Girolamo G, de Graaf R, Florescu S, Gureje O, Hu C, Karam EG, Kawakami N, Kostyuchenko S, Kovess-Masfety V, Lee S, Levinson D, Matschinger H, Posada-Villa J, Sagar R, Scott KM, Stein DJ, Tomov T, Viana MC, Nock MK (2011). Treatment of suicidal people around the world. *British Journal of Psychiatry*. Published online: 24 January 2011. doi:10.1192/bjp.bp.110.084129.

Brunero S, Lamont S (2010). Mental health liaison nursing, taking a capacity building approach. *Perspectives in Psychiatric Care* 46, 286-293.

Buckley S (2010). Caring for those with mental health conditions on a children's ward. *British Journal of Nursing* 19, 1226-1230.

Ciechanowski P, Chaytor N, Miller J, Fraser R, Russo J, Unutzer J, Gilliam F (2010). PEARLS depression treatment for individuals with epilepsy: A randomized controlled trial. *Epilepsy and Behavior* 19, 225-231.

Cohen JA, Mannarino AP (2011). Trauma-focused CBT for traumatic grief in military children. *Journal of Contemporary Psychotherapy*. Published online: 17 February 2011. doi:10.1007/s10879-011-9178-0.

Cooper J, Hunter C, Owen-Smith A, Gunnell D, Donovan J, Hawton K, Kapur N (2011). "Well it's like someone at the other end cares about you." A qualitative study exploring the views of users and providers of care of contact-based interventions following self-harm. *General Hospital Psychiatry*. Published online: 2 March 2011. doi:10.1016/j.genhosppsych.2011. 01.009.

Davies S (2010). Advanced directives and suicidal behaviour: What to do about treatment refusal at 3 am? *British Medical Journal* 341, c5477.

DiazGranados N, Ibrahim LA, Brutsche NE, Ameli R, Henter ID, Luckenbaugh DA, Machado-Vieira R, Zarate CA Jr. (2011). Rapid resolution of suicidal ideation after a single infusion of an N-methyl-D-aspartate antagonist in patients with treatment-resistant major depressive disorder. *Journal of Clinical Psychiatry* 71, 1605-1611.

Dieterich M, Irving CB, Park B, Marshall M (2010). Intensive case management for severe mental illness. *Cochrane Database of Systematic Reviews* 10, CD007906.

Edwards SD, Hewitt J (2011). Can supervising self-harm be part of ethical nursing practice? *Nursing Ethics* 18, 79-87.

Fleischhaker C, Böhme R, Sixt B, Brück C, Schneider C, Schulz E (2011). Dialectical Behavioral Therapy for Adolescents (DBT-A): A clinical trial for patients with suicidal and self-injurious behavior and borderline symptoms with a one-year follow-up. *Child and Adolescent Psychiatry and Mental Health* 5, 3.

Fox C (2011). Working with clients who engage in self-harming behaviour: Experiences of a group of counsellors. *British Journal of Guidance & Counselling* 39, 41.

Goldberg EM, Ferguson F (2010). Treatment modalities for self-injurious behaviors observed in the special-needs patient: 2 case reports *Pediatric Dentistry* 32, 481-485.

Goodkind JR, Lanoue MD, Milford J (2010). Adaptation and implementation of cognitive behavioral intervention for trauma in schools with American Indian youth. *Journal of Clinical Child and Adolescent Psychology* 39, 858-872.

Hadley D, Anderson BS, Borckardt JJ, Arana A, Li X, Nahas Z, George MS (2011). Safety, tolerability, and effectiveness of high doses of adjunctive daily left prefrontal repetitive transcranial magnetic stimulation for treatment-resistant depression in a clinical setting. *The Journal of ECT* 27, 18-25.

Hanssen-Bauer K, Heyerdahl S, Hatling T, Jensen G, Olstad PM, Stangeland T, Tinderholt T (2011). Admissions to acute adolescent psychiatric units: A prospective study of clinical severity and outcome. *International Journal of Mental Health Systems* 5, 1.

Hassanzadeh M, Khajeddin N, Nojomi M, Fleischmann A, Eshrati T (2010). Brief intervention and contact after deliberate self-harm: An Iranian randomized controlled trial. *Iranian Journal of Psychiatry and Behavioral Sciences* 4, 5-12.

Holland J, Tran TV (2010). The use of social workers' emergency certificates and factors associated with linkage to services. *Social Work in Mental Health* 8, 495-509.

Holt C, Agius M, Butler S, Zaman R (2010). An audit to identify factors affecting response to treatment among depressed patients who have documented suicidal ideation/attempts in a Bedfordshire Community Mental Health Team. *Psychiatria Danubina* 22, 63-67.

Horowitz L, Ballard E, Teach SJ, Bosk A, Rosenstein DL, Joshi P, Dalton ME, Pao M (2010). Feasibility of screening patients with nonpsychiatric complaints for suicide risk in a pediatric emergency department: A good time to talk? *Pediatric Emergency Care* 26, 787-792.

Humber N, Hayes A, Senior J, Fahy T, Shaw J (2011). Identifying, monitoring and managing prisoners at risk of self-harm/suicide in England and Wales. *The Journal of Forensic Psychiatry & Psychology* 22, 22.

Hvid M, Vangborg K, Sørensen HJ, Nielsen IK, Stenborg JM, Wang AG (2010). Preventing repetition of attempted suicide-II. The Amager Project, a randomized controlled trial. *Nordic Journal of Psychiatry*. Published online: 20 December 2010. doi:10.3109/08039488. 2010.544404.

Irckle K (2010). At the cutting edge: creative and holistic responses to self-injury. *Creative Nursing* 16, 160-165.

Ingenhoven TJM, Van Den Brink W, Passchier J, Duivenvoorden HJ (2011). Treatment-disrupting behaviors during psychotherapy of patients with personality disorders: The predictive power of psychodynamic personality diagnosis. *Journal of Psychiatric Practice* 17, 21-34.

Johannessen HA, Dieserud G, De Leo D, Claussen B, Zahl PH (2011). Chain of care for patients who have attempted suicide: a follow-up study from Baerum, Norway. *BMC Public Health* 11, 81.

Kobeissi J, Aloysi A, Tobias K, Popeo D, Kellner CH (2011). Resolution of severe suicidality with a single electroconvulsive therapy. *The Journal of ECT* 27, 86-88.

Krumrei EJ, Newton FB, Kim E (2010). A multi-institution look at college students seeking counseling: Nature and severity of concerns. *Journal of College Student Psychotherapy* 24, 261-283.

Lakeman R (2010). What can qualitative research tell us about helping a person who is suicidal? *Nursing Times* 106, 23-26.

Larkin GL, Beautrais AL, Powsner SM, Sanacora G, Krystal JH, Turelli RR, Lippmann MJ (2010). A prospective open label trial of low dose ketamine for acute suicidal states in the Emergency Department. *Annals of Emergency Medicine* 56, 53-53.

Lazenby RB (2011). Depression in the college population: An E-S-A approach to primary prevention. *The Nurse Practitioner* 36, 33-39.

Lindgren BM, Astrom S, Graneheim UH (2010). Held to ransom: Parents of self-harming adults describe their lived experience of professional care and caregivers. *International Journal of Qualitative Studies on Health and Well-being* 5, 3.

Lizardi D, Stanley B (2010). Treatment engagement: a neglected aspect in the psychiatric care of suicidal patients. *Psychiatric Services* 61, 1183-1191.

Marken PA, Zimmerman C, Kennedy C, Schremmer R, Smith KV (2010). Human simulators and standardized patients to teach difficult conversations to interprofessional health care teams. *American Journal of Pharmaceutical Education* 74, 1-8.

McDonell MG, Tarantino J, Dubose P, Matestic P, Steinmetz K, Galbreath H, McClellan JM (2010). A pilot evaluation of dialectical behavioural therapy in adolescent long-term inpatient care. *Child and Adolescent Mental Health* 15, 193-196.

McHugh PC (2011). Tetrahydrobiopterin pathway may provide novel molecular targets for acute and long term efficacy of mood-regulating drugs. *Current Pharmacogenomics and Personalized Medicine* 8, 174-181.

Moran JR, Gross AF, Stern TA (2011). Staying against advice: Refusal to leave the hospital. *Primary Care Companion to the Journal of Clinical Psychiatry* 12, 6.

Moret-Hartman M, Reuzel R, Grin J, Kramers C, van der Wilt G (2011). Strengthening evaluation through interactive problem structuring: A case study of hospital care after attempted suicide. *Evaluation (Sage)* 17, 37-52.

Mullins D, MacHale S, Cotter D (2010). Compliance with NICE guidelines in the management of self-harm. *Psychiatrist* 34, 385-389.

Murphy E, Kapur N, Webb R, Cooper J (2010). Risk assessment following self-harm: Comparison of mental health nurses and psychiatrists. *Journal of Advanced Nursing* 67, 127-139.

Noordin S, Allana S, Ahmad T, Bhatti A-U-A, Zafar H, Wajid MA (2011). Evolution of trauma management at a tertiary care hospital: A cohort study. *International Journal of Surgery* 9, 75-78.

Norelli LJ, Coates AD, Kovasznay BM (2010). Cancer risk from diagnostic radiology in a deliberate self-harm patient. *Acta Psychiatrica Scandinavica* 122, 427-430.

Ougrin D, Zundel T, Ng A, Banarsee R, Bottle A, Taylor E (2010). Trial of Therapeutic Assessment in London: Randomised controlled trial of Therapeutic Assessment versus standard psychosocial assessment in adolescents presenting with self-harm. *Archives of Disease in Childhood*. Published online: 27 October 2010. doi:10.1136/adc.2010.188755.

Ousey K, Ousey C (2010). Intervention strategies for people who self-harm. *Wounds UK* 6, 34-40.

Owens C (2010). Interventions for self-harm: Are we measuring outcomes in the most appropriate way? *British Journal of Psychiatry* 197, 502-503.

Pasieczny N, Connor J (2011). The effectiveness of dialectical behaviour therapy in routine public mental health settings: An Australian controlled trial. *Behaviour Research and Therapy 49, 4-10.*

Perera Ramani EA, Kathriarachchi ST (2011). Problem-solving counseling as a therapeutic tool on youth suicidal behavior in the suburban population in Sri Lanka. *Indian Journal of Psychiatry* 53, 30-35.

Petersen B, Toft J, Christensen NB, Foldager L, Munk-Jorgensen P, Windfeld M, Frederiksen CK, Valbak K (2010). A 2-year follow-up of mentalization-oriented group therapy following day hospital treatment for patients with personality disorders. *Personality and Mental Health* 4, 294-301.

Pitman AL (2010). Why are psychosocial assessments following self-harm not completed? *Psychiatrist* 34, 540.

Prasko J, Diveky T, Grambal A, Latalova K (2010). Suicidal patients. *Biomedical Papers-Olomouc* 154, 265-273.

Robertson LH (2011). Self-mapping in treating suicide ideation: A case study. *Death Studies* 35, 267-280.

Ryan C, Nielssen O, Paton M, Large M (2010). Clinical decisions in psychiatry should not be based on risk assessment. *Australasian Psychiatry* 18, 398-403.

Sandman CA, Kemp AS (2011). Opioid antagonists may reverse endogenous opiate 'dependence' in the treatment of self-injurious behaviour. *Pharmaceuticals* 4, 366-381.

Schbley B (2011). Managing self-harm: psychological perspectives. *Bulletin of the Menninger Clinic* 74, 354.

Schmidt SC, Strauch S, Rösch T, Veltzke-Schlieker W, Jonas S, Pratschke J, Weidemann H, Neuhaus P, Schumacher G (2010). Management of esophageal perforations. *Surgical Endoscopy* 24, 2809-2813.

Serafini G, Pompili M, Del Casale A, Mancini M, Innamorati M, Lester D, Girardi P, Tatarelli R (2010). Duloxetine versus venlafaxine in the treatment of unipolar and bipolar depression. *La Clinica Terapeutica* 161, 321-327.

Shabani A, Taheri A, Azadforouz S, Abbasi CN, Mousavi Z, Zangeneh K, Shariat SV, Nohesara S, Naserbakht M, Taban M, Kokar S, Teimoorinejad S, Hakimshooshtary M, Shirazi E (2010). Bipolar disorder patients follow-up (BDPF): Methods and materials. 15, 229-234.

Shah PJ, Dubey KP, Watti C, Lalwani J (2010). Effectiveness of thiopentone, propofol and midazolam as an ideal intravenous anaesthetic agent for modifified electroconvulsive therapy: A comparative study. *Indian Journal of Anaesthesia* 54, 296-301.

Talseth AG, Gilje FL (2011). Nurses' responses to suicide and suicidal patients: A critical interpretive synthesis. *Journal of Clinical Nursing*. Published online: 1 March 2011. doi:10.1111/j.1365-2702.2010.03490.x.

Tate A (2010). Getting it right: Caring for people who self-harm. *Emergency Nurse* 18, 32-33.

Taylor LM, Oldershaw A, Richards C, Davidson K, Schmidt U, Simic M (2011). Development and pilot evaluation of a manualized cognitive-behavioural treatment package for adolescent self-harm. *Behavioural and Cognitive Psychotherapy*. Published online: 11 March 2011. doi:10.1017/S1352465811000075.

Thompson D, Goebert D, Takeshita J (2010). A program for reducing depressive symptoms and suicidal ideation in medical students. *Academic medicine: Journal of the Association of American Medical Colleges* 85, 1635-1639.

Trueman S (2010). Suicidal patients; Risky business requiring prescience from mental health nurses. *International Journal of Mental Health Nursing* 19A, 48.

Von Wild T, Siemers F, Stollwerck PL, Stang FH, Mailander P, Namdar T (2011). Postoperative wound manipulation after self-mutilation in borderline personality disorder — a plastic reconstructive challenge. *European Journal of Plastic Surgery*. Published online: 10 February 2011. doi:10.1007/s00238-011-0548-3.

CASE REPORTS

Ago M, Hayashi T, Ago K, Ogata M (2011). Two fatalities associated with chloroform inhalation. Variation of toxicological and pathological findings. *Legal Medicine* 13, 156-160.

Anderson A, Sisask M, Airi Värnik (2011). Familicide and suicide in a case of gambling dependence. *The Journal of Forensic Psychiatry & Psychology* 22, 156.

Andrasi TB, Abebe G, Spielberger J, Rohsbach U, Vitolianos N, Vahl CF (2011). Survival after suicidal transsection of the left common carotid artery in octogenarian. *American Surgeon* 77, 50-52.

Arhakis A, Topouzelis N, Kotsiomiti E, Kotsanos N (2010). Effective treatment of self-injurious oral trauma in Lesch-Nyhan syndrome: A case report. *Dental Traumatology* 26, 496-500.

Azazh A (2010). Case series of 2,4-D poisoning in Tikur Anbessa Teaching Hospital. *Ethiopian Medical Journal* 48, 243-246.

Basha VC, Reddy KS (2010). Unusual presentation of medico-legal cases. *Medico-Legal Update* 10, 11-12.

Berens S, Ketterer T, Kneubuehl BP, Thali MJ, Ross S, Bolliger SA (2010). A case of homicidal intraoral gunshot and review of the literature. *Forensic Science, Medicine, and Pathology.* Published online: 13 November 2010. doi:10.1007/s12024-010-9201-x.

Boehm J, Fischer K, Bohnert M (2010). Putative role of TNF- , interleukin-8 and ICAM-1 as indicators of an early inflammatory reaction after burn: A morphological and immuno-histochemical study of lung tissue of fire victims. *Journal of Clinical Pathology* 63, 967-971.

Boscolo-Berto R, Iafrate M, Viel G (2010). Forensic implications in self-insertion of urethral foreign bodies. *The Canadian Journal of Urology* 17, 5026-5027.

Buschmann CT, Guddat SS, Tsokos M (2010). Suicide note written on the body following self-mutilation. *Rechtmedizin* 20, 419-422.

Chen F, Jiang L, Yang B (2011). Visual loss caused by acute cyanide poisoning: A case report. *Clinical Toxicology* 49, 121-123.

Chen SPL, Tang MHY, Ng SW, Poon WT, Chan AYW, Mak TWL (2010). Psychosis associated with usage of herbal slimming products adulterated with sibutramine: A case series. *Clinical Toxicology* 48, 832-838.

Cheng A, Kunchur R, Goss A (2011). Management challenges in psychiatric patients with severe mandibular pain: A case report. *Australian Dental Journal* 56, 82-84.

Chhabra R, Singh I, Tandon M, Babu R (2010). Indoxacarb poisoning: A rare presentation as methemoglobinaemia. *Indian Journal of Anaesthesia* 54, 239-241.

Coentre R, Power P (2011). A diagnostic dilemma between psychosis and post-traumatic stress disorder: a case report and review of the literature. *Journal of Medical Case Reports* 5, 97.

D'Aloja E, De Giorgio F, Ausania F, Cascini F (2011). A case of suicidal suffocation simulating homicide. *Journal of Forensic Sciences.* Published online: 1 March 2011. doi:10.1111/j.1556-4029.2011.01719.x.

Dawood AWA (2011). Medicolegal aspects of 3 cases of bizarre self-mutilation. *American Journal of Forensic Medicine and Pathology* 32, 35-38.

Dickmann JRM, Dickmann LM (2010). An uncommonly recognized cause of rhabdomyolysis after quetiapine intoxication. *American Journal of Emergency Medicine* 28, 9.

Dutta R, Dube SK, Singh DK (2010). Antitubercular drug poisoning in a pregnant woman. *Indian Journal of Anaesthesia* 54, 335-337.

Furukawa S, Takaya A, Nakagawa T, Sakaguchi I, Nishi K (2011). Fatal hypernatremia due to drinking a large quantity of shoyu (Japanese soy sauce). *Journal of Forensic Legal Medicine* 18, 91-92.

Gahr M, Freudenmann R, Schönfeldt-Lecuona C (2011). Non-suicidal self-injury by intravenous application of nicotine in a patient with borderline personality disorder resulting in substance dependence. *Addiction.* Published online: 10 February 2011. doi:10.1111/j.1360-0443.2011.03393.x.

Glatstein M, Garcia-Bournissen F, Scolnik D, Rosenbloom E, Koren G (2010). Sudden-onset tachypnea and confusion in a previously healthy teenager. *Therapeutic Drug Monitoring* 32, 700-703.

George P (2010). An unusual cause of pulmonary oedema and its successful management: A case of phosphorus poisoning. *Journal of Clinical and Diagnostic Research* 4, 3554-3557.

Grosse Perdekamp M, Nadjem H, Merkel J, Braunwarth R, Pollak S, Thierauf A (2010). Two-gun suicide by simultaneous shots to the head: Interdisciplinary reconstruction on the basis of scene investigation, autopsy findings, GSR analysis and examination of firearms, bullets and cartridge cases. *International Journal of Legal Medicine.* Published online: 10 October 2010. doi:10.1007/s00414-010-0517-6.

Hantson P, Villa A, Galloy AC, Negri S, Esabon G, Lambiotte F, Haufroid V, Garnier R (2010). Dimethylformamide metabolism following self-harm using a veterinary euthanasia product. *Clinical Toxicology (Philadelphia)* 48, 725-729.

Harvey M, Cave G, Chanwai G (2010). Fatal methaemoglobinaemia induced by self-poisoning with sodium nitrite. *Emergency Medicine Australasia* 22, 463-465.

Holstege CP, Forrester JD, Borek HA, Lawrence DT (2010). A case of cyanide poisoning and the use of arterial blood gas analysis to direct therapy. *Hospital Practice* 38, 69-74.

Hong BA, North CS, Pollio DE, Abbacchi A, Debold C, Adewuyi SA, Lisker-Melman M (2011). The use of psychoeducation for a patient with hepatitis C and psychiatric illness in preparation for antiviral therapy: A case report and discussion. *Journal of Clinical Psychology in Medical Settings* 18, 99-107.

Hu YH, Yang CC, Deng JF, Wu ML (2010). Methomyl-alphamethrin poisoning presented with cholinergic crisis, cortical blindness, and delayed peripheral neuropathy. *Clinical Toxicology (Philadelphia)* 48, 859-862.

Hurst K (2010). Primary hyperparathyroidism as a secondary cause of depression. *Journal of the American Board of Family Medicine* 23, 677-680.

Inder D, Rehan H, Yadav M, Manak S, Kumar P (2011). IFN-[alpha]-2a (Interferon) and ribavirin induced suicidal attempt in a patient of chronic HCV: A rare case report. *Indian Journal of Pharmacology* 43, 210-211.

Imamura T, Yanagawa Y, Nishikawa K, Matsumoto N, Sakamoto T (2010). Two cases of acute poisoning with acetamiprid in humans. *Clinical Toxicology* 48, 851-853.

Iyyadurai R, Surekha V, Sathyendra S, Paul Wilson B, Gopinath KG (2010). Azadirachtin poisoning: A case report. *Clinical Toxicology (T and F)* 48, 857-868.

Jousset N, Rougé-Maillart C, Turcant A, Guilleux M, Le Bouil A, Tracqui A (2010). Suicide by skull stab wounds: a case of drug-induced psychosis. *American Journal of Forensic Medicine and Pathology* 31, 378-381.

Kadic L, Maandag NJG, Janssen CMM, Driessen JJ, Schultze Kool LJ (2010). An unexpected outcome of cervical near-hanging injury: A case report. *Acta Anaesthesiologica Belgica* 61, 79-81.

Kaliszan M (2010). Multiple severe stab wounds to chest with cuts to the ribs. Suicide or homicide? *Journal of Forensic and Legal Medicine* 18, 26-29.

Kanchan T, Rastogi P, Menezes RG, Nagesh KR (2010). Apparent partial hanging. *American Journal of Forensic Medicine and Pathology* 31, 376-377.

Katayama M, Naritomi H, Oomura M, Nukata M, Yamamoto S, Araki K, Kato H, Kinoshita M, Ito T, Shimode A, Takenobu Y, Watanabe M, Fukunaga R, Taguchi A, Hazama A, Inglin M, Krieger DW (2011). Case reports of unexpected suicides in patients within six months after stroke. *Kobe Journal of Medical Sciences* 56, 184-194.

Kishore K, Sahu S, Bharti P, Dahiya S, Kumar A, Agarwal A (2010). Management of unusual case of self-inflicted penetrating craniocerebral injury by a nail. *Journal of Emergencies, Trauma and Shock* 3, 193-196.

Kumar S (2010). Case report: Suicide by para-phenylenediamine poisoning. *Journal of Indian Academy of Forensic Medicine* 32, 163-164.

Kuzniar TJ, Balagani R, Radigan KA, Factor P, Mutlu GM (2010). Coma with absent brainstem reflexes resulting from zolpidem overdose. *American Journal of Therapeutics* 17, 172-174.

Laberke PJ, Bock H, Dittmann V, Hausmann R (2011). Forensic and psychiatric aspects of joint suicide with carbon monoxide. *Forensic Science, Medicine, and Pathology*. Published online: 16 February 2011. doi:10.1007/s12024-011-9224-y.

Large MM, Nielssen OB, Babidge N (2011). Self-inflicted intracranial self-injury. *Journal of Emergencies, Trauma and Shock* 4, 147.

Lemyze M, Palud A, Favory R, Mathieu D (2010). Unintentional strangulation by a cervical collar after attempted suicide by hanging. *Emergency Medicine Journal*. Published online: 23 December 2010. doi:10.1136/emj.2010.106625.

Lewin-Fetter V (2010). Self-harm on either side of the pond. *The Lancet* 376, 1224.

Liem M, Barber C, Markwalder N, Killias M, Nieuwbeerta P (2010). Homicide-suicide and other violent deaths: An international comparison. *Forensic Science International*. Published online: 8 October 2010. doi:10.1016/j.forsciint.2010.09.003.

Macedo MMK, Werlang BSG (2011). A case of trauma and attempted suicide in an adolescent patient *International Forum of Psychoanalysis* 20, 18-25.

Maebashi K, Iwadate K, Sakai K, Takatsu A, Fukui K, Aoyagi M, Ochiai E, Nagai T (2010). Toxicological analysis of 17 autopsy cases of hydrogen sulfide poisoning resulting from the inhalation of intentionally generated hydrogen sulfide gas. *Forensic Science International*. Published online: 19 October 2010. doi:10.1016/j.forsciint.2010.09.008.

Mahendran R, Liew E (2010). A case of suicidal thoughts with alprazolam. *The Primary Care Companion to the Journal of Clinical Psychiatry* 12, 3.

Mahmood Hashemi H, Asgarian A (2010). Mandible prognathism saved a life: A case report. *Chinese Journal of Traumatology* 13, 319-320.

Mao YC, Wang JD, Hung DZ, Deng JF, Yang CC (2011). Hyperammonemia following glufosinate-containing herbicide poisoning: A potential marker of severe neurotoxicity. *Clinical Toxicology* (T and F) 49, 48-52.

Mehrpour O, Shadnia S, Sanaei-Zadeh H (2011). Late extensive intravenous administration of N-acetylcysteine can reverse hepatic failure in acetaminophen overdose. *Human and Experimental Toxicology* 30, 51-54.

Mohl B (2010). From science to services: Developing a neuroscience-based innovative clinical treatment model to manage severe and repetitive self-harm in a 60-year-old woman with severe personality disorders. *Personality and Mental Health* 4, 319-322.

Moin-Azad Tehrani M-S, Soltaninejad K, Yazdani S, Nelson LS, Shadnia S (2011). Bilateral loculated pleural effusion as a manifestation of acute parenteral organophosphate intoxication: a case report. *Journal of Emergency Medicine*. Published online: 23 December 2010. doi:10.1016/j.jemermed.2010.11.028.

Morgan DR, Musa M (2010). Self inflicted death following inhalation and ingestion of Builders Polyurethane expandable foam. *Journal of Forensic and Legal Medicine* 17, 439-440.

Muzaffar S (2010). To treat or not to treat'. Kerrie Wooltorton, lessons to learn. *Emergency Medicine Journal*. Publishedonline: 5 October 2010. doi:10.1136/emj.2010.100750.

Nobre LF, Marchiori E, Carrao AD, Zanetti G, Mano CM (2011). Pulmonary instillation of activated charcoal: Early findings on computed tomography. *Annals of Thoracic Surgery* 91, 642-643.

Olson DP, Diaz JA, Jereda JD (2010). A fatal case of paraquat ingestion: Clinical course and review of pathophysiology. *Medical Science Monitor* 16, 153-156.

Omalu BI, Fitzsimmons PR, Hammers J, Bailes J (2010). Chronic traumatic encephalopathy in a professional American wrestler. *Journal of Forensic Nursing* 6, 130-136.

Pandit V, Seshadri S, Rao SN, Samarasinghe C, Kumar A, Valsalan R (2011). A case of organophosphate poisoning presenting with seizure and unavailable history of parenteral suicide attempt. *Journal of Emergencies, Trauma and Shock* 4, 132-134.

Payen C, Dellinger A, Pulce C, Cirimele V, Carbonnel V, Kintz P, Descotes J (2011). Intoxication by large amounts of barium nitrate overcome by early massive K supplementation and oral administration of magnesium sulphate. *Human and Experimental Toxicology* 30, 34-37.

Peschanski N, Clamageran C, Dardel N, Vianney A, Lapostolle F (2011). Two knitting needles in the thorax in a suicide attempt diagnosed on day 6 and treated conservatively. *Annals of Thoracic Surgery* 91, 305-305.

Poulton A (2010). Oral megadose methylphenidate ingestion for suicide attempt. *Pediatrics International* 52, 852.

Presecki P, Grosic V, Silic A, Mihanovic M (2010). Infection or idiosyncratic reaction to antiepileptic drugs? *Psychiatria Danubina* 22, 132-134.

Pridmore S, Ahmadi J (2010). Two cases of 'Type 3' suicide. *Australasian Psychiatry* 18, 426-430.

Pridmore S, Reddy A (2010). Suicide by couples from the public record. *Australasian Psychiatry* 18, 431-436.

Rani M, Rohit Dey A, Dikshit PC (2010). An unusual case of hanging. *Anil Aggrawal's Internet Journal of Forensic Medicine and Toxicology* 11, 2.

Rastogi P, Kanchan T, Menezes RG (2010). Postural asphyxia secondary to organophosphorous poisoning. *Journal of Forensic Medicine and Toxicology* 27, 21-23.

Roberts DM, Smith MW, Gopalakrishnan M, Whittaker G, Day RO (2011). Extreme -Butyrolactone overdose with severe metabolic acidosis requiring hemodialysis. *Annals of Emergency Medicine*. Published online: 21 March 2011. doi:10.1016/j.annemergmed.2011.01.017.

Ruder TD, Ketterer T, Preiss U, Bolliger M, Ross S, Gotsmy WF, Ampanozi G, Germerott T, Thali MJ, Hatch GM (2011). Suicidal knife wound to the heart: Challenges in reconstructing wound channels with post mortem CT and CT-angiography. *Legal Medicine* 13, 91-94.

Sakai K, Maruyama-Maebashi K, Takatsu A, Fukui K, Nagai T, Aoyagi M, Ochiai E, Iwadate K (2010). Sudden death involving inhalation of 1,1-difluoroethane (HFC-152a) with spray cleaner: Three case reports. *Forensic Science International*. Published online: 26 September 2010. doi:10.1016/j.forsciint.2010.08.026.

Salzbrenner S, Breeden A, Jarvis S, Rodriguez W (2011). A 48-year-old woman primigravid via in vitro fertilization with severe bipolar depression and preeclampsia treated successfully with electroconvulsive therapy. *The Journal of ECT* 27, e1-e3.

Sarkar J (2011). Complex case from volume 4, issue no. 4-'From science to services: Developing a neuroscience-based innovative clinical treatment model to manage severe and repetitive self-harm in a 60-year-old woman with severe personality disorders': A response to the commentaries by the complex case author. *Personality and Mental Health* 5, 93-94.

Sarkheil P, Werner CJ, Mull M, Schneider F, Neuner I (2010). Depressive episode induced by frontal tumor culminating in suicidal ideation. *German Journal of Psychiatry* 13, 150-153.

Saz EUl, Ucar SK, Ulger Z, Ersel M, Cevik C, Karapinar B (2010). Successful treatment of suicidal mega dose of propafenone intoxication - A case report. *Kardiologia Polska* 68, 1284-1285.

Schmidt U, Rost T, Jungmann L, Pollak S (2010). Suicide of a cyclist. *Forensic Science International*. Published online: 23 December 2010. doi:10.1016/j.forsciint.2010.11.023.

Segal J (2010). Therapeutic process as a means to navigate impasse? Reflections on a complex case of crosscultural adolescent family therapy. *Australian and New Zealand Journal of Family Therapy* 31, 266-274.

Sersar SI (2011). A self-introduced sharp metallic foreign body migrating transcutaneously to the interventricular septum, mistaken as an inhaled pin. *Journal of Thoracic and Cardiovascular Surgery* 141, 603-604.

Shadnia S, Soltaninejad K, Hassan ian-Moghadam H, Sadeghi A, Rahimzadeh H, Zamani N, Ghasemi-Toussi A, Abdollah M (2011). Methemoglobinemia in aluminum phosphide poisoning. *Human and Experimental Toxicology* 30, 250-253. Sharma A (2010). Acute copper sulphate poisoning: A case report. *Indian Journal of Forensic Medicine and Toxicology* 4, 4-5.

Sieberer MG, Garlipp P (2010). Mercury inhalation as a suicide attempt in a patient with depression and narcissistic personality disorder. *Psychiatry (Edgmont)* 7, 12-13.

Su TY, Lin JL, Lin-Tan DT, Tseng HH, Yen TH (2011). Human poisoning with spinosad and flonicamid insecticides. *Human & Experimental Toxicology*. Published online: 7 March 2011. doi:10.1177/0960327111401639.

Subbalaxmi MV, Abkari S, Srinivasan VR, Krishnaprasad A (2010). Methyl ethyl ketone peroxide ingestion: A rare cause of corrosive chemical poisoning. *The National Medical Journal of India* 23, 150-151.

Toogood S, Boyd S, Bell A, Salisbury H (2011). Self-injury and other challenging behaviour at intervention and ten years on: A case study. *Tizard Learning Disability Review* 16, 18-29.

Tournel G, Houssaye C, Humbert L, Dhorne C, Gnemmi V, Bécart-Robert A, Nisse P, Hédouin V, Gosset D, Lhermitte M (2010). Acute arsenic poisoning: Clinical, toxicological, histopathological, and forensic features. *Journal of Forensic Sciences* 56 (Suppl 1), 275-279.

Tsivgoulis G, Heliopoulos I, Vadikolias K, Argyropoulou P, Piperidou C (2010). Ingestion of gasoline in a suicide attempt: an uncommon cause of bilateral basal ganglia T1 hyperintensities. *Neurological Sciences*. Published online: 24 November 2010. doi:10.1007/s10072-010-0452-9.

Waseem M, Perry C, Bomann S, Pai M, Gernsheimer J (2010). Cholinergic crisis after rodenticide poisoning. *Western Journal of Emergency Medicine* 11, 524-527.

Wiper JD, Grant I, Kay SP (2011). Deliberate soft tissue injection of petrol. *Journal of Plastic, Reconstructive & Aesthetic Surgery* 56, 537-540.

Wozakowska-KapLon B, Stepien-Walek A (2010). Propafenone overdose: Cardiac arrest and full recovery. *Cardiology Journal* 17, 619-622.

Zátopková L, Hejna P (2011). Fatal suicidal crossbow injury - the ability to act. *Journal of Forensic Science* 56, 537–540.

Zech W-D, Kneubuhl B, Thali M, Bolliger S (2010). Pistol thrown to the ground by shooter after fatal self inflicted gunshot wound to the chest. *Journal of Forensic and Legal Medicine* 18, 88-90.

MISCELLANEOUS

Aiello-Laws LB (2010). Assessing the risk for suicide in patients with cancer. *Clinical Journal of Oncology Nursing* 14, 687-691.

Alexander J, Wallett A (2010). Mobile phones, suicide and prognostication. *Australian and New Zealand Journal of Psychiatry* 44, 958-959.

Alvin P (2010). "There are 3 kinds of lies": Comments on the article "Teenage suicides and suicide attempts: Finding one's way in the epidemiologic data". *Archives of Pediatrics and Adolescent Medicine* 17, 1728-1729.

An J, Phillips MR, Conner KR (2010). Validity of proxy-based reports of impulsivity and aggression in Chinese research on suicidal behaviour. *Crisis* 31, 137-142.

Ambade VN, Keoliya AN, Deokar RB, Dixit PG (2011). Decomposed bodies - Still an unrewarding autopsy? *Journal of Forensic and Legal Medicine* 18, 101-106.

Anonymous (2010). Army releases suicide report, prevention recommendations. *Military Medicine: AMSUS Newsletter* 6-7.

Anonymous (2011). Underutilized treatments in depression and anxiety. *Psychiatric Annals* 41, 138-140.

Anonymous (2010). You have duty to intervene when treatment is contraindicated. Case on point: Wulbrecht v. Jehle, 2010-20229 NYMISC (6/14/2010)-NY. *Nursing Law's Regan Report* 51, 2.

Arana A, Wentworth CW, Arellano FM (2010). Validity of the codes of suicidality in the THIN database. *Pharmacoepidemioly and Drug Safety* 19, 1316-1317.

Arun M, Palimar V, Kumar GNP, Menezes RG (2010). Unusual methods of suicide: Complexities in investigation. *Medicine, Science and the Law* 50, 149-153.

Bartram DJ, Sinclair JMA, Baldwin DS (2010). Understanding suicidal thoughts and help-seeking behaviour among UK veterinary surgeons: Preliminary results of a semistructured interview study. *Cattle Practice* 18,110.

Bartram DJ, Yadegarfar G, Sinclair JM, Baldwin DS (2011). Validation of the Warwick-Edinburgh Mental Well-being Scale (WEMWBS) as an overall indicator of population mental health and well-being in the UK veterinary profession. *The Veterinary Journal* 187, 397-398.

Bertolote JM, de Mello-Santos C, Botega NJ (2010). Detecting suicide risk at psychiatric emergency services. *Revista Brasileira De Psiquiatria* 32, 87-95.

Bhalla K, Harrison JE, Shahraz S, Fingerhut LA, Global Burden of Disease Injury Expert Group (2010). Availability and quality of cause-of-death data for estimating the global burden of injuries. *Bulletin of the World Health Organization* 88, 831-838.

Bodner E, Cohen-Fridel S, Iancu I (2010). Staff attitudes toward patients with borderline personality disorder. *Comprehensive Psychiatry*. Published online: 3 December 2010. doi:10.1016/j.comppsych.2010.10.004

Busch SH, Frank RG, Martin A, Barry CL (2011). Characterizing declines in pediatric antidepressant use after new risk disclosures. *Medical Care Research and Review* 68, 96-111.

Bruckner TA, Scheffler RM, Shen G, Yoon J, Chisholm D, Morris J, Fulton BD, dal Poz MR, Shekhar S (2011). The mental health workforce gap in low- and middle-income countries: A needs-based approach. *Bulletin of the World Health Organization* 89, 184-194.

Cantrell FL, Minns A (2011). Cybersuicide with "homemade Valium". *Clinical Toxicology* 49, 56-56.

Carragher N, Mewton L, Slade T, Teesson M (2010). An item response analysis of the DSM-IV criteria for major depression: Findings from the Australian National Survey of Mental Health and Wellbeing. *Journal of Affective Disorders*. Published online: 26 October 2010. doi:10.1016/j.jad.2010.09.033.

Carson HJ (2010). Patterns of ecchymoses caused by manner of death and collateral injuries sustained in bruising incidents: Decedent injuries, profiles, comparisons, and clinico-pathologic significance. *Journal of Forensic Sciences* 55, 1534-1542.

Carstairs SD, Schneir AB (2011). Opsoclonus due to diphenhydramine poisoning. *New England Journal of Medicine* 367, e40.

Catts SV, Frost AD, O'Toole BI, Carr VJ, Lewin T, Neil AL, Harris MG, Evans RW, Crissman BR, Eadie K (2011). Clinical indicators for routine use in the evaluation of early psychosis intervention: Development, training support and inter-rater reliability. *Australian and New Zealand Journal of Psychiatry* 45, 63-75.

Cavalcante GI, Capistrano VL, Cavalcante FS, Vasconcelos SM, Macêdo DS, Sousa FC, Woods DJ, Fonteles MM (2010). Implications of efavirenz for neuropsychiatry: A review. *International Journal of Neuroscience* 120, 739-745.

Cecchetto G, Viel G, Amagliani A, Boscolo-Berto R, Fais P, Montisci M (2011). Histological diagnosis of myocardial sarcoidosis in a fatal fall from a height. *Journal of Forensic Sciences* 56, 255-258.

Cerase A, Leonini S, Bellini M, Chianese G, Venturi C (2010). Methadone-induced toxic leukoencephalopathy: Diagnosis and follow-up by magnetic resonance imaging including diffusion-weighted imaging and apparent diffusion coefficient maps. *Journal of Neuroimaging*. Published online: 26 October 2010. doi:10.1111/j.1552-6569.2010.00530.x.

Chandler A, Myers F, Platt S (2011). The construction of self-injury in the clinical literature: a sociological exploration. *Suicide and Life-Threatening Behaviour* 41, 98-109.

Chang HJ, Wu CJ, Lin MF, Chen TW, Cheng AT, Lin KC, Rong JR, Lee HC (2010). Psychometric properties of the Chinese version of the Life Attitude Schedule (LAS-C) in a sample of Taiwanese adolescents. *International Journal of Nursing Studies*. Published online: 21 December 2010. doi:10.1016/j.ijnurstu.2010.10.010.

Charoonnate N, Narongchai P, Vongvaivet S (2010). Fractures of the hyoid bone and thyroid cartilage in suicidal hanging. *Journal of the Medical Association of Thailand* 93, 1211-1216.

Cholbi M (2010). A Kantian defense of prudential suicide. *Journal of Moral Philosophy* 7, 489-515.

Chung S, Joung YS (2010). Oseltamivir (Tamiflu) induced depressive episode in a female adolescent. *Psychiatry Investigation* 7, 302-304.

Chua JL (2011). Making time for the children: self-temporalization and the cultivation of the antisuicidal subject in South India. *Cultural Anthropology* 26, 112-137.

Clement R, Guay JP, Sauvageau A (2010). Fracture of the neck structures in suicidal hangings: A retrospective study on contributing variables. *Forensic Science International*. Published online: 16 October 2010. doi:10.1016/j.forsciint.2010.09.016.

Coldwell I (2010). Killing the mockingbird: Systems failure and a radical hope for re-grounding responsibility and access to health care in a Mallee town community. *Rural Society* 20, 35-50.

Congdon P (2011). Structural equation models for area health outcomes with model selection. *Journal of Applied Statistics* 38, 745-767.

Cubells JF (2011). Concerns over participant suicides prematurely abort a clinical trial of potentially significant impact on public health: how will we make progress in timid times?

Current Psychiatry Reports. Published online: 26 January 2011. doi:10.1007/s11920-011-0179-1.

De Leon OA, Nolan E (2010). Implausibility and evidentiality in schizophrenic delusions: A case of high risk of suicide. *Clinical Case Studies* 9, 383-394.

de Wit MA, Tuinebreijer WC, van Brussel GH, Selten JP (2010). Ethnic differences in risk of acute compulsory admission in Amsterdam, 1996-2005. *Social Psychiatry & Psychiatric Epidemiology.* Published online: 13 November 2010. 10.1007/s00127-010-0312-1.

Dignam PT (2010). Suicide and mental disorder: The legal perspective. *The Medical Journal of Australia* 193, 430.

Dyer C (2010). Doctors continue fight for David Kelly inquest despite release of autopsy report. *British Medical Journal (Clinical research ed.)* 341, c6031.

Fang F, Fall K, Valdimarsdottir U (2010). Re: Immediate risk of suicide and cardiovascular death after a prostate cancer diagnosis: Cohort study in the United States response. *Journal of the National Cancer Institute* 102, 1448-1448.

Ferreday D (2010). Reading disorders: Online suicide and the death of hope. *Journal for Cultural Research* 14, 409-426.

Fiori LM, Turecki G (2010). Broadening our horizons: Gene expression profiling to help better understand the neurobiology of suicide and depression. *Neurobiology of Disease.* Published online: 21 November 2010. doi:10.1016/j.nbd.2010.11.004.

Fortin JL, Judic-Peureux V, Desmettre T, Manzon C, Grimon D, Hostalek U, Fétro C, Capellier G (2011). Hydrogen cyanide poisoning in a prison environment: A case report. *Journal of Correctional Health Care* 17, 29-33.

Franchitto N, Faurie C, Franchitto L, Minville V, Telmon N, Rougé D (2011). Self-inflicted burns: The value of collaboration between medicine and law. *Journal of Forensic Sciences.* Published online: 3 March 2011. doi:10.1111/j.1556-4029.2011.01706.x.

García-Caballero A, Recimil MJ, Touriño R, García-Lado I, Alonso MC, Werlang BS, Jiménez J, Pérez MC, Losada A, Bendaña JM (2010). Adaptation and validation of the Semi-Structured Interview for Psychological Autopsy (SSIPA) in Spanish. *Actas Espanolas de Psiquiatria* 38, 332-339.

Greenberg DB (2011). The signal of suicide rates seen from a distance in patients with pancreatic cancer. *Cancer* 117, 446-448.

Gunn III JF, Lester D (2010). Moral development and perceptions of attempted suicide and physician-assisted suicide. *Psychological Reports* 107, 697-698.

Guthrie R, Westaway J (2011). Compensation for workplace injury leading to suicide in Australia. *Journal of Law and Medicine* 18, 333-343.

Hammad TA, Mosholder AD (2010). Suicide and antidepressants. Beware extrapolation from ecological data. *British Medical Journal* 341, 6844.

Hebert R (2010). An urgent need to improve life conditions of seniors. *Journal of Nutrition Health and Aging* 14, 711-714.

Hoffman RS (2010). Toxicology from across the pond. *Journal of The Royal College of Physicians of Edinburgh* 40, 152-158.

Holtmann M, Buchmann AF, Esser G, Schmidt MH, Banaschewski T, Laucht M (2011). The Child Behavior Checklist-Dysregulation Profile predicts substance use, suicidality, and functional impairment: a longitudinal analysis. *Journal of Child Psychology and Psychiatry* 52, 139-147.

Horon IL, Cheng D (2011). Effectiveness of pregnancy check boxes on death certificates in identifying pregnancy-associated mortality. *Public Health Reports* 126, 195-200.

Innamorati M, Pompili M, Gonda X, Amore M, Serafini G, Niolu C, Lester D, Rutz W, Rihmer Z, Girardi P (2011). Psychometric properties of the Gotland Scale for Depression in Italian psychiatric inpatients and its utility in the prediction of suicide risk. *Journal of Affective Disorders*. Published online: 1 March 2011. doi:10.1016/j.jad.2011.02.003.

Innamorati M, Pompili M, Serafini G, Lester D, Erbuto D, Amore M, Tatarelli R, Girardi P (2011). Psychometric properties of the suicidal history self-rating screening scale. *Archives of Suicide Research* 15, 87-92.

Iwase H, Yajima D, Hayakawa M, Yamamoto S, Motani H, Sakuma A, Kasahara S, Ito H (2010). Evaluation of computed tomography as a screening test for death inquest. *Journal of Forensic Sciences* 55, 509-1515.

Jayasekera H, Carter G, Clover K (2011). Comparison of the Composite International Diagnostic Interview (CIDI-Auto) with clinical diagnosis in a suicidal population. *Archives of Suicide Research* 15, 43-55.

Joiner T (2011). Understanding and overcoming the myths of suicide: What goes on in the minds of those who attempt suicide? *Psychiatric Times* 28, 20-24.

Jordan JR (2011). A child psychiatrist explores the mystery of her mother's suicide. *Death Studies* 35, 90-93.

Jukkala T, Makinen IH (2010). Acceptance of suicide in Moscow. *Social Psychiatry and Psychiatric Epidemiology*. Published online: 26 November 2010.

Khubchandani J, Wiblishauser M, Price JH, Thompson A (2010). Graduate psychiatric nurse's training on firearm injury prevention. *Archives of Psychiatric Nursing*. Published online: 3 December 2010. doi:10.1016/j.apnu.2010.07.010.

Knizek B, Akotia C, Hjelmeland H (2010). A qualitative study of attitudes toward suicide and suicide prevention among psychology students in Ghana. *Omega: Journal of Death and Dying* 62, 169-186.

Kornhauser P (2010). The cause of P.I. Tchaikovsky's (1840-1893) death: Cholera, suicide, or both? *Acta Medico-Historica Adriatica* 8, 145-172.

Krespi Boothby MR, Mulholland I, Cases A, Carrington K, Bolger T (2010). Towards mental health promotion in prisons: The role of screening for emotional distress. *Procedia - Social and Behavioral Sciences* 5, 90-94.

Lankford A (2011). Suicide terrorism as a socially approved form of suicide. *Crisis* 31, 287-289.

Large MM, Ryan CJ, Singh SP, Paton MB, Nielssen OB (2011). The predictive value of risk categorization in schizophrenia. *Harvard Review of Psychiatry* 19, 25-33.

Larkin GL, Rivera H, Xu H, Rincon E, Beautrais AL (2011). Community responses to a suicidal crisis: implications for suicide prevention. *Suicide and Life-Threatening Behavior* 41, 79-86.

Lauth B, Arnkelsson GB, Magnusson P, Skarphedinsson GA, Ferrari P, Petursson H (2010). Parent-youth agreement on symptoms and diagnosis: Assessment with a diagnostic interview in an adolescent inpatient clinical population. *Journal of Physiology- Paris* 104, 315-322.

Lawlor C, Johnson S, Cole L, Howard LM (2010). Ethnic variations in pathways to acute care and compulsory detention for women experiencing a mental health crisis. *International Journal of Social Psychiatry*. Published online: 8 November 2010. doi:10.1177/0020764 010382369.

Leavey G, Rondon J, McBride P (2011). Between compassion and condemnation: A qualitative study of clergy views on suicide in Northern Ireland. *Mental Health, Religion and Culture* 14, 65-74.

Lester D, Hathaway D (2010). Organ donation and suicide. *Psychological Reports* 107, 500.

Lewis SP, Heath NL, St Denis JM, Noble R (2011). The scope of nonsuicidal self-injury on YouTube. *Pediatrics*. Published online: 21 February 2011. doi:10.1542/peds.2010-2317.

Loar C (2010). Medical knowledge and the early modern English coroner's inquest. *Social History of Medicine* 23, 475-491.

Lyne J, Ephros H, Bolding S (2010). The need for preoperative risk assessment. *Oral and Maxillofacial Surgery Clinics of North America* 22, 431-437.

MacCormack G (2010). Liability for suicide in Qing law on account of filthy words. *Nan Nu* 12, 103-141.

Mak MHJ (2011). Youth suicide: Knowledge and attitudes from secondary students' perspectives — A Hong Kong based study. *Illness Crisis and Loss* 19, 41-56.

McCoy KL, Carty SE (2011). Failure is not a fate worse than death. *Archives of Surgery* 146, 62-63.

Mellanby RJ, Hudson NPH, Allister R, Bell CE, Else RW, Gunn-Moore DA, Byrne C, Straiton S, Rhind SM (2010). Evaluation of suicide awareness programmes delivered to veterinary undergraduates and academic staff. *Veterinary Record* 167, 730-734.

Moore R (2011). The stigmatized deaths in Jonestown: Finding a locus for grief. *Death Studies* 35, 42-58.

Mugisha J, Knizek BL, Kinyanda E, Hjelmeland H (2011). Doing qualitative research on suicide in a developing country. *Crisis* 32, 15-23.

Murray A (2010). Did Simone Serdini ('il saviozzo') really commit suicide? *Medium Aevum* 79, 250-277.

Nelson C, Johnston M, Shrivastava A (2010). Improving risk assessment with suicidal patients. *Crisis* 31, 231-237.

Nepon J, Pagura J, Sareen J (2011). Study limitations in report of suicidal behavior among women with co-occurring PTSD and borderline personality disorder. *The American Journal of Psychiatry* 168, 328.

Ng'walali PM, Shigeyuki Tsunenari S (2010). Self-destruction by multiple methods during a single episode: A case study and review of the literature. *African Health Sciences* 10, 273-275.

Nolan PD, Triplett J, McDonough S (2010). Sociology's Suicide: A Forensic Autopsy? *American Sociologist* 41, 292-305.

O'Reilly CL, Simon Bell J, Chen TF (2010). Pharmacists' beliefs about treatments and outcomes of mental disorders: A mental health literacy survey. *Australian and New Zealand Journal of Psychiatry* 44, 1089-1096.

Oquendo MA, Feldman S, Silverman E, Currier D, Brown GK, Chen D, Chiapella P, Fischbach R, Gould M, Stanley B, Strauss D, Zelazny J, Pearson J (2011). Variability in the definition and reporting of adverse events in suicide prevention trials: an examination of the issues and a proposed solution. *Archives of Suicide Research* 15, 29-42.

Patrick AR, Miller M, Barber CW, Wang PS, Canning CF, Schneeweiss S (2010). Identification of hospitalizations for intentional self-harm when E-codes are incompletely recorded. *Pharmacoepidemiology & Drug Safety* 19, 1263-1275.

Perdekamp MG, Kneubuehl BP, Ishikawa T, Nadjem H, Kromeier J, Pollak S, Thierauf A (2010). Secondary skull fractures in head wounds inflicted by captive bolt guns: Autopsy findings and experimental simulation. *International Journal of Legal Medicine* 124, 605-612.

Pestian J (2010). A conversation with Edwin Shneidman. *Suicide and Life-Threatening Behavior* 40, 516-523.

Pilpel A, Amsel L (2011). What is wrong with rational suicide. *Philosophia* 39, 111-123.

Polder-Verkiel SE (2010). Online responsibility: bad Samaritan and the influence of internet mediation. *Science and Engineering Ethics.* Published online: 16 December 2010. doi:10.1007/s11948-010-9253.

Preti A (2011). Do animals commit suicide? Does it matter? *Crisis* 32, 1-4.

Price JH, Thompson AJ, Khubchandani J, Mrdjenovich AJ, Price JA (2010). Firearm anticipatory guidance training in psychiatric residency programs. *Academic Psychiatry* 34, 417-423.

Pridmore S, Majeed ZA (2011). The suicides of The Metamorphoses. *Australasian Psychiatry* 19, 22-24.

Raven M (2010). Interpretation of ecological data: reply. *British Journal of Psychiatry* 197, 332-332.

Ravina MJ (2010). The apocryphal suicide of Saigo Takamori: Samurai, Seppuku, and the Politics of Legend. *Journal of Asian Studies* 69, 691-721.

Salvador-Carulla L, Bendeck M, Fernandez A, Alberti C, Sabes-Figuera R, Molina C, Knapp M (2011). Costs of depression in Catalonia (Spain). *Journal of Affective Disorders.* Published online: 12 March 2011. doi:10.1016/j.jad.2011.02.019.

Sarkar J (2011). Complex case from volume 4, issue no. 4-'From science to services: Developing a neuroscience-based innovative clinical treatment model to manage severe and repetitive self-harm in a 60-year-old woman with severe personality disorders': A response to the commentaries by the complex case author. *Personality and Mental Health* 5, 93-94.

Schulz F, Schäfer H, Püschel K, Tsokos M, Brinkmann B, Buschmann CT (2011). Bowel wall hemorrhage after death by hanging. *International Journal of Legal Medicine.* Published online: 11 January 2011. doi:10.1007/s00414-010-0543-4.

Shiffman S, Gerlach KK, Sembower MA, Rohay JM (2011). Consumer understanding of prescription drug information: an illustration using an antidepressant medication. *Annals of Pharmacotherapy.* Published online: 22 March 2011. Doi: 10.1345/aph.1P477.

Shneidman E (2010). A conversation with Edwin Shneidman. Interview by John Pestian. *Suicide and Life-Threatening Behavior* 40, 516-523.

Schober DJ, Ramaswamy M, Choi WS, Fawcett SB, Hindman J, Martinez JM (2011). Improving collaboration for effective violence surveillance and health promotion. *Journal of Public Health Management and Practice* 17, 174-176.

Short BW (2011). The question of the constitutional case against suicide: An istoriographical and originalist inquiry into the degree to which the theory of the inalienable right to life and liberty is enforced by the thirteenth amendment. *Issues in Law and Medicine* 26, 91-201.

Sinnott RO, Hussain S (2010). Security-oriented workflows for the Social Sciences. *Proceedings - 2010 4th International Conference on Network and System Security*, 152-159.

Speedy J (2011). "All googled out on suicide": Making collective biographies out of silent fragments with "The unassuming geeks". *Qualitative Inquiry* 17, 134-143.

Stack S, Kposowa AJ (2011). The effect of survivalism-self-expressionism culture on black male suicide acceptability: A cross-national analysis. *Social Science and Medicine.* Published online: 15 February 2011. doi:10.1016/j.socscimed.2011.01.028.

Stefansson J, Nordstrom P, Jokinen J (2011). Suicide Intent Scale in the prediction of suicide. *Journal of Affective Disorders.* Published online: 8 December 2010. doi:10.1016/j.jad.2010.11.016.

Sullivan S (2011). The right to die: a discussion of 'rational suicide'. *Mental Health Practice* 14, 32-34.

Tatum PT, Canetto SS, Slater MD (2010). Suicide coverage in U.S. Newspapers following the publication of the media guidelines. *Suicide and Life-Threatening Behaviour* 40, 524-534.

Tierney TF (2010). The governmentality of suicide: Peuchet, Marx, Durkheim, and Foucault. *Journal of Classical Sociology* 10, 357-389.

Tsai SJ, Hong CJ, Liou YJ (2010). Recent molecular genetic studies and methodological issues in suicide research. *Progress in Neuro-psychopharmacology & Biological Psychiatry*. Published online: 23 October 2010. http://dx.doi.org/10.1016/j.pnpbp.2010.10.014.

Tsatsakis AM, Tutudaki M, Tzatzarakis MN, Dawson A, Mohamed F, Christaki M, Alegakis A (2011). Is hair analysis for dialkyl phosphate metabolites a suitable biomarker for assessing past acute exposure to organophosphate pesticides? *Human & Experimental Toxicology*. Published online: 22 March 2011. doi: 10.1177/0960327111403171.

Uher R, Perroud N (2010). Probing the genome to understand suicide. *The American Journal of Psychiatry* 167, 1425-1427.

Vandoninck S, D'Haenens L, Donoso V (2010). Digital literacy of Flemish youth: How do they handle online content risks? *Communications* 35, 397-416.

Veijalainen J, Semenov A, Kyppo J (2010). Tracing potential school shooters in the digital sphere. *Communications in Computer and Information Science* 76, 163-178.

Villalobos-Galvis FH (2010). Validity and reliability of the positive and negative suicidal ideation inventory, in Colombian students. *Universitas Psychologica* 9, 509-520.

Violanti JM (2010). Suicide or undetermined? A national assessment of police suicide death classification. *International Journal of Emergency Mental Health* 12, 89-94.

Vrouva I, Fonagy P, Fearon PR, Roussow T (2010). The risk-taking and self-harm inventory for adolescents: Development and psychometric evaluation. *Psychological Assessment* 22, 852-865.

Wakefield JC, Schmitz MF, Baer JC (2011). Did narrowing the major depression bereavement exclusion from DSM-III-R to DSM-IV increase validity? Evidence from the national comorbidity survey. *The Journal of Nervous and Mental Disease* 199, 66-73.

Walker RL, Flowers KC (2011). Effects of race and precipitating event on suicide versus non-suicide death classification in a college sample. *Suicide and Life-Threatening Behavior* 41, 12-20.

Waraich P, Saklikar RS, Aubé D, Jones W, Haslam D, Hamill K (2010). Quality measures for primary mental healthcare: a multistakeholder, multijurisdictional Canadian consensus. *Quality and Safety in Health Care* 19, 519-525.

Weich S, McBride O, Hussey D, Exeter D, Brugha T, McManus S (2011). Latent class analysis of co-morbidity in the Adult Psychiatric Morbidity Survey in England 2007: implications for DSM-5 and ICD-11. *Psychological Medicine*. Published online: 4 March 2011. doi:10.1017/S0033291711000249.

Westefeld J (2011). A tale of two gavels. *Counseling Psychologist* 39, 171.

Wilks MF, Tomenson JA, Fernando R, Ariyananda PL, Berry DJ, Buckley NA, Gawarammana IB, Jayamanne S, Gunnell D, Dawson A (2011). Formulation changes and time trends in outcome following paraquat ingestion in Sri Lanka. *Clinical Toxicology* 49, 21-28.

Wong PWC, Chan WSC, Beh PSL, Yau FWS, Yip PSF, Hawton K (2010). Research participation experiences of informants of suicide and control cases: taken from a case-control psychological autopsy study of people who died by suicide. *Crisis* 31, 238-246.

Wortzel HS, Gutierrez PM, Homaifar BY, Breshears RE, Harwood JE (2010). Surrogate end-points in suicide research. *Suicide and Life-Threatening Behavior* 40, 500-505.

Yaseen Z, Katz C, Johnson MS, Eisenberg D, Cohen LJ, Galynker II (2010). Construct development: The Suicide Trigger Scale (STS-2), a measure of a hypothesized 'suicide trigger state'. *BMC Psychiatry* 10, 110.

Zimmerman M, Galione JN, Chelminski I, Young D, Dalrymple K, Witt CF (2010). Validity of a simpler definition of major depressive disorder. *Depression and Anxiety* 27, 977-981.

www.ingramcontent.com/pod-product-compliance
Lightning Source LLC
Chambersburg PA
CBHW080235270326
41926CB00020B/4249